Pogroms, Peasants, Jews

Pogroms, Peasants, Jews

Britain and Eastern Europe's 'Jewish Question', 1867–1925

Sam Johnson

Senior Lecturer in Modern European History, Manchester Metropolitan University

palgrave
macmillan

First published 2011 by
PALGRAVE MACMILLAN

Palgrave Macmillan in the UK is an imprint of Macmillan Publishers Limited, registered in England, company number 785998, of Houndmills, Basingstoke, Hampshire RG21 6XS.

Palgrave Macmillan in the US is a division of St Martin's Press LLC, 175 Fifth Avenue, New York, NY 10010.

Palgrave Macmillan is the global academic imprint of the above companies and has companies and representatives throughout the world.

Palgrave® and Macmillan® are registered trademarks in the United States, the United Kingdom, Europe and other countries.

ISBN 978–1–4039–4982–0 hardback

This book is printed on paper suitable for recycling and made from fully managed and sustained forest sources. Logging, pulping and manufacturing processes are expected to conform to the environmental regulations of the country of origin.

A catalogue record for this book is available from the British Library.

A catalog record for this book is available from the Library of Congress.

10   9   8   7   6   5   4   3   2   1
20   19   18   17   16   15   14   13   12   11

Transferred to Digital Printing in 2011

Pro sovy a náš příběh.
Rukopisy nehoří...

Contents

List of Illustrations

Acknowledgements

The process that facilitated the completion of this manuscript would not have been possible without the assistance and resources of a number of institutions: for financial support in aiding archival visits to the United States, I acknowledge the assistance of the Cardiff University Young Scholars' Scheme and the Manchester European Research Institute at Manchester Metropolitan University. My thanks also go to numerous librarians and archivists, most especially at the British Library, St Pancras; the British Newspaper Library, Colindale; the Central Library, Manchester; Wendy Thirkettle at the Manx National Heritage Library, Isle of Man; the London Metropolitan Archives; the Board of Deputies of British Jews, who gave me permission to investigate their archives; the Rothschild Archive, London; the archives of the *Alliance Israélite Universelle*, Paris; the National Library of the Czech Republic, Prague (where large parts of the manuscript were written); the YIVO Institute of Jewish Research and Columbia University Library, New York City.

On a personal note, thanks must also be extended to my family, especially my mum; friends old and new – particularly for their support during some exceedingly trying times – Beth, Robyn and Penny Reed; distant and immediate colleagues on two continents in the field of Jewish studies; most especially Alexander Ivanov, who unearthed several Russian references and has kept me up-to-date with the most recent historiographical and archival developments in the Russian Federation; Małgorzata Domagalska for some Polish references; Dagmar Hájková and Z.A.B. Zeman, who have favoured me with their hospitality in Prague over many years. Particular gratitude must go to those who carefully read the manuscript prior to its dispatch to the publishers; Malcolm Crook, my former history tutor and fellow football obsessive; and Gennady Estraikh.

Unfortunately, during the period the manuscript was being written, the field of Jewish studies lost two of its most eminent and pioneering scholars, and I owe a debt of gratitude to them both. First of all, to the late Jonathan Frankel, a most generous scholar and man, I am but one of many who benefited from his advice and encouragement. I will always be thankful for his assurance that he was 'interested' in the topic.

And, finally, though his place is first and not last, my heartfelt thanks for innumerable things go to the late John Doyle Klier. Despite his unwilling absence in the latter stages of this manuscript's completion, he continued to accompany me, his positive spirit a constant presence. John made my life better, in every aspect, and I will never cease to be grateful for the blessing of knowing him. Thus, my humble endeavours stand not only for him, but because of him.

Manchester – Praha – Piter – Bristol
April 2010

Introduction

Confidence and uncertainty: New Jewish questions

Upon the elevation of Nathaniel Mayer de Rothschild to the peerage in 1885, the nineteenth-century dilemmas about the Jewish place in public life, in politics and in education appeared to have finally passed in Britain. Emancipation, achieved in stages from the 1830s onwards, bore successful consequences, and British Jewry was perhaps justified in feeling satisfied at the place it had secured within wider society. Such accomplishments and the apparently acculturated condition of British Jews, whose religious observance was concealed by stiff Victorian garb, led many commentators to claim that Britain had no Jewish question.[1] A *Times* editorial in 1882, for instance, asserted that British Jews had learnt 'to identify their own prosperity with that of their fellow-citizens'.[2] In other words, Jewish attainments of wealth and status were of benefit to wider society, not just a self-interested and enclosed community. The ancient fetters of the ghetto – psychological, social and economic – happily left no visible scars upon the emancipated Jews of the British Empire.

In Britain, the Jewish question appeared solved. This scenario, true or not, was contrasted, by nineteenth-century British observers, with the situation on the continent, particularly in Eastern Europe. There, in Tsarist Russia, Romania and parts of the Habsburg Empire, Jew-baiting, antisemitic politics and Judeophobic sentiment seemed to dominate daily life. Why this was the case preoccupied British public opinion throughout the period. It puzzled over Romania's persistent failure to grant Jewish civil equality, shuddered in horror at Russian pogroms and, most of all, poked and prodded at the Eastern European Jew himself.[3] After all, it was wondered, perhaps the reason the Jewish question would not go away in all continental Europe was the unique character of the Jew himself. As *The Spectator* indelicately expressed it, when explicating the deliberate destruction of a synagogue in Neustettin, Imperial Germany in 1881: 'the Jews everywhere are foreigners, and in Europe, Asiatic foreigners, separated from the people by lines which, though sometimes indefinable, are ineffaceable.'[4]

Until the 1880s, the more obvious 'foreign' nature of East European Jewry, observed from afar, prompted British curiosity, bewilderment and a reliance on generalisations that deemed Jews clannish and religious outsiders. Geographical distance and little direct contact afforded a degree of tolerance, if it may be called that, conditioned undoubtedly by greater domestic and imperial concerns. The Irish question, for instance, remained persistently in the foreground of parliamentary and editorial worries. This somewhat complacent Victorian attitude towards continental Jews and their inherent (though not British) problems experienced a gradual shift from the mid-1880s onwards. The arrival of thousands of East European Jews to British shores – from Galicia, Imperial Russia and Romania – prompted a renewed examination of all Jewish questions. Public and parliamentary discussion of 'dirty, poverty-stricken and degraded' Jewish immigrants ebbed and flowed according to the contemporary economic climate.[5] Their numbers, from the 1880s until the eve of the First World War, amounted to between 120,000 and 150,000.[6] By the twentieth century, the Jewish population of Britain had more than doubled and the resultant discussion, summarised by both contemporary commentators and historians as 'the aliens debate', bore political consequences. A number of parliamentary enquiries occurred, most notably the 1902 Royal Commission on Alien Immigration. The 1905 Aliens Act, passed in its wake, was Britain's first piece of immigrant legislation. At the turn of the twentieth century, Britain surely had its own Jewish problem, albeit one almost exclusively tied to the 'alien, pauper Jew'.

Given these circumstances, British consideration of Eastern European Jewish matters, particularly the emigrants' country of origin, acquired additional importance. Commentators wondered, for instance, about the reasons for emigration and its connection to Jewish persecution in their homelands. Were the two matters connected? If they were, what could be done to remedy the situation? Herein lay a major dilemma for many observers. How could Britain hope to shape the internal affairs of Romania, or the Tsarist and Habsburg Empires? Were the Jewish policies in foreign states of any concern to Britain? If the tables were turned, for example, it would certainly shun any foreign intention to interfere in its own domestic policy and, as *The Graphic* observed, 'consider it an impertinence'.[7] Even if the foreign persecution bore apparently direct consequences in a tide of seemingly unstoppable emigration, could British representatives seriously hope to effect intervention, beyond stirring the consciences of foreign leaders? Such questions recurred at regular intervals from the 1880s onwards, particularly during moments of Jewish crisis, such as the pogroms of 1881–1882 and the expulsions from Moscow and St Petersburg in the early 1890s.

Nevertheless, despite these anxieties, it did not follow that Britain maintained an objective disinterest in all forms of anti-Jewish persecution in Eastern Europe. Indeed, every crisis, whether in Romania, Tsarist Russia or elsewhere, prompted an outcry. The press played its part in commenting and reflecting on various incidents. British popular indignation was manifest in petitions and public protests, such as occurred at the Mansion House and Guildhall, in 1882 and 1890, respectively. In the wake of the Kishinev pogrom in 1903, a mass demonstration was held in London's Hyde Park. Parliament similarly condemned anti-Jewish persecution, with MPs and peers asking insistent questions as to the possible reactions of Her (and later, His) Majesty's Government. The Foreign Office, though bound by discrete diplomatic etiquette, was involved in investigating persecution at first-hand, its findings published as parliamentary Command Papers. Thus, although there was widespread hesitancy about interference in the affairs of a foreign state, it did not follow perforce that British public and political opinion was hamstrung by it. If a regime claimed to rank among the civilised, but continued to pursue a persecutory policy by, say, refusing to grant civil emancipation or allowing anti-Jewish violence to occur on its watch, then surely it was incumbent upon British public opinion to highlight, in no uncertain terms, this iniquity? The methods by which this was undertaken form a central theme of this study. So, too, are the consequences of this response in terms of Britain's attitude towards 'foreign' Jews, largely in Imperial Russia, divided (later reunited) Poland and Romania. It also considers Britain's relationship with its own Jews.

* * * * * * * * * * * *

The nineteenth and early twentieth centuries spanned an age of intense intellectual enquiry in Britain, a period host to an array of questions related to the political, international, social and economic *status quo*. Alongside the Jewish and Irish questions could be found, for example, the Eastern or Balkan question (how could the Great Powers deal with the disintegrating Ottoman Empire?); the woman question (should half the adult population have the vote, or not?); the labour or socialist question (what could be done to ensure the working classes were not drawn to socialism?); and, of course, the alien question, which was usually, but not always, concerned with whether East European Jews should, or not, be permitted to come and live in the United Kingdom. There were many more such questions, some of lesser longevity, and others that arose during particular moments of domestic and international difficulty, such as the Congo question in the decade before the First World War.

Formulating these questions was straightforward enough, less so the process of finding adequate and workable answers. This was perhaps more true of the Jewish question than any other, since the confounding nature of Jewry, especially in Eastern Europe, thwarted rational efforts at amelioration. There were no straightforward political solutions, such as the redrafting of treaties or international borders, the division of land, the granting of the vote or the institution of parliamentary government (of course, these were by no means easy solutions either, but according to contemporary perceptions they were more straightforward in their precedence). In the matter of the Jewish question, for instance, was mass emigration from Eastern Europe and elsewhere a possible solution? Could part of Africa, or even South America, be designated as a Jewish state, or would Palestine serve? Should there be a Jewish state at all? Were Jews a race, a religion or a nation? Was assimilation the solution (especially in an age when wholesale religious conversion was unacceptable, in Europe at any rate)? Or, should pressure be exerted on governments, rather than on Jews themselves? If the Jewish question was perhaps not as important in its immediacy and proximity as, say, the Irish question, it can nevertheless be argued that it was more problematic, not least because Jews were to be found in every European state. Moreover, its inherent complexity and its Eastern European variant were as difficult for British Jews to negotiate as their gentile contemporaries.

Hitherto, historians have paid scant attention to British perspectives towards Eastern Europe's Jewish question. Whilst there have been studies of British responses to particular events and incidents of crisis in Eastern Europe, there has been no study that has examined the British narrative of the Jewish question in relation to its Eastern, or for that matter, Western European counterpart.[8] Instead, the Jewish experience, and the construction of antisemitic discourse in Britain, has mainly been considered within the intellectual and geographical limits of Britain itself. For instance, the earliest studies of the aliens question, worthy though they may have been, did not compare the British response to its continental counterpart, despite the fact that the issues with which Eastern European Jewish immigration was fraught were just as controversial in Imperial Germany, France and the Habsburg Empire.[9] No doubt as a consequence of this, individuals deemed to have explicitly promoted an antisemitic agenda in Britain, such as Arnold White and Joseph Bannister, have been exceptionalised in the British context.[10] Others, such as Hilaire Belloc and G.K. Chesterton, have mostly been half-heartedly compared with the most extreme antisemitic variants on the continent, as though virulently Jew-hating Nazis constitute the only viable point of reference.[11]

More recent studies, it is true, have partially moved away from this compartmentalised analysis and attempted to investigate the broader construction of the figure of 'the Jew' in popular and political discourse, and considered the ramifications for late Victorian and Edwardian society.[12] Nonetheless, even this has largely been undertaken within the context of the aliens debate, or the South African Wars, or the development of conspiracy theories that linked Jews to the press, to Germany and socialism on the eve of the First World War. In other words, only the domestic context has been considered, and no convincing comparison to any continental equivalent has been undertaken. Surely, however, in an age of mass communication, when it took just a matter of minutes to send a telegram from one city to another, when newspapers in every land reported what was happening in another in great detail, the British relationship with the continent and the wider world requires examination?[13] This is particularly apposite in relation to the Jewish question and the development of modern antisemitic discourse, which, even in the twenty-first century, employs language, images (both literary and visual) and frames of reference that are remarkable in their universal endurance, appeal and intent.

An underlying assertion in the historiography of British attitudes towards Jews and the Jewish question has been that the British position was unique, that developments on the continent were entirely separate and any comparison simply falls at the first hurdle. This interpretation began long before any historiographical explanation was attempted. Even when Britain experienced incidents of anti-Jewish violence, such as in the East End of London in 1903–1904, in South Wales in 1911 and Leeds during the First World War, these were dismissed as freakish events, as utterly inconsistent with anything occurring in Eastern Europe, despite the fact that something as apparently minor as the smashing of a window in a Jewish shop actually constituted a pogrom in Imperial Russia, even if an individual was not physically attacked in the process.[14] Indeed, as we shall see, many of the problems inherent in interpreting the Jewish experience in Eastern Europe, which often originated in tandem with specific contemporary events, remain an obstacle in some historiographical interpretations to this day.

My own view is that neither geopolitical boundaries, nor the physical separation that is the English Channel, constitute an impenetrable border in the development of attitudes towards Jews and the Jewish question. On the contrary, I believe that late nineteenth- and early twentieth-century Britain was intrinsically and intricately linked to the continent of Europe by a multitude of intellectual, cultural and political ties. To be sure, Britain may be popularly characterised as existing in 'splendid isolation' in the diplomatic arena on the eve of the First World War, but I regard this as a facile and simplistic explanation in any context. In the period with which this study deals, intellectual and cultural exchange existed on many levels, and, given the array of information available at the fingertips of a society with a universal literacy rate just shy of 100 per cent, it was nigh impossible to formulate attitudes in isolation on many matters.[15] This was especially the case in relation to the Jewish question. Even if one's own interests lay primarily with immigration, consumers of the daily and weekly press could not fail to be influenced by articles that exclusively discussed East European Jewish life in Romania, divided Poland and Russia.

It is my belief that akin to those directly observing developments in the late nineteenth and early twentieth centuries, historians of British antisemitism and the Anglo-Jewish experience only consider matters from a Western European standpoint. As a consequence, 'the East' persists in appearing an exotic, 'different' and (most frustratingly, not to say disparagingly) a 'backward' entity, utterly removed and detached from 'the West'. Yet, from a British perspective in the late nineteenth century, the experience in 'the East' was far from intellectually untrammelled, despite the varieties of difference and distance that had to be overcome. In the earliest stages of this study, I was especially drawn to individuals for whom, like me, 'the East' was just as important as 'the West', the British pioneers of East European studies who laid and managed a tricky path of investigation. The questions I formulated about these individuals inevitably marked my intellectual point of departure: what did Russia/Poland/Romania mean to them? How did they imagine and portray these lands? Were the intellectual origins of their explorations driven by domestic or foreign agendas? What forms of cultural baggage did they carry on their journeys, metaphorical or otherwise, back home? And how, most importantly, did this impact on manifestations of the Jewish question in the British imagination?

Individuals such as Charles Saroléa, Bernard Pares and E.J. Dillon spurred my initial interest in British perspectives of the Eastern European Jew, but since I did not want to write a biographical study of one or more of these individuals, it was therefore essential to consider the broader aspects of their influence and, more particularly, the construction of the wider British narrative on the Jewish question. This is what I have attempted to do below, and, instead of exceptionalising the British experience, I have endeavoured to highlight its continental connections, its similarities and its inseparable relationship in matters related to the Jewish question. I am primarily concerned with the public arena, the written and, sometimes, the spoken word, the allusions, tropes and metaphors it generated, as well as their place, utility and function in contemporary discourse on the Jewish question. As will be seen, in this most crucial aspect of the modern Jewish experience, the way that Jews were imagined and described (by both non-Jews and Jews), Britain certainly did not dwell in isolation, splendid or otherwise.

* * * * * * * * * * * *

This study begins with an analysis of Romania in the late 1860s, a state that has heretofore merited little historiographical interest in relation to its Jewish question and the ramifications for the British context. Yet, contrary to expectations that might assume Tsarist Russia was the prime British concern in this period, it was Romania that dominated newspaper columns throughout the late 1860s and 1870s. The claim to 'being civilised' lay at the root of this anxiety, and whether or not Romania could be characterised as such. For this reason, Romania's refusal to emancipate its Jews ensured that British indignation was regularly roused throughout the latter decades of the nineteenth century. Of course, such considerations were not unique to the British context. Civil emancipation was a widely accepted requirement by the 1870s (it had already been granted, among other states, in Imperial Germany, France, Italy, Greece, Switzerland, the Kingdom of Poland and the Habsburg Empire), and its absence on any state's statute book raised crucial questions about civilisation's progress since the dark, medieval centuries of religious bigotry. For this reason, Jewish emancipation occupied a part of the agenda at the Congress of Berlin in 1878, which subsequently saw the institution of legal and civil equality for the Jews of Serbia and Bulgaria. From a British perspective, therefore, Romanian values did not belong to the nineteenth century and it needed to be brought into line.

Yet, as we shall see, even in dealing with a relatively minor player on the European stage, Britain's effort to prick the Romanian conscience mostly failed. Interference was greatly resented and emancipation was only finally granted in 1923, largely as a consequence of pressure exerted at the Paris Peace Conference. How, then, did British moral indignation fare when encountering the might of the Tsarist Empire? In this case, the approach was somewhat different. Notwithstanding the unwillingness of the Tsar(s) to grant emancipation to the Empire's Jewish subjects in the western provinces (modern Ukraine, Belarus, etc.), British interest in this corner of Europe was mostly reactive. Generally, there was only a limited effort in British opinion to encourage the Tsarist regime to follow the path that was required of Romania. Instead, concerns arose during moments of particular crisis and, as a consequence, in light of specific anti-Jewish legislation, such as the continued existence of the Pale of Settlement, the part of the Tsarist Empire to which the majority of its Jews were required to reside.

The tone of admonition was sometimes more cautious when dealing with Tsarist Russia. Even in the aftermath of the Kishinev pogrom, to which the world responded in shrill horror, British opinion was often fairly restrained about any indictment overtly directed towards Tsar Nicholas II. No doubt this was conditioned by international considerations, since Britain and Russia were Imperial rivals for much of the period under discussion. Nevertheless, the issue of religious rights took their place in the British narrative of Imperial Russia's Jewish question. Indeed, it was no coincidence that at the two most significant anti-Russian meetings in 1882 and 1890, proceedings were dominated by leading Christian figures. But what did this reveal about late Victorian society? More specifically, what did it reveal about the nature of British Jewry and the reality of its position within wider society? These are the questions this study considers.

By the turn of the twentieth century, the hope that had heralded earlier decades seemed wholly unfounded. Outbreaks of anti-Jewish violence in Eastern Europe became ever more commonplace, especially in the Tsarist Empire. And, notwithstanding the massive political upheaval Russia witnessed in the decade before the Great War, no concessions were made to Jews. In another part of the Tsar's realm, the Kingdom of Poland, a new variety of anti-Jewish sentiment made its ugly debut. Political and racial antisemitism formed a crucial component of the ideology of the Polish National Democratic Party, led by Roman Dmowski, which from 1912 promoted an anti-Jewish economic and social boycott throughout divided Poland. The opening salvoes of the First World War portended the beginning of a prolonged period of tragic and terrifying turmoil for Eastern Europe's Jews. Caught at the heart of battle, expulsion, refugeedom, hostage-taking, pogroms and famine all became mainstays of the Jewish experience in these years. Even the optimism generated by the Russian Revolution in February 1917 was short-lived, despite the fact that it was accompanied by civil emancipation. Nor did the Great War's end bring any respite in tragedy. In 1918, Poland's rebirth was accompanied by yet more devastating pogroms, as was the internal encounter in the former Russian Empire during the Civil War. Trapped between the armies of Red and White, Jews were victims of both. By this stage, Jews also encountered an insidious allegation that suggested they were behind the Bolshevik *coup d'état* of October 1917. It was a lie that bore countless consequences.

From the British perspective, all these events – war, revolution, the redrawing of national and ethnic boundaries – were vitally important. But how high on the scale of consideration was the East European Jew in these times of troubles? How did Britain respond to the daily accusations of disloyalty and espionage that Jews were forced to negotiate throughout the Great War in the East? What could be done in terms of material relief? These matters continued to be relevant during the Russian Revolution and the Civil War. By this stage, of course, the discourse of the period had wrought additional ramifications for Jews. The advent of racially based intellectual developments, the reconfiguration of 'the Jew' as not only a religious but also an ethnic outsider, was hugely significant by the first decade of the twentieth century. In the years after the Great War, it was particularly relevant in light of Poland's rebirth, where the question of ethnic minority rights occupied the thoughts of negotiators at the Paris Peace Conference. As we shall see, the Jewish position in the new Poland was, to say the least, somewhat ambiguous.

Throughout the period under scrutiny, the issue of the Jewish image, how Eastern European Jews were imagined and described, merited major consideration in the British narrative of the East European Jewish question. Any catastrophe, whether in Romania, Poland or Russia, inevitably prompted a re-assessment of the nature of the Eastern Jew, and his religious, social and political habits. The extent to which this was fixed, whether the same characteristics were applied to all East European Jewry in the period under question, forms another theme of this study. Were Romanian, Polish and Russian Jews regarded in the same terms, or were different attributes ascribed? In this regard, this study examines internalised visions of national, ethnic and religious otherness, for which, as we shall see, there was effectively a double bind in the British context. After all, where were the most singular lines of otherness to be delineated in Eastern Europe? Did British observers consider the Russian/Polish/Romanian gentile less or more exotic than the Russian/Polish/Romanian Jew? Sometimes the precise orientation of these attitudes was difficult to discern. A truly significant answer to this question only really coalesced under the threat of a mass exodus of Jews from Eastern Europe, which, in turn, ensured that the East European Jewish question inherently carried a domestic resonance. For British public opinion, what happened to the Eastern European Jew mattered and this continued to be the case for many decades to come.

* * * * * * * * * * *

From the 1860s, British print journalism acquired an increasingly important role in day-to-day life, which gradually, as a consequence of advances in print technology and the telegraph, brought Britain ever closer to Eastern Europe. By the 1880s, there was barely a corner of the United Kingdom without a representative newspaper, and even the most locally orientated, maintained an increasing interest in the world beyond the local, the county and the national. During the 1860s and 1870s, for instance, apparently parochial dailies like the *Leeds Mercury*, the *Hull Packet and East Riding Times* and the *Bristol Mercury* were interested in the fate of Romania's Jews. In London, the capital city of a vast Empire, its printing presses barely stood still for a second, as newspapers were churned out morning and evening, on a daily and weekly basis. Fascination for the Eastern European Jewish question grew in step with Britain's print media and, given the increasing sophistication by which newspapers operated by the twentieth century, the role of foreign and special correspondents became hugely important.

Inevitably, newspapers make up the most significant source in this study, though I cannot claim to have examined every single British newspaper published between 1867 and 1925. Oftentimes, the chronology of specific events, such as pogroms, international congresses and the like, has dictated my examination of particular newspaper runs. Similarly, because of space limitations, not every single reference to the East European Jewish question that I located in the British press appears in the footnotes. Nevertheless, I have tried to be as thorough as possible and consider the various colourings of the British press – liberal, right-wing and, in particular, the Jewish perspective; after all, to this day Britain remains home to the world's oldest continually published Jewish newspaper, the *Jewish Chronicle* (founded in 1841). I have also ensured that my investigations were not confined to the extensive London press and have, therefore, utilised titles published throughout the United

Kingdom. In the matter of image, of course, events did not necessarily dictate the sources, such as the unravelling of British attitudes to Polish Jews over several decades. In this instance, it was the narrative itself that marked the point of departure.

Even in the nineteenth century, there was not a single British newspaper that formulated and disseminated its opinions in isolation. Rather, every newspaper, every weekly and monthly journal, no matter where it was published, formed a network of complex linkages, of references and counter-references, of ideas shared and rejected and of polemic upheld and disparaged. Even *The Times*, which oozed a certain form of Imperial self-confidence and belief, often referred to other publications, to other correspondents and, of course, assisted in constructing and illustrating a narrative formulated beyond the world of newspapers. But these networks stretched much further than the national arena. By the 1890s, British newspapers, especially those based in London, were connected through all manner of ties to their continental and international counterparts. This included, as we shall see at the time of the Kishinev pogrom, Yiddish and Russian language newspapers. The growth of news agencies, such as Associated Press (founded 1846) and Reuters (1851), obviously assisted in the wider broadcast of information and opinion. In a similar vein, developments in transportation facilitated the progress of rapid communication across the continent, which also enabled the physical movement of continental newspapers and their representatives. Leading newspapers in St Petersburg had subscribers in London and *vice versa*.[16] And freelancers plied their wares throughout the continent.[17] Naturally, this carried significance beyond the world of newspapers. The century also witnessed the creation of international institutions, including Jewish organisations, which allowed interested parties to swiftly convene a sympathetic meeting, send a petition or an appeal in any given city. By the twentieth century, whatever was happening to Jews in Kraków, Kiev or Bucharest was often as much British news as it was Polish, Ukrainian or Romanian.

Naturally, print media is a way for historians to examine popular attitudes, since, even in the 1860s, it was incumbent upon newspaper editors to publish news that was interesting to their readers. Otherwise, why would anyone buy their newspaper? But the press also had an intrinsic connection to the political world. For example, parliamentary proceedings appeared verbatim in almost every daily newspaper. Government policy, domestic and foreign, was scrutinised in editorials and leading articles. And, in the case of Eastern Europe's Jewish question, meetings between Jewish representatives and government ministers were regularly reported. It was the political world, of course, that represented the true agency of change. Popular meetings were not only intended to highlight the obloquy of a foreign miscreant. They were also designed to attract the attention of HMG, which, it was hoped, would use the appropriate official channels to register British disdain. For this reason, several major political sources are used in this study, including a number of official publications, as well as parliamentary debates. Occasionally, it was on the floor of the House of Commons that the most strident opinions on Eastern Europe's Jewish question were expressed.

The kind of communication channels and transnational linkages available to observers and correspondents in the period under investigation, whether in the newspaper or political world, facilitated the transmission of not only news, but opinion and prejudice. In the matter of the Jewish question, this naturally has significant resonance. It enables, for instance, the historian to compare various 'national' attitudes towards Jews and the Jewish image, to measure them in different cultural contexts. In this aspect, whether or not expressions of anti-Jewish sentiment were similar in Britain and Eastern Europe is of special significance. More particularly, did one influence the other? In this study, principal interest lies in the degree to which Russian/Polish/Romanian discourse on the Jewish question was absorbed into the British narrative. Were the same images, allusions and stereotypes deployed? By the same token, did British newspaper reportage of a particular crisis mirror its East European counterpart? In other words, how was Britain intellectually, culturally and prejudicially linked to Eastern Europe? These are questions that will be considered below.

* * * * * * * * * * *

The anti-Russian meetings of the 1880s and 1890s and other seemingly positive British responses to particular Jewish crises have previously been viewed by historians within the context and as a reflection of alleged 'philosemitism' in the United Kingdom.[18] In this aspect, public meetings, editorials and individual champions of a given Jewish cause have been regarded as evidence of extensive British tolerance towards religious and ethnic differences in general, and the Jewish case in particular. Inevitably, within themselves these notions pay homage to the apparent reason that meetings were convened in the first place, which, in turn, render British values in the era under investigation as inherently fore-bearing and open-minded. Clearly, this is a somewhat unsophisticated approach to an inevitably complex matter. From the outset, therefore, this study, in its analysis of the British response to the Eastern European Jewish question, dispenses outright with 'philosemitism' as unhelpful delineation. For, even in the organisation of a single public meeting, as we shall see, responses were infinitely more multifaceted than a straightforward demarcation of 'good' or 'bad' gentiles, as the 'philosemitic' interpretation suggests. What is more, meetings, condemnatory editorials and speeches in parliament were far from unique to the British context. Nor, for that matter, were they even confined to 'enlightened' Western spheres of influence. Even at the throbbing heart of the anti-Jewish beast (as the Tsarist Empire was widely regarded by the late nineteenth century), individuals and communities responded to Jewish crises with their own public meetings, petitions and newspaper editorials.[19] Moral indignation was not the unique preserve of the British, no matter how highly or smugly they placed themselves on civilisation's scale.

In addition, a second problematic expression deserves attention here. As already indicated, the Victorians were more than aware of ideological developments on the continent. For instance, the earliest use in *The Times* of the term 'antisemitic' occurred in November 1880, in connection with developments in Germany.[20] Whereas the term 'antisemitism' did not make its debut until October 1882, this time in light of political divisions in Vienna, evident in the Habsburg *Reichsrat*.[21] To be sure, this was not long, in fact, after it had been coined (or at least decisively used) by the German ideologue, Wilhelm Marr, in his 1879 pamphlet *Der Sieg des Judenthums über das Germanenthum* ('The Victory of the Jews over Germandom').[22] Thus, as a foreign definition of anti-Jewish feeling, it was absorbed remarkably rapidly into regular English language usage; indeed, in the 1880s and 1890s, it oftentimes retained the capitalisation it bore in the original German. However, its use was imagined in very specific terms, which applied exclusively to manifestations of anti-Jewish sentiment in the political and ideological arena, as Marr himself intended. Therefore, Karl Lueger in Vienna, Édouard Drumont in Paris and Marr in Berlin fell under the antisemitic rubric, as did the political parties that attempted to present an anti-Jewish petition to German chancellor Otto von Bismarck in 1881. Occasionally, the term was deployed to describe other manifestations of anti-Jewish feeling, such as the Russian pogroms and expulsions.[23] But in the matter of anti-Jewish violence, commentators usually fell back upon other expressions, such as 'Jew-baiting', 'outrages' and 'Hep! Hep!' (as we shall see, 'pogrom' did not enter regular usage until 1904–1906).[24] Similarly, legal restrictions in Eastern Europe were seldom described as antisemitic, regardless of the motivations that lay behind their implementation. This remained the case for much of the period under discussion, and it was only really in the decade leading to the First World War that the expression began to acquire a wider meaning, beyond political division and ideology.

For this reason, I have chosen to avoid overuse of the term 'antisemitism', since, like the Victorians and Edwardians, I also believe it refers to a specific brand of anti-Jewish sentiment, which is particularly relevant in the period under investigation. In this context, I do not think it especially useful to deem any individual who is discussed below as an 'antisemite', though they may be described as holding antisemitic attitudes. To do so would, in my view, reduce the import of the term itself and the concepts to which it relates/espouses. Furthermore, this study is in no way intended to be some kind of witch-hunt, hopeful of uncovering an apparent truth about late nineteenth- and early twentieth-century British society, that it was inherently antisemitic and populated by antisemites. That, in fact, Britain was no better than some of its continental neighbours. Whilst there is a truth that might be argued here, it remains an unhelpful objective in this kind of study, which focusses on a broad response and the deconstruction of a wide narrative, over three or four generations.

Instead, the principal objective of this study is to demonstrate that attitudes towards Jews – that is towards the Jewish question – were innately complex. 'Antisemitism' and 'philosemitism' suggest, of course, a world of opposites, a dichotomy, which by its very nature squeezes out all non-categorical attitudes, or at least renders them less significant. Yet, as we shall see, there was not a single attitude held by an individual, nor a single sentence, article or comment in a newspaper that could be usefully deployed in summary of late nineteenth- and earlier twentieth-century British views on Eastern Europe's Jewish question. As a consequence, this study recognises that all responses merit attention, whether good, bad or indifferent.

Image 1   Eastern Europe, 1902

Map outlining Major William-Evans Gordon's tour of Eastern Europe in 1902, published in his book *The Alien Immigrant* (see Chapter 4 for discussion of this trip). As the crow flies, Evans-Gordon's journey encompassed some 4500 kilometres, and took in the Habsburg and Tsarist Empires, as well as Romania, an indication of geographical range in which the Jewish communities of Eastern Europe dwelt at the beginning of the twentieth century. Many of the cities he visited, such as Vilnius (Vil'na), Kraków, Warsaw and Lemberg (L'viv), were hugely significant in Jewish terms in this period. Thus, this was not simply an extraordinary journey in geographical terms, but culturally and intellectually, too. The Pale of Settlement is depicted in the map with diagonal stripes - and, as usual, it is erroneously rendered, since it is shown as including the Kingdom of Poland, which was not a part of the Pale (see Chapter 4 for the problems this presented for the British perspective).

1
Romania: 'Cruelty to an Unprecedented Pitch', 1860s and 1870s

Nothing can be more insolent than the complacent continuance of the system of ill-usage of the Jews in Romania – a state which only exists by the indulgence of the great powers of Europe.

Jewish Chronicle, May 1872

The more liberty [Romanians] obtained, the more illiberal they became.

The Scotsman, June 1877

Romanian freedom: 'a sad beginning'

Had British commentators been asked in the 1860s where in Europe the Jewish lot was at its worst, there is no doubt the majority would have pointed a condemnatory finger at Romania. Throughout the decade, reports of anti-Jewish violence and expulsions, outbursts of antisemitic polemic and legally instituted discrimination were regularly relayed to the British press from this corner of the Balkans. The *Jewish Chronicle*, leading newspaper of Anglo-Jewry, often featured items relating to the desperate plight of Romanian Jews. For instance, in July 1866 it reported the malicious destruction of a Bucharest synagogue.[1] That same month, hostile parliamentary speeches delivered by Romanian politicians were reprinted, with one deputy denouncing Jews as 'wretched pariahs'.[2] In June 1867, the *Chronicle* described an 'outbreak of fanaticism' in the actions of the Romanian Prime Minister Ion C. Brătianu who was accused of carrying out 'measures from which a savage potentate in the interior of Africa would have recoiled'.[3] Again, damage to Jewish life and property was detailed. The same

16

year, a horrifying report of the drowning of four Jews in the town of Galatz (today, Galaţi) received intense coverage.[4] The victims had, according to the *Chronicle*, been forced into the river Danube because of a Turkish–Romanian border dispute.[5] A year later, the mainstream press reflected on a recent bill presented to the Romanian chamber of deputies, which aimed to regulate Jewish life in the finest of detail. It required, for example, that Jews seek permission to reside in both countryside and the town, forbade them to own land or property and, in a particularly spiteful gesture, to sell food or drink directly or indirectly to Christians.[6] In 1869, provincial newspapers highlighted another slice of unpleasant oratory from a Romanian politician, Mihail Kogălniceanu, in which he described Jews as 'vagrants' and 'a real pestilence'.[7]

For the *Chronicle* and other British newspapers, these manifestations of anti-Jewish sentiment in Romania, which recurred to an alarming degree, were not only the source of undisguised revulsion, but disappointment too. Romania's path to independence began in 1862 with its liberation from the Ottoman yoke and the unification of the principalities of Moldova and Wallachia. These actions were an indication to British minds of the Romanian potential to move into the orbit of Western European civilisation. Alas, these expectations were soon dashed. In large part, the Romanian leadership's Jewish policy was to blame. 'What', asked the *Chronicle*, was the 'first use of [Romania's] newly-acquired freedom?' The answer, it seemed, was the 'oppression of an inoffensive race [and] inexcusable violence directed against a peaceable' community. 'A sad beginning', indeed, to the embryonic years of Romanian liberation, as the oppressed swiftly turned oppressors.[8]

The British preoccupation with Romania's Jewish question persisted throughout the 1870s. Official enquiries by both Houses of Parliament revealed that the significance of anti-Jewish persecution in Romania was not confined to newspaper columns and editorials.[9] In 1872, 10 years before its notable Russian equivalent (see Chapter 2), a meeting was held at London's Mansion House, home to the Lord Mayor and located in the heart of the capital's financial district. It roundly condemned 'the outrages' committed on Jews in Romania, events regarded as a 'disgrace to Christianity', and was attended by a range of influential figures drawn from society's religious and political ranks.[10] All resolutions at this meeting were proposed and seconded by non-Jews, but British Jews also played a considerable part in publicly supporting their Romanian co-religionists.

In the House of Commons, questions were often tabled by the Liberal MP Sir Francis Goldsmid, who had originally made his mark as England's first Jewish barrister.[11] As a result of the incident at Galatz, the aged Sir Moses Montefiore, venerable doyen of Anglo-Jewry and a widely respected philanthropist, attempted a personal intervention and travelled to Romania to negotiate with representatives of the regime.[12] Other leading communal figures, such as the Chief Rabbi Dr Nathan Adler, the lawyer Sir John Simon MP and Alfred de Rothschild gave their weight to the campaign; all were present at the Mansion House in 1872. In later decades, prominent members of the community's major institutions, the Anglo-Jewish Association (AJA) and the Board of Deputies, continued to draw attention to the cause. These included Romanian-born religious leader Moses Gaster and Lord Nathaniel ('Natty') Rothschild. During the half century until the outbreak of the First World War, Romania was never absent from Anglo-Jewry's litany of international concerns.

In many ways, however, promoting this particular Jewish case was a complex task. In comparison to Imperial Russia, for instance, which was to feature as the continent's greatest persecutor of Jews from the 1880s onwards, Romania rarely registered on Britain's diplomatic or political radar. Its geographical remoteness and economic insignificance ensured that it only intermittently figured in the reportage of Eastern Europe. In line with similar process in and South-Eastern Europe, its movement to full independence was monitored with interest, especially during the final ratification process at the Congress of Berlin in 1878.[13] But Romania attracted few intellectual and political converts in Britain, in contrast to Imperial Russia's numerous aficionados. From the early twentieth century, the academic and journalist R.W. Seton-Watson was its principal and, for the most part, only advocate.[14]

Akin to those commentators who extolled the virtues and achievements of the Tsarist Empire, Seton-Watson romanticised Romania, heralding it as the 'sentinel of Latin culture in the East of Europe, a racial link with Italy and France amid a world of alien peoples'. During the First World War, he described it as the 'Belgium of the East', a comparison with tremendous resonance at that particular moment.[15] In an account that admired Romania's recent economic achievements (its 'oilfields and wheat granaries'), its scenic beauty ('wild forests and upland valleys') and its apparent progress since liberation from the retrograde dominance of Turkey, Seton-Watson also examined the nature of its Jewish question. Reflecting on the preceding 50 years, Romanian Jews had, he wrote, 'many just grievances' and an 'anomalous' legal status.

They were, in fact, 'citizens of no-man's-land'.[16] Even though Seton-Watson was himself unsympathetic towards the Romanian Jewish cause, he pithily encapsulated the difficulties that had tormented Romanian Jews for over half a century. Notwithstanding the violent assaults – both verbal and physical – that frequently marred Jewish lives, or the extensive legal restrictions on their economic and social activities, the central theme of British consternation with this South-East European state was the Jewish right to Romanian citizenship. It was a subject to which commentators constantly returned, in every single decade from the 1860s onwards. For British observers, the failure of the Romanian government to confer citizenship upon its Jews, despite a myriad of external pressures, succinctly defined the entire Jewish experience in Romania until the Great War. In Edinburgh, during the 1867 Galatz incident, *The Scotsman* had described Romanian actions as 'cruelty to an unprecedented pitch'.[17] For British public opinion, such a phrase might easily have stood for all aspects of Romania's Jewish policy.

Reality and myth: Jewish life in Romania

The nineteenth century was a significant period for the Jewish experience in Romania for a number of reasons. The community witnessed, for instance, a considerable demographic expansion. At the end of the previous century, Romania's Jewish population had numbered less than 20,000.[18] By 1899, according to the census of that year, it had increased to almost 300,000, a figure representing around 4.5 per cent of the entire population.[19] These statistics bear testimony to more than demographic change. In the first half of the nineteenth century, the community grew as a result of in-migration from Galicia and the Russian Empire that was encouraged, in its earliest phases, by Romanian landowners, who actively sought Jewish talents in servicing the merchant and middle ranks of an overwhelmingly peasant society.[20] Until the early nineteenth century, a substantial proportion of Romanian Jews were of Sephardic descent and spoke Ladino; by 1899, Yiddish-speaking Ashkenazim formed the majority.[21] Indeed, Europe's first professional Yiddish theatre was founded in Jassy (Iaşi), in 1876.[22]

Romanian Jews mostly resided in major urban centres, such as Jassy and Bucharest, principal cities of Moldova and Wallachia, respectively. In common with the bulk of the their East European counterparts, their occupational skills ranged from various commercial and middle-man activities, including money-lending and exchange, to manual labour and tavern-keeping.[23] By the end of the nineteenth century, a great many, if not the majority, lived beneath the poverty line, a situation hardly assisted by the Jewish policies of the regime. As in Russia, Congress Poland and Austrian Galicia, the dire economic circumstances faced by Romanian Jews prompted many to emigrate in the late nineteenth and early twentieth centuries. By 1912, the Jewish community had shrunk to around 240,000, and it now represented about 3.4 per cent of the total population.[24]

It is unlikely that economic deprivation was the sole motivating factor for emigration, since the regime took steps to hinder the progress of Jewish life in Romania on many levels. Various pieces of legislation, such as those that proscribed the ownership of farms, taverns and property, curbed Jewish membership in the professional classes, as well as the upsurge in Romanian nationalist ideology and popular anti-Jewish resentments, all contributed to a situation from which there seemed no escape within Romania itself. Jews were effectively regarded by the Bucharest regime as unwanted foreigners or aliens. As part of the gradual process leading to independence, Romania's first constitution was codified in 1866, and it declared, in what became the notorious and symbolic Article 7, that only Christians could hold Romanian citizenship.[25] This provision subsequently ensured that individual Romanian Jews, no matter how many generations they and their families had resided in Romania, were prevented from obtaining citizenship. Beyond religious conversion, ways of circumventing the law were circuitous and even those who served in the armed forces (Jews were obliged to serve, though they were not permitted to become officers) were by no means guaranteed constitutional parity with their ethnic Romanian counterparts. These limitations exercised many Western Europeans, especially in Britain and France, where Jewish emancipation and civil equality was (sometimes) viewed as a *sine qua non* of nineteenth-century civilisation.

Such proscriptions were legitimised by the prevailing intellectual climate in Romania.[26] In the view of one historian, the Romanian parliament also became a forum in 'which deputies gave free vent to invectives against the "Jewish invasion"'. In that same arena, Ion C. Brătianu, who often drew the venom of the *JC*, described Jews as a 'social disease', a 'wound' and a 'plague' on Romania.[27] To be sure, in many ways, manifestations of anti-Jewish sentiment in Romania were little different to those in other parts of Europe, especially in the East. Jews were viewed as a destabilising social and moral influence, the very antithesis of the peasant, who formed Romanian society's majority.[28] Jewish economic activities, whether as tavern-keepers or 'vagabonds', were deemed exploitative and their image 'transmuted into a symbol for all the socioeconomic tensions racking' nineteenth-century Romania. Regardless of political affiliation within its parliamentary and intellectual ranks, antisemitic ideology was an 'omnipresent corollary' of the Romanian nationalist idea.[29] Brătianu and Kogălniceanu were not isolated figures; in fact, they represented mainstream political currents. Further down the social scale, Judeophobia bared its teeth in other ways and, well into the twentieth century, Romania was host to anti-Jewish rioting, vandalism and the like. The Great Peasant Revolt of 1907, in particular, witnessed an assault on Jewish property and lives.[30]

How did British observers interpret this undisguised anti-Jewish sentiment in Romania? Was a connection made between the regime and its people? If so, in which direction did the influence flow? In 1867, in the wake of the Galatz incident, *The Times* was under no illusion as to the link between the two. There was evidence, it said, that Romanian officials had tried to blame the Galatz deaths on Turkish malfeasance, but there could be no doubt who was really responsible. As consequence of the laws that restricted residency in the countryside, Romanian officials had rounded up and deported hundreds of Jews throughout 1866 and 1867.[31] Galatz was viewed as a component of this policy. For *The Times*, the ruling system in Romania simply reinforced and legitimised anti-Jewish sentiment at the lower end of the social scale:

> under the influence of M. [Brătianu], the [Romanian] Government urged the local authorities to remove vagabonds or vagrants from the country. This order seems to have been aimed particularly at the Jews, many of whom are, of course, natives of neighbouring countries who have settled in [Romania] for the purpose of trade, and who are now looked upon with the usual dislike both by the dealers whom they undersell and by the buyers with whom they drive hard bargains. But whatever the intention of M. [Brătianu's] Circular, it has undoubtedly given an opportunity of ill-using the Jews, which an ignorant and bigoted people has not been slow to seize.[32]

In some ways, of course, this was a questionable perspective. *The Times* criticised the Romanian regime's anti-Jewish attitudes, whilst simultaneously upholding the veracity of a negative Jewish stereotype, the hard-bargaining trader. Nevertheless, that prominent Romanian figures held outspoken and sometimes extreme views on the Jewish question is indisputable. However, the matter of whether or not incidents of localised anti-Jewish violence in Romania were linked to government policy has not, in Western historiography at any rate, been proven. But in the 1860s, the dots were easily joined up. It was assumed that popular brutality towards Jews was, at worst, ordered from above. At best, vehement anti-Jewish polemic expressed in the chamber of deputies simply served to justify individual attacks on Jews and their property.

No British reporter was to be found in Romania at this moment. Any judgement made in the columns of the British press resulted, therefore, from analyses of material sourced elsewhere. Most reportage was dependent upon transcontinental telegraphic agencies and, in particular, the *Alliance Israélite Universelle* (AIU), the principal international Jewish organisation of the period. Led by Adolphe Crémieux, a republican member of the French chamber of deputies and vice-president of the *Consistoire Central des Israélites de France*, the AIU was instituted in 1860 to deal specifically with the kind of crisis manifest in Romania.[33] In the main, it aimed to explore and put pressure on various diplomatic channels in the hope of remedying the social and political ills of contemporary European Jewry. But it was also a great engine of publicity, collecting and disseminating material to interested parties throughout the continent and the United States.[34] Inevitably, since Romania was its priority in the 1860s and 1870s, its findings regularly appeared in the British press.[35] The activities of the AIU, particularly Crémieux's attempt at personal intervention during a visit to Bucharest in 1866, served to confirm the British belief that the Romanian regime was in active and hateful pursuit of its Jews.[36]

Other important sources of information at this time were the British diplomatic reports on Romania presented to parliament in 1867. Given the recurrent incidents of anti-Jewish violence, as well as the implementation of legal limitations on Jews, British consular officials in Bucharest, Jassy and elsewhere were in regular contact about these matters with the Foreign Office. They also met with members of the Romanian regime in order to ascertain official perspectives and to outline the British response. These reports essentially confirmed the Romanian government's manipulation of anti-Jewish feeling and Brătianu was once again held culpable. In an interview with the British Consul in Jassy, A.B. St Clair, the Romanian minister revealed that his circular on vagrants was aimed at getting 'rid of the helpless and filthy Jews who found no occupation [in Romania], as their agglomeration in large towns contributed mainly to the extension and creation of epidemic diseases'.[37] Such a concept, absent from *The Times'* assessment, was hugely significant. If these were the words that Brătianu spoke (it is not unlikely), then he accused Jews not only of financial exploitation but also of harbouring and spreading life-threatening diseases. This was a revealing indictment, indicative of the dangers that 'the Jew' posed in the Romanian nationalist mindset.

But what of an examination of the part played by the lower orders in the promotion and acceptance of anti-Jewish sentiment in Romania? What were their motivations? Why were they apparently so easily led? No analysis in the British press, or official reports, posed these kinds of questions. It was the regime and its members that drew the focus of attention. Romanian society itself was a shadowy presence in British interpretations and there was little insight into its structure. To be sure, the lower orders were easily led, though there was an implicit suggestion that they also needed to be led. Newspaper and consular reports inferred that persecution could not occur without the role and permission of the authorities. In consular accounts, for instance, various Romanian officials were viewed as instrumental to the violent outbreaks of the 1860s. This was not only true of senior government ministers, such as Brătianu, and it was revealed, for instance, that in implementing various regulations 'subordinate employees had acted without judgement'.[38] Thus, the political promotion of anti-Jewish sentiment and legal proscriptions in Romania had a trickle-down effect. It was for this reason that in the 1870s, the British anti-Romanian campaign primarily focussed on trying to stir the Christian consciences of Romania's leaders. If Brătianu and others of his ilk could be steered onto the correct path, the rest of Romanian society would surely follow.

Mansion House 1872: marshalling indignation

The 1870s witnessed a renewed international interest in the fate of Romanian Jewry. In 1870, the United States, for instance, appointed a special consul-general to Bucharest, Benjamin Peixotto, whose brief was specific to the Jewish question.[39] His interventions sometimes appeared in the British press.[40] In the recently unified Germany, Gerson von Bleichröder, Jewish banker and advisor to its chancellor, Otto von Bismarck, began a discreet campaign on behalf of Romanian Jews. Regularly in communication with Crémieux throughout the 1870s, Bleichröder was to play a crucial role at the Congress of Berlin in 1878, where the issue of Romanian Jewish emancipation featured on the agenda.[41] The early 1870s were also significant from the Anglo-Jewish perspective. Two public meetings were held in support of Romanian co-religionists. The first took place in Birmingham, and the second, as already mentioned, was in London at the Mansion House. There were to be similar gatherings in subsequent decades, each of them indicative of British reactions to incidents of anti-Jewish discrimination, especially in its physically violent manifestations, throughout the continent. This marshalling of collective indignation was made possible by an earlier development, the creation in 1871 of the Anglo-Jewish Association, effectively the British arm of the AIU. It was formed by influential Jews, including the barrister Jacob Waley, who became its first president, alongside Sir Francis Goldsmid and Sir John Simon.[42]

The heightening of collective and communal abhorrence in 1872 was invoked by anti-Jewish disturbances in Ismail (Izmail) and Cahul (Kagul), both then located in Moldova. The crisis precipitated in the former town caused the most concern, where the riot's incitement was found in the allegation that a Jew had stolen the 'holy vessels' from a church.[43] According to one British consular report, this included 'a gold and silver cross, a silver casket containing the consecrated bread, and two spoons used in the Holy Communion'.[44] In another report, Colman Goldenberg, a British Jew resident at Ismail, informed his consulate that the stolen items were '100 ducats and two spoons'.[45] But there was no question over what had subsequently occurred. A mob, fuelled by alcohol and vengeance violently set upon any Jew that crossed its path.[46] Men, women and children were 'beaten, wounded, plundered [and] driven out of their houses'.[47] Two synagogues were reportedly destroyed and rapes committed against women, each violation of the worst imaginable kind.[48] Terrified for their safety, hundreds of Jews sought refuge in various consulates and 'on board an Austrian steamer'.[49] The Romanian response to this violence was not encouraging. The *Pall Mall Gazette* reported that a rabbi in Cahul and four other 'innocent men' had been 'condemned to three years dungeon for the robbery committed in the church'.[50]

As will become evident in subsequent chapters, this description of a sustained and violent attack on individual Jews and their communities presaged the standard manner in which Russian pogroms were repeatedly portrayed by British commentators in the late Imperial period. The role of alcohol, rape and indiscriminate cruelty universally featured in descriptions of pogroms. Moreover, the religious origins of the local populace's hatred oftentimes proved to be of similar significance. In this Romanian case, the items that were allegedly stolen in Ismail, as well as the location of the theft, indicated that religious animosity was the root cause of the subsequent riot. A church was not merely robbed, but desecrated; in one account, it was suggested that the site was defaced or defiled in the 'most filthy and disgusting manner'.[51] Of particular importance was the theft of the 'silver casket containing the consecrated bread'. This revealed a connection to a medieval anti-Jewish accusation, host desecration.[52] Thus, the townspeople were not driven to attack their Jewish neighbours because of a simple case of theft; rather, it could be ascribed to their fear that Jews were planning to do harm to the sacramental bread, to the body of Christ. Although such specific notions were not explored in the British response to these events, the wider religious aspect was often highlighted. During an earlier incident in September 1871, for example, the *Manchester Guardian* reflected upon a blood libel accusation in Bucharest and subsequent mob violence.[53] These interpretations, of course, affirmed the widely held belief that Romanian society was primitive, superstitious and out of step with contemporary civilisation. The same would also be said of Imperial Russia.

Undoubtedly, it was these religious elements and the issue of religious equality that drove the convening of the two anti-Romanian public meetings held in Britain during 1872. In Birmingham a gathering was organised in the city's town hall by a noted local secularist, Charles Cattell. Despite its good intentions, however, the protest was a failure. In the first place, many of the renowned figures invited by Cattell were unable to attend, including the Liberal politicians and local MPs, John Bright and George Dixon.[54] But it was not the absence of these notables that undermined the meeting's message. Under the influence of Sir Moses Montefiore, few members of the local Jewish community attended. Montefiore had made it widely known that it was 'inadvisable' to hold a public meeting on Romania at this moment. This was because Montefiore believed interventions should be made discreetly, preferably behind closed doors. In this action, he revealed a connection to wider, well-established continental Jewish diplomacy, the practice of *shtadlanut*.[55] Since Montefiore's word was much respected, Jewish communal leaders in Birmingham decided not to join protestors at the town hall.[56] When a small group finally convened on 28 March 1872, only two members of the Jewish community attended, Louis Stern and J. Creamer. The latter wrote a disgruntled letter to the *JC*, which reflected upon the disappointing character of the meeting and the absence of leading Jews.[57]

The divisions tacitly expressed in this response to the Birmingham meeting were typical of the many internal problems that Anglo-Jewry would be forced to negotiate in future decades. As we shall see, dissension arose on every occasion that a public meeting related to a specific act of foreign persecution was proposed. In 1872, Anglo-Jewish society was certainly not united in rejecting or boycotting the Birmingham meeting. Although he did not attend, for instance, Sir Francis Goldsmid made it known that, although he was personally unable to be present, he fully backed Cattell and his aims.[58] Goldsmid was very active in publicly and privately promoting the Romanian Jewish cause throughout 1872. He wrote directly, for example, to the Foreign Secretary and requested the British Government make representations to Bucharest.[59] On 27 April 1872, he made a long speech in the House of Commons, in which he adumbrated Romanian abuses since 1866.[60] In the weeks that followed, Goldsmid was instrumental in the formation of the AJA's Romanian Committee, which comprised several other prominent figures, including Sir David Salomons and Lionel de Rothschild.[61]

Although the AJA had engaged in an international protest in the year since its foundation, the Romanian campaign was a real opportunity to justify its existence.[62] At this moment, it did not claim the unanimous support of Anglo-Jewish society.[63] In the *Jewish Chronicle*, for example, letters of objection were published which argued that since the subscription fees were comparatively high, the AJA had been founded on a class basis. There was also the question of what the Board of Deputies future role would be. With Moses Montefiore as its president, the Board was the oldest communal organisation in Britain. Although mostly concerned with domestic issues, it sometimes got involved with international matters, but preferred to conduct its protests behind closed doors. In 1872, for instance, Montefiore sent polite and private letters to the Foreign Office on the Board's behalf, but did not give any bold public statements.[64] The establishment of the AJA, therefore, represented the possibility creating a more dynamic influence on the British response to the Eastern European Jewish question. Its initial reaction was, however, fairly conventional as a philanthropic campaign was mounted on behalf of victims in Ismail and Cahul.[65]

By March 1872, the AJA attempted to publicise the wider ramifications of the crisis. It strongly believed that Britain's 'remonstrance [of Romania] must surely be effective'.[66] The upshot of these ambitions was the Mansion House meeting, at which a full cohort of prominent British Jews convened in strident defence of their Romanian brethren. At this moment, there was evidently a palpable sense of wider responsibility and conviction in the abilities of British Jews to act collectively beyond the ministration of relief. Indeed, the *Chronicle* deemed the Mansion House meeting as an 'era, a red letter day, in the annals of the Anglo-Jewish community'.[67] But the meeting not only served to highlight the Anglo-Jewish community's sense of itself and its responsibilities within the Jewish world. Perhaps the proudest achievement at Mansion House was the degree to which non-Jews were involved, and the social ranks from which they were drawn. One of the most distinguished figures of Victorian society, the Earl of Shaftesbury, was the principal speaker and proposer of the first resolution. A host of Members of Parliament also attended, both Jewish and non-Jewish, several Christian religious leaders such as the Bishop of Gloucester, and it was presided over by the Lord Mayor of London, Sir Sydney Waterlow.[68] A clear agenda at the meeting was emphasised with the distribution of a pamphlet written by a leading member of the AJA, Israel Davis.[69]

It is evident from the proceedings at Mansion House, as well as comments in the *Jewish Chronicle*, that the AJA and its prominent leadership (most of whom were parliamentarians) believed that any condemnation issued to Romania could not take the form of a Jewish message alone. It had to be a British message, one that united Christians with Jews. Communal ties were subsumed to a greater intention and, in many senses, identity. In urging people to attend the meeting, the *JC* encouraged everyone to cast aside political, class and religious affiliations, whether Jew or Christian: 'Minor differences of opinion must be sunk in the great object of supporting momentous interests involved in this question.' At the same time, the outside world must see that Jews were not 'lukewarm in a Jewish cause'.[70]

Thus, the meeting at Mansion House was about much more than the sufferings of Romanian Jews. It also concerned the standing of Anglo-Jewry within British society. Emancipation had not occurred overnight in Britain, and in 1872 its final steps remained a part of living and, sometimes, personal memory.[71] Leading British Jews were not, under any circumstances, about to throw away the advantages of their recently acquired civil and political equality. On the contrary, Mansion House provided an opportunity to show that Jews and gentiles shared the same values, that they were built of the same moral fibre and could, when called upon, equally demonstrate the true nature of what it meant to be British. 'A great outcry has gone forth from this country', said the *Jewish Chronicle*, 'declaring the detestation felt by Englishmen for cruelty, intolerance and fanaticism'.[72] It happened to be the case that the cruelty was experienced by Jews, but it was not simply for a Jewish cause that the cry had been raised. 'Romanian bandit-patriots' would do well to take heed of English values too.[73]

Following the events at Mansion House, the unequivocal support British Jews acquired for their Romanian campaign encouraged further action. In early June 1872, a small deputation met with the Foreign Secretary, Lord Granville. It was led, once again, by Lord Shaftesbury and attended by, amongst others, Goldsmid, Salomons and Chief Rabbi

Adler.[74] Granville assured the meeting of his interest and concern in the fate of Romanian Jews, and affirmed that he had already communicated with his continental counterparts on the matter. Russia, it seemed, had regretfully declined to become involved. Nevertheless, the *JC's* subsequent report on Granville's assurances burst with enthusiastic optimism. In particular, it reflected positively on the involvement of leading Christians. It clearly hoped that Granville and Shaftesbury's denouncements would prick the conscience of Romanians on the grounds of shared faith, if not the same church.[75]

Thus, by default and design, it was a Christian message that was emphasised at this moment. Did Anglo-Jews detect any irony in this? It appears not. Rather, the emphasis on Christian values – which Jews in turn emphasised as 'English' values – and their denigration by Romania was viewed as a political advantage. Similarly, Anglo-Jews chose to ignore the fact that Lord Shaftesbury had, for many years, acted as the president of an evangelistic organisation, the London Society for Promoting Christianity Among the Jews.[76] Who, on any grounds, could gainsay the involvement of such a towering figure of Victorian society? Shaftesbury's presence simply added weight and, more importantly, publicity to an already potent argument. As we shall see, in subsequent decades Anglo-Jewish society would be similarly moved to compromise in defence of its foreign co-religionists.

Romanian Jews in the British mindset

On the face of it, British society, especially in parliamentary spheres, appears to have been sympathetic to the Romanian Jewish cause. The basis of Romanian persecution and their 'civil death', as one observer termed it, made the case reasonably straightforward from a British perspective.[77] Jews were as much entitled to constitutional parity as their Romanian Christian counterparts. There was, therefore, simply no legal or civilised basis for the Bucharest government's persistent pursuit of discriminatory legislation. From a contemporary perspective, the British desire to bring Romania to book was comprehensible, straightforward and wholly justifiable.

However, simplifying the Romanian Jewish question in this manner rendered Romanian Jews themselves somewhat obscure, anonymous and passive figures in the complex manoeuvrings of international politics. The principle of civil equality was the paramount consideration, not the economic, social and cultural characteristics of the Romanian Jew. Geographical distance afforded this particular kind of objectivity, especially since at this time, beyond the diplomatic corps, few British commentators actually had any kind of first-hand contact with either Romania or its Jews. As will become apparent in subsequent chapters, this contrasted with the Russian and Polish contexts of later periods. But what of those who had direct experience of Romania? How did Romanian Jews fare in their imaginations? Such questions are clearly important in considering the immediate context prior to the Congress of Berlin.

As has already been inferred, Romanian Jews were depicted as victims, who laboured under a wide range of restrictions, both social and economic, that were enforced by a repressive regime. This was apparent in the many Romanian tales of discrimination, violence and denunciation that were published in the British press during the 1860s and 1870s. Indeed, articles almost always featured a run-down of the various pieces of legislation that restricted Jewish life, from those concerned with vagrancy and tavern-keeping, to others that prevented the acquisition of citizenship and land. Yet an insightful piece in *The Scotsman*, which, as usual, outlined every piece of legislation, actually attempted to understand the motivations behind Romanian discrimination. Why, it wondered, did Romania's rulers hate their Jews? After all, it observed, Romanian Jews were capable of 'greater industry' when compared to their gentile counterparts. They had many talents as artisans, 'bricklayers, roof-coverers, horse dealers and painters'. Unfortunately, this correspondent argued, these achievements were the subject of jealousy in Romania, where a suspicion of foreigners reigned supreme. Anti-Jewish prejudice was thus implicitly deemed as xenophobia, rather than Judeophobia; as a corollary to this, the dislike of other minority ethnic groups, such as Greeks, was also highlighted.[78] According to another article in *The Scotsman*, discrimination in Romania had become 'a system; it is but the consequence of a hatred to strangers generally'.[79]

Without these laws, said *The Scotsman*, Romanians believed that the whole of the country would be in the 'hands of the Jews'.[80] The article eschewed the notion that there was any possibility of this occurring, but it is worth noting that the notion of any state potentially falling into 'the hands of the Jews' was an important antisemitic trope in the nineteenth century. In later decades, it was not a notion simply connected to political takeover (local or national), but to economic dominance in a world, moved by modernity, which had become ever more complex. In a state such as Romania, where most of the population were peasants, the clever manipulations of 'the Jew' were of major resonance and certainly formed a component of nationalist discourse. Thus, *The*

Scotsman's correspondents delved into yet more interesting and revealing political currents in Romania. At the same time, although readers would have gleaned a sense of the spheres in which Jews were employed, even in this sympathetic piece they mostly remained voiceless victims.

Not all commentators, however, were as measured and temperate in their analyses. A paragraph from an article in the *Saturday Review*, from April 1872 (not long after the Mansion House meeting), recorded a quite different perspective:

> It is not merely religious fanaticism that sets the Romanians against the Jews. It is the old story. The Jews are too clever for the Christians. They are more thrifty, more intelligent, more united. They make money when the degraded Christians do not make it. They lend money and get hold of the property of their debtors, and this the Christians resent. There is something certainly very sweet to the barbarous mind in first taking a man's money, and then, when he wants his money back, kicking him and beating him and half killing him on high religious grounds. The Romanians are in this respect only in the mental state in which Englishmen were in the thirteenth century. [...] Wherever money is to be made, and [Jews] are permitted to hold life even as a persecuted and miserable race, they flourish, multiply and grow rich. No spot is too remote, no form of trade too disgusting, no climate too unhealthy for the Jew. He does not fear isolation or discomfort, for he and his people have been for centuries isolated and miserable. He is sustained by the hopes of his religion and by the contemplation of the gold he accumulates. In Romania the Jews are said to be hated more than in the other semi-barbarous countries in the vicinity, because there are so many of them there. They aggravate the Christians by multiplying as the sands of the sea, where they are most trodden underfoot and persecuted; and fear of a power they cannot crush is one of the strongest influences at work to animate the fury of the Romanian population. [...] There is no real difference between the Romanian Jews and the Jews of Galicia or Bohemia, nor can they in their turn be separated from the Jews of Germany, of France, or of England. The dirty greasy usurers of Romania are the humble brethren of the financier of London and Frankfort, and that the Jews are a great power in Europe is incontestable.[81]

It seems unlikely that this commentator actually went to Romania, a 'semi-barbaric' state upon which he (or she?) had very little positive to say. Instead, they simply utilised Romania's Jewish question as a hook upon which to hang a whole range of undisguised Judeophobic antipathies. Excessive fecundity, greed, dirt and the ability to live in unhealthy conditions were all allusions to the fact that, in the mindset of this unnamed author, Jews were far from being passive victims. Their greed, money-making endeavours, selfishness and immorality indicated a community that was proactively engaged in fleecing its neighbours, whether rich or poor. But these circumstances were hardly unique to Romania. Rather, this was a warning that required heeding throughout the continent, including Britain. The final sentence, in particular, indicated a general attitude to all Jews, rather than the specific Romanian case. Put simply, Jews were Jews and exhibited the same characteristics no matter where they resided. It comes as no surprise to learn that the *JC* was swift to denounce these sentiments.[82]

For those with day-to-day contact with Romania, the diplomatic correspondence of the late 1860s and 1870s illustrates a variety of British attitudes towards Jews. The Consul at Galatz, George B. Ward, for example, wrote sympathetic reports to the Foreign Office about a number of incidents, including the actions of a mob in late 1868. The origins of this riot, in his view, were of religious significance and some kind of blood libel accusation appeared to have been made: 'this disturbance arose out of the vulgar belief that Jews use human or Christian blood for certain purposes connected with their religious ceremonies.' Ward then noted the subsequent physical assaults made on individuals and property, as well as the failings of the local authorities in quelling the actions of the rioters. For the most part, Jews appeared once again as hapless victims, though Ward also reported efforts at self-defence: 'the Jews suddenly appeared in force, and belaboured the mob furiously with sticks.' Both Jews and non-Jews were wounded in a disturbance that lasted for 'about three hours'.[83] This was a glimmer into a quite different rendering of Jewish–gentile relations in Romania, in which Jews appeared as proactive participants in their own destiny, but it was not explored further.

Ward suggested that the origins of anti-Jewish sentiment in Romania were reliant on religious animosity and ancient accusations, for which he clearly held no truck. But not all officials upheld such judicious perspectives. Vice-Consul St John, resident at Jassy in the 1870s, did not invoke or embrace the blood libel, but he called to mind an array of Judeophobic allusions in his reports to the Foreign Office. Referring to the Jassy community, for instance, he observed that most were wealthy, possessed 'frugal habits' and had 'succeeded in monopolizing every trade or calling by which money can be turned'. These activities were responsible, according to St John, for the legislation that limited Jews from selling alcohol, and, from the regime's perspective, it was a simple matter of protecting the already 'demoralized' working class. In explaining anti-Jewish sentiment in Jassy, St John asserted that:

> The marked antipathy existing in this town towards Jews arises not so much on account of the difference of religion as from their persistency in not conforming to civilized habits and dress, and more particularly from their palpable want of cleanliness – a fact which any one may easily ascertain by passing a few hours at Jassy.[84]

In another report, St John reiterated these views, observing that 'filth [...] together with usury, and a desire to prey on the Christian community, seem to be their sole objects in life; hence their unpopularity'.[85] Some Romanian nationalists would have found much to concur with here, though, as we shall see in subsequent chapters, even in the British context they were not unique.

At this moment, just a year or two after the Mansion House meeting, several leading Anglo-Jews and the AJA continued to exert pressure upon the British government on behalf of their Romanian brethren. Sir Francis Goldsmid remained especially active and wrote regularly to the foreign secretary, Lord Granville, on the subject. He also had access to some of the reports sent by British representatives in Romania, including those by St John. Reflecting on the notion that Romanian Jews were 'uncivilized', Goldsmid wrote:

> As to the remark with which [St. John's] report concludes, that the antipathy existing at Jassy towards Jews arises from their want of civilized habits, I have certainly heard it before; but I have been assured by competent persons, well acquainted with the country, that there is no ground for it, because although perfectly true that the Romanian Jews are imperfectly civilized, it is equally true that the rest of the population is more uncivilized still.

These reflections indicated that St John's words were not perhaps as offensive to Goldsmid as might have been imagined. Rather, as an Englishman and a Jew, Goldsmid's measure of civilisation was, in some ways, equal to that of St John, particularly given the assertion that ethnic Romanian society was 'more uncivilized' than its Jews. Nevertheless, Goldsmid asked, how could Jews be deemed an 'inferior civilization' when the same report described their success in 'every trade by their industry, perseverance and frugality'?[86] Of course, such characteristics with their Smilesian echoes, despite their negative usage by St John, formed the bedrock of Victorian values.

Goldsmid was not the only prominent member of the community to tackle British Judeophobic discourse on the Romanian Jewish question. Sir John Simon found himself at the centre of a heated discussion in 1876, played out in the pages of the *Pall Mall Gazette*. The dispute began with an item in which Simon revealed that anti-Jewish persecution in Romania was entirely the product of religious intolerance.[87] Four days later, a letter responding to these views appeared under the pseudonymous signature 'Veritas'.[88] According to this correspondent, the truth of the Romanian Jewish question had nothing whatsoever to do with religious persecution. On the contrary, Romania was a state in which all religious creeds were tolerated. The real source of aggravation, it turned out, were the practices and behaviour of Jews themselves. In essence, the correspondent argued, they had flooded into Romania from Russia and Galicia, and subsequently attempted, quite deliberately, to take over every aspect of Romanian economic life. What was more, their numbers were growing at an exponential rate. 'Fancy, Sir', Veritas wrote, 'if every fifth person you met in London was a Jew! If every fifth shop was closed on the Jewish as well as the Christian Sabbath!' According to Veritas, Jews held in their hands 'all the business, from banking to the selling of matches'. Evidently, there was little to recommend in these views, and they embraced a wide range of Judeophobic sentiments, for which there was domestic resonance. It is unlikely, however, much like the correspondent in the *Saturday Review* that Veritas had ever been to Romania – though this is speculation. Nevertheless, he had been influenced by Romanian nationalist discourse, since words attributed to Mihail Kogălniceanu were directly cited.[89]

Inevitably, Sir John Simon was swift to refute these perspectives. He sent two letters to the *Pall Mall Gazette*, each of which carefully anatomised and undermined Veritas' accusations.[90] Similar criticism was made in a letter from the editor of the *Jewish Chronicle*, Abraham Benisch.[91] In the years since the Mansion House meeting, Anglo-Jewry had kept the subject of Romanian Jewry alive through various means, in parliamentary questions, as well as the columns of newspapers. Since the foundation of the AJA, a good deal of experience in campaigning on a larger stage had been acquired. In October 1872, for instance, several of its representatives had attended an international congress of Jewish organisations in Brussels.[92] A similar meeting occurred in the same city in 1876.[93] All of which was experience for an even greater arena, the Congress of Berlin. Here, Anglo-Jews, along with their continental counterparts, could, in theory, do more than simply raise the topic of Romanian Jews in the press or in private conversations with government ministers. This time, there was the possibility of playing a very real role in realigning Romania's Jewish policy. Perhaps Anglo-Jews would ultimately assist in resolving once and for all an issue that had troubled their consciences for many years. This was the optimistic intent that Anglo-Jewish society bore in its heart on the journey to Berlin.

Berlin: the final hurdle?

Europe's Great Powers, Russia, Germany, France, Italy, Austria-Hungry and Britain, met at Berlin in June 1878 to reconfigure the map of South-East Europe in the wake of the Russo-Turkish War (1877–1878). Their lengthy agenda comprised various border revisions in the Balkans, the independence or autonomy of Montenegro, Serbia, Bulgaria and Romania, and, somewhat further down the list, an intention to resolve the Serbian and Romanian Jewish questions.[94] The principal British delegates were the Prime Minister Benjamin Disraeli (by then, the Earl of Beaconsfield), the Foreign Secretary Lord Salisbury and Lord Odo Russell, ambassador to Germany. Naturally, the protection of British imperial ambitions lay at the heart of their intentions. From the Jewish perspective, in Britain, France and Germany, the Congress was seen as an opportunity to raise the issue of civil equality for Romanian Jews in an extremely powerful arena. These aspirations were initially raised by Crémieux and the AIU, which, in turn, utilised the influence of Gerson von Bleichröder.[95]

In Jewish circles in Britain, the possibility of exerting pressure on the international resolution of the Romanian Jewish question had been broached with the highest authorities even before the outbreak of the Russo-Turkish War. Following the April 1876 Bulgarian uprising against the Ottomans, an international conference convened in Constantinople. Meeting with the then foreign secretary, Lord Derby, a group of influential Jews, including John Simon, Julian Goldsmid (an MP and nephew of Sir Francis) and Henry de Worms, urged the British government to table at the conference the issue of Jewish religious and civil equality in Romania and Serbia.[96] This elicited a few approving sentences from Derby, but no subsequent action. Not disheartened by this failure, Anglo-Jewry enthusiastically grasped the next international opportunity and from March 1878, began an open discussion of its hopes for the Congress of Berlin. Francis Goldsmid discussed the issue in parliament, as did Baron Henry de Worms.[97] In early June, a week or so before the Congress convened, a public meeting was held by the AJA in Islington, north London. Attended by a range of prominent figures, it reaffirmed the community's aspirations. In his speech, de Worms stressed the need to remove 'the unjust ban imposed upon nations by reason of their creed', and he urged Jews to press their claims forcefully at Berlin:

> If you cannot make yourselves loved, you must make yourself feared, not in the usual acceptation of the word, not feared by acts of violence or illegality, but feared by the position which intelligence can command when backed up by indomitable energy and perseverance, and crowned by the most absolute integrity.[98]

There was an evident recognition in these words and the general tone of the meeting that Jews must no longer act in a passive manner, that they could and should take an active role in determining their own future. It did not matter if they made enemies in the process, for crucial principles were at stake. These principles were far from being applicable only to Jews. Such sentiments were expressed in open letters sent by the AJA, the Board of Deputies and Baron Lionel de Rothschild to the British delegates at Berlin.[99]

Beyond Anglo-Jewish spheres, other British commentators were naturally interested in the proceedings at Berlin, though mostly, it must be said, in their wider ramifications. *The Times*, however, made special mention of Romania's Jewish question. It observed, in the first place, that Jews had already proven their entitlement to full constitutional rights, given the patriotism that many had displayed in serving the Romanian army during the recent hostilities against the Ottoman Empire in its war with Russia. Secondly, it noted that the disabilities the Romanian government had implemented against its Jews had little to do with religious discrimination. Rather, Romania was, somewhat foolishly, 'terrified at the [possibility of the] over-powering competition of Jewish capitalists'. However, if Romania granted equality to such a skilled, industrious and ambitious people, it could only be beneficial to a society that was basically socially and economically backward. Finally, the removal of anti-Jewish laws in Romania was advised, once again, on the grounds of civilisation:

This is not so much a question of the interest of the Jews, or of any other nationality, as of the recognition of principles which Western Europe has long ago come to look upon as the chief tests of a liberal and progressive civilisation.[100]

These perspectives clearly chimed with those of the Anglo-Jewish community. Evidently, all of Eastern Europe needed to embrace Western European standards, otherwise its social and economic progress would continue to stall. This was especially relevant to Romania.

Just like any other international congress, proceedings at Berlin were not straightforward and every delegation brought its own agenda. Historians have made much of Bismarck's role, both in the final ratification of various borders and national rights, as well as matters related to the Jewish question.[101] In early July 1878, Bleichröder sent a telegram to Moses Montefiore in London advising that the Congress had concluded that religious equality was a condition of Romanian independence.[102] The Great Powers, he said, would only ratify Romania's existence if its government rewrote its constitution and dismantled every piece of anti-Jewish legislation. But even this was a complicated affair. Article 44 of the Treaty of Berlin, for instance, noted the qualifications for Romanian citizenship, which, at face value, might be regarded as a victory for those who had fought for a solution to the Jewish question:

In Romania the difference of religious creeds and confessions shall not be used against any person as a ground for exclusion or incapacity in matters relating to the enjoyment of civil or political rights, admission to public employments, functions and honours, or the exercise of the various professions and industries in any locality whatsoever. [...] The freedom and outward exercise of all forms of worship shall be assured to all persons belonging to the Romanian state as well as to foreigners, and no hindrance shall be offered to either the hierarchical organisation of the different religious communities nor to their spiritual leaders.

But, although this seemed fairly broad in its limitations, another clause of Article 44 was dropped. It had read: 'The Jews of Romania who do not belong to a foreign nationality have the right to acquire Romanian citizenship.' This was a crucial omission, resulting from another Bismarckian *démarche* that, as Carol Fink has indicated, 'doomed Jews to another generation of discrimination'.[103]

Nevertheless, from an Anglo-Jewish perspective the initial response to the Treaty of Berlin sounded a note of triumphalism. At the annual meeting of the AJA, held in July 1878, Baron Henry de Worms spoke of the 'successes' at Berlin and indicated his belief that the Congress surely heralded a new phase for Jewish political activism on the world stage:

> The only real weapon the Jews have at their disposal is that of publicity. It is our duty to hold up to public obloquy all acts of oppression and violence [...] we should demonstrate to the world that there is no reason for the oppression of the Jews, that the Jew is entitled to the same rights and privileges as other men, and that the wrong is on the side of the oppressor and not the oppressed. [...] We must show the world that we are ready to do battle for our rights.

Of course, it was perhaps a simple matter to speak in such strident terms, given the relatively comfortable position in which British Jews found themselves by the late 1870s. Such a perspective would not have been quite as certain had it been viewed through the eyes of Romanian Jews. Nevertheless, this speech and the actions of the AJA were significant in light of their broader context. The Berlin Treaty demonstrated that Jews, including British Jews, were capable of organising themselves in the cause of their distant co-religionists, that they carried political influence and that they need not fear the repercussions. In addition, de Worms justified the AJA's existence and its essential difference from other Anglo-Jewish institutions, such as the Board of Deputies, by emphasising that it was 'not an eleemosynary body'. Instead, its two principal tasks were, firstly, the emancipation of the un-emancipated and secondly, the elevation of 'our brethren above the level of our oppressors'. The second task was to be achieved via the promotion of educational schemes, an objective chiming with the ambitions of the AIU.[104]

In the history of the Anglo-Jewish experience, 1878 was undoubtedly a significant year. But was it for Romanian Jews? The Treaty of Berlin was a bitter pill for the Romanian leadership to swallow. Territorial gains were made, independence was recognised, but the conditions were disagreeable. External interference in domestic affairs was much resented, especially when it came from Western Jewish organisations.[105] Yet, inevitably, this interference persisted, especially on the part of Anglo-Jews. In July 1879, for instance, a full year on from the Congress, a deputation of prominent Jews, including Henry de Worms, met with the Foreign Secretary Lord Salisbury. The meeting expressed the hope that Britain would accept 'no compromise' on the issue of Jewish emancipation in Romania.[106] The AJA also issued a pamphlet on the matter in 1879 and distributed it to all members of parliament, in both the Commons and Lords.[107]

By this stage, July and August 1879, British observers were aware that, following discussions in the Romanian parliament and beyond, the provisions of the Treaty of Berlin were going to be ignored, or, at the very least, circumvented. At this stage, Romania attempted some damage limitation, and in August 1879 Foreign Minister Vasile Boerescu was sent to negotiate its position with various European governments.[108] In an interview with the French Prime Minister W.H. Waddington (who had been a French representative at Berlin), Boerescu revealed that it 'was impossible to confer naturalisation indiscriminately' on the Jews of Romania. It could only be given to 'those whose intelligence gave them an interest in the stability of Romanian institutions', a somewhat vague diagnosis of Romanian intentions and attitudes.[109] Boerescu's mission was met with disdain in the British press, and he was accused of ignoring Romanian 'crimes and errors of the past'. What was more, he represented a regime that had tried to delay 'a rational settlement of its Jewish question simply to save a handful of boyars from the natural consequences of their own worthlessness and incompetence'.[110]

A similar outlook was laid before Western Europeans by other Romanian politicians in 1879. Ion Ghica, who had twice been Romania's prime minister in the 1860s and 1870s and was appointed Romanian minister to London in 1880, wrote a letter to *The Times*. In response to a recent debate in its columns about the Jewish question, Ghica was uncompromising in the views he expressed. He noted, for instance, that all Romanian capital was 'in [the] hands' of Jews and that, as a result of excessive fecundity and immigration, they represented about 15 per cent of the total population. He also observed that there were two distinct communities, one of Spanish origin, the other Polish. Ghica was positive about the Sephardim, whom he said were, in many ways, little different from ethnic Romanians. But Ashkenazi Jews lived 'by low means or extortion', 'in the greatest filth' and had nothing 'in common whatsoever with the customs, feelings [and] aspirations of Romanians'.[111] The *Daily News* recorded correspondingly categorical perspectives held by the Romanian minister to Paris, N. Callimaki-Catargi.[112]

The Romanian parliament took over a year, until October 1879 in fact, to finally pass a law that rewrote Article 7 of the constitution.[113] Instead of expressly stating that only Christians could hold Romanian citizenship, it now read: 'Difference in religious beliefs and confessions does not constitute, in Romania, an obstacle to the obtainment of civil and political rights, nor to the exercise of these rights.'[114] Whilst the Great Powers accepted this rephrasing, the Romanian reality was that a great many obstacles were constructed, which, in no uncertain terms, aimed to prevent the Jewish acquisition of citizenship. These included a requirement to personally petition the Prince (later King), followed by a 10-year period of residence, during which the petitioner had to prove his 'usefulness' to Romania. Even Jews who served as soldiers were only infrequently granted citizenship. Thus, rather than emancipate all its Jews in a single legal act, as other European states had done, in the Romanian case individual Jews were required to prove their worthiness to the nation. Between 1879 and 1900, according to the estimate of one historian, only 85 Jews became naturalised citizens in Romania.[115] The majority remained, in the eyes of the regime, foreigners. In a very short time, the widespread hope that Romania's Jewish question had been resolved at the Congress of Berlin rapidly came to grief.

* * * * * * * * * * * *

Throughout subsequent decades the matter of Jewish religious equality in Romania regularly appeared in British newspaper columns, as did atrocity stories. In 1884, for example, *The Times* concluded that the 'war against Hebrews is being waged with greater determination than ever' in Romania.[116] From 1880 to 1886, the British Minister in Bucharest, Sir William White, made regular appeals to the Romanian regime about its Jewish question.[117] For its part, despite the disappointments and frustrations of Berlin, Anglo-Jewry continued to agitate on behalf of its co-religionists. In the 1880s, for example, Henry de Worms regularly asked questions in the House of Commons and sent letters to newspapers highlighting Romania's continued contravention of the Berlin Treaty.[118] In the opinion of the *Jewish Chronicle*, the worst features of persecution were the perpetual legal assaults on Jews, such as the law on hawking of 1884, which threatened to remove every economic opportunity from Jews in the Romanian countryside.[119] The following year, the AJA sent another deputation to the Prime Minister Lord Salisbury, which hoped for government intervention in Romania's failure to adhere to the Berlin Treaty.[120] That same year, Britain welcomed a Jewish exile from Romania, Moses Gaster, who rapidly became a beacon of faith for his compatriots. Appointed as *Haham* of Britain's Sephardic community in 1887 (although he was actually Ashkenazi), in the decades to come Gaster often spoke out on Romanian Jewish matters and also provided financial assistance to Romanian immigrants in Britain.[121]

These efforts at intervention continued for many years to come, for full civil equality was not granted to Romanian Jews until after the First

World War. But, notwithstanding these recurrent appeals, by the early 1880s Romania was no longer the priority – from both a Jewish and non-Jewish perspective. Its place as the continent's greatest menace when it came to the Jewish question was usurped, in the most terrifying manner, too. In some ways, for Anglo-Jews what happened in the Russia Empire in 1881–1882 came as a surprise. Surely, nothing could be worse than the shocking nature of Romanian Jewish policy, the riots, the blood libels, the expulsions and the vicious political speeches? Indeed, reflecting in 1877, the editor of the *Jewish Chronicle* had noted that many Jews had fled Romania to seek succour in more enlightened states. At this moment, it turned out that Jews were 'treated with more humanity' under the rule of Romania's neighbours, the Hapsburg and Tsarist Empires.[122]

Yet, within a year or so of Romania finally being granted independence in February 1880, following a tacit approval of its new constitution by Britain, France and Germany, a new Jewish crisis presented itself. This time, the epicentre of anti-Jewish violence was located in a different realm, the Russian Empire. Beginning in April 1881, a series of anti-Jewish riots gripped the communities of the south-western provinces of the Empire. Thereafter, for almost 2 years, Tsarist Russia was convulsed by recurrent and destructive waves of violence that, from a British perspective, seemingly knew no end in their intensity and hatred. As British commentators – Jewish and non-Jewish – soon came to learn, the pogroms of 1881–1882 would surpass even Romanian persecution in their intensity and consequences.

2
Imperial Russia: Troubles in the South, 1880s–1890s

The Jew and *muzhik* are fire and tow. A spark, and we have, as in the present case, a conflagration.

Jewish World, May 1881

The Russian mob are about the last in the world either to attempt a breach of the peace, or to succeed in their efforts [...] unless with the connivance of the authorities.

Morning Post, February 1882

Not all fiddlers: Jews in the lands of the Tsars

From the 1880s onwards, in the matter of Eastern Europe's Jewish question the British imagination was predominantly focussed on events in Imperial Russia. This is, of course, no great revelation. The pogroms of 1881–1882, the expulsions of the early 1890s and 10 years later a major convulsion in the form of the Kishinev pogrom all ensured that the British spotlight of enquiry inevitably shifted from Romania to Imperial Russia.[1] Domestic matters reaffirmed this significance, since many thousands of Russian Imperial Jews, who were regarded as the first-hand victims of Tsarist persecution, upped sticks and crossed the continent to make new lives in Western Europe and beyond. Of all European cities, London was the most popular destination, where the East European Jewish immigrant founded new communities that altered in remarkable aspect the imperial capital's ethnic, religious and, in many ways, political landscapes. In the latter part of the 1880s, the British narrative of the East European Jewish question was oftentimes intrinsically entwined with the more domestically pressing 'alien problem'.

It goes without saying that for Russian Imperial Jewry, the 1880s was a momentous decade. The 1881–1882 pogroms afflicted a broad geographical swathe of the Russian Empire, taking in cities as far apart as Ekaterinoslav, Kiev, Odessa and even Warsaw.[2] Hundreds, perhaps thousands of Jews were rendered homeless and their livelihoods shattered. Subsequently, further interference was wrought upon Jewish life, this time in the actions of the Russian Imperial government. The so-called May Laws of 1882, which, amongst other restrictions, limited Jewish residency in the countryside, were viewed in the West as a high point of the regime's undoubted anti-Jewish outlook. In addition to the Jewish difficulties at the hands of Tsarist officials and laws, Jewish society experienced hardship in other ways. Demographic change, for instance, had a considerable impact, and by the end of the nineteenth century the Jewish population of the Russian Empire had grown to almost 4 millions, according to the 1897 Imperial census. This figure represented just 4 per cent of the entire population of the Empire, but around half of the world's Jewry.[3] In turn, this population growth heightened the economic privations experienced by the majority of Russian and Polish Jews. Like their Romanian counterparts, scratching a living became increasingly hard, hence the difficult decision to emigrate that was taken by so many.[4]

Not all was grim, however. Although, as we shall see, contemporary commentators often portrayed Russian Imperial Jewry *en masse* as passive victims, the reality was, in many ways, not so clear cut. The final decades of the nineteenth century were especially significant from the perspective of Jewish politics in Imperial Russia. We might note, for example, the formation of the socialist Bund in Vil'na (Vilnius) in 1897, which claimed activists in many fields of Jewish life.[5] There were other noteworthy political affiliations. Jewish nationalism and Zionism, in its many forms, were hugely important in the Tsarist Empire from the 1880s onwards.[6] And, as many late nineteenth-century observers were only too keen to point out, Jews also played a role in various revolutionary organisations in the Empire, from the Socialist Revolutionaries and Social Democrats (Bolsheviks and Mensheviks), to various terrorist groups.[7]

It was not only political spheres in which Jewish difference was discernible. Like the rest of Russian Imperial society, Jews experienced a good deal of social change and, sometimes, advancement. Despite the *numerus clausus* in operation from the 1880s for many professions, Russian Jews succeeded in becoming doctors, lawyers, professors, teachers and the like.[8] Others, such as the Gintsburgs, Poliakovs (the Jewish 'railway kings') and Brodskys (the 'sugar barons'), bore names which, from a Jewish perspective in Russia, were synonymous with the Western achievements of the Rothschilds.[9] At the bottom of the social scale, by the end of the nineteenth century Jews were more likely to be found working as artisans, shopkeepers and factory hands, than as the traditional peddler figure that formed such an important component of Western European imaginings of 'the Jew'. As was the case with gentile life in Russia, modernity challenged and recast Jewish society in many realms, the social, the economic and the intellectual. By the turn of the twentieth century, it had made an indelible mark on both the internal and external dynamics of Russian Imperial Jewry.

Thus, it would be folly to search for the 'typical Jew' of late nineteenth-century Imperial Russia. Somewhat inevitably, however, in the British narrative of this period, there was little to separate the portrait of the Russian Imperial Jew from that of his Romanian counterpart. All East European Jewry was ascribed singular and universal characteristics. In essence, the Jews of the Russian Empire, like their Romanian co-religionists, were depicted as 'oriental', religiously orthodox, Yiddish-speaking and conservative in their social and political habits. Economically, their typical occupation was deemed to be tavern-keeping, peddling or trading. These narrative elements were not simply homespun devices to explicate the mysteries and miseries of Eastern European Jewish life. Even in the 1880s, the British press drew great influence from the writings and journalistic contributions of Russian and Polish correspondents, both Jewish and non-Jewish.

In July 1880, for instance, the *Jewish Chronicle* published three articles by a Russian Jew, Henry Iliowizi, which presented a detailed account of Jewish life in several western provinces of the Tsarist Empire.[10] Iliowizi's first-hand experiences rendered a depiction of Russian imperial Jewry that entirely conformed to perceptions inherent to the British context in which he was writing. His world was confined to the *shtetl* (market town, Yiddish; *mestechko*, Russian), an environment free from external influences, tied to a daily routine inherited from times past that had very little connection to the patterns of life beyond its borders. Religious obligations were inculcated from an early age and, consequentially, it was nigh impossible to break free from their rigorous strictures. Poverty was ubiquitous, social advancement unachievable. The only aspect of division Iliowizi encountered in this otherwise homogeneous society was, like everything else, concerned with matters of religious faith, and he revealingly discussed the separations between *Hasidim* and *mitnagdim*.[11]

Iliowizi was courted by the *Jewish Chronicle* as an authentic voice of Russian imperial Jewry, a reliable informant. No doubt he fulfilled each of these expectations. However, it would be wrong to consider him representative of every Jew of the Pale, though this was probably the manner in which he was perceived by the *JC* and its readership. To be sure, many elements of his worldview could be compared to that of his Russian Imperial co-religionists, but his emigrant status already guaranteed him a different path to those that remained. The tone of his piece suggested, too, that in some ways he rejected the traditional patterns of existence that lay at the heart of his narrative. As we shall see, such perspectives and delineations of otherness broadly conformed to British attitudes, both Jewish and non-Jewish, towards the East European Jew in this period.

In light of this wider discourse, Iliowizi's Jews could have resided in any part of divided Poland, Russia or Romania. But there was one sphere in which British commentators believed Jews played a specific role in the Tsarist Empire and it was absent in Iliowizi's analysis. By the 1880s, nihilism was a vague aphorism used to describe any revolutionary organisation in Tsarist Russia, regardless of its ideological leanings, and gradually it became associated intrinsically with 'the Jew'. Indeed, little was understood of the precise political adherences of various groups that fell under nihilism's remit, and emphasis was instead placed upon their anti-monarchist or general trouble-making tendencies. Sometimes a much older frame of reference was employed to highlight these political agitators. 'It cannot be denied', said *The Times* in 1880, 'that the sect which has hoisted the pirate's black flag in the midst of the Russian Empire comprises many members of the Jewish denomination.'[12] Pirate suggested, of course, an intention to lawlessness, rather than political revolution. Nevertheless, such political affiliations, no matter how vague, were not ascribed in this period to Romanian Jews and, thus, the Russian and Polish Jew began to appear somewhat less passive than his counterpart across the Tsarist Empire's south-western frontier. However, the full ramifications of these political connections were not felt until many decades later, nor were they fully absorbed into British discourse until the turn of the twentieth century.

The apparent Jewish embrace of revolutionary and criminal solutions to their problems in the Russian Empire was easily deduced in the British narrative.[13] Jews were a hapless people, who desperately clung to an anachronistic lifestyle, but they were, above all else, victims. Even before the introduction of the May Laws and other legislation, the Tsarist regime was believed, just like its Romanian counterpart, to be in deliberate pursuit of a counterproductive and persecutory policy when it came to its Jews. This persecution was precisely the reason that the Russian and Polish Jew remained mired in superstition and poverty. The hounding of Jews, whether by word, deed or law, encouraged the development of disagreeable characteristics. The *JC* noted, for example, that 'in Romania and Russia oppression drives our people into the back slums and bye-ways of life.'[14] Cut off from civilising influences, it was little wonder that the Jews remained in the condition depicted by Iliowizi. It was, therefore, the negative aspects of the Jewish experience in the Tsarist Empire that were overwhelmingly stressed by British commentators. This was the case whether Russian and Polish Jews were observed from within or without. For some historians and even for twenty-first century Jewish collective memory, a single word has come to embody this pitiable existence – pogrom!

Mythologising the pogroms of 1881–1882

Almost from the outset, the events of 1881–1882 generated their own mythology. The notion that the pogroms were officially inspired and directed remains a singular attitude that, notwithstanding the meticulous research of modern historiography, has proved nigh impossible to shift. In general terms, the events of 1881–1882 have been depicted as a never-ending outburst of unparalleled collective violence against a defenceless community, which resulted in wholesale murder. It was accompanied by crimes such as vandalism and, more seriously, mass rape. In the last 40 years or so, much dedicated scholarship has convincingly challenged this definition and, crucially, concluded that, in 1881–1882, the Tsarist regime was not responsible for organising or encouraging pogroms.[15] Moreover, of the 200 or so individual events that made up the pogroms of these years, no single pattern is discernible. Various incidents, of varying intensity, were classified as 'pogroms' by the regime, though it rarely used the term: *besporiadki* ('disorders') was preferred. These ranged from mob assaults on Jewish property and persons to the smashing of windows by individual assailants. As for the common indictment of mass rape in 1881–1882, historians have proven that it was greatly exaggerated by contemporary commentators.[16]

All of this, of course, is not to lessen the import of the 1881–1882 pogroms. They were, in many ways, defining events.[17] But the point here is to analyse the degree to which the British perspective played a key role in the genesis of this mythology and definition of the term pogrom. This is not only important in relation to 1881–1882, but in light of later events, such as Kishinev in 1903, the pogroms of 1905–1907, as well as those that occurred during the First World War and its aftermath. In many ways, British reportage of 1881–1882 was instrumental in the construction of a single pogrom narrative for all of these events, when in fact they were each very different, especially in their consequences.[18]

Undoubtedly, as other investigations have shown, the coverage of some British newspapers in 1881–1882, especially *The Times* and the *Jewish World*, was crucial in ascribing culpability to the regime.[19] And, although the British press did not use the term pogrom in this period (contrary to another myth, which usually notes that 'pogrom' entered regular usage in the English language in 1881–1882; instead, terms such as 'disorders', 'riots', 'outrages' and 'atrocities' were employed), it nevertheless laid the foundations for a metonymy in which pogrom came to stand for extreme physical violence, murder and mass rape.[20]

There are a number of issues to consider when examining the British response to the 1881–1882 pogroms. For instance, was the emphasis on brutality and rape connected to the manner in which Russian life was generally perceived in the British mindset? In January 1882, the novelist Charles Reade set out in forthright terms his attitude towards Tsarist Russia, its leaders and its people. Russians, he said, were 'barbarians governed by varnished savages, [...] picture-worshipping idolaters and cowardly murderers'.[21] This was a perspective widely held in Britain, and it quite possibly followed that no matter how terrible the acts of cruelty depicted in the press, they were believable since they occurred at the hands of Europe's most uncivilised of peoples. Perhaps, therefore, the Russian context was the most significant aspect in determining acceptance of the most sensational reportage. This will, of course, be considered below. So, too, will that very matter of sensationalism, and the degree to which the press coverage gathered its own momentum, or whether it occurred precisely in tandem with the intensity of events in Russia.

The apotheosis of the British fascination with the pogroms became apparent in January and February 1882, in the wake of events in Warsaw during 25–28 December 1881. This pogrom appears to have inspired some of the most lurid accounts of the wider phenomenon of anti-Jewish violence, but why? Did newspapers draw significance from a pogrom in 'different', Catholic, more 'Western' part of the Empire, or was it the mere fact that the violence overall showed no sign of stopping? That such was the momentum and intensity of the pogroms, national frontiers were easily crossed. Inherent in such reportage was, of course, a repeated analysis of the causes of the pogroms. Did these remain the same throughout the 2 years, or were differing arguments and interpretations proffered? The manner in which the press covered the pogroms clearly had an impact on how the broader dimensions of anti-Jewish violence were depicted and analysed. But, as we shall see, it also influenced the degree to which British society was motivated in defence of Jewish interests.

Early testimony and interpretation: May–July 1881

The first pogrom occurred in Elisavetgrad, Kherson province on 27 April 1881 (OS 15 April[22]). It was followed by a series, or wave, of similar events, throughout the province, and many towns witnessed an attack of some kind. The pogroms were essentially urban phenomena, beginning in large towns or cities, their aftershocks reverberating outwards to outlying settlements. As will be observed below, a widespread view in 1881 held that the pogroms were perpetrated by peasants, which suggested a movement in the opposite direction. But it was the prejudices of the town and its inhabitants that primarily wrought havoc on Jewish lives and livelihoods in 1881 and 1882.

By 8 May 1881 (OS 26 April), other provinces were struck, most notably Kiev and Chernigov. News of these events filtered only gradually into the British press, which is hardly surprising given the obstacles presented by geographical distance and, to a degree, Tsarist censorship.[23] It was not until a week after the riot in Elisavetgrad that the first reports appeared. On 3 May 1881, the *Morning Post* published a short paragraph detailing 400 arrests as a result of largely unspecified 'excesses' in Elisavetgrad, where a 100 houses had been pillaged.[24] A week later, the *Daily News* and the *Evening Standard* reported a series of 'disorders' in Kiev.[25] Such was the scale of destruction, troops had opened fire on the crowds and 500 were arrested. The death of a woman was also noted.[26]

Coverage of events in Russia continued throughout 1881, though by June and July interest had more or less tailed off. There were, in essence, several discernible narratives, and a particular distinction can be drawn between Jewish and non-Jewish interpretations. For mainstream publications, such as *The Times, Evening Standard, Daily News, St James's Gazette* and *The Graphic*, all published in London, the anti-Jewish riots in Russia were considered amongst a myriad of other domestic and worldwide events. At home, for instance, the death of the former Prime Minister Benjamin Disraeli in April 1881 was widely covered. Further afield, French activities in North Africa were eyed warily and, in July 1881, London was shocked by an attempt on the life of US President James Garfield, who eventually died from his wounds. However, it was, of course, Tsar Alexander II's assassination in March 1881 that formed the principal Russian context in which the pogroms were viewed. In the British imagination, it created a backdrop of unremitting chaos, revolutionary fervour and social disintegration in Russia. No journalist, therefore, appeared surprised by the outbreak of the pogroms.

For Jewish publications, the emphasis was different. Of course, all these events were pondered upon, not least Disraeli's death, but the Jewish angle of any event was understandably the primary focus for the *Chronicle* and the *World*. It inevitably followed that the pogroms received more intense and prolonged coverage in these two newspapers than any other. Moreover, in 1881, they were the only newspapers that contained substantial personal testimony, provided by special correspondents. In the case of the *Jewish Chronicle*, a regular column entitled 'Narratives from the Borders' was provided by David Gordon, editor of the Hebrew-language Prussian newspaper, *HaMaggid*. Whilst in the *World*, between June and September 1881, a section entitled 'The Russo-Jewish Question' was authored by an anonymous correspondent working from within the Russian Empire. Subsequently, in these newspapers a more detailed analysis was undertaken of the causes and consequences of the pogroms. It formed a narrative that sometimes chimed with the views expressed in the mainstream press, but which occasionally did not. Additionally, although the mainstream press was not ordinarily influenced by its Jewish counterpart, in 1881–1882 there is no doubt that for some periods Anglo-Jewish reportage dictated the wider narrative of the pogroms. This is important when considering the degree to which anti-Jewish violence came to be regarded as a deliberate Tsarist policy.

In May 1881, however, the causes attributed to the pogroms took three specific lines of enquiry that firstly examined the role of various external influences, and then the part played by the Russian peasant. In some cases, commentators made a connection between events in Russia and those that had occurred in Imperial Germany earlier in the year, when, in particular, a synagogue had been burned to the ground in Neustettin.[27] As a consequence, the violence in Russia was regarded as a foreign import, though precisely how the pogromists were cognisant of the actions in Germany was not explored.[28] In somewhat simplistic terms, however, nigh simultaneous outbreaks of anti-Jewish violence in Germany and Russia could not be viewed as mere coincidence. The influence of German antisemitic ideologues like Heinrich von Treitschke and Otto Stöcker was also observed, and the *Jewish World* accused the Russian peasantry of 'putting into practice the theories of their German friends'.[29]

The role of external influence was examined in other ways in the earliest reportage. In many reports, for instance, the local inhabitants of a given town appeared to have been exhorted to attack their Jewish neighbours via proclamations, pamphlets and placards.[30] These were accompanied, in some cases, by widespread rumours of an imminent attack.[31] In these instances, the organisers were assumed to be nihilists.[32] This is no surprise, for two reasons. First of all, the regime itself also initially accused nihilists of being responsible for the disorders, and secondly, because it was an analysis that readily resonated with the British perspective on Russia's general political climate.[33] Indeed, a seemingly separate story appeared alongside pogrom reports and revealed that the Moscow police had discovered printed revolutionary proclamations concealed inside painted wooden Easter eggs.[34] It was not difficult to make a connection between all of these actions, all the more so since British newspapers reported that the ringleaders and main protagonists of the pogroms were outsiders.[35] For instance, the Odessa pogrom of 15 May 1881 (OS 3 May) was apparently instigated by Muscovites.[36] Many journalists no doubt had in mind the so-called Going to the People of the 1870s, undertaken by the revolutionary Populists (*Narodniki*), when young intellectuals headed to the countryside in the hope of persuading the peasantry to rise against the Tsar.[37]

The next line of enquiry was connected to the nihilist explanation and also to a long-established British narrative of Russian life; the failings of the credulous, ignorant and (usually) inebriated peasant. Every newspaper disregarded the urban nature of the pogroms and instead resorted to a long-established simplistic view of the Russian experience. In the British narrative, Russia contained only peasants, nobles and bureaucrats. Russian society was envisioned on deterministic lines, and Jews fitted into a social pattern that was essentially medieval. This was especially the case in the religious delineation of the Jewish–gentile relationship in the Empire *The Morning Post*, for example, described the 'social incendiaries', who had been able to:

> use in great measure the superstitious rancour and sectarian haste of the ignorant *muzhiks* against the Israelites, it is now an open secret that the attack on the Jews is only part of a gigantic intrigue for revolutionising the lower strata of Muscovite society.

Consequently, the outbreaks were, in part, the result of external encouragement that played upon religious animosity between Christians and Jews. Some reports, for instance, noted the riots began at the time that such hatred traditionally rose to the surface – Easter. Russian peasants clung to 'horrible stories of ancient superstition', though no specific mention of the blood libel was made.[38] At moments when a riot was anticipated, it was even noted that Christians put crucifixes and candles in their windows to deter attackers.[39]

But it was not only religious difference that prompted the peasant to assault Jews. Almost every mainstream British newspaper expressed a belief in the unbalanced nature of social and economic relations between Jews and peasants. A striking phrase in *The Scotsman* explained the matter thus: '[the peasantry] look upon the Jew as the vampire that sucks their life-blood.'[40] In other words, the Jew fulfilled a role as the exploiter of the 'semi-barbarian' peasant's weaknesses.[41] Several newspapers considered the ancient accusation of Jewish usury as a reason for the pogroms.[42] According to *The Graphic*, had the peasant been sufficiently articulate to express his frustration in words, his complaint would be: 'with us the Jews swarm, they shirk hard work whenever they can, they have a genius for money-lending and they have got our poor peasants in their nets.' Instead, of course, the speechless, dumb peasant sought recourse to the only solution he knew: violence. And, although the violence was not in itself justifiable, there was 'something in the [peasants'] protest'. 'Make what excuses we will', said *The Graphic*, but 'money-lending will never be popularly regarded as a reputable way of getting a living.'[43] A Catholic newspaper, *The Weekly Register*, concurred with this perspective: '[the violence] is probably a sort of inarticulate expression, among a population who have no means but insurrection in making their grievances known, against the absorbing predominance of a wealthy class [i.e. Jews] who have gradually and insensibly become the possessors of a large share of the property of the country.'[44]

Unsurprisingly, such insinuations were refuted in the Anglo-Jewish press. *The World* angrily retorted that 'the cry of Jewish usury as a factor in the present disturbances is utterly untrue.'[45] Nevertheless, as the title of this article – 'Jew and *Muzhik*' – suggested, the Anglo-Jewish narrative was similarly concerned with the role of the peasant and his anti-Jewish proclivities. In an earlier article, the *World* described the pogroms as a consequence of the bitter anti-Jewish feeling that characterised the *muzhik*'s outlook.[46] The *Chronicle* also explored such matters. 'The unsettled state of the country', it said, had allowed 'the evil passions of the peasantry to be let loose'.[47] Thus, in May 1881, the British commentary, whether Jewish or non-Jewish, bore similarities in terms of its analysis of the causes of the pogroms. But where did the authorities fit into this analysis? Was there a single British narrative at this stage, or not?

The Tsarist regime: *Kto Vinovat?*

Already in May 1881, in considering who was guilty (*kto vinovat?*), there was some divergence of opinion. In the mainstream press, the role of the authorities was certainly analysed. In many cases, the police appeared unprepared and helpless when it came to dealing with the riots. Additionally, there was evidence that troops drafted to deal with the disorders were sometimes unwilling to act against the mob.[48] There was even the suggestion that the police had permitted the pogrom to occur in Kiev 'under special protection'.[49] This was also inferred in a drawing that appeared in the *Illustrated London News* and bore the title 'assault on a Jew in the presence of the military'.[50] But beyond this, there was no implication that the authorities in St Petersburg were complicit or had deliberately planned the violence. There was no overtly expressed belief in a conspiracy. On the contrary, officials in the capital and various provincial governors were reported as having instigated both preventative and remedial steps. Kiev's governor, General Aleksandr Drenteln, ensured that 'energetic measures [were] taken by the authorities to protect' the Jews.[51] Martial law was proclaimed in Kishinev (Bessarabia), troops were observed bivouacking in the streets of Odessa and, as was noted in Ekaterinoslav, sometimes they opened fire on the crowds and hundreds of arrests were made in many cases.[52] At the end of May 1881, the *Daily News* noted that:

> There is no reason to believe that the Russian authorities, whatever else may be said against them, attach too little importance to the forcible maintenance of order; and the despatch of troops to the localities where the worst outrages have occurred is a satisfactory symptom of vigour.[53]

By early June, reports of various courts martial appeared throughout the British press, with guilty sentences handed down to many *pogromshchiki*.[54] The regime, it appeared, fully attempted to punish those who incited violence, plundered and attacked Jews.

However, although there is no evidence at this stage that the mainstream press suggested the violence had been deliberately orchestrated in St Petersburg, the regime was indicted in another way. It may not have been complicit, but it was careless. Its general manner of dealing with its Jews demonstrated to the wider Russian population that anti-Jewish feeling was acceptable. Given the 'strikingly significant animus inspiring the Emperor's advisors to treat the Children of Israel, no matter what their nationality or social status, as enemies of the Russian state', it was little wonder the 'grossly ignorant' peasant acted in the way he did.[55] The *Morning Post* could not understand why enlightened elements in the Tsarist bureaucracy had failed to bring their influence 'to bear to prevent the commission of atrocities which are a scandal to Christendom'.[56] But since it was an Empire that was generally 'behind [the West] in true civilisation', these bureaucratic inefficiencies were understandable.[57] Yet, the regime must prepare to reap the whirlwind of its errors, as an editorial in *The Times* counselled:

> The prejudice with which Russian rulers [...] tamper is preparing for them a terrible perplexity throughout the Empire. They may find in the savage fanaticism countenanced by their own attitude towards native and foreign Jews, a difficulty only second to the more impalpable plotting of socialists. The Russian peasant, when he stones or pillages a Jew, indulges all his passions which it ought to be the first aim of a Government like that of Russian to quell.[58]

And, although the Tsar was lauded for his apparent disgust at the pogroms, made evident during audiences with leading Petersburg Jews, Alexander III's aloofness or isolation from major affairs of state was frequently observed.[59] His 'complete seclusion at Gatchina', the imperial residence located 30 miles to the south of St Petersburg, was often commented upon.[60]

How did these attitudes compare with the Jewish perspective? Both the *World* and the *Chronicle* agreed on the bigotry of the Russian peasantry. It was noted, however, that the Russian bureaucracy was 'lukewarm in its desire to protect the Jews'.[61] According to the *World*, it was not in the interests of the regime to 'remove the existing prejudice against the Jews', as it suited a sinister purpose. Only this could explain the authorities' apparent 'blindness or indifference' to the Jewish plight, even when they had been forewarned.[62] By the beginning of June, as the realisation set in that the violence showed no sign of ending, the *World* expressed itself in no uncertain terms:

> we hold, and fearlessly assert that the Russian government and the Russian government alone, are responsible for the outrages to which

the Jews have been and are being subjected. [...] the ignorant *muzhik* is only imitating the conduct of his leaders [and] will never learn the lesson of tolerance towards the Jews whilst the government inculcate it by example; by placing the Jew equally with the Christian.[63]

Yet even these strident opinions did not suggest that the regime had deliberately and systematically arranged the pogroms. Rather, a link was once again made between the government's policies and the peasantry's Judeophobia. One influenced and justified the other. But, at the same time, unlike the mainstream press, Anglo-Jewish newspapers were much more prepared to challenge the regime. This was an attitude also manifest in wider Anglo-Jewish society. Jewish MPs, for instance, asked questions in the Commons about events in Russia; the AJA and Board of Deputies pondered a public meeting; and a parliamentary deputation met with the Foreign Secretary Lord Granville.[64] Ultimately, a public meeting only occurred in February 1882, in the aftermath of the Warsaw pogrom.[65] Nevertheless, in the intervening months, the Anglo-Jewish press constantly raised the spectre of Tsarist guilt.

This was most evident in the contributions of the *Jewish World*'s special correspondent, whose column first appeared in late June 1881. The identity of this London-based journalist was not revealed in the *World*, but is seems likely that he was one Meier Bankanovich, a name identified in other sources.[66] He was despatched to the Russian Empire in mid-June 1881 and appears to have been suitably qualified in all the requisite languages for such a journey – Russian, Ukrainian, Polish, Yiddish and Hebrew. The copy he filed on a weekly or fortnightly basis provided dramatic testimony of a tour of the Empire's western provinces, which took in Lemberg (today L'viv in Ukraine; then located in Galicia, Austrian Empire, near the border with Russia), Kiev, Elisavetgrad, Odessa and Aleksandrovsk. Bankanovich met with leading Jews in these communities, scoured the columns of the Jewish and non-Jewish press and took a singular stance on the causes and consequences of the pogroms.

Bankanovich did not spare the sensibilities of his audience in describing the brutality enacted upon the Jews of south-western Russia. In his accounts, babies and children were burnt to death, numerous women were horrifically raped and tortured and entire villages destroyed. In Berezovka (Kherson province), Bankanovich told the story of 'forty mothers and their children' who were forced into the river.[67] This litany of abhorrent acts could go on and many, many were published in the columns of the *Jewish World*. Yet, they must be viewed with extreme caution, since most of these claims were exaggerated.[68] Nevertheless,

Bankanovich's articles generated their own momentum, in which one atrocity story after another was relayed in the finest detail and the notion that the regime had deliberately instigated the pogroms became increasingly plausible.

Bankanovich's first port of call, in connection with the Kiev pogrom, was the press. In early July 1881, 'The Russo-Jewish Question' suggested that there was a link between the Judeophobic newspaper *Kievlianin*, and the ruling authorities in Kiev.[69] 'Subsidised by governing powers', *Kievlianin* was officially allowed to publish anti-Jewish articles. There were major consequences, as it facilitated the transmission of a 'virus [that] penetrated downwards, until a favourable opportunity occurred to inoculate the peasantry *en masse*'. This bore resemblance to accusations in other newspapers that connected Tsarism's example with the *pogromshchiki*'s actions. But Bankanovich went further: 'the outbreaks were well-organised [and] funds [were] supplied to certain well-known persons to carry out the agitation.'[70] The names of these individuals were not identified.

Next, Bankanovich looked at the role of the police, again in connection with Kiev. In mid-July 1881, he asserted that the Kiev pogrom was 'pre-arranged', that the authorities were indifferent and the police had simply 'looked on' as chaos ensued.[71] In early August, he claimed the head of police in Elisavetgrad had been cognisant of the pogrom's arrangements in early April.[72] Bankanovich's report from Odessa, published in late August 1881, suggested that there was a link between Moscow and the local authorities. The disturbances had been 'anticipated'.[73] Although these reports did not directly point a finger of suspicion at the Tsar and his ministers in Petersburg, a *Jewish World* editorial in July fully suggested official incitement:

> [The] Russian atrocities are absolutely *sui generis*. They were deliberately got up in a time of peace against quiet traders and order-loving citizens by persons legally and morally responsible for their protection. [...] We plainly and publicly impeach the Russian official class as directly responsible for the late enormities in Kiev.[74]

Such perspectives were re-visited in September 1881. Louis Cohen, director of a well-known stockbroking firm that helped to distribute relief money in Russia, wrote to *The Times* about a recent reoccurrence of violence. In explaining these events, Cohen cited official indifference at local level, but decried any involvement of the Imperial regime in the violence.[75] In its refutation of these views, the *World* claimed that 'during the whole of the riots [of 1881], *not* a single order was given to make a stand against the mobsmen.'[76] This was also a patent exaggeration, since throughout 1881 the British press had carried many reports that described Tsarism's efforts at curbing the pogroms.

Evidently, by the autumn of 1881 the regime's role in the pogroms was under renewed scrutiny. This was, in part, encouraged by the publication in St Petersburg of a circular by the Minister of the Interior, General N.P. Ignatiev. It was issued to local commissions in pogrom-ridden provinces, which were required to examine the dimensions of the Jewish question in their locality.[77] The tenor of the circular suggested that the minister, who undoubtedly held Judeophobic views, was in search of proof that the economic activity of the Jews was 'specially injurious to the prosperity of the [non-Jewish] population'.[78] Evidently, if the regime hoped to dispel the notion that it pursued a deliberately anti-Jewish policy, such circulars would not assist its cause. Later on, it would add grist to the mill of those who believed the pogroms were a deliberate government policy.

Christmas 1881: the Warsaw pogrom

The Warsaw pogrom occurred over Christmas 1881 and lasted for 3 days.[79] By the end of December, the first, somewhat confused reports about the pogrom's origins appeared in the British press. On 26 December 1881, the *St James's Gazette* published a paragraph about an incident of 'panic in a Warsaw church'.[80] Three days later, the *Daily Telegraph* wrote of the 'alarming state in Warsaw', where it doubted the 'authorities [had] attempted seriously to restrain the rioters.'[81] Inevitably, the *Jewish World* expressed its own view of these events in no uncertain terms: 'the whole affair turns out to have been, just as in the case of the South Russian atrocities, a planned business.'

> We, in Western Europe, can scarcely understand a condition of things in which such scenes as those enacted last week in Warsaw, without police or military interference during two [*sic*] whole days, are possible. We can scarcely conceive how a riot can be planned, organised and carried into execution in open day, and under the very noses of the so-called guardians of the peace and actually with the active assistance of the police themselves. But that the narratives in our columns of the recent occurrences in the South have familiarised us with the invariable course of these anti-Jewish risings, the record of pillage and outrage, and murder, at Warsaw would indeed be incredible.[82]

This paragraph proved just how significant was the part played by Bankanovich's testimony in making up the mind of the *World* on the origins of the pogroms. In the following week's edition, its editorial was suggestively entitled 'the secret springs of anti-Judaism in Russia'. Again, blame was attributed to 'official tyranny', which was vividly compared to a 'large snake [...] twined round the national life, crushing it in its deadly folds, while besliming it with its filthy slaver, and poisoning it with its venomous breath.'[83]

By this stage, mid-January 1882, British interest in the anti-Jewish rioting in the Tsarist Empire attained heightened levels of reportage. What is more, almost every newspaper and journal concluded that there was a degree of official planning behind the pogroms. Instrumental in encouraging this notion was a series of articles that appeared in *The Times* during the second week of January. Written by Joseph Jacobs, a Jewish historian and author, who was also involved in the recently instituted Russo-Jewish Committee (see below), they appear to have been influenced by Bankanovich's accounts.[84] To be sure, the degree to which the brutality of the pogroms was depicted in these articles bore parallels with their equivalents in the *World*. Jacobs described children being 'dashed to death, or roasted alive in their own homes', the raping of 30 women at Elisavetgrad alone and the 'razing of whole streets inhabited by Jews'.[85]

The following week, a number of newspaper published articles authored by or derived from Bankanovich's work, including *The Scotsman*, the *Daily News* and the *Evening Standard*.[86] They replicated his columns in the *World*, in terms of tone, content and melodrama. Reflecting upon this, an editorial in *The Scotsman* cautioned that the testimony might be exaggerated. Nevertheless, it also argued that the higher ranks of Russian society believed 'their own personal or political ends can be served by a crusade against the Hebrew community.'[87] Successive editorials in other newspapers concurred with this perspective and, by the end of January 1882, the separate interpretations on the origins of the pogroms had coalesced into one. The peasantry remained the perpetrators, but Tsarist officials, at the lowest and uppermost levels, were the planners and instigators. There was some difference in degrees of emphasis, but the essential argument was universally incorporated into the British narrative.[88]

For instance, the *Birmingham Daily Mail* believed, like *The Scotsman*, that the outrages had been 'represented in too lurid a light'. But it was under no illusion that the pogroms had been 'instigated by the state'.[89] The *Morning Post* spoke of the 'connivance' of the authorities.[90] *The Spectator*, commenting on the articles in *The Times*, believed the number of outrages on women had been underestimated, but that the 'guilt of the Russian government in this business is very great'.[91] Yet, the *Pall Mall Gazette* regarded the 'accounts of violations [as] pure inventions'.[92] A few days after these comments, the *Gazette* contributed its own personal testimony to the discussion in the form of two articles provided by an anonymous correspondent in St Petersburg. They broadly conformed with other supposed eyewitness accounts, though in less dramatic terms than either those by Bankanovich or Jacobs.[93] This shift in attitude was noted by the *World*, which had been effected, it believed, by the work of its own special correspondent. In a suitably self-laudatory tone, it observed: 'We take it upon ourselves to say that had it not been for the *Jewish World* the Jews and the Press of this country would not have been aware of a tithe of the outrages which have.'[94]

Was, however, the work of the *World* the only significant factor in influencing the creation of a universal narrative on the pogroms? How important, for instance, was the Polish context in consolidating this perspective? As will be discussed in Chapters 4 and 6, Poland was regarded in different terms to Russia, especially in light of its Catholicism and somewhat martyred status on the European stage. Certainly, its 'Western' characteristics were often, if only tacitly, recognised and appreciated; Poles, albeit Catholics, were deemed marginally closer to the British, especially in their intellectual development, than Orthodox, 'Eastern' Russians. Given this background, the Warsaw pogrom came as something of a surprise, as the *Morning Post* observed:

> Poland, in spite of oppression, is by far the most advanced and cultivated portion of the Tsar's dominions, and the most unchecked spread of anarchy in such a region speaks volumes for the domestic situation in more remote backward districts.[95]

Additionally, Jewish–gentile relations in Poland were regarded as more stable and amicable than in Russia. Poles were often credited with a tolerance unsurpassed in the rest of Eastern Europe. This perhaps reiterated the necessity for external interference in the pogroms, since Poles were apparently not naturally inclined to hate their neighbours, let alone violently attack them. Indeed, it is no revelation that the ringleaders of the pogroms were identified by one report as being 'well-dressed men of Russian origin'.[96] Yet, curiously, no commentator stopped to consider what the Tsarist regime had to gain by encouraging violence in a part of the Empire it monitored more carefully than most. The 1863 Polish Uprising, for instance, remained a fairly recent and uncomfortable memory, and its consequences were considerable for Poles and the manner in which they were ruled.[97] The Tsarist authorities were especially anxious to ensure that any kind of rebellion in Poland was strangled at birth. Surely, therefore, there was a risk that any unchecked violence in Warsaw, directed towards property and persons, might swiftly encourage the perpetrators to turn to other enemies? Such questions were unasked, let alone answered, in the British narrative.

Against this background of intensive interest in the fate of the Jews of Russia, the Anglo-Jewish community debated, both publicly and privately, the urgent matter of what was to be done. In private spheres, the Russo-Jewish Committee (RJC), founded by the AJA and Board of Deputies in November 1881,was mandated to 'consider and adopt measures [regarding] the amelioration of the Jews in Russia'.[98] But its activities, much to the chagrin of the Anglo-Jewish press, were conducted in secret. Thus, it appeared by early January 1882 to have done 'nothing, absolutely nothing'.[99] This was not the case, since various negotiations were conducted behind the scenes, but its first public gesture appeared to reconfirm its useless dabbling. In late January, the RJC attempted to present a petition to the Russian Ambassador in London, Prince Alexei Lobanov-Rostovskii. Acceptance was refused.

To illustrate the Tsarist regime's apparent disdain for the plight of Russian Jews, the RJC sent its memorial to the British press. It was subsequently published in an number of newspapers and most were bemused at the Embassy's response.[100] The *Jewish World* was not. In a curt editorial, it suggested the RJC's failure was of its own making, since the Embassy's refusal to accept the petition was only in keeping with Imperial Russian interactions with the outside world. Instead of approaching the regime's representatives in London, it advised, a far better method of gaining Alexander III's attention would be to show that: 'the outrageous persecutions of the Jews and the repressive laws affecting [them] are known in England, and the hollowness of [Russia's] pretensions [...] to rank as a civilised country is fully appreciated by Englishmen, Christians as well as Jews.'[101] Evidently, the *World* was in total support of a public meeting that would, in no uncertain terms, reaffirm the iniquity of Tsarist rule in British eyes.

The possibility of a meeting was discussed in the Jewish and non-Jewish press throughout January 1882. In contrast to the response to similar proposals in May/June 1881, there was an evident appetite for broader action. This was reflected in a slew of letters to various newspapers, including one from the Earl of Shaftesbury in *The Times*.[102] As with the Romanian crisis a decade earlier, the disabilities suffered by the Jews of Russia were sufficiently terrible to inspire wide indignation. Moreover, in contrast to attitudes in the previous year, when the mainstream press had advised against a public meeting, in January 1882 there was significant support on this issue. The *Daily Telegraph*, for instance, called for an 'emphatic protest against the Tsar' by Her Majesty's Government.[103]

The protest meeting was eventually held on 1 February 1882, in London's Mansion House. It attracted a large number of participants, culled from a range of influential figures in late Victorian society. Shaftesbury was there, of course, as was Cardinal Henry Manning, Catholic leader of England, and Dean William Farrar was present in lieu of the Archbishop of Canterbury. A host of MPs attended, both Jewish and non-Jewish, and a number of letters from prominent absentees were read out. It included one from Alfred Tennyson, the poet laureate, and another from Hugh Grosvenor, Duke of Westminster. If anything, the collective chorus of this Mansion House protest was even more impressive than its Romanian predecessor.[104] But, once again, it was a Christian message that was stressed. Indeed, the AJA advised regional branches that when organising 'indignation meetings' they were to be 'convened by Christians' and that Jewish speakers were to 'confine themselves to proposing and seconding votes of thanks to the respective chairmen'.[105]

In the wake of the London meeting, a number of noteworthy gatherings were held outside the capital. Those convened in Glasgow and Manchester in late January were especially well-attended and unanimous in their condemnation of Tsarist policy.[106] But all of these meetings were somewhat cautious in their approach. The *Jewish Chronicle* had hoped for the expression of 'passionless opinion' at Mansion House, which inevitably hinted at a rejection of the *World*'s rabble-rousing, feisty style.[107] And it got this, with each speaker at Mansion House choosing his words carefully. There was to be no question of insulting the Tsar or his ministers, rather the object was to highlight the foolhardiness of the regime's recent Jewish policy. The Russian response to these actions was as might be expected.[108]

A month after the Mansion House meeting, in March 1882, less caution was evident in the representations made by Baron Henry de Worms in the House of Commons. He presented a resolution, which aimed to encourage a direct intervention in the Russian crisis by Her Majesty's Government, in order to 'prevent the recurrence of similar acts of violence'. In his evidence, de Worms listed in graphic terms the number and details of the atrocities that had occurred since May 1881: 'Two hundred and one women have been violated, 56 Jews killed, 70 wounded, 20,000 rendered homeless and £16,000,000 worth of property wrecked.' For sure, he was encouraged in the assertion of these statistics by the articles of Bankanovich and Jacobs. Most significantly, he accused the

Tsarist government of having 'connived' in the outrages.[109] But de Worms' indignation was also engendered by the activities of the British government as he reflected on the recent presentation of a 'Blue Book' (Command Paper) on the pogroms to both Houses of Parliament.

Parliament eventually published two 'Blue Books' on the events in Russia, which included extensive diplomatic reports by British representatives throughout the western provinces of the Empire.[110] In part, they were placed before parliament in early February 1882 as a result of the recent eruption of anti-Tsarist feeling, as evidenced at the Mansion House meeting.[111] In terms of their outlook, these reports were a ragbag of assorted prejudices and judicious opinions, similar to those that had been published about Romania in the previous two decades. Several British consuls visited various pogrom areas and sent back detailed accounts to London, none of which concluded that the regime had deliberately sponsored, enacted or encouraged the violence against Jews. Additionally, the degree to which the regime attempted to prevent or halt a pogrom was much discussed. In Warsaw, for instance, it was revealed that the Governor-General had taken numerous military precautions. Many explanations as to causes were proffered, such as the condition of Jewish-peasant relations and the role of politics, especially in relation to nihilism. It was also frequently suggested that the British press, even in 1881, had exaggerated many of the events.

Inevitably, de Worms took great exception to these reports, claiming that he had 'never seen any official document [as] unsatisfactory'. He deemed them 'absolutely and totally unreliable', [...] nothing more than hearsay reports of what took place, gathered many hundreds of miles from the seat of the outrages themselves'. Patently, this was untrue, since the reports actually painted a picture of careful evidence gathering, by observers closer to the scenes of violence than he was willing to admit. But from de Worms' point of view, certain eyewitness accounts published in the British press were more accurate, though given the parliamentary context he was unable to make reference to the *Jewish World* or *The Times*.[112]

Although de Worms' resolution was supported by many MPs, some of whom delivered equally emotive speeches, it was ultimately rejected by the House of Commons. There was no appetite for a direct intercession in the affairs of another nation. Indeed, even the *Jewish World* regarded de Worms' actions as injudicious.[113] Moreover, whilst many MPs sympathised with the victims of the pogroms, not all agreed that the regime was guilty of a deliberately violent policy. Crucially, the Prime Minister William Gladstone spoke against de Worms, as did a Jewish MP, Arthur Cohen. Both concluded that the Russian government was innocent of any connivance in the pogroms.[114] Thus, in the British context the conspiratorial narrative of the 1881–1882 pogroms did not achieve a victory in every arena. Government and parliament were each unprepared to wholly accept this theory at face value. Nevertheless, there were consequences and undoubtedly these were felt the next time Russia was convulsed in paroxysms of anti-Jewish rage.

Aftermath: expulsions in the 1890s

In mid-1890, the British press began to feature regular articles that revealed a renewed legal assault on Russian Jews was in the offing in St Petersburg.[115] The noises emanating from the Imperial capital promised a closer implementation of the May Laws, the corollary to which was the threat of expulsion for those Jews residing outside of the Pale of Settlement, especially from the two capitals. It also threatened those living without permission in certain cities within the Pale, particularly Kiev. *The Times* and other newspapers carried detailed accounts of the precision by which the 1882 May Laws circumscribed Jewish life and, once again, correspondents spoke of a Russia that was heading towards another 'chapter in the annals of despotism'.[116] For the *Leeds Mercury*, the auguring of more narrowly pursued legal methods of persecution represented a far more barbarous state of affairs than even the pogroms of the previous decade, as it believed a 'war of extermination' had been set in motion.[117] In light of these reports, questions were broached in both Houses of Parliament, though without any satisfactory government response.[118] Lord Salisbury's reply to the AJA's letter on the matter, for instance, denied that the Russian regime had proposed to instigate any new laws at all.[119]

In November 1890, a small Jewish delegation consisting of the acting Chief Rabbi Hermann Adler and Oswald John Simon MP presented a petition to the Lord Mayor of London, Joseph Savory.[120] It was a request to convene a public meeting, signed by an array of influential Christian figures, including the Archbishop of Canterbury, the Duke of Westminster and Lord Tennyson.[121] A few weeks later, the Guildhall, just a few streets from the Mansion House, was packed to the rafters with the great and good. This impressive gathering was chaired by Savory, and, once again, all the motions were proposed and seconded by Christians.[122] In another echo of British protests in 1882, the Petersburg authorities refused to accept the Guildhall protest and it was returned to the Lord Mayor in early 1891.[123] Clearly, British admonitions stood for nothing and this was affirmed within a matter of months as the Jewish situation in Russia disintegrated yet further. In April 1891,

Tsar Alexander III issued an edict ordering the expulsion of certain categories of Jews from Moscow and Kiev, many of whom lived illegally, according to Russian law, in these cities. The expulsions occurred on the first day of Passover, though it is doubtful the authorities intended to make some kind of ironic comment in their actions.[124] As a consequence, the British clamour for change became increasingly louder, though by mid-1891 it was underpinned by anxieties closer to home.[125]

The expulsions of the early 1890s prompted a wide-ranging debate in Britain for a number of reasons. In the first place, many commentators were horrified by the manner of Tsarist rule as the expulsions appeared just as cruel as the pogroms. All newspapers and weekly journals carried harrowing tales of dispossession, of helpless Jews in thrall to bigoted officials and the wholesale destruction of synagogues and their congregations.[126] Nevertheless, despite this condemnatory tone there were many voices that spoke against Russian Jewry and their alleged habits, inferring that in some sense they were responsible for their fate at the hands of Tsarist officials. Particularly noteworthy in this regard were the contributions in late 1890 of Olga Novikova, a Russian noblewoman resident in London. Her letters to *The Times* suggested that Jews had nobody but themselves to blame, particularly since their only function in Russia was as money-lenders. This was far from the only Judeophobic component of her argument, and she attempted to make great capital out of the allegation that Russian and Polish Jews were draft-dodgers. She also cautioned that if Britain continued to interfere in Russian internal affairs, it may reap an unfortunate and unwanted whirlwind, namely a massive and unstoppable influx of immigrant Jews.[127]

By mid-1891, the fears hinted at by Novikova gained ascendancy in the British analysis of the Russian Jewish question. Yes, there remained a good deal of sympathy for the Jewish predicament, but the unabated persecution ensured that the primary concern shifted to matters closer to home. The 1880s had seen some anxiety generated on the aliens question and, to a degree, it had been linked to anti-Jewish persecution in the Tsarist Empire. By the early 1890s, however, the recurrent expulsions led to all manner of expectations for the British context. The terms 'exodus', 'swarms' and 'tides' were frequently utilised, which in turn induced a sense of panic.[128] A House of Commons' debate on the issue was given the title 'the Russian Jew invasion' by one newspaper.[129] According to another, the *Pall Mall Gazette*, the 'harrying of the Russian Jews threatened a wholesale emigration' to Britain. The numbers suggested totalled around 60,000, a figure that guaranteed in a single fell swoop to more than double Britain's existing Jewish community.[130] Naturally, there was a good deal of exaggeration in these statistics, but the worry it generated was such that correspondents began to investigate emigrants at their points of departure on the continent. In the Berlin suburb of Charlottenburg, for instance, immigrant Jews were housed in hostels before being permitted by the Prussian authorities to travel further.[131] British journalists visited Charlottenburg and attested to the dirt, poverty, disease and sheer wretchedness amongst these migrants, many of whom proposed to make the United Kingdom their final destination.[132]

Inevitably, there was a clamour to halt this threatening tide in certain quarters. The Earl of Dunraven, for instance, founded the Society for the Suppression of Immigration of Destitute Aliens in May 1891.[133] Others outlined the need for legal restriction in various monthly journals.[134] But solutions of a quite different tenor were suggested elsewhere, which promised to tackle the apparent root cause of the emigration, the Tsarist government. One such answer was seen in the power of the Rothschild banking house. Reports suggested that a loan promised to St Petersburg by the French branch of the organisation had been withheld.[135] It was vainly hoped that this might encourage the Russian government to reassess its Jewish policies. A second powerful Jewish name also came to the fore in 1891, proffering a quite different solution.

In September 1891, Baron Maurice de Hirsch, the German Jewish philanthropist, instituted the Jewish Colonisation Association (JCA), which proposed to establish Jewish colonies in South America and elsewhere.[136] The process that culminated in the JCA's creation was followed intensively in the British press.[137] After all, Hirsch's wealth presented the hope of a radical and long-lasting solution to Russia's Jewish problem. Not only would Jews be able to leave behind their mean Russian *shtetlekh*, but by retraining them in agricultural, artisanal and other crafts a more 'useful' Jewish society would be fashioned. In other words, Hirsch's scheme undertook to grant East European Jewry the possibility of rebirth, to 'straighten the ghetto bend' as the popular allusion would have it. One newspaper, the *Northern Echo*, described Hirsch as the 'new Moses', who would lead his people out of a different kind of slavery.[138] To many British commentators, these ambitions looked to erase forever the disagreeable characteristics of the Russian Jew. Indeed, a British publicist, Arnold White, believed the promise of Jewish colonies in South America would herald social, economic and racial redemption for East European Jewry. Although a prominent anti-alienist, White wholeheartedly embraced the JCA's mission and was appointed an emissary by Hirsch in early 1891. During a visit to Russia that same year at Hirsch's behest, White saw glimmers of a better future in the Jewish agricultural colonies in Southern Ukraine (see Chapter 7).[139]

Image 2 From the Nile to the Neva, *Punch*, August 1891
Punch's take on the expulsions of the early 1890s. Despite its apparent sympathy for the plight of East European Jews, the satirical weekly could not but help employ the most obvious of antisemitic stereotypes, the Shylockian money lender, as also reflected in image 3.

Image 3   'Blood versus Bullion', *Punch*, May 1891

Arnold White has often been cast as an arch antisemite by historians of British antisemitism and, indeed, many of his contemporaries also found his views disagreeable. He was regularly a target for the Anglo-Jewish press, for instance. But at this moment, 1891, White was actually courted for his apparent expertise on the Russian Jewish question.[140] In particular, his views were positively embraced by a supplement published irregularly by the *Jewish Chronicle* throughout 1891–1892. Sponsored by Sir Isadore Speilmann and the RJC, *Darkest Russia* aimed to publicise more widely the plight of Russian Jewry.[141] It drew contributions from a range of influential figures, including William Gladstone (then occupying parliament's Opposition benches) and Alfred Tennyson.[142] White's name appeared on several occasions and, although *Darkest Russia* did not support his emigration schemes, it nevertheless appreciated his indictment of the financial status of the Tsarist Empire. Russia's 'bankruptcy' was effectively underwritten, White argued, by its persecutory policy towards Jews. His heartrending, apparently first-hand descriptions of the Jewish plight in light of recent events were also valued. White wrote emotively about the expulsions, of 'the scattered homes, of husbands parted, of the old deprived of hope, of the young old before their time, gaunt with want, ignorant of laughter, of starved hospitals, and schools deprived of support'.[143]

White pleaded with Tsar Alexander III to alleviate the untold misery of the Pale by dismantling the regime's entire anti-Jewish legal structure 'with a stroke of his pen'.[144] Once again, however, the mobilisation of British moral indignation failed to produce the desired consequences. Rather, the legal proscriptions on Jewish life appeared to worsen with every year. Unlike the pogroms, the expulsions were, of course, the direct consequence of Tsarist policy and legally managed by both statutes and officials. No doubt, these actions proved that Tsarism's overriding attitude towards its Jewish question was, at the very least, unsympathetic and, at worst, malicious.[145] Naturally, the expulsions were not viewed in isolation. Commentators did not fail to make a connection to the events of 1881–1882. The overwhelming perception, therefore, was of Russian regime that was prepared to use all manner of tactics to proscribe and inhibit Jewish life in the Empire. Consequently, in British analyses of Russia's Jewish question, the past (1881–1882) and the present (1890–1892) experiences of Russian Jews were conflated. In turn, such a perspective facilitated the creation of an oppressive and singularly miserable narrative. Pogroms and expulsions were all of a piece. Violent, barbaric, anachronistic, they were government inspired, directed and implemented.

3
Romania and Kishinev: Crises Intertwined, 1900–1906

> Whoever has been able to watch the agonized look of the animal under the air pump, when it slowly begins to realize that the life-giving air is disappearing, can picture to himself vividly the look upon the face of the Jews of Romania.
>
> *Haham* Moses Gaster, November 1902

> The *pogrom* is a national institution [in Russia].
>
> *The Times*, December 1903

The new century: old and new anxieties

By the turn of the twentieth century, British unease about Eastern European Jewish immigration was in the process of reassertion.[1] In many ways, this was understandable, since the preceding decade had witnessed a larger movement of East European Jews to the United Kingdom than ever before. As we have seen, there had been passing moments of official and popular concern in the 1880s and 1890s, but by 1901 parliament was set on a new course that intended to resolve the aliens question once and for all. In 1902 and 1903, a Royal Commission investigated its causes and consequences, interviewed a wide range of witnesses, from the lowest to highest social circles, both Jews and non-Jews. The list included officials, clergymen, policemen, businessmen, trades' union leaders, members of the medical profession and regular east enders.[2] At the heart of this examination lay the status and condition of Russian, Polish and Romanian Jews, particularly the reasons they chose to emigrate. In the Russian case, the Commission concluded that a combination of persecution and economic deprivation was the cause, whilst in Poland, where the legal limitations placed

upon Jewish life were very different (see Chapter 4), economic oppor-
tunism was deemed the motivation. By contrast, in the Romanian case
persecution was revealed as the solitary 'expulsive force'.[3] Eventually,
these prolonged deliberations resulted in Britain's first piece of immigrant legislation, the 1905 Aliens Act. Thus, Britain began the new era
by attempting to resolve its own Jewish question with unprecedented
restrictions.

Despite the flush of optimism that accompanied the opening throes
of the twentieth century, Europe's Jewish question, to which had been
added fresh British concerns, was apparently becoming ever more complex. Immigration, which also occupied the thoughts of contemporary
observers in France, Germany, the Habsburg Empire and the United
States, gave rise to new, or at least reasserted, popular and political
resentments against Jews. In the United Kingdom, for instance, the new
century witnessed an increase in domestic anti-Jewish feeling as a consequence of the South African War (1899–1902).[4] Allegations that readily
surfaced in a continental context bared their ugliness in Britain (though
hardly for the first time!), and Jews were accused of profiteering from
the war, promoting pro-Boer propaganda and failing to embrace a truly
patriotic spirit. Little wonder that the *Jewish Chronicle* published double-
page accounts of Anglo-Jewish military service in South Africa, complete
with photographs of serving Jewish soldiers.[5]

The increasing complexity of Britain's Jewish question was especially
observable from an Anglo-Jewish standpoint. Immigration, after all, was
not simply a gentile concern and it directly impacted upon Anglo-Jewish
life, most especially in the matter of self-perception. Moreover, Anglo-
Jewish society's internal dynamics underwent a profound change in this
period. For sure, immigration played a part in swelling the community's numbers, thereby altering its social and economic composition.
But, reflecting changes in continental Jewish society, there were also
key political influences in force by this time and, in particular, Theodor
Herzl's Zionism claimed many British adherents.[6] Territorialism was
also important and British playwright Israel Zangwill was instrumental in the creation of the Jewish Territorial Organization (ITO), which
aimed to find a Jewish homeland outside Palestine.[7] Other political ideas
swirled in the Anglo-Jewish imagination. Much debate, for instance,
was devoted throughout 1903 to the disposal of the so-called Hirsch
Millions, the substantial legacy of the Jewish Colonisation Association's
Baron Hirsch.[8]

Against this myriad of domestic, political and, in many ways, philosophical matters, what was happening on a day-to-day basis to Jews

outside the British Empire might seem of lesser importance. And, certainly, in the mainstream British narrative, infrequent attention was devoted to Jewish struggles in Eastern Europe. At least, this was the case until the Kishinev pogrom of 1903. Prior to this crucially significant event, discussed below, any interest in East European Jewry was mostly confined to Anglo-Jewish circles and it concentrated largely on Romania. Yet, just as two generations before, promoting the cause of Romania's Jews was an uphill struggle. It remained an internationally insignificant state, and although Romanian Jews emigrated to the United Kingdom, they did so in far fewer numbers than their Russian and Polish co-religionists. Indeed, according to evidence presented to the Royal Commission by L.L. Cohen, President of the Jewish Board of Guardians, in 1901 only 84 Romanian Jews emigrated to the United Kingdom, whilst a year later the figure stood at just 30.[9]

What was more, in this period there were no diplomatic manoeuvrings comparable to the Congress of Berlin. The means by which Romanian persecution might be halted were consequently restricted. Indeed, judging by a response to a question addressed to the House of Commons in 1900, the limitations imposed by the Berlin Treaty were largely forgotten, or at least regarded as of marginal significance.[10] But by no means was the Romanian Jewish plight completely overlooked. Although, as already noted, it was recognised that few Jewish immigrants were of Romanian extraction, the precipitants of their exodus were fleetingly examined by the Royal Commission. A member of the Commission and MP, Major William Evans-Gordon, undertook an investigative tour of Eastern Europe in the summer of 1902. The final destination of his journey, at least its purposeful part, was Romania, where he visited Bucharest, Jassy and other towns. Here he discovered that the Romanian government pursued a 'malignant policy against the Jews'. Excluded from many professional avenues, and even hospital treatment, Romanian Jews were compelled to serve in the armed forces despite their continued legal status as aliens. Although the Romanian part of Evan-Gordon's findings occupied just a few columns in the Commission's thousand-page report, it nevertheless aided the reinvigoration of the Anglo-Jewish campaign in the public arena.[11]

Romania: public and private campaigns

Evans-Gordon's comments, which will be discussed below, occurred at a significant moment in the Romanian campaign. Hitherto, whilst the

Anglo-Jewish community had long been interested in Romania, from the 1890s onwards the pursuit of wider publicity for the cause was fairly restrained and there were limited efforts to intervene. Occasionally, confidential memoranda were presented to the Foreign Office.[12] From 1900 to 1901, the AJA collected funds for the material relief of Jews in Bessarabia and Romania, distributed via the AIU in Paris and Baron Aleksandr Gintsburg, nominal head of the Jewish community in St Petersburg.[13] In early 1902, the *JC* and *JW* were both greatly involved in discussing the renewed legal assault on Jews in Romania. Many articles were published, which often listed the legislation that Romanian Jews were forced to negotiate on a daily basis.[14] And, by April 1902, the *Chronicle* advised that the situation had grown sufficiently desperate to merit the convening of a public meeting in London.[15]

But the Anglo-Jewish establishment did not adjudge this an opportune moment for such a meeting. The AJA was especially reluctant to publicise the Romanian case too heavily. Indeed, in February 1902, its Austrian equivalent, the *Israelitische Allianz zu Wien*, proposed, under the guidance of Theodor Herzl, that a conference of international Jewish organisations be assembled in order to discuss Romania.[16] The AJA gave the proposal some thought, but initially declined to participate on the grounds that it was not 'desirable that Jews should act in political matters as an international body at all' – a somewhat surprising diagnosis, to say the least. Furthermore, it alleged that it was 'unwise' for foreign Jews to try and extract concessions, particularly as it might render impotent Romanian Jewish attempts to alleviate their lot.[17] Yet, when the conference finally met, in April 1902, Herman Landau (founder of the Poor Jews' Temporary Shelter) represented the AJA in Germany, though the reason for the change in heart is not recorded. Perhaps, however, it was related to pressure from other Anglo-Jewish institutions, especially the English Zionist Federation, which sent a letter to *The Times* urging the AJA and Board of Deputies to acquiesce to the conference.[18] Landau's report was, however, only orally presented to the AJA's ruling committee, with negligible written evidence being produced (or at least preserved).[19] The conference was merely granted a sketchy reference in the *JC*, too.[20]

Further hesitancy on the Romanian issue was evident in an AJA meeting held in mid-April 1902, at which, presumably in the wake of Landau's Cologne report, it was decided that Romania would be given increased 'consideration'.[21] By July, a bit more evidence had surfaced as to the conference's intentions, but beyond a desire to revoke or modify Romanian law, little constructive policy appears to have been agreed upon.[22] This was reflected in the comments of the Zionist Joseph Cowen at the annual meeting of the AJA in mid-July 1902. Remarking upon the dearth of information about the AJA's policy towards Romania in its recently published Annual Report, Cowen begged for a more 'explicit' account. The Cologne conference, held in an 'obscure place', he deemed 'hole and corner'. How could it hope to have any effect? Neither did he see how 'public opinion would be greatly influenced in favour of the Romanian Jews by the issue of a Romanian Bulletin by the Jewish press.' He suggested, ironically, that a column instead be taken out in the *Daily Mail*. This latter comment was greeted with laughter from the assembled AJA members.[23]

In referring to a Romanian Bulletin, Cowen drew attention to a rather recent development. In an effort to heighten interest in Romania the *Jewish World* began an irregular supplement in early June 1902.[24] It was not dissimilar in tone and content to *Darkest Russia* and stressed the various legal proscriptions enacted against Romanian Jews. Additionally, as Arnold White had done in relation to Imperial Russia in 1891, the Bulletin attempted to highlight Romania's financial instability.[25] But, unlike its predecessor, it was unable to provide much dramatic copy; forced expulsion and legislative discrimination were entirely different matters in their intensity and ramifications, one providing more opportunity for sensationalist reportage than the other. The early issues of the Bulletins were, therefore, somewhat arid and uninspiring in their propagandising.

From a public perspective, it appeared that the Anglo-Jewish establishment had put Romanian agitation on the back-burner. Certainly, there seems to have been a degree of reticence on the matter from early to mid-1902. However, in private spheres things were very different. For instance, in addition to simultaneously playing a leading role in the Royal Commission, Lord Rothschild sent regular entreaties to the Foreign Office as to British policy in Romania.[26] Given his powerful position within the British establishment, he was able to consult detailed memoranda dispatched to the Foreign Office by HMG's representative in Bucharest, Sir John Kennedy.[27] Rothschild was especially interested in two pieces of proposed legislation, the 'Bill on Organised Trades' and the 'Police Bill for Rural Communes', both of which threatened to undermine further the economic and social position of Romanian Jewry.[28] Although there was little that Rothschild could do beyond promoting the matter in influential circles, he nevertheless repeatedly stressed to the foreign secretary, Lord Lansdowne, the hope that Germany and Austria-Hungary might also take an interest. In particular, he emphasised the possibility of an increase in Romanian Jewish emigration to these lands, the threat of which might precipitate renewed German and Austrian pressure on the Bucharest government.[29]

By late May 1902, the AJA and Board of Deputies were also making direct, private appeals to the Foreign Office. As on previous occasions since the 1880s, they urged the British government to remind Romania of its obligations as set out in the Treaty of Berlin.[30] A large dossier accompanied one petition, which described in detail Romania's anti-Jewish legislation and the regular international infringements it had made since 1878.[31] Whilst each of these letters, like Lord Rothschild's, received sympathetic replies, it was evident that at this juncture HMG was not willing to undertake too proscriptive a stance on Romania and its Jewish policy. Indeed, Kennedy believed that such actions would be counterproductive, even if supported by the other signatories of the Berlin Treaty. It would, he indicated in one memorandum, 'be harmful to the Jews, and it would probably lead to a ministerial crisis and provoke a political agitation' in Romania that would benefit the propaganda of antisemitic nationalist circles.[32] Nevertheless, despite outward appearances, Anglo-Jewish individuals and institutions were attempting intervention in mid-1902.

By late 1902, a change of direction and atmosphere was detectable in the public arena. In particular, a visit to Galicia and Romania by the French writer, publicist and *Dreyfusard* Bernard Lazare received a good deal of publicity.[33] His express purpose was to examine the Jewish question in these parts and his conclusions were widely disseminated in publications in France, Britain, Germany and Romania.[34] Moses Gaster also took a trip to his former homeland in July and August 1902, where he was granted an audience with the King.[35] By September, Anglo-Jewish hopes for the encouragement of wider interest in Romania's Jewish questions coalesced in light of further international activities. The US Secretary of State, Colonel John Hay, presented a note to the seven signatories of the Berlin Treaty that urged pressure on the Romanian authorities.[36] Since the United States was not a signatory, it is evident that Hay's motives resulted from internal political agitation in Washington DC, partially connected to concerns about immigration.[37] Indeed, this was actually highlighted in the memorandum and emphasised in British reportage.[38] There was additional pressure on the US government at this moment from prominent American Jews, such as Oscar Strauss, Cyrus Adler and Jacob Schiff, who were to become major figures in the international manoeuvrings of the Jewish question.[39]

The Hay's Note elicited a frisson of excitement in Anglo-Jewish circles.[40] The *Jewish World* believed that Romanian policy had 'at last evoked official reproof' and its Bulletin, most recently published in July 1902, reappeared.[41] The September issue included supportive letters from the Archbishop of Canterbury, Joseph Chamberlain and the Bishop of London, proving that there was indeed a wider appetite for change.[42] Major Evans-Gordon also added his name to the campaign. His letter urged the 'great Jewish Banking Houses' to bring 'financial pressure of a serious kind to bear when the Romanian Government next needs assistance'. It can merely be speculated upon whether in expressing such a perspective, Evans-Gordon betrayed the hint of a conspiratorial mindset.[43]

Nevertheless, Major Evans-Gordon had an intriguing relationship with Anglo-Jewish society. In 1900, he stood for a second time as the Conservative parliamentary candidate for Stepney in the East End, which, of course, included a large immigrant Jewish population.[44] Evidently aware of this, Evans-Gordon cultivated local Jewish opinion and occasionally included Jewish charity amongst his public interests.[45] In 1900, he also obtained Lord Rothschild's approval of his political candidacy.[46] Two years later, his report on East European Jewry to the Royal Commission was greatly appreciated for its honesty and insight by the *JC*.[47] It was equally heralded at the annual meeting of the Poor Jews' Temporary Shelter, a leading institution for destitute immigrant Jews.[48] Yet, at the same time, Evans-Gordon was an active proponent of legislation to limit immigration and, more significantly, played an outspoken role in the British Brothers' League. The League had vaguely proto-fascist leanings and held mass meetings in the East End that brashly proclaimed its prejudices.[49] Evans-Gordon stood on platforms at several meetings and published a book in 1903, *The Alien Immigrant*, which was pretty unrestrained in its disdain for the 'alien Jew'.[50]

There were, therefore, many contradictions inherent in Evans-Gordon's Jewish relationship. Yet, Anglo-Jewish society was hardly unaware of this. When, in late 1902, Evans-Gordon pressed the British government for information about its stance towards Romania, his actions were greeted with a chorus of approval.[51] At the same time, the *JC* could not refrain from pointing out that such interest in its Romanian co-religionists came from 'unlikely quarters'.[52]

Discussion of Major Evans-Gordon might, at this stage, appear somewhat of a digression. However, he is a useful example of the curious contradictions that were often inherent in Anglo-Jewish interventions on behalf of their foreign brethren. Already, we have seen that in the earlier Romanian campaign of the 1860s and 1870s, Anglo-Jewry sometimes utilised the support of Christians who were not averse to proselytising amongst Jews. In the 1890s, the *JC*'s *Darkest Russia* supplement employed the journalistic services of individuals, such as

Arnold White, who held problematic views on the Jewish question. The same tactic was deployed in the Romanian campaign of 1902–1903, and much was made of Evans-Gordon's interest in the matter. Whilst he came low down on the scale of pan-European antisemitic devilishness, the degree to which Anglo-Jews were willing to take advantage of his less disagreeable opinions is reflective of some wider Jewish political manoeuvrings in this period.[53]

Evans-Gordon asked two parliamentary questions about the plight of Romanian Jews, and also wrote a supportive letter to the *Jewish Chronicle*'s special Romanian bulletin in December 1902.[54] As a consequence, his interventions in late 1902 helpfully augmented the Romanian campaign. So, too, did the repeated coverage in *The Times*.[55] The appearance of a Romanian supplement in the *Chronicle* was also not without significance. Undoubtedly, it was tangible proof of the Anglo-Jewish establishment's growing confidence in the prospects for the Romanian cause afforded by the recent publicity. In the main, though, the *JC*'s supplement was practically a verbatim version of that published by the *World*.[56] Yet, this joint action revealed the necessity of appealing to as wide a constituency as possible, since each newspaper catered for very different sections of Anglo-Jewish society. The *Chronicle* was deeply rooted in the Anglo-Jewish establishment, whereas the *World*, as was evident during the 1881–1882 period, stood at the more popular end of things.

In affirmation of wider and international interest in Romanian affairs, Moses Gaster published an article in a US journal in November 1902. By this stage, 2 months after the Hay's Note had been sent to the seven Berlin signatories, its effect seemed limited. To the relief of the Anglo-Jewish press, the British Government explicitly supported the actions of the United States. But every other Berlin signatory declined to participate in the proposed collective action against Romania. Gaster explored the reasons for this disappointing response:

The Governments of Europe are playing a political game, and every pawn on the chess-board counts. In order not to drive one of these smaller states into the arms of one of the two groups of Powers, they have refrained from exercising any pressure on Romania [...] There is further the old adage of the 'beam and mote' which could be applied, should any of the Central European Powers interfere too strongly in the Jewish question in Romania. Antisemitism, which is rampant in these countries [Austria-Hungary, Germany], gave a kind of support and countenance to the action of the Romanians, and thus the only argument which would be of any weight was wanting – the moral condemnation of the treatment of the Jews in Romania. [...] Of greater importance was the economic factor, which determined the benevolent neutrality of the Central European Governments. By ignoring the Jewish question, and by playing into the hands of the different political parties, one Power after the other got some bargain in exchange.[57]

An editorial in *The Times* concurred with this gloomy analysis, predicting that the Note could only hope to induce a 'moral effect'. German, Austrian and Russian self-interest – each state was tied economically to Romania – dictated the degree to which they might influence Romania, and it was always a greater priority than the rights of Romanian Jews.[58] Sir John Kennedy expressed the same view in private correspondence to the Foreign Office. He also remarked upon Romania's resentment at this international interference in its internal affairs.[59]

Indeed, perhaps the only truly significant consequence of the Hay's Note was a resurgence in anti-Jewish sentiment in Romanian nationalist spheres. A telegram sent to Paris by the AIU's correspondent in Bucharest, Isaac Astruc, noted the 'enormous sensation' the Anglo-American pressure had produced in the Romanian press.[60] Subsequently, a flurry of justificatory propaganda appeared in several languages, including a pamphlet by Radu Rosetti, Romanian historian and author, written under the pseudonym Verax ('Truth'). Rosetti's treatise pulled no punches. He condemned Romanian Jews for exploiting the peasantry, for driving them to drink and for generally destabilising the Romanian economy. Jews even, he asserted, failed to adequately fulfil their solitary civic expectation, since they made rather pathetic soldiers. As will be discussed in Chapter 7, such allusions often lay at the heart of East European Judeophobia in this period. Similarly, in the matter of Jewish citizenship in Romania, Verax inevitably took an equally uncompromising stance. His pamphlet, wholly Judeophobic in its orientation, once again insightfully revealed the manner of the Romanian nationalist mindset.[61] This was precisely the kind of response that Kennedy feared and he pessimistically observed in late 1902, that 'no amount of pressure or representations could force the [Romanian] Government – whether Liberal or Conservative – to fulfil the provisions of Article XLIV of the Treaty of Berlin.'[62]

Conversely, by late 1902 and early 1903, any residual doubt had more or less been cast aside in Anglo-Jewish ambitions for the Romanian cause. At least, this was the case outwith the highest echelons of the establishment. In mid-January 1903, Herbert Bentwich, founder of the English Zionist Federation and a close associate of Theodor Herzl, delivered a lecture on Romanian persecution to members of the B'nei Zion Association.[63] Bentwich had recently returned from a visit to Romania and, like Lazare, Gaster and others, bore the same unfavourable outlook of Romanian Jewish life and government policy. But his solution was not the publication of a supplement, nor an approach to the British government. He wanted a public meeting, along the lines of those held in 1872, 1882 and 1891, preferably at the Guildhall. Perhaps he was encouraged in this by earlier developments when the Jewish Lord Mayor of London, Sir Marcus Samuel (founder of Shell Oil, later Viscount Berstead), had intentionally excluded the Romanian Minister from the annual Lord Mayor's Banquet.[64] This action, regarded in the *Chronicle* as 'an illustration of what English freedom means', reaffirmed the confidence with which some British Jews were prepared to confront Romania by late 1902.[65] It encouraged Bentwich, who declared that 'there is no force so strong as that of public opinion', and he appealed to the 'national [i.e. Jewish] consciousness to help solve the Jewish question'.[66]

During and after the lecture, many attendees concurred with the sentiments articulated by Bentwich. But, perhaps yet again reflecting the establishment's core perspective, the *Chronicle* was somewhat hesitant in supporting the proposal of a public meeting. In particular, it expressed concern in relation to the manner of persecution in Romania. Not that the *JC* wished to underestimate the consequences for Romanian Jews. But since there was nothing comparable in this persecution to, say, Russian pogroms and expulsions, it regarded the stimulation of wider British condemnation as difficult. 'A series of local laws', it observed, 'passed in a country many hundreds of miles distant is hardly of a nature to raise a moral storm.'[67]

The public meeting did not occur. Yet, the *JC*'s observation was significant, even if we merely consider it so with the advantage of hindsight. Not long after Bentwich's lecture – about 12 weeks in fact – another calamity befell the Jews of the Russian Empire in the form of the Kishinev pogrom. As a consequence, Romanian Jewry's crisis of recurrent legal discrimination and civil inequality was immediately and dramatically overshadowed. There was no difficulty in raising 'a moral storm' over events in Bessarabia. Intriguingly, the *Jewish Chronicle* initially attributed the origins of the pogrom, which occurred in a province with a large Moldavian population, to Romanian antisemitism.[68] At various points in the nineteenth century, the Principality of Moldova had fallen under the Romanian remit and, as a consequence, these separate ethnic groups were often conflated (a matter which remains controversial). Thus, at first glance, it seemed as though Romanians had directly exported their particular brand of antisemitic agitation into Bessarabia. But the *JC* was soon to alter this insight, and by mid-1903 Romania's Jewish question had been all but purged from the priorities of the British narrative by the blood spilled at Kishinev.

Kishinev: the pogrom myth consolidated?

If the new century's optimism remained tangible in early 1903, any lingering hopes for a solution to the Jewish question in Eastern Europe shortly evaporated. The Kishinev pogrom of April 1903, which witnessed 2 days of sustained violence in the Bessarabian capital, resulted in 51 deaths (49 of them Jews), countless physical injuries and the widespread destruction of property.[69] At the time, it was difficult to conceive of a more terrifying event and, for several reasons, it undoubtedly marked a 'turning point' in the Jewish experience of the modern period.[70] For sure, Kishinev's immediate impact was more discernible than the 1881–1882 pogroms. It was, for example, as a result of advances in printing and photographic technology, the first time a pogrom entered the world's consciousness in visual terms. Hitherto, descriptions of pogroms had been accompanied with sketches, cartoons and caricatures. But within weeks of Kishinev, photographs were published in the *Jewish Chronicle* and elsewhere. They showed the bodies of victims laid out in a makeshift mortuary, the chaos of ransacked buildings and pavements strewn with shattered furniture and glass.[71] Today, nothing better symbolises the barbarity of this pogrom than the single photograph of a small child's corpse, its faced transfixed in silent agony. A century after it was taken, it is an iconic image that retains the power to shock.[72]

There is no doubt that the events of Kishinev were deeply shocking to contemporaries throughout Europe and North America, both Jews and non-Jews alike. In many cases, the immediate practical response was the raising of philanthropic committees and the convocation of condemnatory meetings. In New York City and other places in the United States, numerous meetings were held, each suffused with outrage and indignation.[73] Similar gatherings took place in Paris, Berlin and Vienna. In the British Empire, such steps were taken in cities in Canada, Australia, South Africa and, at home in Great Britain, in London, Manchester, Glasgow, Edinburgh and many, many other places. (Though there was no meeting 'officially' endorsed by the Anglo-Jewish establishment, a matter to be discussed below.)

Such a reaction was, of course, entirely predictable. Moreover, given the degree to which the density of newspaper reportage had altered in the two decades since the 1881–1882 pogroms, coverage of Kishinev was comprehensive, graphic and informed by a large array of sources that emanated from the Tsarist Empire. A good many newspapers also had their own correspondents in Russia, or relied on information from the increasingly sophisticated news' agency networks, such as Reuters and Associated Press. For those in Russia who opposed the Tsarist regime, regardless of their political colouring, Kishinev afforded an excellent opportunity for publicity. If Western observers entertained doubts as to the iniquity of Tsarism's Jewish policy, or even its broader political outlook, the Kishinev pogrom was certainly capable of dispelling such reservations. Of this propaganda advantage, the Jewish Bund and other political organisations inside and outside the Russian Empire were more than well aware.

To what extent, however, was British coverage determined by the antecedents of violence in 1881–1882? Was Kishinev viewed as a continuation of a 20-year government policy in the Tsarist Empire, or was it regarded as a singular event, which had nothing whatsoever to do with the earlier pogroms? In other words, can a single pogrom narrative be traced from 1881 to 1903, or not? After all, from a twenty-first century perspective, it is easy enough to compress those intervening 20 odd years into an apparently short period of time. And, certainly, for some contemporary observers of Kishinev, 1881–1882 remained a living memory. It would not be impossible, therefore, if these events were instinctively regarded as linked. Others, of course, had no such memories; Kishinev was a drama wholly of the present, not the past. Whether or not Kishinev generated its own pogrom myth, or embraced those of the former period, will be considered below.

The earliest reference to events in Kishinev in the British press appeared on 24 April 1903 in *The Times*, just 5 days after the pogrom occurred on 19–20 April (OS 6–7 April). A short paragraph, taken from a Reuters communiqué, summed up the little that was known at this point:

> The workmen at Kishinev made an attack on the Jews [...] as a result of which twenty-five were killed, about seventy-five severely wounded, and about two hundred slightly wounded. The Minister of the Interior has ordered special measures to be taken to preserve order in the town and district of Kishinev.[74]

The same paragraph was reproduced in other British newspapers, including *The Scotsman*, the *Jewish Chronicle*, the *Jewish World* and the *Manchester Guardian*. It took a week or so, however, for this news to sink in, for the full horror of Kishinev to be realised and described. This time, in contrast to 1881–1882, the *JC* was instrumental in unfolding the tragedy of the 2-day pogrom. Better connected than its rival the *World*, the *Chronicle* utilised an assortment of Russian sources to underscore its coverage.[75] These included the newspapers *Sanktpeterburgskie Vedomosti* ('St Petersburg Bulletin'), *Pravitel'stvennyi Vestnik* ('Government Herald'), *Novosti* ('News'), *Novoe Vremia* ('New Times'), the Russian-Jewish *Voskhod* ('Sunrise') and the Yiddish *Der Fraynd* ('The Friend'), as well as émigré publications *Osvobozhdenie* ('Liberation', based in Berlin) and *Free Russia* of London. Each of these represented a different strand of Russian political life. But the *Chronicle* made little effort to indicate the essential differences between, say, the Yiddish language liberal daily *Der Fraynd* and the Russian language reactionary daily *Novoe Vremia*. Each was filleted for its most dramatic coverage of Kishinev, providing a graphic piquancy to the British depiction of the pogrom.

The exposure granted by *The Times* to Kishinev was also pretty intense. Unlike the *JC*, the pre-eminent newspaper of the British Empire had its own correspondents in Russia. They included Dudley Braham, a British Jew, who was expelled from the Empire shortly after the pogrom, allegedly as a result of *The Times'* reportage that directly tied the Tsarist regime to events in Kishinev (see below). Other newspapers gave further depth to the narrative. Moreover, since the pogrom's ramifications were truly international, this was an aspect carefully monitored by every newspaper. The British response was not viewed in isolation, but in conjunction with that of other nations, especially the United States. It all added up to a potent mixture of harrowing detail, moral outrage and more than a hint of sensationalism.

In contrast to the events of 1881–1882, which were comprised of a series of pogroms that emanated in waves across the Empire's southern provinces, Kishinev took place in a single city, in a neatly bookended period of time. The reportage was therefore concentrated, distilled and facilitated greater insight into the pogrom phenomenon. For observers in 1881–1882, the *Jewish World*'s articles had made this possible. But Bankanovich's testimony, even if we disregard his tendency to exaggeration, was surely tempered by the fact that he wrote about many events which occurred over a comparatively longer period of time (over 12 months, as compared to 2 days). To be sure, he conflated numerous (alleged) incidents, none of which he had witnessed personally. In contrast, in 1903 the British media was able to ask questions about a single pogrom.[76] And the *Jewish Chronicle*, the *World*, *The Times* and other newspapers were able to provide answers using Russian sources. As we shall see, the manner of this coverage contributed to the creation of a clearly defined pogrom paradigm.

In terms of how the pogrom began, a number of variants were proffered and they altered in the weeks the followed. In the earliest *JC* articles, the beginnings of the 2-day riot lay in a mob's verbal taunting of local Jews, who then took things a step further by throwing stones at them. Following this, the agitation shifted up several gears, and the mob moved to the 'systematic wrecking of Jewish houses and the sacking of Jewish shops'.[77] Similarly, in *The Times'* reports of early May, the pogrom took the same graduated course and began in the wake of a lengthy church service that started at midnight. The rabble emerged from the church in the early hours of the morning, according to *The Times*, and initially attacked nearby Jewish shops, only moving onto other districts and assaults on individuals several hours later.

In these early stages, many publications made much of the fact that the pogrom occurred at the most momentous period of the Orthodox Christian calendar, Easter. Festivities during and following Easter Sunday, celebrating Christ's resurrection, formed the preamble to the pogrom.[78] It was not an insignificant assumption to make and, in turn, it was tied to the animosities that had recently been stimulated by a ritual murder accusation in the nearby town of Dubossary.[79] As a consequence, the rivalries inherent within the Jewish–gentile relationship in Kishinev were deemed religious, rather than ethnic or social. Indeed, the *JC* referred to the earliest pogromists as a 'band of Christian youths'.[80] These aspects chimed, of course, with renderings of the 1881–1882 pogroms. But, in actual fact, as recent historiography attests, the animosity towards Jews in this diverse city located at the fringes of Empire was more likely to have been ethnic and social.[81] This is not to say that Kishinev was devoid of religious tension. But it might be argued that religion actually served to heighten and accentuate ethnic and social differences (or even *vice versa*?) at a time of year that was acutely significant for both Judaism and Christianity. In 1903, Easter and Passover occurred at the same time; Easter Sunday, the day the pogrom began, was also the last day of Passover.

Thus far, the immediate details of Kishinev were little different to the manner in which the 1881–1882 pogroms had been depicted in their earliest stages. But this was soon to alter, and by the second week of

May 1903, the horror, brutality, the noise, the smell and aftermath of the 2-day riot were revealed in all its blood-curdling intensity:

> The noise of the smashing of windows and of the cracking of doors mingled with the screams of the maltreated Jews and the cries of terror of their wives and children – a terrific cacophony. [...] Every Jew who was encountered was beaten until he lost consciousness; one Jew was dragged under a tramcar and smashed to death. The miserable dwellings of the poor were rifled of their contents, which were removed and piled in the street. Immense clouds of feathers rose in the air.

Kishinev's brutality was minutely analysed and some gruesome detail recorded. There were references to disembowelled corpses, whose eviscerated bodies were stuffed with feathers. Other cadavers were mutilated, their eyes gouged out and ears chopped off.[82] One victim had nails driven into his temples.[83] More were 'literally slaughtered and hung up in the butchers' shops'.[84] And, as in 1881–1882, women were 'outraged'; they aimlessly wandered the streets, their lives having been stolen in the worst way imaginable.[85] In the *Daily Express*, an alleged German eyewitness account, originally published in *Berliner Tageblatt*, described the despair of a husband who had been compelled to watch the rape and mutilation of his wife. In the same paragraph, more grisly incidents appeared: 'a baby aged one was blinded with red-hot irons, the eyes being literally burned out [and] a man had both his legs sawn off.'[86] According to the *Daily Mail*, 'women were hung up by their hair to trees, human heads were stuck on poles.'[87] The *Jewish World* published a list of the dead and injured, their losses and their wounds: lips and tongues were cut out, heads stabbed and nostrils pierced with nails.[88] Added to all this was a distinct sense of the atmosphere that engulfed the city, both during and after the pogrom. The air was choked with 'clouds of feathers', an image that repeatedly occurs:

> [the streets] were strewn with debris, various articles of furniture, pianos, pictures, crockery [...] covered with a thick layer of feathers and down, which, whirled in the breeze, darken[ed] the atmosphere.[89]

Other sensory elements could be detected. In the aftermath of the pogrom, for instance, an eerie silence pervaded the city, as its inhabitants stayed indoors. A tang of paraffin hung in the air from the many fires that had been deliberately set.[90]

These many facets of the Kishinev pogrom – the sadistic violence, the broken glass, the feathers and its tremendous racket – continued to occupy a significant place in the British narrative throughout 1903. For instance, in late May *The Spectator* referred to the 'flinging of children from the balconies on to the stones below', and to the torture and mutilation that occurred: 'nails were driven into one man's head, and bodies were found which had been disembowelled.'[91] In early June 1903, the émigré publication *Free Russia* highlighted similar details, including 'babies thrown from upper storeys, helpless old men [pushed] under tramcars to be crushed'.[92] In August 1903, Arnold White, who was less than sympathetic towards the Jewish cause by this stage, wrote in the *National Review* of violated young girls, murdered children and 'Jewish corpses [that] were eviscerated and stuffed with feathers'.[93]

It is impossible to know how many, or whether, these horrific acts actually occurred in Kishinev. Undoubtedly, the loss of life was great, the manner of death of the most abhorrent kind. At least 500 people carried injuries and reported to the local hospital. Most were wounded on the head and face, having been beaten by 'clubs, canes and crowbars'.[94] V.H.C. Bosanquet, the British Consul-General at Odessa visited Kishinev 2 months after the pogrom and collected information from various individuals, both Jewish and non-Jewish. He discountenanced many of the claims of mutilations and 'deliberate torture', pointing out that in the majority of cases the wounds were to the head and face. He was informed that a 'women [had] been wounded in the stomach,' but found no corroborative evidence.[95] Nevertheless, it is clear that the British press revelled, for whatever reason, in sensationalising the blood, gore and stench of Kishinev. Time and again, the same metonymic image occurred. For contemporaries, the corpse stuffed with feathers undoubtedly represented the entire inhumanity of those 2 days in Bessarabia. Only *The Times* declined to publish such detail, claiming the 'mutilations as too abominable for description'.[96]

Of course, many of these provocative images were actually taken from the Russian press. There was no British reporter present in Kishinev, either during the pogrom or in the weeks that followed. For the *JC*, *Der Fraynd*, *Voskhod*, *Novosti* and *Pravo* provided this kind of striking detail.[97] *The Times* and *Daily Telegraph* also used similar sources.[98] And all of it was taken at face value, since there is no evidence that these sources were ever questioned – at least publicly. Thus, although Russia was regarded as uncivilised, barbaric, its moral universe rooted in the medieval, it was clearly the case that these images were equally shocking and evocative in different cultural contexts.[99] A disembowelled corpse stuffed with feathers required no frame of reference – cultural, ethical or otherwise – in order to highlight the particular savagery of this murder. Naturally, the British press did not reflect upon this, but rather attempted to accentuate the moral distance it usually placed between Russia and Britain. It did this most especially by making much of the alleged spectators who came to witness the fury of the pogrom in action. The *Jewish World*, for instance, reported that a 'fashionable portion of the population [drove about] in carriages watching the acts of savagery perpetrated by the mob with all the enjoyment of a spectacle.'[100] This was an exaggeration, though like any unchecked riot, as the pogrom gathered momentum and spread through various districts of the city, bystanders became opportunistic looters as onlookers threw in their lot with the *pogromshchiki*.

But who, in 1903, made up the mob? In 1881–1882, every newspaper had assumed the *pogromshchiki* were peasants. Two decades later, the identity of the Kishinev rioters was noted from the very beginning and, rather than peasants, they were workmen.[101] Their weapons were 'stones, sticks, crow-bars and revolvers'.[102] Later on, further social specifics came to light, and the *World* referred to 'gangs of stonemasons, carpenters, labourers [armed] with sticks, clubs and knives'.[103] Such tools and weapons, although pretty general, were not agricultural (i.e. they were no pitchforks, scythes, etc.) and emphasised that it was townspeople, not peasants, who took part in the pogrom. Again, this was more insightful than renderings of the 1881–1882 pogroms. For the most part, Kishinev's *pogromshchiki* were male urban workers, though on the second day there is evidence, interestingly, that nearby peasants arrived to join the throng.[104] The *World* also claimed that Kishinev was 'engineered by the organisers of the politically disaffected secret associations of the Russian industrial classes, whose ramifications are taking root all over the country'.[105] It is not clear whether the political orientation of such organisations was to the left or right, though these sentiments foreshadowed, in many ways, events that were to occur during the revolutionary years of 1905–1906. But, in 1903, they hinted at an underground, controlling influence upon the prejudices of Kishinev's gentile inhabitants. Unsurprisingly, such manipulation was discovered in many quarters.

For instance, the provocative actions of individuals in Kishinev and beyond were closely scrutinised. At local level, the role of the antisemitic newspaper *Bessarabets* ('The Bessarabian'), edited by P.A. Krushevan, was held responsible for stirring up anti-Jewish hatred amongst ordinary

Kishinevites.[106] Once again, Russian sources endowed the British press with this information, since any understanding of the Tsarist provincial press was beyond its remit. On 22 May 1903, the *Jewish World* published a report presented by the Kishinev Jewish community to an official St Petersburg official. How the *World* got hold of this report is unclear, as is the identity of the official, but it made evident the role of local agitation in the pogrom's instigation:

> The present riots are without precedent – even in the history of antisemitic troubles – and so much against the usual life of the people of this region that the causes must be sought in the events of these last years, and particularly in facts observable during the actual excesses. In the first place, the influence of the local press whose sole representation in the *Bessarabets*, must be mentioned. This journal, during the last few years, has made it its business to inculcate hatred of the Jews, with a violence unprecedented in the Russian press. The population heard daily, 'The Jews are our enemies, they are harmful, they must be annihilated'. [...] It is therefore quite natural that the mass of the people should become imbued with the opinions of this journal, which did not consider the annihilation of the Jews merely desirable but possible. The *Bessarabets* frequently employed the words 'death to the Jews', as a means of bringing about a solution of the Jewish question.[107]

In the *World*'s view, Krushevan's 'evil sheet' had deliberately whipped up popular anti-Jewish animosity in Kishinev. The *Chronicle* took the same perspective, noting its 'incessant appeals to race hatred and to the worst passions of the people'.[108] Once again using a Russian source, *Voskhod*, the *JC* revealed the inflammatory nature of *Bessarabets*, illustrating it with the 'following pearls' from the latter's pages:

> 'Russia will not allow seven to ten millions [and exaggeration by between one and four millions] to dwell in their midst, oppressing the people, working against them, and undermining their welfare'. [...] In the same number of *Bessarabets* (No. 238) there is a whole series of wild cries such as: 'It is time Russian life were free from parasites!' 'Death to the Jews!' 'Jewish corpses shall be bound to cartwheels!' [...] The editor of the *Bessarabets* proclaims solemnly: 'The Jewish question has assumed a critical phase and threatens the Jews with a terrible, nay, insupportable tragedy'.[109]

This local incitement was also acknowledged elsewhere, particularly in *Free Russia* and *The Times*.[110] And, of course, it contrasted with the manner in which 1881–1882 had been supposedly orchestrated; what use would the written word have been to peasants?

However, in relation to the local and national authorities, there was a major link between the narratives of 1903 and 1881–1882. From the outset, the indifference and occasional encouragement of the local police were noted in Kishinev.[111] So, too, was the role of the Vice-Governor V.G. Ustrugov, who also acted as the local censor. *The Times* held him culpable for permitting *Bessarabets* to heighten the antisemitic atmosphere in Kishinev in the months and weeks before the pogrom.[112] The Bessarabian Governor, R.A. Raaben, came in for similar criticism, particularly in his apparent restraint at deploying ready numbers of troops.[113] Undoubtedly, condemnation of local incitement (Krushevan), indifference (Ustrugov and Raaben) and inefficiency (the chief of police) was not without justification.[114] But then British newspapers swiftly moved higher up the Imperial scale, and the buck inevitably stopped with V.K. Plehve, the Minister of the Interior.

As has often been recounted, in May 1903 *The Times* published a notorious 'despatch', dated March 1903, purportedly from Plehve, which indicated that he knew a pogrom would occur in Bessarabia.[115] It ordered the Provincial Governor to avoid using excessive force in dealing with future violence.[116] To this day, the author of this forged document remains unknown, yet the response it precipitated in Britain, the United States and elsewhere can be easily anticipated. Nor is it difficult to imagine the shock it induced for the Tsarist regime. In fact, it must be surmised that Braham, *The Times*' correspondent, was expelled precisely as a result of this incident. Even if the regime did not believe him directly responsible, he unfortunately became a Jewish scapegoat.[117] For many years thereafter, the 'Old Thunderer' and the Russian government were on uneasy terms.

Predictably, the authenticity of the despatch was not questioned, and one after another every British newspaper, metropolitan and provincial, roundly condemned the regime for its deliberate pogrom policy.[118] The Russian government and its ministers were guilty to a man. It was a plain and simple fact and, actually, it was widely believed prior to the release of the despatch. Even though the 1903 narrative was, in many ways, different to that of 1881–1882, a line of descent could be traced in the degree to which the theory of official connivance was embraced. In 1881–1882, it had only acquired gradual acceptance; but in 1903, it was the conclusion to which all immediately jumped. Although

1881–1882 was barely referenced amongst the reportage of Kishinev, the most salient 'fact' of the earlier outrages was certainly remembered. Moreover, the detail of Kishinev added to the theory, from the stone-throwing to the roles of *Bessarabets*, low and high officials, from the smashing of property to the horrific violence inflicted on individual Jews. Indeed, for the first time the term 'pogrom' was used in the British narrative. The earliest reference appears to have been on 22 May 1903, in the *Jewish World*.[119] But no definition was attempted. It was not until the Gomel (Homel, Minsk province) pogrom of 9 September 1903 (28 August OS) that an exploration of the term was instigated, initially in the *Manchester Guardian*.[120] In December 1903, a Russian correspondent of *The Times* defined in full the mechanisms of a pogrom. It is worth citing in full (my bold; italics in original):

It is perhaps because the word *pogrom* is not understood in Western Europe that the occurrences at Kishinev and Gomel were described as massacres. There is an important distinction, for the **pogrom is a national institution**, and it was not a massacre in the ordinary sense of the term, but a *pogrom* that took place in the towns. The word *grom* means thunder and the word *pogrom* implies a desire to shatter or destroy as a thunderstorm destroys. A mob assembled for purposes of devastation does not, however, constitute a *pogrom* unless it follows **certain well-established and characteristic rules**. Thus, until now, *pogroms* have only been directed against Jews, though **the system** could be extended to other sections of the population. The *pogrom* was first **instituted** after the assassination of Alexander II, in 1881, when anti-Semitism and reaction flourished under General Ignatiev. The *pogrom* was encouraged as a means of terrorising the Jews.

The **method** is as follows:- first there is a **period of incubation**. Hints are received 'from above' by the local police that it would be well to give the Jews a lesson. It will then so happen that some three or four months before Easter a **propaganda** is commenced in dram shops, cheap restaurants, and other places of popular resort. **Rumours** are circulated that the Jews are exploiting the people, that they are enriching themselves, that they have killed for ritual purposes a Christian child. Then, when Easter comes, the smallest incident suffices for a *pogrom*. At Kishinev it was a squabble with a Jew who was managing a merry-go-round; at Gomel it was a dispute with a woman selling herrings. **The first manifestation of a *pogrom* is made by small boys**. They march around the town shouting, throwing stones, and smashing windows of houses inhabited by Jews. If the *pogrom* has commenced spontaneously or its occurrence is **not considered desirable by the authorities**, the police arrest some of the small boys, give them a flogging in a public square, and there the matter ends. But if on the morrow it is ascertained that no boys have been flogged, a mob of adults gathers and matters become more serious. The houses of the Jews are entered, though as a rule, no one is hurt, and only the furniture is smashed. But, above all, **the great feature of a *pogrom* is the bringing of bedding to the windows and discharging the feathers it contains into the street below.** The Jews are very great consumers of poultry and they carefully keep their feathers. Thus, **feather beds become a mark of social distinction and indicate the wealth of a family.** To slit open a feather quilt cuts at once at the pride and purse of the Jew. The scattering of the feathers also greatly amuses the crowd, and it is considered a fine sport. The **police stand aside**, only interfering should the Jews resist; then they separate the contending parties.

On the morning of the third day the Governor or the local authorities issues proclamations, professing to be very grieved at what has occurred and forbidding the people to assemble in the streets. Perhaps two or three *muzhiks* are arrested and publicly flogged. Here the *pogrom* generally terminates, and such *pogroms* have now taken place off and on for more than 20 years, that they fail to cause any particular concern unless they are **allowed to continue** for the third day. By that time the criminal instincts have developed, and the professional criminal ceases to fear the police. **Then it is that men are murdered and women violated.** A *pogrom* is, therefore, a five-act drama. First there is the propaganda; secondly, some squabble that provides the pretext; thirdly, little boys go forth and see if the authorities are willing, and if they are not punished for smashing the windows, then the fourth act begins and the mob breaks the furniture and scatters the feathers of the bedding. Finally, at the fifth act, the lowest passions finding themselves unrestrained, rape and murder terminate the drama. But **from the very first pebble thrown by a small boy to the last murder committed, all is absolutely under the control of the Government.**[121]

A great deal could be said about this extract, not least that the context, consequences and Jewish response to the Gomel pogrom were all quite different to Kishinev. In particular, the Gomel Jewish community was much larger and better prepared; local branches of the Bund had already organised self-defence units in anticipation of possible violence. And the local police and military were considerably more efficient in quelling the pogrom.[122] Thus, Kishinev was not a model pogrom that was subsequently imitated in the rest of the Russian Empire. On the contrary, of the 43 pogroms in 1904, and the 54 that occurred between January and October 1905, none were identical in context, form, detail and impact. There were similarities, but also differences.[123]

Cleary, however, this commentary in *The Times* was hugely significant regardless of its historical accuracies and inaccuracies. In the British narrative, a pogrom paradigm had been defined. Despite the fact that this paradigm did not even follow the manner in which the Kishinev pogrom had occurred (where, according to some observers, murders occurred on the first day), it facilitated an insight into a Russian 'national institution' that permitted British observers to understand both motive and method.[124] It could be applied to both past and future outbreaks, regardless as to whether in every case the 'well-established rules' and or 'system' were followed to the letter. As long as some/most of the rules were followed, it was a pogrom. In this paradigm, the pogrom 'method' and its essentials were clearly laid out; 'a period of incubation', 'propaganda' and 'rumours' often connected to ancient Judeophobic accusations, stone-throwing by small boys and, somewhat inevitably, the destruction of feather mattresses and pillows.[125] Only then, after testing the waters, would the perpetrators move to violence against individuals and the vandalism of property. To qualify as a pogrom, there had to be mass destruction, murder and rape; but there also had to be order discernable from chaos.

Yet the key aspect of this paradigm was, of course, the role of the authorities. From the local to the national, everything was in their hands and, if they did not want a pogrom to occur, they would not allow it to happen. Various signals were used to indicate the wishes of the authorities. Thus, it was not simply a kind of game, as suggested by the feather business, it was institutionally organised. It was a policy and, in a society in which the state apparently controlled everybody's lives to the most extreme degree. It could not happen, under any circumstances, without the approval of the highest officials in St Petersburg.

Kishinev's impact – and the years of revolution

Having considered the manner in which the Kishinev pogrom was portrayed by British reportage in the first few months after April 1903, we must now turn to the matter of Britain's practical response and the long-term consequences. What could be done? And, more to the point, what was done? As has already been noted, a number of meetings were organised in London and various provincial cities. These not only condemned the Tsarist regime, but were also philanthropic and raised funds for distribution amongst the victims of Kishinev. In every synagogue in the British Isles, rabbis preached against the pogrom and urged all Jews to unite in defence of their brethren.[126] The most important and well-attended gathering was a demonstration in Hyde Park, held under the auspices of the Jewish labour and trades' union movement.[127] But, unlike preceding decades, the Anglo-Jewish establishment did not organise or promote a meeting, nor did any Christian organisation. This was a matter that puzzled the Russian émigré publication, *The Anglo-Russian*, edited by Jakov Prelooker:

> That England is as much shocked with the Kishinev massacres as any country nobody will doubt. The English Press has given full accounts of the tragedy and reflected pretty well the feeling of the public at large. Yet one is painfully astonished that practically nothing has been done in this country in the way of an organised and influentially-supported public protest. [...] Is there not something the matter with England? Is there not something radically wrong with the present day England?[128]

To be sure, there was plenty of condemnation in the British press and, for its part, the Anglo-Jewish establishment was not completely silent. A significant letter from the Board of Deputies and AJA appeared in *The Times* on the same day as the publication of the Plehve dispatch.[129] However, despite a universal consensus on the true horror of Kishinev, there was no agreement on the matter of what was to be done.

Why was there no 'official' meeting in the wake of Kishinev? Certainly, many quarters pressed the Board of Deputies and Anglo-Jewish Association on the issue. The *Jewish World* led the call in the public arena. In late May 1903, there were also heated exchanges at the monthly meeting of the Board of Deputies. Sir Samuel Montagu, for instance, fretted that a Guildhall or Mansion House-style meeting might encourage a Nihilist or some such radical to shout out 'Down with the Tsar!'[130] The *World* was understandably scathing about this concern. If this was all that could be said 'against the public meeting of protest at the heart of the Empire of freedom and tolerance', it was surely a risk worth taking.[131] After all, part of the point was to give Petersburg officials pause for thought about the system under which they lived and worked, not whether it was ever acceptable to insult a monarch. But, herein lay the dilemma for the Anglo-Jewish establishment. Whilst its membership was as appalled as every other British Jew at events in Kishinev, it was reluctant to criticise the Emperor Nicholas II and to consequentially appear in cahoots with the revolutionaries of the East End and beyond. If such a public gathering occurred under the aegis of the establishment, the entire cause would be irredeemably weakened. Moreover, there was concern that such a meeting would appear too Jewish. At a discussion held by the Conjoint Foreign Committee, for example, Leopold de Rothschild noted that his brother, Lord Rothschild, was 'of the opinion that a meeting would only be useful if convened by leading Christians'.[132] In the absence of such a event, it was better to attempt intervention quietly, behind the scenes, with the assistance of the CFC. Evidently, many of the lessons of 1881–1882 had not been learnt; this was precisely the same unpopular route that had been taken by the Russo-Jewish Committee.[133]

The tensions that existed between the various components of Anglo-Jewish society, which undoubtedly came to a head during the Kishinev crisis, were both social and generational.[134] By this stage, the Board of Deputies and Anglo-Jewish Association were mostly staffed by distinguished, but elderly individuals, all from respectable bourgeois stock, each grounded in the deferential mores of the century into which he had been born. The exception in generational terms was Lucien Wolf, who, as we shall see, did mount a campaign against Tsarist Russia in subsequent years; but in 1903, he was chair of the CFC and followed the official line. Similarly, the *Chronicle* mirrored the establishment's anxieties and, on the eve of the Hyde Park demonstration, it expressed the hope that the meeting would 'not give way to violent denunciation, particularly in their references to the Tsar'.[135]

Political divisions also asserted themselves during the domestic fallout from Kishinev. Socialist and Zionist allegiances were usually found amongst those who most fiercely wielded the anti-Tsarist baton. Indeed, it was Zionist individuals within the Board of Deputies who chiefly fought for a meeting.[136] Outside these exalted realms, ripples of consternation ran through the Jewish East End. Working-class, unionised and chiefly recent immigrants, East End Jews were less than impressed at the refusal to hold a meeting. At a socialist gathering in Mile End in June 1903 at which 5000 were present, a printed address to the 'Workers of England' ended with the following triumphal sentences: 'Down with Russian absolutism. Long live the Social Democratic Labour Party of Russia. Long live the Bund.'[137] The loyalties of class overrode religious and ethnic affinity, which had the potential to draft many more supporters than could be dreamt of by the Anglo-Jewish establishment. (Though it is difficult to imagine that Lancashire cotton workers or coal miners in South Wales felt much affinity with the Jews of Kishinev.) Subsequently, the enthusiasms of the East End gave rise to the International Kishinev Protest Committee, though it only survived until July 1903.[138]

Outwith the Anglo-Jewish community the practical response to Kishinev was somewhat lukewarm. Two questions were asked in the House of Commons, each tabled by the Jewish MP, Sir Stuart Samuels.[139] There was no debate, such as had taken place in 1882, though the government did request a first-hand account from a British official in Russia. V.H.C Bosanquet's report has already been mentioned and it was presented to the House in August 1903. Mostly dedicated to describing the pogrom, the report attributed blame to *Bessarbets* and the slow response of the local authorities. No connection was made to the Ministry of the Interior.[140] In light of this evidence, the British government made no effort to intervene in Russian domestic affairs.

Like all crises, however terrible their intensity and consequences, British interest in Kishinev gradually diminished. Towards the end of 1903, it was revisited in the Jewish press, firstly as a result of events in Gomel and, in the second place, because the trials of the perpetrators began in Imperial Russia.[141] But by 1904, other Tsarist matters preoccupied the mainstream British narrative, shifting the Jewish question down the agenda. In particular, the Russo-Japanese War, the Dogger Bank Incident that almost precipitated war between Britain and Russia, and, by the end of the year, the early rumblings of the 1905 Revolution.[142]

The years of revolution were traumatic for the Jews of the Russian Empire. Notwithstanding the political manoeuvrings of this time, such as the October Manifesto that resulted in the granting of civil liberties and a parliament, the victories of 1905 were ambiguous for Russian Jews.[143] There was no emancipation, the May Laws were not repealed, nor was the Pale of Settlement abolished. And the pogrom was as much a hallmark of these years as strikes, peasant rebellions, urban demonstrations and revolutionary publications. Historians have estimated that between October 1905 and September 1906, around 650 pogroms occurred throughout the Empire. Many broke out in the same southern provinces that had witnessed anti-Jewish disorders in 1881–1882: Chernigov, Kherson, Ekaterinoslav and Kiev. Others occurred in

Congress Poland, Bessarabia and Vil'na. In terms of the number of victims, the statistics are staggering. Over three thousand were killed, many more thousands were wounded, rendered homeless and left destitute.[144] In Odessa alone, where a pogrom took place in October 1905, between 400 and 800 people were murdered.[145] It was only in the wake of this pogrom, that the Anglo-Jewish establishment finally agreed to organise a public meeting, though it was inevitably dominated by Christian voices.[146]

This dramatic upsurge in anti-Jewish violence did not pass unnoticed in Britain and, for the first time, the word 'pogrom' entered regular usage.[147] Thus, it was not 1881–1882, Kishinev or Gomel that allowed from the full absorption of this Russian word into the English language, but the pogroms of 1905 onwards.[148] Yet, inevitably, for the mainstream press the revolution often took precedence over the Jewish experience; after all, many momentous moments occurred – Bloody Sunday, the October General Strike, the Manifesto, the Moscow Uprising and much else besides. Oftentimes, it actually looked like the autocracy might crumble under the forces of popular and nigh-universal protest. Of course, the Anglo-Jewish press also monitored the revolution. In spite of the pogroms, there were moments of tangible optimism, when the hope of a solution to the Jewish question was visible on the horizon. The *Jewish Chronicle's* response to the signing of the October Manifesto, for instance, was to declare that the 'Tsar has been beaten to his knees.'[149]

But the pogroms of these years could hardly escape attention. In both the mainstream and Anglo-Jewish press, the pogrom that began in Odessa on 30 October 1905 (17 October OS) and in Białystok on 13 June 1906 (1 June OS) drew the most coverage. The reportage in the *JC* was as detailed and horrifying as it had been during 1903, with a reliance on Russian and other continental sources again evident. The initial report on Odessa, which ran beneath the headline 'Many 1000s Killed and Injured', filled up six whole pages – each edged in black. Like Kishinev, the *JC* reported that it began with the distribution of antisemitic propaganda that proclaimed 'Death to the Jews', further agitating the already heady and excited atmosphere in the city. The context was the open celebration of the October Manifesto. Red flags were draped in the streets, and a celebratory atmosphere pervaded many quarters. Meanwhile, bands of 'cutthroats', 'ruffians', Cossacks and policemen, angry at this revolutionary air of victory, mounted a full assault on Odessa's Jews. A 'wave of fury' ran through the city, as *pogromshchiki* laid waste to property, butchered anybody in their way, mutilating them in the process – eyes were gouged out, pregnant women disembowelled, temples nailed – countless women were raped, the elderly were drenched in petroleum and burnt alive. Every street was strewn with corpses, the carnage unimaginable. And the whole ghastly massacre was 'pre-arranged'. Although many local elements were culpable, the controlling influence was in St Petersburg.[150]

In *The Times*, some equally dramatic testimony was filed, and it mostly concurred with the *Chronicle's* perspective.[151] Two articles, however, provoked controversy. The first emphasised the Jewish role in provoking the pogrom, in particular, its wholesale embrace of revolutionary sentiment in Russia. Indeed, *The Times'* correspondent went so far as to suggest that a non-Russian Jewish organisation had deliberately agitated in favour of revolution in Odessa, sending its own emissaries for that exact purpose. Additionally, it inferred that it was mainly/only Jews who bedecked the city in red flags, that they tore the strips of blue and white from the Russian national flag (leaving just the red) and destroyed pictures of the Emperor and other Tsarist emblems. In other words, the revolution was actually Jewish; most other inhabitants of the city, all identified as Russian, did not participate in any revolutionary act – save for a few students. Only Jews were revolutionaries; no true and patriotic Russian would ever mutilate a portrait of the Tsar! Additionally, in defending themselves Odessa's Jews inflicted a great deal of damage on the city, dropped countless bombs from balconies and generally aided in the establishment of anarchy.[152]

Naturally, many Jews in Odessa and throughout the Russian Empire supported the revolution at some level. Some were even members of revolutionary parties, but the majority were not, as has been relentlessly demonstrated by historians (see Chapter 7). Certainly, many celebrated the October Manifesto, hopeful that it marked a step towards Jewish emancipation, but most insinuations in *The Times* were false and revealed as much about the mindset of the correspondent as they did about the revolution and the pogroms. This did not pass unnoticed and, a few days later, a letter from Moses Gaster was published. It challenged each assertion; no emissaries were sent to Odessa, Jews had no advantage to gain from the establishment of anarchy, and where on earth did they acquire all the bombs that were supposedly dropped onto unsuspecting townspeople?[153] In other words, according to Gaster, *The Times'* correspondent was guilty not only of exaggeration but also of actual falsehoods.[154] A similar contretemps occurred a few weeks later. Once more, it was claimed that Jews had, by their revolutionary actions, provoked the violence.[155] This time a critical rebuttal by Lucien Wolf was published.[156]

Like most of the Russian Empire, Odessa was a maelstrom of political extremes in 1905. In many ways, the pogrom, with all its terrible intensity and brutality, represented the confrontation between these extremes. Despite the revolution's universal elements that took in many social classes and ethnic groups, for the extreme right, which opposed the revolution, the Jew lay at the heart of it all. Any concessions granted by the regime were regarded by the extreme right as weakness, a sign of Jewish influence. There was only one way to respond to this, to the revolution itself. This aspect of the revolution did not pass unnoticed in the British narrative. During 1905, observers became aware of extreme right-wing elements in the Russian political spectrum, in particular the Black Hundreds (*Chornaia sotnia*). As historians point out, the Black Hundreds was not a political party, but rather a 'amorphous entity that acted as a semi-autonomous arm of the Russian right', its 'vigilantes and terrorists'; their rallying cry was 'Beat the Jews'.[157] Often it was associated with a more legal organisation, the Union of the Russian People. But both groups were active in Odessa and played their part in the pogrom of 1905.[158]

However, the appearance of the Black Hundreds and other extreme right groups in the British narrative was significant not as a result of an appreciation of the many layers of political orientation in the Russian Empire. Rather, it was taken as yet further indication of the official origins of the pogroms. In the *Jewish Chronicle*, they were deemed the regime's 'hirelings'.[159] The same perspective was embraced elsewhere. Indeed, *The Times* noted that the Black Hundreds and other elements of the Russian population, especially 'hooligans', 'were organized by the reactionaries to reverse the policy of the [October] Manifesto by provoking riots and baiting the Jews'.[160] To be sure, in Odessa and elsewhere, there was a link between the extreme right and individuals with the local bureaucracy and police. But there was no link to St Petersburg. At least, there was no link in terms of the Black Hundreds being used to pursue a deliberate pogrom policy.[161]

But, inevitably, a connection was made in the British narrative and, once again, the essential definition of a pogrom lay in its official origins. This was writ large in every assessment of 1905. Two distinguished commentators on Russian affairs, Bernard Pares and Maurice Baring, penned an unsigned article on the matter for the *Quarterly Review*. They were convinced that the pogrom was a 'weapon of reaction', and their article focussed especially on events in Odessa.[162] Pares repeated the claim in a book dedicated to the 1905 revolution.[163] Whilst neither Pares or Baring overtly suggested that officials in St Petersburg were involved, it was not difficult to make the connection given the evidence they presented. Lucien Wolf came to the same conclusion in his many contributions on Russia's Jewish question in the years leading to the First World War. He wrote the introduction of a book by E.P. Semenov, the not insignificantly titled *The Russian Government and the Massacres*. Wolf wrote:

> The political advisors of the Tsar deliberately and systematically use massacre as an instrument of government [...] as a normal expedient for assuring the stability of the Autocratic system! The [massacres were] the natural impulse of such an anachronism [i.e. the regime] fighting for its life.[164]

In later years, in Wolf's view the term 'pogrom' became a metaphor for the entire Jewish experience in the Russian Empire, and in *Darkest Russia* he observed that 'the Jews are subjected to one long pogrom, which grinds down their lives with pitiless monotony.'[165] It seemed that the pogrom was indeed a 'national institution' in Russia.[166]

4
Partitioned Poland: Physical and Ideological Encounters, 1880s–1914

> [Poland] is poor and the Jew, laid like the rest on this anvil of national poverty, must submit in addition to be the hammer of priestly and popular oppression.
>
> *Jewish Chronicle*, January 1903

> Stick to your own kind!
>
> Slogan of the Polish National Democratic Party

Without the Pale: Polish Jewry

For many British observers, the Pale of Settlement, the area in which the majority of Jews were legally required to reside in the Tsarist Empire, embodied the status of the Eastern European Jew as a victim. Instituted in stages from the late eighteenth century onwards, the Pale's origins can be traced to the partitioning of Poland. Empress Catherine II not only acquired new territory as a consequence of the 1772, 1792 and 1795 partitions, but also acquired a large population of Jews. Indeed, Russia's Jewish question can be said to have begun in the wake of the first partition, since few Jews had hitherto resided within the confines of the Tsarist Empire.[1] The Pale, *cherta osedlosti* in Russian, covered a vast area – around a million square kilometres, roughly twice the size of France. By the end of the nineteenth century, according to the 1897 Imperial census, approximately 3.9 million Jews lived within its boundaries.[2] The majority were legally restricted to living in towns in the Pale, with a minority living in the countryside.[3] In the nineteenth-century British narrative, it was depicted as a stifling, stunted place, overcrowded and not dissimilar in its day-to-day limitations to the manner in which the medieval ghetto was imagined. In fact, the term 'ghetto', often capitalised, was sometimes synonymous with 'the Pale'. In various publications, the following perspectives on the Pale were recorded: Jews were 'forced to live together [in the Pale] crowded together in filth and misery'; Jews were sentenced to the 'dusky ghettoes of the Pale, the victims cramped and crushed, starved of air and space and food, with scarcely roof or rags to cover them'; 'the greater part of six million Jews are caged up in the few plague-stricken towns and villages of the Pale'; Jews were 'cooped up in a vast sort of ghetto'; Jews were 'herded together [like animals?] and decimated by disease bred in an unnatural manner'.[4] These were universal images, widespread in the Jewish and non-Jewish narratives.

The Pale's existence precipitated much confusion for not only British, but Western observers generally. For example, a report by a US Congressional committee, published in *The Times*, concluded that the Pale was 'about the same dimensions as the state of Texas [...] a flat, sandy country that hardly seemed capable of sustaining the population upon it'.[5] Quite what inspired this desert-like rendering of lands that were host to some of the most agriculturally fertile parts of the Tsarist Empire is not clear, yet it reaffirmed the outcast status of Russian Imperial Jewry – condemned to live in an arid, barren, hostile region.

But the most important misunderstanding with regard to the Pale was where its borders began and ended, precisely which parts and provinces of the Tsarist Empire fell within its remit and which did not. As a rule, Western observers believed that Congress Poland (the *Kongresówka* – formerly the Duchy of Warsaw established by Napoleon Bonaparte in 1807 – ceded to the Tsarist Empire in the wake of the Congress of Vienna in 1815) was a part of the Pale.[6] It was not.

That the *Kongresówka* was without the Pale is significant for many reasons. First of all, Polish Jews living under Tsarist rule did not labour under the same restrictions as their co-religionists in the 15 provinces of the Pale.[7] Polish Jews were exempt, for instance, from residence restrictions, from the 1882 May Laws and the various *numerus clausus* instituted under Tsar Alexander III. Moreover, unlike in the 15 provinces, emancipation was actually achieved in Congress Poland, a process that effectively began in the late eighteenth century and was finalised in 1862.[8] Thus, although there were often similarities between Russian and Polish Jews, such as in matters of religious observance and language (though not dialect), social and economic opportunities were sometimes more advantageous in the *Kongresówka*. Not by coincidence, many Jews from the Pale migrated into Congress Poland in the latter part of the nineteenth century.[9] This was a source of resentment, not only for ethnic Poles, but Polish Jews, too. Few British observers recognised these important details, and the temptation to conflate Poland with the Pale was often overwhelming.

Of course, notwithstanding these legal differences, life was not perfect for the Jews of Poland. This was as much true for the pre-partition period as it was in later decades. In this overwhelmingly Catholic part of Europe where Jews had resided since the tenth century, blood libel accusations made regular reappearances in the seventeenth and eighteenth centuries, with consequences for individual Jews and the broader Jewish–gentile relationship.[10] And, as we have already seen, Warsaw experienced a significant pogrom in 1881. In all parts of partitioned Poland – the *Kongresówka*, Prussian Poland, Austrian Poland (Galicia) – Jews encountered poverty, legal intrusion, social disadvantage and outbursts of anti-Jewish rhetoric from neighbours, officials and politicians alike. In 1897, a new Polish political party was created, the National Democratic Party. Led by Roman Dmowski, whom we shall encounter below, the *Endecja*'s worldview was radically nationalist and racial antisemitism formed the keystone of its ideology.[11]

Despite these difficulties and habitual flare-ups of anti-Jewish feeling, the British perspective on the Jewish experience in Poland almost always followed the same path. Poles were a tolerant people, particularly when it came to their Jews. Poland itself was regarded as an historical haven for fugitive Jews, who had fled in earlier centuries from less enlightened regimes.[12] This was Poland's past, but it also informed its outlook in the nineteenth century. Such perspectives were further compounded by the widespread belief that Poland itself was a victim. Thrice divided by neighbouring powers, one observer writing in 1913 described it as an 'open sore' on the European body politic.[13] That same year, Bernard Pares employed the same evocative image of this wounded, bleeding, pain-wracked country:

> There is nothing more tragic in history than the running sore of Poland [...] It is a terrible thing to live in a house of which all the doors have been broken in, with a threefold dividing line the runs over one's very hearthstone. There is no subject in European politics which it is more difficult to treat.[14]

Poland's status as a European martyr held great sway in the British mindset, even in spite of its Catholicism, which usually prompted suspicion. And, as we shall see in Chapter 6, during the opening salvoes of the Great War it was comparable in its martyrdom to Belgium, another

Catholic state. In Britain, Polish culture was admired and the work of Henryk Sienkiewicz, who won the Nobel Prize for literature in 1905, was especially highly regarded.[15] Monica M. Gardner, a self-taught Polish speaker, published a number of well-received books on Polish themes, including a biography of Sienkiewicz, in the years before and after the First World War.[16]

But where did the Jews fit into this rendering of Poland? If they lived in a supposedly tolerant society, how were incidents of anti-Jewish sentiment interpreted? As we have already seen, the 1881 Warsaw pogrom was deemed an external provocation, the result of malign Russian influence. Was this the manner in which all outbreaks of Judeophobia and antisemitism in Poland were analysed, explained away, or were other reasons proffered? In answering these questions, this chapter will consider early British receptions of Polish National Democracy, in terms of individuals, ideology and policies. In its final assessment, it will consider responses to the venomous anti-Jewish boycott that the National Democrats instigated on the eve of the First World War. First of all, however, this chapter will examine the occasions on which a separate narrative of Polish Jewry is discernible, and consider whether the Polish Jewish experience was ever truly depicted without the Pale. In other words, from the British perspective, precisely who was the 'Polish Jew'?

The divided Polish 'Ghetto': crossing borders

In 1882, two works of fiction dealing with 'life in the Eastern ghetto' appeared in English translation: 'From the Ghetto' (*Aus dem Ghetto*) by the Czech Jew Leopold Kompert and 'The Jews of Barnow' (*Die Juden von Barnow*) by his Podolian counterpart Karl Emil Franzos.[17] Both authors were subjects of Austrian Emperor Franz Joseph I, and their contributions recorded Jewish experiences in very different parts of the Habsburg Empire. The former in Bohemia, the latter in Galicia. The vision of the 'ghetto' in these books, and the Jews that resided within its clutches, was grim, miserable and welded to an outmoded way of life. Franzos, who is best remembered for his oft-misused dictum 'every country has the Jews it deserves', described his ghetto, Barnow, as: 'A small town, a squalid nook in a God-forgotten corner of the earth, where the great current of life hardly seems to cause the faintest ripple.'[18] Isolated, untouched by modernity, the ghetto represented a pattern of traditional Jewish existence from which both Franzos and Kompert were keen to escape and distance themselves. For these authors, the possibilities of social and moral advancement lay beyond the ghetto's metaphorical walls, amongst assimilated Jewish society. Or, to paraphrase one historian, for them the ghetto represented death, whilst assimilation was the affirmation of life.[19] These fictional works encapsulated many strands of the debates and anxieties that occupied European and American Jewish society throughout the nineteenth and twentieth centuries.

From a British perspective, the appearance and embrace of these exotic tales were no doubt influenced by recent events in Europe (the various attacks in Imperial Germany and the Russian pogroms) as publishers were keen to take advantage of heightened interest in the continental Jewish question. They might give substance and form to the otherwise anonymous victims of persecution, as well as the communities and environment in which they lived. After all, in the British imagination it was quite difficult to separate Bohemia from Galicia, and from the Pale of Settlement; were they really so different in terms of their Jews? It appeared not. *The Times*, for instance, regarded both volumes as 'instructive as to the customs of Polish Jews and life among the lower orders of Polish society'.[20]

Of the two books, *The Jews of Barnow* precipitated the most lasting interest and, until his death in 1904, Franzos' work was popular in the United Kingdom. Indeed, the translation of his 1889 book 'For the Right' (*Ein Kampf ums Recht*) included an appreciative introduction by William E. Gladstone, former and future prime minister.[21] In the words of one reviewer, Franzos' work shed light on the 'most incomprehensible of human beings', the 'mysterious' East European Jew.[22] For another critic, the international border that separated the Pale of Settlement from Galicia, in which Barnow was supposedly located, was undetectable in Franzos' stories[23]:

> There is little to distinguish the Ghetto of a town here from one in Russian Podolia. We see the same curls and caftan, we hear the same jargon, and it is only when we get further into the interior of Russia that we begin to find the characteristics of the Russian Jew vary in some respects from his Polish brother. Among the Jews themselves, Polish Jews are the least esteemed; but they are not on that account the less interesting as a study.

This was an unhelpful perspective for British readers. Although the reviewer indicated that apparent differences could be discerned between Galician Jews and Jews of the Pale, s/he did not identify what they were. Were they social, religious, cultural? There was no indication. Moreover, this review later noted the degree to which Jewish life in Galicia had lately improved, 'owing to the enlightened policy which characterised the Austrian administration of the province'.[24] But how? Again, the author did not elaborate on this matter. In 1882, few contemporaries could have doubted that the official rule to which the Jews of the Pale were subject was the precise opposite of enlightened. This, then, was surely a major difference.

Other borders, divisions and separations were visible in Franzos' Barnow – particularly the 'barriers' between Jew and gentile. And they seemed to have altered little over the course of many centuries, according to a review in the *Daily News*: 'These glimpses into the inner life of the Podolian Ghetto [...] are like visions of mediaeval times [...] The Jews have been forbidden to hold or practise any of the professions. To accumulate coin is all that is left to them.'[25] To be certain, since the advent of Austrian rule, the Jewish experience in Galicia had been of mixed fortune, but, by the 1880s, in legal terms at least, things had changed greatly. In 1867, in the wake of the *Ausgleich*, the political union of the Austrian and Hungarian crowns, all the Jews of the Habsburg Empire received full civil emancipation. Amongst the many things this facilitated was the purchase of land.[26] Of course, the abolition of poverty and localised anti-Jewish prejudice was not so straightforward, and for most Jews there was no immediate improvement in their day-to-day condition. Yet, to imagine Galicia in these terms was too simplistic, dependent on long-established stereotypes, though it once again reaffirmed the overwhelming status of the East European Jew as a voiceless victim.

Ten years after the appearance of *The Jews of Barnow* in English, Franzos' influence on British attitudes was marked in other ways. In the early 1890s, East European Jewry faced a crisis in the form of the aforementioned expulsions in the Tsarist Empire. As a consequence, in late 1891 the well-known writer Sir Thomas Hall Caine was invited to investigate the Jewish question in Eastern Europe.[27] Hall Caine was a literary celebrity in the 1890s and, although his work has not endured, it seems clear that his sympathetic disposition towards the Jewish question prompted the invitation, though by whom is unclear.[28] Earlier in 1891, he published a much appreciated novel entitled *The Scapegoat*, which dealt with the persecution of Jews in Morocco.[29] And prior to his Eastern European excursions, Hall Caine was fêted by Anglo-Jewish society and gave talks, for instance, to Chovevi Zion and the Maccabaeans (in its inaugural year).[30]

By the time Hall Caine arrived on the continent, another catastrophe threatened Jewish and other lives. A cholera epidemic, which traversed every conceivable boundary – whether geopolitical, social or cultural – began in Afghanistan, spread rapidly through the Russian Empire, then into Galicia and finally made its halt in the German port of Hamburg. The epidemic was closely monitored in Britain and the United States, and in the popular, and occasionally official, imagination there appeared to be a link to Jews.[31] Of course, for East European Jews, Hamburg was one of their most important points of departure from the Old to the New World; they often interrupted their journey westwards with a temporary sojourn in London, Southampton, Liverpool and other British ports.[32] Whether Jews could transport or transmit this 'plague' across the continent and oceans was a major worry, and cholera was added to the list of diseases with which Jews had been maliciously associated since the Black Death.[33]

Prior to Hall Caine's first-hand investigations in divided Poland, he visited Karl Emil Franzos in Berlin. Who better than Franzos to seek advice on the life of Galician and Eastern Jewry, but also to provide insight into the obstacles and trials that might be endured in the hazardous journey eastwards? It was Franzos who set the tone not only for Hall Caine's expedition but also for the writings he produced in its wake. And it is evident that, more than any other anxiety he may have ruminated upon, it was the threat of cholera that dogged Hall Caine's every step:

> You are going in by Galicia [advised Franzos] and will come out by the Baltic provinces and return home by Hamburg. Now, if you hear of even one case [of cholera] in Hamburg pack your bag and be gone instantly. One case today will mean forty cases tomorrow and a hundred the day after. Remember this and lose no time.[34]

Little wonder, then, that the articles Hall Caine subsequently wrote for *The Times* were entitled the 'Shadow of the Great Death'. In fact, he seems to have been greatly fearful of his own well-being, anxiously spotting the cholera menace in every dark corner – in the individual Jews who departed the continent without the aid of Jewish organisations, in the cargoes of rags he saw unloaded from his ship on return to Grimsby, in the produce sold on Galician market squares and in the faces of panic-stricken Jews at prayer in synagogues. It cannot be said that Hall Caine believed that only Jews were harbingers of this life-threatening disease, that he imagined it was a 'Jewish disease'. But, cholera was his point of departure on heading East, and it informed his entire discourse on the Eastern European Jewish question.[35]

The notion of frontier, of division and separation recurred in several aspects in Hall Caine's *Times'* articles, and also in the two pieces he subsequently produced for the *Pall Mall Magazine* in 1893. Immediately upon his arrival in the East, for instance, he was struck by the geographical lines of partition in this 'triangular region where three territories meet'. He referred to three towns – Katowice, Sosnowice and Kraków – that summed up for him the essential difference between Prussian, Russian and Austrian rule in Poland. Prussian Katowice, for instance, had paved streets, whereas the Russian town of Sosnowice did not. The people of Katowice were poor, but 'civilised'; in Sosnowice they were 'half-civilised' and many hundreds were reduced to pathetic beggary. Just a few kilometres of territory separated these towns, but 'on the one side', he said, was 'decency and civilisation and some measure of safety from disease; on the other side, [there was] semi-barbarity, discomfort, squalor, filth, and imminent danger from every epidemic that comes within a score of miles.' As for Kraków, in some ways it was a mixture of these extremes. It had grand and noble architecture, but the Jewish quarter was 'squalid and dirty, foully drained, and abounding in rank, slimy open gutters, where filth lies rotting in the hot sun and sending up at midday a palpitating haze of sickening vapour'.[36] No doubt Hall Caine also saw, quite legitimately in this instance, the shade of cholera in this primitive sewerage system.

But to what extent were these differences and similarities, the gulfs and the gullies connected by Hall Caine to the Jewish inhabitants of each city? It seems evident that in all three cases, the generalised terms in which he spoke of Katowice, Sosnowice and Kraków were applicable to all classes, ethnic and religious groups. In the first two instances, no mention of the Jewish population was made. It was only when Hall Caine got to Kraków that Jews began to preoccupy his pen. This part of the world, Galicia, was important to Hall Caine because of its proximity to the Pale of Settlement and the frontier gripped his imagination. Whilst at the border, standing besides the yellow-and-black-striped border posts, he encountered yet more personal distress in the form of a pleading, beggarly old woman who had crossed into Galicia from the Pale. 'This', he said, 'was my first experience of Russia and I was appalled.' For him, this old woman personified the difference between the manner of rule under which Jews struggled in Russia as compared to Austrian governance of Galicia, where a more liberal environment enabled the Jew to 'betray more freely his racial qualities'.

These 'racial qualities' were apparent to Hall Caine in many aspects. For example, immediately upon reaching the frontier separating Russia from 'the countries of northern Europe', he was struck by 'the costume and general appearance of the Jews'. They were 'feeble, sickly pallid', had 'long and thin' faces, 'more than the ordinary proportion of aquiline nose, and [...] a shifty expression in the egg-shaped eyes'. He noted also their *peies*, 'long kaftans' and 'hats [with a] peaked cap like that of an English yachtsman'. According to Hall Caine, who did not explore the religious meanings of Jewish modes of dress in the East, this costume was actually 'a visible sign that the Jew is a voluntary alien who keeps and guards his peculiarities'. And, 'undoubtedly it cut off the Jew from the people about him.' Thus, the differences that existed between Jew and gentile were emphasised by Jews themselves, in their attire and side-locks. Nevertheless, although Hall Caine encountered Russians and Austrians who opposed these habits, believing this apparent proclamation of 'foreign nationality' to be an offence, he himself bore an open-minded attitude. 'I should be sorry to miss the variety which the Jewish costume gives,' he noted. Clearly, the exoticism of the Polish Jew was worthy of preservation, his differences to be appreciated rather than shunned, otherwise any cause to look upon him would vanish: 'the uncultured Polish Jew, can badly spare the one thing that makes him worth a second glance. Poverty and oppression have already crushed out of his poor featureless body nearly all sense of the picturesque.'[37]

It must be said that in many aspects, Hall Caine's attitudes were somewhat similar to those elaborated upon in *The Jews of Barnow*. Jewish separateness, a people 'ghettoised' from their neighbours, their visible differences and even the mysticism found amongst some East European Jews in the form of wonder rabbis and the like were similarly fundamental to Franzos' interpretation of the community into which he had been born, but had chosen to reject. Indeed, it might be argued that Hall Caine arrived with preconceptions and tightly formed attitudes about East European Jews that were forged under the influence of Karl Emil Franzos. This was best represented by Hall Caine's regurgitation of Franzos' view that 'every nation gets the Jews it deserves because it has made them what it deserves to find them.'[38] But also the notion that there was something 'picturesque' about them, that they were curious in their social and religious habits – living anachronisms, museum pieces upon which to gaze with amazement, a passive people from which there was nothing to fear. Beyond these obvious influences, it is evident that a good deal of intellectual traffic passed between the two authors. One newspaper even reported that Hall Caine was 'busy with a novel' on the Russian Jew, assisted by none other than Franzos who was providing the 'peculiar historical knowledge and local colouring that perhaps none but a Jew could give'.[39] Alas, the book did not materialise, as Hall Caine pursued greater interests within his own domestic environment.[40]

What did Hall Caine's work reveal about British attitudes to Polish Jewry? In essence, although it was sympathetic, occasionally verging on the patronising – Hall Caine could not in any way be accused of antisemitism – it was a somewhat confusing account. Yet again, the stumbling block was divided Poland and the matter of where the Pale of Settlement began and ended. Hall Caine began his writings by described the Pale's vital statistics, erroneously stating that there were around six million residing in it borders. He also made much of its apparently poor physical geography, that it was 'not a region enriched by nature', that there was 'hardly in all the earth a land less favoured by God'. It was 'flat and featureless', 'swampy and ague-stricken', 'a weary waste', its towns 'neither picturesque nor comfortable. [...] the prevailing colour is yellow, the dominant odour is noxious, the ways are narrow and often unpaved'.[41] Clearly, like many other commentators he disliked the Pale and found it to be an uninspiring, desperate and inhumane place. And, like many of his contemporaries, he exaggerated the number of Jews residing within its borders, probably as a result of conflating the 15 provinces with the *Kongresówka*. He also interchangeably used the terms 'Russian Jewry', 'Polish Jews' and 'Galician Jews', their apparent fluidity further emphasised in the title of his *Pall Mall Magazine* articles: 'Russian Jewry. Scenes of Home Life in Poland and the Pale'.

Yet, it seems evident that most, if not all, of Hall Caine's expedition to Eastern Europe took place in Galicia. Apart from Sosnowice and Katowice, no other towns in Congress or Prussian Poland were mentioned in his writings. And Kiev was the only city of the Pale referenced, though this was in connection to an outline of residence restrictions. Hall Caine did not discuss any visit of his own to the Ukrainian capital, which he surely would have done had he actually been there. Nor was there mention of the obligatory encounter with a Tsarist official, oftentimes the Minister of the Interior or some such, and one wonders, in any case, whether a British subject would have been permitted to enter the Russian Empire through the border with Austria.[42] The towns that appeared most frequently in Hall Caine's Eastern European writings – Kraków, Lemberg and Brody – were all located within Galicia, where the Jews had once been a part of the Polish lands, but now resided under Austrian rule. For certain, they were not and had never been subjects of the Russian Empire; they were not Russian Jews.

Hall Caine's journey, therefore, mostly (probably wholly) confined to Galicia, meant that he merely observed the Pale from the border, the

Austro-Russian frontier. As a consequence, his first-hand knowledge of Russian Jewish life was limited, and no doubt relied on pre-existing perceptions of life in the Pale. In essence, Hall Caine simply transposed his experience of Jewish life in Galicia to the Pale and, therefore, it was impossible for him to extricate or appreciate any possibility of separate narratives; to his mind, Jews in Galicia and Congress Poland were no different in any aspect from their co-religionists in the Pale. In this regard, like many British commentators he was apparently overwhelmed and fascinated by the presence of the Pale, the 'ghetto' it symbolised. And, for Hall Caine, it defined the life of the 'Polish Jew', wherever he happened to reside.

Face-to-face with Polish Jews: Evans-Gordon and Baskerville

About 10 years after Hall Caine's visit to Galicia, two other British observers came face-to-face with Polish Jewry. This time, the circumstances and context of their investigations were very different. As we have already learnt, as a consequence of the aliens debate, the early years of the twentieth century were extremely important in the development of British perspectives on Eastern European Jews. Major William Evans-Gordon, as noted in Chapter 3, embarked upon a long journey through Eastern Europe in 1902 in order to specifically investigate the Jewish question and how it was connected to emigration. Unlike Hall Caine, Evans-Gordon's journey was perhaps as extensive as was physically possible at this time. He began in Berlin and thence travelled to St Petersburg, Dvinsk, Riga, Libau, Vil'na, Kovno, Pinsk, Warsaw, Łódź, Kraków, Budapest, Bucharest and Lemberg. His expedition covered, as the crow flies, around 4500 kilometres, and he not only visited the Pale but also visited two components of divided Poland – the *Kongresówka* and Galicia.

By the time Evans-Gordon set off his grand tour, another British observer was already a resident of Warsaw, where she was to live for 8 years. Beatrice Baskerville, about whom little is known, was a journalist and author who, like Monica Gardner, appears to have been a self-taught Polish speaker. In 1906, Baskerville published a book entitled *The Polish Jew. His Social and Economic Value* that detailed her first-hand experiences in the Polish capital. This work was an obvious effort to analyse and encapsulate the essence of the Jewish question in Poland. In particular, it tried to stress the significance of Polish Jewry in relation to the aliens debate in Britain. 'Although neither Great Britain nor the United States have reason to fear being "swamped" by the

Semitic race', wrote Baskerville, 'it is not improbable that even the supreme Anglo-Saxon would profit by observing the methods, customs and character of that wonderful people whom no amount of oppression, persecution or injustice has been able to conquer.'[43]

These two encounters were, in some senses, quite different. Evans-Gordon's visit covered a huge amount of territory, was of limited duration and as a consequence he was only able to acquire snapshots of Jewish life in Eastern Europe. Although he detailed visits to individual towns and cities, he did not reveal precisely how long he stayed in each, nor how many weeks his entire journey lasted. Throughout, he was escorted by guides and translators, who were mentioned in the book he produced about the tour, *The Alien Immigrant*, and sometimes they appeared in the accompanying photographs. In contrast, Baskerville's experience was forged over a considerable period of time, occurred in single part of the Tsarist Empire and largely in the same city. Therefore, she viewed matters from much closer quarters and, since she seems to have been a Polish speaker, she was able to seek out information under her own guidance. Moreover, she had the possibility of conversing on her own terms with Poles, both Jewish and non-Jewish, of reading daily newspapers and intensively monitoring the day-to-day experience in Warsaw. Additionally, Evans-Gordon went to Eastern Europe for very specific reasons related to the Royal Commission and his agenda was governed accordingly. When observing the Polish Jew 'at home', he often had in mind the Polish Jew 'abroad', especially in the East End of London. As for Baskerville, although she did not reveal precisely why she was in Poland – she was not employed by a newspaper at this time – her priorities were not so clear cut, despite the references to the alien question, and we might reasonably expect that they fluctuated throughout the 8 years of her stay. Indeed, a reviewer in the *Times Literary Supplement* noted that the Aliens Act, which was passed the year prior to the appearance of her book, was merely a 'peg on which to hang her thoughts' about Poland's Jewish question. And, in fact, *The Polish Jew* had been 'unconsciously written rather for a Polish than for an English public'.[44]

Given Evans-Gordon's well-established vehemence on the aliens question, as evidenced at public meetings of the British Brothers League, an interesting facet of his East European travelogue was his remarkably open-minded approach. Indeed, he seems to have positively relished the experience and did not utilise the personal discomfort and other difficulties he experienced in order to cast negative light on East European Jewry. Some parts of his journey in the Pale, for instance, were undertaken on the back of a horse-drawn cart, over many kilometres of unsealed roads. But since he had seen active service as a soldier, maybe these drawbacks were not as problematic for Evans-Gordon as they might have been for a less adventurous traveller.[45] Additionally, whilst he was surely armed with preconceptions about the Polish Jew, which in consequence of the aliens question were undoubtedly negatively tainted, he was nevertheless fully appraised of the Jewish legal position in Eastern Europe, and how it differed in the *Kongresówka* as compared to the Pale and Galicia. He also knew precisely where the Pale began and ended, and made use of statistics from the 1897 Imperial census in an accurate fashion.[46] Unlike other commentators, such as Hall Caine, he did not conflate the Jewish population of Congress Poland with that of the Pale.[47] In his report to the Royal Commission, which was mostly measured and temperate, he was quite clear about all of these important matters.[48]

In terms of how Evans-Gordon regarded the Polish Jew, this very much depended upon where he found himself. In Warsaw, for instance, he observed the deep poverty, the restriction of economic opportunity made all the more difficult due to profound demographic change. But on the whole, he thought Warsaw Jews were economically much better off than their co-religionists elsewhere in Poland. In Łódź, the so-called Polish Manchester, he investigated the local spinning and weaving trades, the large factories owned by Jews that employed hardly any Jewish workers. At the less technologically sophisticated end of the trade, amongst the handloom industry where Jewish workers were in the majority, he encountered conditions that were simply 'appalling'. 'I shall never forget', he said, 'the terrible places and rooms in which I saw this trade being carried on. [...] I have never seen human beings living under more awful conditions', who had the appearance of 'half-starved consumptives'. In analysing Polish Jews, poverty was certainly the overwhelmingly defining factor for Evans-Gordon, which he of course linked in turn to the common desire to emigrate. It was, he believed, the most materially poor, the most unskilled and therefore the least suitable Jews, who were likely to leave and seek new opportunities elsewhere. To be sure, he did not want their destination to be the East End of London.[49]

At the same time, despite his anti-alien outlook, it is evident that Evans-Gordon had some sympathy for Polish Jews, often pitied them and, for the most part, refrained from speaking of them in derogatory or racialised terms. There were no references in his report, for example, to any notions about a supposed specific Jewish physique or physiognomy. Moreover, he endeavoured to view matters from all angles and much admired, for instance, the efforts of the wealthier members of Poland's Jewish community to provide various charitable actions, such as soup kitchens, though, at the same time, he felt that not quite enough was being done. Nowhere was the need for philanthropic intervention greater than in Galicia, where the Jewish middle classes were beleaguered with all kinds of causes. In Kraków, especially, where the overcrowding was incredible, the amount of people who apparently lived on nothing had attained desperate numbers; Evans-Gordon actually used the Yiddish term *luftmenschen* ('men of air') to describe them. The poverty was all-consuming and reduced many thousands to living literally upon nothing.[50]

It was as a consequence of his visit to Galicia that Evans-Gordon spoke for the first time in visualised terms about Jews. Here they willingly adhered to 'the costume of the middle ages' and presented the outsider with a 'remarkable and picturesque appearance'. Indeed, a photograph of two *Hassidim* in Kraków, attired for Shabbat, was used as the basis for the front cover of the *Immigrant Alien*. Like Hall Caine before him, Evans-Gordon was clearly fascinated by the other-worldliness of Galician Jewry, which he had not encountered in the Pale. Indeed, it was in connection with these Jews that his most negative, and perhaps most telling, comment was made. 'Their costume', he observed, 'is typical of the stage of evolution they have reached.' Thus, their outfits were not merely a reflection of religious practice, but an adherence to times past, an unwillingness to advance forwards. Such an outmoded worldview had no place in the United Kingdom and it was no coincidence that the photograph of the *Hassidim* was used for the front cover of *The Alien Immigrant*.[51]

It was inevitable that Evans-Gordon linked the lives of Polish Jewry to the alien question. As we have seen, he made regular direct comparisons between the material poverty in Polish cities and that of the East End of London. Moreover, he believed there were all kinds of economic ties between London and Poland that, were they to fail, would incur disastrous consequences for Britain. In particular, if the chronically unstable textile industry of Łódź were to crash, the 'ashes and debris' would be carried as far as Whitechapel. In contrast, he believed economic affairs were more secure in the Pale, and regarded Jewish endeavours 'of benefit to the peasantry'. In Poland, there were simply too many people and the economic jam was spread far too thinly.

Moreover, unlike the Pale, he regarded anti-Jewish feeling in Poland of much greater import, connected intrinsically to Polish nationalism and liable to erupt violently at any opportunity.[52]

That Evans-Gordon was reasonably informed and somewhat judicious in his views reflected, of course, the nature of the forum in which his report was received. An intolerant, overtly reactionary perspective would have been shunned by the Royal Commission, an arena governed by a parliamentary etiquette that necessitated considered and substantiated opinion. In particular, other knowledgeable members of the Commission, not least Lord Rothschild, would undoubtedly have challenged a harshly unforgiving portrait of Polish Jews. Indeed, throughout the Commission's proceedings, expressions of unwarranted and unjustifiable perspectives on Jews in London or elsewhere as observed by various witnesses were regularly discountenanced by Rothschild and others.[53]

Such limitations did not exist for Beatrice Baskerville, whose work was exclusively addressed to a general audience. She had no cause for restraint in expressing her opinions and it showed. Her account, *The Polish Jew. His Social and Economic Value*, was intemperate, negative and highly racialised in its approach. Readers were not spared a wide range of evocative allusions. She used colourful language in describing the visual and sensual aspects of Polish Jewish life, as well as the environment in which they dwelt. The following paragraph more than amply sums up her attitudes:

> The first impression of the Jewish quarter [of Warsaw] is not so much poverty as the stifling atmosphere, the smell of garlic and of dirt which pervades the streets and seems to roll from the houses in waves. So strong is it, in summer months especially, that it seems to be something tangible. In the winter, the cold suppresses it in the streets, only to coop it up in double strength in the rooms where six feet afford sleeping, living and working accommodation for a dozen people, whose aversion to soap and water is proverbial and whose favourite food is herrings and garlic. [The streets] are crowded and the people who pass one another have nearly all the Jewish type. The men are dressed in the long *Halat*, or skirted coat which reaches nearly to the ankles, and the peaked cap, or *Jarmulka*. Some of the younger women have their hair plaited; others wear the hideous wigs of the married women which can be seen like the trophies of some Indian chief, piled up in baskets in the market place. Every degree of Hebrew beauty and ugliness is here: the stunted boys and girls,

the offspring of diseased parents; young men with Christ-like faces, others with mean ones; old men wrinkled and calculating, with eyes in which lust for money glints as hard as the golden idol; old women who look like witches invented to frighten naughty children.

There is little need to reflect substantively upon these comments, since a less unsympathetic analysis can hardly be imagined. This was reflected elsewhere in the book, as she described, for instance, Jewish patterns of speech as 'gesticulating and gibbering'. In physical terms, Jews were cowardly, had an awkward 'gait and ungainly feet' and 'talked through [the] nose'.[54] In other words, Baskerville's work was barely devoid of a single antisemitic stereotype it was possible to embrace at this time. She found absolutely nothing redeemable in the Polish Jew, in either his religious or social habits. In essence, he was a parasite, who preyed upon the weaknesses of the Pole, who in turn was defined as a spineless creature, lacking in 'grit'.[55] There was nothing mysterious, nor picturesque about the Polish Jew, such as suggested by Hall Caine and Evans-Gordon. *Streimel*, *peies*, *talit* and *sheitl* were regarded by Baskerville as symbols not only of religious or racial difference but also of a voluntary separation that spelled social and economic doom for Poland. The Jew had 'crept into every Polish household from the palace of the manor, from the farmhouse to the cabin. [...] Were he to make a mark on all his hands have touched, not a field or pasture, not a brick or stone, not even a beast of burden but would bear the trace of the despised son of Israel'.[56]

Baskerville examined other ways in which Jews apparently undermined the integrity of Poland, most particularly in the political arena. Jewish activities in socialism and Zionism were especially objectionable. During the 1905 revolution, she observed that Warsaw's Jews 'prevailed amongst the red banners and rags', behaving in stark contrast to the universally patriotic processions of Poles.[57] As for Zionism, this was an equally insufferable Jewish political faith and, according to Baskerville, had been utterly counterproductive in its ambitions, since it had resulted in an increase in antisemitism:

To the Polish nature, easy-going though it be, there is something particularly obnoxious in the contemplation of the better part of a million Jews, whose forefathers found a refuge in a country at a period when the Semite was chivied [*sic*] and chased from all parts of Europe, who have lived upon that country for centuries, some of whom have even amassed fortunes, assuming an attitude of hostile exclusiveness towards the very people to whom they owe so much, flaunting the cult of the jargon, the *halat* and the Talmud before their eyes, and eagerly looking forward to the time when they will have amassed a sufficient quantity of Polish gold to bear them over the seas and establish them in Palestine to continue the cult practised in the land of exile.[58]

Undoubtedly, these were extreme perspectives and one wonders with whom Baskerville interacted socially and intellectually in Poland, which newspapers she read and whether she had any involvement, at some level (even if only intellectually), with the Polish National Democratic Party. Alas, she gave no indication as to these matters; there were no references to individuals she knew, nor specific reading material and the like. But, as we shall see, in many ways the ideas she embraced undoubtedly mirrored those of Roman Dmowski and his *Endek* colleagues, who championed the most extreme ideological response to the Jewish question in Poland.

At first glance, given his role in the Royal Commission it appears almost inevitable that Evans-Gordon's encounter with Polish Jewry would have the most lasting impact on the British context and narrative. His evidence undoubtedly assisted in realising a long-held personal desire for restrictive immigrant legislation in the United Kingdom. And, surely, the report's restrained nature aided him in his cause. By the same token, it might be argued that Baskerville's book would or could not have had too great an impact on legislation or British opinion, since it was probably not widely disseminated (it was an expensively priced book in its day at 10 shillings and 6 pence), and was perhaps mistimed as it appeared the year after the Aliens Act's passage through Parliament. However, despite its extreme vision, *The Polish Jew* surely encapsulated many widely held British perspectives. Certainly, it reflected attitudes presented by less restrained witnesses to the Royal Commission, as well as those bandied about in the East End by members of the British Brothers' League and the like.[59] The stereotype of the Polish Jew of the East End was comparable to that in Baskerville's book; politically unreliable, religiously and racially exclusive, intent on making money at the expense of the non-Jewish (and sometimes the Jewish) community and prepared to endure the worst degrees of poverty in order to achieve his goals. Yes, there were differences in emphasis, and Baskerville was exceptional in the vehemently expressive manner in which she embraced these stereotypes. Nevertheless, Baskerville's little-known work, which has barely been touched upon by historians, actually embodied the popular attitudes that resulted in the somewhat hasty parliamentary passage of the Aliens Act. In this instance, the 'Polish Jew' was none other than the 'alien Jew', an allusion with resonance not only in the British, but the Polish context, too.

Ideological challenges: British interactions with Polish National Democracy

In the period before and during the First World War, the single most important British figure connected, both culturally and intellectually, to the Tsarist Empire was Bernard Pares. Founder, in 1907, of the first Department of Russian Studies in the United Kingdom, at the University of Liverpool, Pares was instrumental in securing a legitimate place for the study of Eastern Europe in British intellectual life. In later years, during the Great War, he played a hugely significant role in the founding of the School of Slavonic and East European Studies, then housed at King's College London.[60] Pares was a Russian speaker and frequent visitor to the Tsarist Empire. In the period during and after the 1905 Revolution, he travelled extensively through the Tsar's lands, where he observed peasants embroiled in heated political meetings, witnessed violence on many city streets and discussed the issues of the day in the Imperial capital with leading members of Russia's emerging political elite.[61] Moreover, he was actively engaged in promoting Anglo-Russian friendship and was instrumental in the instigation of two symbolic exchanges of amity, intended to reaffirm the cordiality of these relations. The first, a visit of Duma deputies to London in 1909 was followed 3 years later by a reciprocal delegation of various British officials to St Petersburg.[62] And, as we have already seen in the article he wrote on the pogrom phenomenon in 1905, Pares regularly wrote for the British press in this period on a wide range of Eastern European and Russian themes. If a newspaper required an expert on the Russian Empire, it was invariably Bernard Pares to whom they turned.

One of the most important personal and political encounters Pares made in this period was with Roman Dmowski, leader of the Polish National Democrats. In 1906, Dmowski was elected by Warsaw as a member of the Imperial Duma, the parliament granted in the wake of the 1905 October Manifesto. In the Duma, Dmowski and his Polish compatriots formed a coalition, known as the Polish Koło ('circle'), comprised of various political orientations.[63] Dmowski was unquestionably the most charismatic of the Polish cohort in the Duma. Uncompromising as a champion of the nationalist cause, he swiftly became a well-known figure within and without the Petersburg political set. As a regular observer of the verbal jousting in the First and Second Dumas, Bernard Pares witnessed Dmowski in full flow and he was, it seems, impressed by the National Democrat leader from the first. Indeed, in reflecting upon Dmowski's political credentials on the eve of the First World War, Pares believed him to be the 'the most robust and able of all political workers whom Poland has produced during [its] hundred years of desolation.'[64] A year into the War, Pares claimed there was 'no better political head in Europe'.[65] Much later, he reiterated this admiration in his memoirs, describing Dmowski as a figure who reminded him of Camillo Cavour, a key architect of Italian unification, and the Irish nationalist Charles Parnell.[66] Before 1914, he was not alone in this flattering assessment and the leading French specialist on Tsarist Russia, Henri Leroy-Beaulieu, portrayed Dmowski as 'the man who today represents the best of the aspirations of the Polish people'.[67]

In his time, Roman Dmowski was often a controversial figure and he remains so to this day. Active in the Polish nationalist arena from the 1890s, Dmowski was uncompromising and radical on many issues, but most particularly the Jewish question. Indeed, it can justifiably be argued that, in some manifestation or other, the Jewish question dominated his thinking on a whole range of matters. In this context, in order to gain a more insightful understanding of his worldview, rather than match him with nineteenth-century nationalist leaders, such as Cavour or Parnell, it is more useful to compare him with contemporary figures associated with various antisemitic ideologies. In particular, in intellectual and political terms, Dmowski was linked to those for whom the idea of 'the nation', and the racial basis upon which it should or should not exist, was of the utmost significance. These included, for instance, Édouard Drumont in France and Heinrich von Treitschke in Germany. Although it may appear a facile comparison, it was not mere coincidence that the slogan of the National Democrats during their anti-Jewish boycott, which began in 1912 and will be discussed below, was *Swój do swego po swoje!* ('Stick to your own kind!'). Whilst in France, Drumont's antisemitic weekly, *La Libre Parole*, bore the tag line 'France aux Français!' ('France for the French!') on its front page. Certainly, the configuration of the 'nation' espoused by these three ideologues was different in terms of emphasis, but, most significantly, their visions were exclusionary – especially when it came to Jews.[68]

Prior to his election as a Duma delegate, Dmowski had already been active in Polish politics for almost a decade. He co-founded the National Democrats with Zygmunt Balicki in 1893, and also edited a journal for many years, *Przegląd Wszechpolski* ('All-Polish Review'), published in

Lemberg, in which he was able to give full vent to his often complex belief system. In 1903, his thoughts coalesced into a single volume, *Myśli nowoczesnego Polaka* ('Thoughts of a Modern Pole'). Six years later, after having been a member of the Duma for a number of years, he published *La question polonaise*, an effort to address the wider, international concerns of Polish geographic and political partition.[69] Collectively and individually these publications revealed the full breadth of Dmowski's ideological and racialist stance on the Jewish question. In essence, he believed that it was impossible for Jews to assimilate into Polish life and the threat they posed to the integrity of the Polish nation existed on many levels. Fundamentally, as Brian Porter has argued, it was the image of the Jew as a parasite that shaped National Democratic antisemitism. This parasite wore many disguises, from socialism to capitalism, from the racial to the religious. The ephemeral, changing and often indeterminate nature of 'the Jew' was intrinsic to *Endek* ideology. Ultimately, the National Democrats envisioned the recreation of a future Polish state that would be 'compelled to insulate itself behind high walls of exclusion and hostility'.[70] In other words, there would be no Jews.

Hindsight, of course, facilitates an all-too-apparent and somewhat disturbing comprehension of the significance of Roman Dmowski and Polish National Democracy in the development of twentieth-century antisemitic ideology, especially in the political domain. In fact, so apparent is this significance, it is unnecessary to comment further, especially given the chronological limitations of this study. But what did British observers before the First World War make of this radical political outfit and its exclusionary vision for the future Poland? Naturally, in assessing these responses, we must dispense with the advantages that hindsight grants, and consider Dmowski and his party in their contemporary context.

From a British perspective, of course, most extreme political variants on the continent lacked resonance in home-grown politics during the late nineteenth and early twentieth centuries. Although there were organisations of both the extreme right (the British Brothers' League) and extreme left (the Social Democratic Federation, for example) in the United Kingdom, they were small beer when compared to their contemporaries in Europe.[71] They began and remained small, specialist factions, which commanded the interest and loyalty of relatively few. Moreover, extreme right-wing ideology, especially in connection with the nationalist idea, did not acquire a significant role on the British political stage until the advent of Oswald Mosley in the 1930s. Similarly, political antisemitism found few British adherents and was certainly not incorporated into mainstream political rhetoric, even if social and cultural manifestations of antisemitism were widely found in everyday life. Thus, for a number of quite legitimate reasons, Polish National Democracy was perhaps difficult for British observers to comprehend in its many aspects, not least in its stance on the Jewish question.

Such a response was certainly evident in the first substantial article written about the *Endecja* for a British journal, by a contributor who simply signed him or herself 'G.W.'. In exploring *Endek* ideology, this piece emphasised the degree to which prominence had been given to Polish education and propaganda, as well as its outspoken intention to pursue 'future independence [by the] gradual extension of national consciousness'. Once again, Dmowski was compared to Cavour, and portrayed as a leader who simply believed that it was 'the natural right of each nation to a national government'. Like many other authors, as already noted at the beginning of this chapter, 'G.W.' emphasised Poland's status as a martyr. Consequently, as far as he or she was concerned, from an international standpoint the reunification of this divided state was of the utmost importance. To reaffirm this significance, a quotation by the Danish publicist Georg Brandes prefaced the article: 'Poland is synonymous with our hope or our illusion as to the advance of our age in culture. Its future coincides with the future of civilisation. Its final destruction would be synonymous with the victory of modern, military barbarism in Europe.'[72]

If the Polish national cause was this crucial, then it was nigh inevitable that, in turn, British observers would be tempted to admire and support Dmowski and the National Democrats. What mattered most was their noble goal of independence, their intention to repair a shattered Poland and undo a grave wrong committed many decades before, not the kind of state they envisioned in the future. Indeed, if the *Endek* vision was stripped down to its apparent bare essentials – the right to a national government and the extension of Polish 'consciousness' – it was straightforward enough to compare this brand of nationalism with its early nineteenth-century Romantic precursors. Most especially, though this was not explicitly mentioned by 'G.W.', it was possible to portray Dmowski as the inheritor of a Polish tradition, passed down through the decades from Mickiewicz, Kosciusko and the like. Undoubtedly, it was a misreading of *Endek* nationalism. Nevertheless, this was the historical context in which it was viewed; commentators referred only to a martyred Polish past, and a more satisfactory, if imprecise, future. This was evident in 'G.W.'s reference to Polish 'consciousness', which did indeed lay at the heart of the *Endecja*'s conception of 'the nation'. But it was an amorphous consciousness, and the consolidation of 'the nation' was not a pedestrian or simple affair, such as 'G.W.' might have imagined. Indeed, in *Endek* rhetoric, Porter has likened 'the nation' to a faith, rather than a physical reality, describing its view of Poland as a 'transcendent social entity'. To be Polish entailed a spiritual connection; geographical borders were of lesser importance.[73] Appreciably, such a concept was difficult to grasp and, instead, 'G.W.' and other British commentators fell back upon examples of successful nationalist leaders and their achievements. First and foremost, the rebirth of Poland was imagined in geographical terms and, as a consequence, no consideration was given as to where Poland's Jews might – or might not – fit into the scheme of things.

As we have seen, in comparing Dmowski to Cavour and Parnell, Bernard Pares no doubt also considered Polish nationalism in these relatively straightforward terms. Unfortunately, Pares did not explore on these matters in his own writings. But in reflection of the high esteem in which he held Dmowski and his *Endek* co-founder Balicki, both men were invited to contribute to the *Russian Review* on the eve of the Great War. This journal, which Pares created and edited, was the first academic journal devoted to Eastern European studies in the United Kingdom. Given Pares' extensive personal and intellectual connections to the continent, the *Russian Review* was able to draw upon the skills of a range of continental commentators, from Russia, Poland and elsewhere.[74] It was an ambitious and admirable academic project, its short life thwarted by the Great War.

Dmowski's contribution appeared first, in 1913, and was devoted to the 'Political Evolution of Poland'.[75] Zygmunt Balicki's article was published the following year, and discussed a similar theme, the development of politics in Poland in the years since the 1863 uprising.[76] Pares could no doubt claim a great coup in dragooning these two experts on Polish affairs, and each was granted a fair amount of space in which to discuss their ideas. So what did they reveal? Both articles appeared at a time of heightened antagonism towards Jews in the *Kongresówka* and Galicia, as a result of the boycott. But, though it was mentioned by Balicki, this was not central the topic of their writings, even if for a modern reader it hovers faintly in the background. In essence, both men made a historically legitimate case for the Polish national cause. Each outlined the manner in which Polish politics had developed since the 1860s, how it had subsequently matured, moved away from positivist ideals and how it was now ready to seek the ultimate aspiration, reuni-fication and independence. In essence, Dmowski and Balicki made a case for the National Democrats as the party most able to take Poland forward.

For the most part, Jews did not appear in Dmowski's articles, gain-ing only tacit reference. Of course, we cannot know whether this was deliberate or not and whether he attempted to construct an argument suitable for British audiences that he perhaps felt had no interest in the Jewish question. By the same token, its absence is worthy of mention, since the Jewish question occupied a central tenet of his ideology, which his *Russian Review* articles otherwise intended to justify and underpin. In *La question polonaise*, for instance, which was also aimed at Western opinion, Dmowski made lengthy reference to the Jewish matters. Here, Jews were represented as a threat to the political, economic and eth-nic integrity of a future Polish state.[77] Thus, the non-appearance of the Jewish question in the *Russian Review* was curious, at the very least.

As for Balicki, who produced one lengthy article, compared to Dmowski's three, the Jewish question played a significant part in his argument. National Democratic ideology was evident here, in all its var-ied colours. For instance, in assessing the 1863 uprising, Balicki blamed its failure on the Jews. From the beginning, rather than attempting a nationalist revolution in 1863, in Balicki's view, Poles had increas-ingly attempted to make it socialist. This was the consequence of the revolution having been 'permeated [...] with the Jewish spirit of its creators', and, subsequently, Polish youth had been incited to throw 'themselves into the whirlpool of revolution beneath the banner of cosmopolitan socialism'. Here, of course, 'cosmopolitan' synonymously stood for 'Jewish'. But Jewish influence did not end there, and Jews appeared in the *Russian Review* as national separatists, controllers of the European press, economic agitators and anti-nationalists. And, should there be any doubt about these allusions, since many were buried in the attempted historical interpretation of 1863 and beyond, one sentence amply summed up Balicki's views: 'It was observed [in Poland] that the Jews had an evil influence on the Polish nation, introducing disunion, cosmopolitanism and even moral disorder.'[78]

These were typical *Endek* antisemitic tropes and recurred frequently in their propaganda and pronouncements, before, during and after the Great War. Whether or not they meant anything to British observers is another thing entirely. As the editor of the *Russian Review*, Pares was not tempted to excise these references. But why might he have done? On reflection, perhaps these sentiments simply did not resonate in the British context. And for Pares and other British observers they were entirely peripheral when considering the reconstitution of Poland. Dmowski's *La question polonaise*, for example, was reviewed by the Oxford professor and Member of Parliament, J.A.R. Marriott. He described it as a 'singularly interesting and temperate treatise'.[79] In contrast, a Polish observer lamented the influence Dmowski's book commanded in Western circles, calling it 'a prejudiced product of modern journalistic haste, which, unfortunately, thanks to efficient advertising, passes abroad for a valuable source.'[80] The need for a deeper intellectual connection to Polish political context was evidently essential in trying to understand the *Endecja*. In its absence, the National Democrats appeared to be like any other national group striving for independence.

At this stage – on the eve of the First World War – Dmowski and his allies were integrated into the British narrative as nationalist leaders, who simply wished to reassert Poland's pre-partition borders, to re-claim Polish national sovereignty. Since Poland was viewed as a martyr, it was understandable, when it was examined, that the *Endek* cause commanded sympathy. Other aspects of their political ideology and intentions were, for the most part, unnoticed. Perhaps it was difficult to incorporate the *Endek* response to the Jewish question into British interpretations, since it was mostly reliant upon the long-established view that configured Poles as a tolerant, progressive people.[81] Any appearance of anti-Jewish sentiment in Poland was either, as observed in 1882, a product of Russian influence. Or, as Evans-Gordon remarked, when Polish in origin it could be explained as economic rivalry.[82] Baskerville took a similar perspective:

Hitherto [i.e. until 1905 or so] antisemitism has not aroused the Poles to organise a campaign against the economic influence of the Jews. Here and there an increased disinclination to buy from them may be seen, and of late much has been written about the need of organising the Polish commercial element into guilds which will defend its interests, for there is a growing conviction that, as the Jews intend to preserve their own national individuality, some means of protecting the Polish element must be found. But as yet it is too early to foretell what these means will be. In Poland, where men think rapidly and act slowly, questions even of such importance as this one do not get the prompt attention they deserve. No, though antisemitism prevails in all classes of the Polish community, it is, as yet, nothing more definite than the instinctive dislike of the Slav for the Semite, not because he is dangerous, politically or economically, not because he talks through his nose, and talks Yiddish, is difficult to throw off, is half a toad-eater and half arrogant, because he has a hooked nose and a high colour, but because he wears a *halat* and his wife wears a wig.[83]

Here, again, tensions were put down to economic difficulties, but more especially as a consequence of Jewish difference. Baskerville simplified Polish Judeophobia to its most basic, ancient form, a fear of religious outsiders. Yet, at the same time, although she could not have known it, she also alluded to the early stirrings of a quite different outburst of anti-Jewish sentiment in Poland. The economic boycott of Jewish businesses, doctors and the like, was far from being a simple matter of theological rivalry, or a fear of the other. It marked, instead, the appearance of a belligerent form of antisemitism, which sought drastic answers to the Jewish question in Poland. How did British observers respond to the boycott, and to what extent did it prompt a reappraisal of Dmowski and the National Democrats?

The anti-Jewish boycott: 1912–1914

The origins of the *Endek* inspired anti-Jewish boycott in Poland have long been explored by historians. The immediate cause has often been assumed to lay in the 1912 municipal elections in Warsaw, when Jews voted for the socialist candidate, thereby, from the *Endek* perspective, apparently revealing their narrow self-interests over the 'national' interest of Poland.[84] Yet, as Robert Blobaum has illustrated, the deeper, long-term context of Polish political and social change, especially of the previous two decades, was just as important. In particular, he notes the impact of rapid industrialisation, the political hangover from the 1905 Revolution and the wider appeal subsequently commanded by the *Endecja*. In 1912, the *Endecja*'s self-belief bolstered its confidence in encouraging the boycott. An effort to stir up anti-Jewish feeling throughout Poland, not only the *Kongresówka*, the boycott placed emphasis on alleged Jewish economic dominance and the need for Poles 'reclaim' their nation.[85] Despite the National Democrats' appeal in Poland, the boycott was pretty much a failure and did not acquire widespread support, especially in the countryside. And, rather than making any kind of economic impact, its true significance was political, its ramifications reverberating long into the future, since it secured a legitimate place for antisemitism in twentieth-century Polish political culture.[86]

So what might British observers make of the boycott? How was it viewed in light of Poland's renowned tolerance? And, was National Democracy reassessed in consequence, or were these events explained in traditional fashion? In other words, was the Tsarist government blamed? One of the earliest substantial references to the boycott in the British narrative actually appeared in Balicki's *Russian Review* article. He noted the motivations behind it and, predictably, it was the Jews themselves who were responsible for the actions perpetrated against them:

> In the elections to the fourth Duma, the Jews obtained purely ille-
> gal privileges from the government in the electoral census, and so
> obtained a majority in Warsaw and carried the election of a socialist
> candidate devoted to Jewish interests. This was the last straw. Over
> the whole country passed the watchword to buy only from Poles,
> breaking off all relations with the Jews and resolutely resisting their
> influences. This is commonly called the 'Jewish boycott in the king-
> dom', which, thanks to the Jewish press, has made so much noise all
> over Europe. It is, in the nature of things, purely an act of national
> self-defence, a deliberate policy of Polonising the towns, raising the
> Polish middle class and protecting it from the harmful influence of
> people who are really enemies to everything Polish. In reality an eco-
> nomic boycott of Polish trade and industry had been quietly practised
> by the Jews long before the idea ever occurred to the Poles.[87]

This interpretation revealed a great deal about the *Endecja*, its motivations in organising the boycott, its view of Polish society, not to say
its (mis)representation of the boycott's 'success'. According to Balicki's
interpretation, it was universally supported, from the very beginning,
not least, it turned out, as Jews had been boycotting Poles for many a
year already! The exploitative Jewish instinct was further emphasised
with Balicki's conspiratorial reference to the Jewish press.

The *Endecja*'s co-founder would have been none too surprised, therefore, to discover that in Britain it was the Jewish press that devoted the
most copy to the Polish boycott. For the mainstream press, it was of
minor interest. After all, it was hardly on a comparable scale to the
pogroms of a few years earlier. One or two references were made, but
there was no substantial examination. Events in Poland were eclipsed
by various international crises, such as the Balkan wars, all of which
foreshadowed events soon to come. There was a mention in a book
about Imperial Russia, for instance, by the foreign editor of *The Times*,
Harold Williams. Hinting at the boycott's existence, he remarked on the

'embittered economic struggle which is now being waged between the new Polish middle-class and the Jews in the kingdom of Poland'.[88] But this was his only examination and reduced the boycott to its economic dimension alone. Evidently, the boycott did not prompt a mainstream reappraisal of Polish National Democracy. This would be significant in the latter years of the Great War, when Dmowski actually came to the United Kingdom to publicise his cause; it will be discussed in Chapter 6.

It fell, therefore, to Jewish observers to publicise and assess the boycott. Both the *Jewish Chronicle* and the *Jewish World* inevitably devoted several columns to the theme, though they were mostly devoted to detailing the events constituting the boycott.[89] The *JC* rarely editorialised on the boycott, but viewed its origins in the consequences of Russian rule: 'the boycotts of Jewish business men; assaults; [...] all the miseries in what may be called the grammar of Russian persecution'.[90] Most comment, however, came from Lucien Wolf, who, in 1912, had overseen the resurrection of *Darkest Russia*. Unlike its predecessor of the 1890s, Wolf's protest sheet appeared weekly and was sponsored by the Jewish Colonisation Association. In terms of target, Wolf's remit was very broad and he tackled a range of injustices, from Finnish autonomy and working-class rights, to Tsarist financial instability and anti-Jewish legislation. He was careful, therefore, not to overly emphasise Jewish matters, and attempted to grant equal space to the national rights of Poles, Finns, Georgians, Ukrainians and Jews.[91] The enemy of all these peoples was, of course, the Russian state, which, in terms of the Jewish question Wolf configured as institutionally antisemitic and promoter of pogroms. So, what did *Darkest Russia* make of the boycott? How did it balance its support of Polish national rights with its reaction to the destructive activities of the *Endecja*?

Undoubtedly, these events presented a dilemma for *Darkest Russia*, which from its first edition had promoted the Polish national cause.[92] Akin to the wider British narrative, Wolf had hitherto represented Poland as a tolerant nation, that had long had good relations with its Jews. Consequently, in its initial analysis, *Darkest Russia* relied upon its usual manner of explicating incidents of anti-Jewish activity in Eastern Europe. In other words, the Tsarist government was to blame, if not directly, then indirectly since it apparently made no effort to halt the boycott. This interpretation also relied on established notions and the degree to which the St Petersburg regime was believed to hold Poland in its mighty grip. Surely, nothing could happen in the *Kongresówka* without the Tsar's approval, tacit or otherwise.[93] Indeed, according to Wolf, 'the Russian authorities [had] discovered [...] a welcome opportunity of discrediting the Poles, and [were] making good use of their advantage.' In addition, there was a suggestion that the boycott, and the form of antisemitism it embraced (especially its violent aspects), was a somewhat alien presence in the Polish political landscape:

> Those usually clear-headed Poles who, stung by the defeat of the 'Concentration' candidate for the Duma at the hands of the Jewish voters of Warsaw, lost their self-control and allowed themselves to be rushed by the anti-Semites into the blunder of a Jewish boycott should be sobered by the latest result of their suicidal policy. [...] For many years, the [Russian] Administration strove to effect a split in the Polish ranks, and at the same time to degrade the country in the sight of the world by encouraging the organisation of anti-Jewish pogroms. The Poles, however, were too civilised a people to be caught in the snare, and for what was accomplished in the pogrom line the responsibility rests with the Russian soldiery.[94]

This explication rested upon long-established British notions, such as were evident during the aftermath of the 1881 Warsaw pogrom. The Tsarist regime used antisemitism as a form of *divide et impera* in Poland, whilst, at the same time, Poles had been able to preserve their tolerance in the face of such provocation. Elsewhere in *Darkest Russia*, antisemitism was described as a 'virus', presumably spread by the regime and its officials, which threatened to 'deeply infect' Polish society and the 'whole body politic'.[95] That Wolf took such a perspective is not surprising, as he long adhered to the theory that pogroms in the Tsarist Empire were officially sponsored.[96] Yet, *Darkest Russia* also realised that attempting to understand the actions of Poles in the boycott was perhaps not so straightforward. For instance, it observed that the ' "economic" boycott [had] been transformed into a campaign of fire and blood', and that its 'methods of Jew-baiting [were] unofficial, and therefore more primitively barbarous.' By 'unofficial', did Wolf mean that the regime was not involved? Or, simply that in some parts of Poland, the boycott had mutated into unintended violence? It is unclear, though the boycott presented evident dilemmas and not a little confusion.

To be sure, events in Poland generated anxiety as to the exact nature of Polish nationalism and its principal representatives, the *Endecja*. *Darkest Russia* supported Polish autonomy (not independence, it should be noted), so what did the boycott suggest might be the future for Jewish–gentile relations in an autonomous Poland? 'What support or sympathy', *Darkest Russia* asked, 'can the Poles hope to gain from Europe

for their claim to autonomy when it is realised that they are dealing with the Jews just as vilely as the Russian government is dealing
with them?'[97] It seemed, therefore, that the Polish nationalists found
in the *Koło* in the Imperial Duma, actively supported in the pages of
Darkest Russia, were not as admirable in their intentions as had first
been imagined. In this regard, before the First World War, Anglo-Jewish
commentators were as unaware of the *Endecja*'s outlook as their gentile contemporaries.[98] But from this moment, Wolf was in no doubt of
Roman Dmowski's antisemitic agenda, a discovery that was to endow
their political encounters during and after the War with venomous
mistrust and enmity.[99]

Similar anxieties occupied Israel Zangwill, who was greatly troubled
by the dilemmas the boycott presented. He took the opportunity to
mention it during the opening weeks of the Great War, when rumours
about the possibility of Tsarist Russia granting civil rights to its Jews circulated in the press.[100] Although Zangwill supported Polish autonomy
in principle, he retained reservations about the manner in which an
independent Poland might develop:

> It is, alas! far from improbable that the Poles, now engaged in a
> barbarous boycott of their Jews, would be stupid enough to imitate
> Russia and deny them [i.e. Jews] equality. In that case the Jews now
> in Austria and German Poland would lose their hard-won rights [...].
> And Russian Jews would only assuredly count as human beings if
> Russia, instead of conquering German and Austrian Poland, herself
> loses to Germany. [...] Is it not tragic that in this instance civiliza-
> tion should have more to gain from German militarism than for our
> Eastern ally?[101]

Evidently, Zangwill was concerned about the civil status of Jews in a
future, reconstituted Polish state and, ironically, it seemed that it was the
barbarous German invaders from whom the Poles could learn a lesson
or two. As we shall see in subsequent chapters, these concerns were not
without foundation as the war unfolded in the Eastern theatre.[102]

5
Imperial Russia: The International Arena and the Great War, 1907–1917

Linking up the torch of liberty with the torture chamber.

Joseph Cowan on the Anglo-Russian Convention,
Jewish Chronicle, December 1907

England has been all she could be to Jews, Jews will be all they can to England.

Banner outside the *Jewish Chronicle* office
during the Great War

An unnerving friendship: Britain and Tsarist Russia

On 22 August 1914, just 2 weeks after Britain declared war on Imperial Germany, H.G. Wells highlighted a certain trepidation felt within liberal society towards Tsarist Russia. In an article published in *The Nation*, Wells characterised the 'fear of Russia' as of such significance, it might potentially disrupt the hitherto friendly relations of the two states.[1] He further elaborated on this subject in a book published later on that year, the optimistically titled *The War That Will End War*.[2] Already, within the early stages of pan-European hostilities, it was evident to Wells that there was 'a very considerable dread of the power and intentions of Russia likely to affect the attitude of British liberalism both towards the continuation of the war and towards the ultimate settlement'. In particular, he cited Russia's 'conspicuous conflict with the Jews' as furthering British antipathy and the possibility that this 'racial resentment [might] break the united front of western civilization'. 'We are not', he cautioned, 'so sure of victory that we can estrange an ally.'[3] Elsewhere, a notable contemporary, G.K. Chesterton, concurred with these concerns.[4]

125

Wells' comments in the stirring weeks of August 1914 were not wholly inaccurate. Notwithstanding the ratification of the Anglo-Russian Convention in late 1907, British perspectives on Tsarist Russia generally remained suspicious, disparaging and pessimistic. It was both an unnerving and, in many ways, shocking alliance. The Russian Empire's domestic situation, as evidenced over many decades, contributed to this perception, but so, too, did the continuing imperial rivalry between these two great powers.[5] Consequently, disgruntlement at the Convention was heard from many quarters, across the political divide. But to what extent were these misgivings the consequence of Russia's Jewish policy? It is evident that the Convention was opposed for many reasons, but, in most cases, the Jewish question did not come atop the list.

At first glance, for instance, one might assume that Lucien Wolf, as Secretary of the Conjoint Foreign Committee of the Board of Deputies and AJA, would make Jewish matters his prime bone of contention in opposing the agreement. Yet it is evident that, in public at least, Wolf was always careful to stress – long before his reinstitution of *Darkest Russia* – a range of anti-Russian grievances. In his weekly column in *The Graphic*, in which he commented upon foreign affairs, he readily admitted: 'It is difficult to imagine a worse perfidy than the Russian attitude towards us in the last ten years.'[6] But, in this instance, the perfidy was non-specific. Two years later, in light of the proposed visit of Tsar Nicholas II to the United Kingdom, Wolf engaged in an epistolary quarrel with Bernard Pares in the columns of the *Morning Leader*.[7] He was careful to highlight numerous vital matters that Russia needed to confront urgently in order to claim its place among the civilised nations of the world.[8] In particular, Wolf was critical of the harsh treatment of Finland, of the Field Courts Martial introduced by Prime Minister P.A. Stolypin (essentially punishment courts instituted in the wake of the 1905 revolution, which dispensed summary justice), the Tsar's patronage of the 'Reactionary League' (i.e. the Union of the Russian People and the Black Hundreds) that had 'openly organised massacres and connived at the assassination of prominent Liberals' and the subjugation of the Jews which had 'no parallel in history'.[9] Life under Tsarist rule remained a sorry litany of despair for all, not just Jews.[10]

Of course, privately Wolf no doubt placed total emphasis on the Jewish question, but in the mainstream arena he was more cautious. In many ways, this reflected a general dilemma for the Anglo-Jewish establishment, of which Wolf was a representative. Prior to the agreement's ratification, for example, the *Jewish Chronicle* occasionally muttered its opposition. However, once the deal was done, it concluded:

We have not hesitated to express [...] our opinion as to England, whose name all the world over is synonymous with freedom and justice, entering into any pact with Russia, whose record of oppression and persecution calls to Heaven for vengeance. The point of view we have urged has, we doubt not, been fully weighed by the Foreign Office and those who are responsible for the policy England is pursuing. It is one which we feel sure must have impressed them, for they are fully alive to the horrors through which our people in Russia and other Russian subjects have passed, and, as we write, are passing, in the Empire of the Tsar. Having, notwithstanding all this, concluded the convention we are forced to assume that the interests of this country in its foreign affairs [...] imperatively demanded that course. We venture to express the hope that one result of the agreement [will] be to enable the Government of this country – without, of course, venturing to interfere in the internal affairs of Russia – to exercise its influence with the Tsar on the side of right and justice and mercy to Jews living under his sway.[11]

These sentiments represented an uneasy compromise, which balanced a loyal belief in the talents of Britain's political classes with the desperate hope that the Convention could do nought but good. The *JC* did not wish to be accused of lacking patriotism, of putting Jewish before British interests. Without this international agreement, its proponents might have argued that Britain would be forced to stand alone in any future conflict with Germany, a major preoccupation at this moment. The *Chronicle* was not prepared to countenance such a scenario for Britain or any consequent accusation in light of its own views – at any price.

Not everybody, however, was willing to sacrifice or compromise Jewish interests in Russia or elsewhere and, perhaps in reflection of the ambiguousness privately felt about the Convention by the *Chronicle*'s editors, the newspaper published several letters that strongly opposed any formal gesture of friendship towards Russia. One, from H.S. Alexander, the representative of Brondesbury (north London) on the Board of Deputies, took the opportunity to take a swipe at the 'puerile' activities of the Jewish establishment in dealing with international matters since 1881. In particular, he derided the 'influence of the rich [and] powerful':

Interesting interviews with successive Foreign Ministers, pretty platitudes expressed in windy communications to Government officials, mass meetings held in public halls, may be and are the source of gratification to gentlemen ensconced in the security of their homes protected by law and order, but they mean nothing to the starving Poles [i.e. Jews], threatened with the brutal onslaught of hired mercenaries.[12]

These were strong words and, as was obvious during the Kishinev crisis, even on Russia's apparently clear-cut Jewish question Anglo-Jewry was unable to speak in a single voice. In relation to the Convention, such a consensus was impossible. This also became increasingly evident during the Great War, when similar dilemmas and patriotic emergencies arose.

Nevertheless, despite the conciliatory attitude towards the alliance espoused by the Anglo-Jewish establishment there was, as H.G. Wells' acknowledged, a component of mainstream liberal discourse in Britain that wholly rejected the diplomatic rapprochement with Tsarist Russia, not least because of its Jewish policy. Many notable individuals contributed to this discourse, such as C.P. Scott, editor of the *Manchester Guardian*, and the parliamentarian H.N. Brailsford. Scott's newspaper was markedly anti-Tsarist in this period and well-known for promoting the Jewish cause through its active support of Zionism.[13] Brailsford, too, was somewhat sympathetic to the plight of Russian Jewry. In 1912, he wrote a pamphlet outlining the moral disadvantages of Britain's relationship with the Tsarist Empire, and his assessment was especially gauged in light of the regime's treatment of its Jews.

'The progress of any European society towards civilisation', Brailsford noted, 'may be measured infallibly by its treatment of its Jews.' Inevitably, the Russian standard fell somewhat short of the mark and, indeed, 'had actually retrogressed during the period of the English understanding'. Despite the absence of pogroms in recent years, he observed that 'a more artistic form of torture [had] taken place, and the Jews [had] experienced instead a sort of dry terrorism, a bloodless persecution by legal and economic methods.' Amidst a wealth of detail about anti-Jewish legislation, Brailsford especially focussed on the regular expelling of Jewish families from various places outside the Pale. Despite the desperate plight of Russia's Jews, the fact that Britain was, by default, associated with this oppression, was the source of greatest despair:

To harry the Jews who have settled outside the Ghetto, to aggravate the over-crowding, the competition and the exploitation within it, to deny knowledge and to close the avenues through which knowledge led to freedom, such has been the policy of the Russian government during the period of its intimacy with a British Liberal administration.[14]

No doubt Brailsford's analysis was influenced by matters in Russia before 1914. Prior to the Great War, there were three significant Russian domestic events that commanded the world's attention. First of all, in September 1911, Russia's Prime Minister P.A. Stolypin was assassinated in Kiev. Around the same time, a Ukrainian Jew, Mendel Beilis, was arrested in the very same city on suspicion of murder. Then, in April 1912, the Lena Goldfields' massacre took place in Siberia, where a group of striking mineworkers were gunned down by soldiers of the Russian Imperial army.[15] Political and social chaos appeared once more to grip Russia and any residual optimism Britain felt for the democratic progress of its ally surely dissipated. But it was the subsequent rise to prominence of the Beilis Case, and the resurrection of the blood libel accusation that highlighted, more than anything else, the apparent influence of the medieval on the Tsar and his regime.

Revisiting the medieval: the Beilis Case

The indictment, in late 1911, of ritual murder against Mendel Beilis, a manager at a brick factory in Kiev, was not, as some commentators suggested at the time, Imperial Russia's Dreyfus Affair.[16] On one level, it undoubtedly illustrated, like *l'Affaire* in the French Third Republic, domestic political divisions in Imperial Russia, and, for a time, Beilis was a *cause célèbre*. But this was where any similarity with Dreyfus began and ended.[17] For the allegation made against Beilis, that of killing 13-year-old Andrei Yushchinskii in order to drain his blood for religious purposes, was barely believed by anybody, even in backward, darkest Russia.[18]

In Britain, as during the pogrom period, letters of protest were published, including an impressive missive sent to *The Times* in May 1912. Denouncing the entire notion of the blood libel as 'a relic of the days of Witchcraft and Black Magic', it was signed by a host of prominent Christians, headed by the Archbishop of Canterbury, leading politicians such as Arthur J. Balfour and Austen Chamberlain, a slew of university professors from Oxford, Cambridge, London and elsewhere, literary celebrities such as Thomas Hardy and Arthur Conan Doyle, and newspaper editors, including C.P. Scott.[19] It mirrored similar efforts in France, Germany and Imperial Russia itself, where a petition brimming with notable names was published.[20] There were no Jewish names among the British signatories and Anglo-Jewish institutions had nothing to do with the letter's appearance. Nevertheless, a laudatory appreciation from Sir Stuart M. Samuel MP was published in *The Times* a few days later, in which he noted the 'thrill of satisfaction' that all British Jews were bound to feel at this 'generous protest'.[21]

A year later, upon commencement of Beilis' trial in September 1913 (he had been imprisoned in solitary confinement since late 1911), British interest in the Case was revived and condemnatory meetings swiftly convened. In October 1913, the Memorial Hall in Farringdon, central London, hosted a protest under the auspices of the English Zionist Federation. It was chaired by Sir Francis Montefiore (great-nephew of Sir Moses), with a strong resolution proposed by the Oxford professor, A.V. Dicey.[22] In Glasgow, a meeting was held at which almost every speaker was gentile, including several Christian leaders of many denominations; all condemned the accusation outright on theological grounds.[23] The Parliamentary Committee of the Independent Labour Party passed a resolution urging the Foreign Secretary, Sir Edward Grey, to issue a protest to the Russian government.[24] In the United States, a petition was signed by prominent Christians and forwarded to the US ambassador in Washington DC.[25] A mass meeting was held in Chicago.[26] And, in New York City, the *Independent* newspaper published a strongly worded 'open letter' addressed to Tsar Nicholas II.[27] Czech intellectuals also issued their own petition, mirroring a protest during another blood libel accusation, the Hilsner Affair of 1899.[28] The chorus of disapproval appeared, therefore, universal and overwhelming.[29]

In Britain, the accusation itself, 'a monstrous falsehood', a 'calumnious' and 'incredible' charge, was viewed with utter bewilderment and dismissed out of hand.[30] Even as a straightforward murder case, according to the *Jewish Chronicle*, there was not a single shred of evidence against Beilis 'worthy of bringing him before a Court of Justice'.[31] Alongside the world's press, the *JC* and the *JW* followed the trial intensively, illustrating the absolute unity of Anglo-Jewry on this particular matter.[32] Such were the appalling circumstances of the Beilis Case and the role which Tsarist officials, in both St Petersburg and Kiev, had clearly played, Anglo-Jews did not even hesitate to criticise the Emperor. Nicholas II was named an 'arch antisemite' in the *Chronicle*, an epithet unthinkable a decade earlier, even in the aftermath of the Kishinev pogrom.[33]

Yet, despite this chorus of condemnation, there were occasional voices in Britain that indicated not every commentator was willing to stand with the majority. *Darkest Russia*, which reappeared just as the Case was taking shape and was as a useful hook for Lucien Wolf to hang his wider anti-Tsarist arguments, discovered that British perspectives were occasionally as wanting as their Russian counterparts.[34] In particular, it highlighted an article on the Beilis Case by Dr Emile J.Dillon, published in the Sunday newspaper, *The Observer*.[35] Dillon was a long-term commentator on Russian affairs. He originally made his mark in the 1890s with a book entitled *Russian Characteristics* and wrote for a number of publications, including the *Daily Telegraph*, the *Contemporary Review* and *Fortnightly Review*.[36] Based in St Petersburg and a fluent Russian speaker, his views were widely respected.

In March 1912, Dillon reported the background to the events leading to the arrest of Beilis in *The Observer*. These were early days, but he already believed the case to be 'one of the most sensational on record'. Like almost every other commentator, he refuted the veracity of a ritual murder accusation in this particular instance. Nevertheless, Dillon hinted that there might be an estranged Jewish sect somewhere in the Pale of Settlement that engaged in such heinous activity. Even the 'mildest form of Christianity' (i.e. Russian Orthodoxy), he said, had 'sects which mutilate their members, sects which encourage suicide, sects which preach deliberate murder with the assent of the victim'. How could, therefore, 'a Jew maintain with *a priori* and with infallible certitude that no such religious abortions are possible among his co-religionists?' Simply because the 'Hebrew faith condemns absolutely all murder and bloodshed [...] it by no means follows that a sect can never arise among them which encourages them.' For Dillon, Beilis' supporters protested too much and made 'exaggerated use' of Judaism's strictures. In light of these considerations, Dillon wished to reserve judgement on the Beilis Case until it was tried in Russia's courts.[37]

It is not difficult to anticipate the response that these allegations elicited from Lucien Wolf. *Darkest Russia* rapidly condemned Dillon, noting that:

> his former studies in comparative theology [*sic* – Dillon was once a professor of philology at the University of Kharkov] should convict him out of his own knowledge of a particularly gross attempt at slander by means of an untenable analogy. Not one atom of proof has ever been forthcoming in the support of a ritual murder charge.[38]

The suggestion that there was some truth in the ritual murder accusation was relatively rare in British discourse, but Dillon's insinuations were by no means unique. *The Times*, for instance, published a letter by the Russian Ambassador to Britain, Baron Alphonse Heyking, which similarly implied that Beilis belonged to an 'illicit sect'.[39] Once again, Lucien Wolf immediately sent a letter repudiating these comments, as did *Haham* Moses Gaster.[40]

Elsewhere, among the realms of British intellectual life which may, to some extent, be deemed peripheral, ritual murder and blood libel were reasoned as not only possible, but probable. In the weekly journal the *New Witness*, the brainchild of the Catholic, right-radical portmanteau, the Chesterbelloc, the notion of an obscure 'heretical sect' was pursued.[41] Originally conceived by Hilaire Belloc and G.K. Chesterton, the *New Witness* was greatly preoccupied at this time with denouncing the British political system, to which it took great exception.[42] There can be no doubt that components of antisemitic ideology underpinned its uncompromising views and frequent insinuations were made as to the existence of an international Jewish conspiracy, particularly in the press, politics and finance. The terms in which these views were expressed were equally uncompromising. Indeed, the journal detected one or two concerns in connection with the Beilis trail and advised readers 'to regard with the gravest suspicion all the reports of the proceedings in Kiev which appear in the English papers'. After all, it asserted, 'practically all the news-agencies are Jewish and nearly all the newspapers are in one way or another subject to Jewish pressure.'[43]

In light of these remarks, it comes as no surprise to discover that several contributions in the *New Witness* were wholly convinced of Beilis' guilt and subsequently asserted that he was, indeed, a ritual murderer. For instance, a regular contributor, F. Hugh O'Donnell, a former Member of Parliament, made several allegations to this effect.[44] In addition, in 1914 – by which time the trial had taken place – Cecil Chesterton, at this stage the editor of the *New Witness*, reviewed Israel Zangwill's recent play *The Melting Pot*. Contending Zangwill's one-sided depiction of Russian attitudes towards Jews, Chesterton remarked[45]:

> if we are asked to believe that Russians do abominable things to Jewish children, we should at the same time be asked to regard it as incredible (note that I do not say 'unproved', but 'incredible') that Jews do abominable things to Russian children – at Kiev, for instance – unless, of course, we are to accept it as a dogma that all Jews are good and all Russians are bad.[46]

It must be said, that the final sentence was not without merit. After all, it was not especially useful to imagine Jewish–gentile relations in Russia in such simplistic, monochromatic terms. But the preceding comments revealed a good deal about Chesterton's mindset, even allowing for the supposedly ironic tone in which it was written. Zangwill, naturally, did not find this article even faintly amusing and his angry response appeared in the following week's issue. 'What is "incredible"', he said, 'is that the murder could be "ritual" since there is no such rite.'[47] This was not the first or last time that Zangwill and the *New Witness* came to blows, and throughout its lifetime the journal was a battle-ground on which their mutual and undisguised antipathies were played out. Yet if there were cause to doubt Chesterton's attitude towards Beilis, his subsequent reply argued that he belonged to a 'ferocious secret society among the Russian Jews'.[48]

Why did the *New Witness* believe there was a chance the Blood libel was true, especially when every other British journal and newspaper rejected it wholesale? It might be argued that this was simply a mischievous effort to stir up home-grown anti-Jewish feeling, in order to highlight the journal's own political grievances. In other words, the Beilis Case was utilised to reiterate the *New Witness'* belief, as we have seen, in a Jewish conspiracy connected to the press, to corruption in politics, the business world and even the personal sphere. Of course, the suggestion that there existed an estranged Jewish sect had a wider resonance, which insinuated that Judaism itself was a religion shrouded in mystery, that, in turn, rendered Jews dishonest and underhand. The corollary to this, naturally, was the intimation that Jews possessed inherently bad racial characteristics (and Jews were absolutely a race for the Chesterbelloc), instilled by centuries of arcane religious rituals. These characteristics, no matter how the Jews tried to conceal them, by changing their names (a major *bête noire* in the *New Witness*), or other assimilatory methods, would, like scum, always rise to the surface.[49] Thus, whether or not the *New Witness* truly believed in the probability of ritual murder was, in reality, a moot point. Beilis was a Jew. He was bound to be guilty of something.

Moreover, the *New Witness'* perspective of the case was conditioned by its attitude towards Tsarist Russia. Although neither of the Chestertons nor Hilaire Belloc had a direct connection to Russia, it nevertheless occupied a significant place in their worldview. In particular, they were attracted to the simple lifestyle of the Russian peasant and the allegedly pure form of Christianity to which he adhered. 'Every person', wrote G.K. Chesterton, 'who has come in practical contact with Russia, has had the electric shock of Christianity.'[50] Russia appeared devoid of the influences of modernity the Chesterbelloc so detested. Its anti-modern outlook ensured a belief that 'Jew and the peasant' were at 'cross-purposes all over the world', but most especially in Russia.[51] The Russian peasant represented, therefore, a Christian bulwark against the modernising influences of the Jew; the one rooted to the soil, the other not.

It was, in fact, peasants who comprised the 12 members of the jury at Beilis' trail, a reflection of the trust the Tsarist regime also placed in this supposedly conservative social element. For 34 days, the jury was presented with a good deal of complex 'evidence', and confronted by a bizarre range of witnesses, including a Catholic priest, Father Justin Pranaïtis, who was practically laughed out of court.[52] As both historians and contemporary commentators noted, the entire process alternated between high drama, farce and vaudeville.[53] In the end, the judge requested that the jury consider two questions. The first asked, in some detail, whether Andrei Yushchinskii had been murdered in Kiev. It was deliberately leading, since it explicitly referred to the number of wounds on his body and the severe loss of blood (five glasses, enough for a precise rite ...), though it did not overtly refer to ritual murder. However, the second question was unequivocal. It asked whether Beilis had, with unnamed confederates, planned and committed the crime in the name of religious fanaticism. Evidently, this was a concerted effort to manipulate the jury and to obtain the desired verdict. However, the jury responded 'yes' to the first question, and 'no' to the second. Beilis, therefore, was acquitted.[54]

Inevitably, the verdict was greeted in Britain with a combination of joy, relief, justification and a good deal of indignation.[55] Only the *New Witness* attempted to make alternative political capital from the verdict, by claiming, in typically contrary fashion, that the jury had, in fact, upheld the ritual murder conviction.[56] But for the majority, the acquittal was perhaps not an unexpected result, given the widespread and long-established belief in Beilis' innocence. Yet, many observers were cautious. After all, the whole business had been unpredictable from the outset; who was to say the authorities, who had gone to desperate lengths to justify the trial in the first place, might not tamper with the verdict? Although this pessimistic perspective did not come to pass, it was nevertheless difficult for many observers to feel totally vindicated. By its own actions, Tsarist Russia had proven its barbarous status once again. As the *Jewish Chronicle* noted, it had situated itself 'outside the ambit of modern civilisation' and preferred instead to remain governed by a 'backward medievalism'.[57] At this stage, of course, Britain was firmly locked in its alliance with Russia, alongside France. Six years on from the signing of the Anglo-Russian Convention, according to the *JC*, the gulf separating these states seemed to have widened, not narrowed: 'The Beilis Case has put a barrier against anything like true friendship or brotherly feeling between Russia and the people of either France or this country.'[58] Other newspapers concurred with this perspective.[59] But within less than a year, the world was to reverberate with the opening salvoes of the Great War. For everyone in Europe, whether Jew or gentile, there was no going back.

The Great War: loyalty questioned

Historians have long considered the First World War a troubling time for British Jewry.[60] Like many of their continental counterparts, from the early weeks of the conflict British Jews faced recurrent questions about their loyalty to the cause. Allegations of spying and political unreliability went hand in hand with accusations of cowardice and shirking. German-sounding surnames prompted fantastical imaginings, whilst immigrant Polish and Russian Jews were deemed pacifists. The Anglo-Jewish establishment endeavoured to correct this skewed perspective through a discreet propaganda campaign and, from mid-1915, an active and visible recruitment drive in the East End of London. A sentence from a leading article published in the *Jewish Chronicle* in August 1914, rapidly became a slogan that was embraced and reiterated throughout the war: 'England has been all she could be to Jews, Jews will be all they can to England.'[61] Individual Anglo-Jews even pledged their allegiance by sending so-called loyalty letters to *The Times*.[62] From its earliest stages, the Great War was perceived as a test-bed for Jewish patriotism by Jews themselves.

As for immigrant Russian and Polish Jews in Britain, accusations surfaced against them in the middle of the war and were connected to a supposed shirking of military duty. Many Russian and Polish Jews resident in Britain had not, up to this point, applied for naturalisation and were thus eligible only for service in the Imperial Russian army. Only a handful honoured the regime's call to arms. This matter was little noticed in Britain until 1916, when the government enacted compulsory military conscription for wide sections of the population. As a result, the issue of Entente nationals resident in the United Kingdom was highlighted. Russian Jews who refused to fight for either their country of birth or adoption were accused of cowardice, lack of patriotism and revolutionary intent. A recruitment drive was hastily convened, in which Lucien Wolf, Lord Rothschild and the Home Secretary, Herbert Samuel, all played a role, but which achieved varying degrees of success.[63] Eventually, in 1917, a Jewish legion in the British army was formed.[64]

Despite these endeavours, questions about Jewish loyalty were not vanquished. This was not unique to the British context. Throughout the theatre of war, on every side, the dedication, military fitness and patriotism of Jews, both combatant and non-combatant, were regularly queried. Within the Tsarist Empire, for instance, barely a day passed when an allegation was not made. Like their British counterparts, the Jews of the Russian Empire were derided by the press and popular discourse. Suspicion about spies and underground movements was widely disseminated, especially in right-wing newspapers like *Znamia* and *Novoe Vremia*. Akin to Britain, 'Jewish' was often conflated with 'German', and both ethnic groups, whether separate or conjoined, were widely regarded as an internal enemy. In Moscow, St Petersburg, Warsaw and other Polish cities, Jewish and German businesses were ransacked by marauding mobs.[65] But, terrible as these events indisputably were, they were small beer when compared to the broader aspect of the war's impact on the Jews living under Tsarist rule.

From the outset, the Russian Imperial army was hostile to Jews. This was informed, in part, by a long-standing element of Russian Judeophobic discourse that questioned whether the Jew was capable of possessing martial characteristics.[66] Throughout Imperial Russia's nineteenth century, Jews had been deemed cowards and draft-dodgers (see Chapter 7). By 1914, such perspectives dominated the views of Russia's military commanders and components of the Ministry of War.[67] This was all the more significant as in regions occupied by the Russian Imperial army during the war, military rule effectively usurped civil government. Thus, almost the whole of the Pale of Settlement, which was eventually *de facto* abolished in 1915 (out of necessity, rather than any kind of emancipatory gesture), fell under the remit of the Russian Imperial army. The consequences were horrendous.

The Russian military's solution to allegations of spying and disloyalty was straightforward enough; deportation eastwards, summary execution and, from 1915, the taking of hostages. Tens of thousands of families were forcibly uprooted, decimated and terrorised – simply because they were Jews. In Eastern Galicia, occupied by the Russian army at various stages in the war, where it behaved as the most appalling kind of imperialist, further hardship was endured. Many restrictions were imposed on Jewish life; Jews were forbidden to sell alcohol, copper and other metals, they were dismissed from the judiciary, from hospitals and schools, and newspapers in Yiddish and German were prohibited.[68] Deportations occurred here, too, though many thousands of Galician Jews also fled Westwards, crowding into Vienna.[69] Human displacement was a huge problem in the East and historians have estimated that at as many as one million Jews were rendered homeless between 1914 and 1917.[70] Then, from late 1914 onwards, there were pogroms – the first and last in which there was an official Tsarist connection. The victims were numbered in their thousands.[71]

These actions unquestionably confirmed the worst fears that many in Britain had harboured in the wake of the Convention with Russia. Certainly, as we shall see below, for Anglo-Jews, the only surprising aspect of these events was their intensity, not that they happened in the first place. But what was the wider British response to these matters? Was it possible to consider them, given Britain's own, immediate wartime commitments? After all, it was the blood and mud of the Western Front upon which the British imagination was primarily, and naturally, focussed. Given the daily casualty lists published in newspapers, the evident and catastrophic human consequences of the war, it would be understandable if little thought were spared as to the plight of those in the East.

Notwithstanding British self-interest, it was difficult to shed light on the Eastern theatre of war. Pressure from the Government and Foreign Office ensured that most newspapers only emphasised the positive aspects of the Eastern conflict. Any effort to disparage the Tsarist regime was not only discouraged, but often excised by the censor. In mainstream reportage, reference to the hardships faced by Eastern Jews was almost entirely absent, though, as might be expected, the Anglo-Jewish press tried to cover events as much as possible (see below).[72] In large part, information from the East depended on the work of reporters who had obtained some degree of official recognition. Amongst the most significant observers, who regularly filed to the British press, were Bernard Pares, Stanley Washburn – an American special correspondent of *The Times*, E.J. Dillon and the freelancer Stephen Graham.

Pares and Washburn spent the early years of the Great War on the Eastern Front, attached as official newspaper reporters (today, they would be 'embedded', proving that only the terminology is new) to the Tsarist Army.[73] Given this status, their accounts of the currents of military action in the East were pretty one-sided. Had they been overly critical of the Tsarist regime, their press passes would have been swiftly revoked. Though, by the same token, it is doubtful that such interpretations would have made it to the columns of a British newspaper. In his reports from the front, for instance, Pares attempted to present the

Russian soldier as a noble, brave and, indeed, moral individual, worthy of marching arm in arm with his British and French counterparts.[74] Despite accompanying Tsarist forces to Eastern Galicia, he made no reference in any of his accounts as to the nature of Russian rule there; the wholesale executions, expulsions and cultural vandalism all escaped his attention.[75] Indeed, Pares appeared to endorse Russian aspirations in this part of the Habsburg Empire, observing that 'we were the advance guard of the liberation of Slavs.'[76] Washburn's account was little different. He observed in the same field of battle that 'everyone seems to be taking the Russian occupation quite easily.'[77] Of course, to be fair, it must be said that both journalists were stymied in their endeavours by the censor. But what of the Jews?

In the account of his Eastern adventures, Pares revealed that there was a considerable Jewish presence in this part of the world, though Washburn overlooked this entirely. In Pares' writing there was a positive description, for example, of an encounter with Jews who gave bread and milk to the soldiers. He also observed a 'strong, masterful old Jew with dignified bearing striding silently with his two sons over his land, a sight which is hardly seen in Russia'. Beyond this, however, his rendering of Galician Jewish life was cast in the negative. In particular, Pares referred to the 'severest bondage' and 'obeisance' in which the Jews held the Galician peasant, leaving only 'starvation wages to the tenants of their farms'. Apparently, the Jewish lease-holders took 'ten-elevenths of the profits' from the tenant farmer, a contrast to Russia where they only took 'two-thirds'.[78] This was, of course, a classic depiction of the Jewish–gentile relationship in Eastern Europe, as has already been observed in discussion of the 1881–1882 pogroms. Indeed, it was not too far removed from Pares' established perspective, having already noted in an entry he wrote for the *Cambridge Modern History* that Jews had a 'complete economic superiority' in the Pale of Settlement and used it 'to the full'.[79]

But what relevance did this have in terms of the war? How did the war impact upon the conduct of Jews and their neighbours? In his infrequent references to Jews, Washburn nonetheless alluded on every occasion to their apparent tendency to disloyalty:

> The manner and faces of the people [in Galicia] showed neither fear or suspicion of the troops quartered about; and with the possible exception of the Jews, there was not a hostile look. The Jews, on must admit, looked pretty sulky, though on all occasions they were effusively polite.

Elsewhere, Jews were described as German in their 'sympathies'.[80] As for Pares, in the published version of *Day by Day with the Russian Army*, he had very little to say on this matter, apart from the following hint: 'the local Jews constantly circulated rumours of an Austrian return, and the Russian tenure of Galician remained precarious.'[81] But there was no explicit and wholesale condemnation of Habsburg Jewry. In contrast, the interpretation in Pares' unedited manuscript was quite different. Here he reiterated the claim that Poles and Ukrainians were in 'acute economic relations' with Jews. However, although he understood Galician Jewry's allegiance to Emperor Franz Joseph, Pares was less reconciled towards the presence of Jews in the Russian Imperial army:

> The complication [in terms of loyalty] was carried much further by the presence of so substantial a Jewish element in the Russian army itself. [. . . .] There are many instances of brave Jewish soldiers; several have the George Cross, but among the Jewish contingent of any regiment, the number of 'missing' has taken the largest proportions. In a struggle like this, the man who goes over carries with him information which is felt without delay in grievous losses to those whom he has left.[82]

Of course, whilst acknowledging those Jewish soldiers who admirably served their country, Pares simultaneously implied that the majority was not quite as patriotically inclined. The term 'missing', for instance, was not intended to infer that these soldiers had been lost in battle, but rather that they had deserted or deliberately placed valuable information into the hands of the enemy. In other words, they were traitors. Such perspectives similarly dominated a private letter sent from Pares to Benjamin Wilenski of the City of London College. Here, Pares elaborated upon his belief that the Jewish attitude in the theatre of war had been 'of very great assistance to the enemy', and in many units 'nine tenths' had gone over to the enemy. Furthermore, on the home front the threat was just as great, especially in Petrograd, since the war had induced a 'furious speculation and commercial prospecting' amongst Jews.[83]

Pares suggested that the letter might be published. It was not. Instead, it was sent, via David Alexander, president of the Board of Deputies, to Lucien Wolf. The response was predictable, with Wolf refuting Pares' insinuations wholesale. Unfortunately, there is no extant evidence to indicate that the correspondence progressed any further. Nevertheless, Wolf deemed Pares 'quite free from antisemitic prejudice' and there was some truth to this analysis. Instead, Wolf argued, that in his duties as a war correspondent Pares had moved in 'an antisemitic atmosphere'.[84] Again, this was not wholly inaccurate and the circles in which his work was conducted, the senior soldiers with whom he interacted on a daily basis undoubtedly influenced Pares' outlook.[85] Notwithstanding these allowances, it is evident that in private, at least, Pares was inclined to peddle unquestioningly the Tsarist Army's official line on the Jewish question.[86] But in the public arena, for whatever reason – though it is impossible to speculate effectively upon this – he (and/or his publishers) chose to downplay his views.

But what of other correspondents? Did their accounts match these interpretations, or was an alternative vision presented? For E.J. Dillon, the proceedings of the war were mostly observed from Petrograd, his sources were taken from Russian newspapers and daily encounters with ordinary and not-so-ordinary Russians. Like Pares and Washburn, he moved in exalted circles. In a book published in 1918, for instance, he revealed contacts with leading liberals, as well as the first Russian Prime Minister Count Sergei Witte.[87] It is little wonder, therefore, that Dillon sincerely embraced the Imperial Russian cause, as well as aspects of its war-time military discourse. In a report filed to *The Observer*, for example, he noted the assistance given to the enemy by 'the insidious espionage nourished by Baltic Germans and the disloyal element among the Jews'.[88] Additionally, he believed Russia was 'the greatest State in Christendom' and had raised the largest army in the Entente to 'fight the enemy of Christendom'.[89] The appeal of religious imagery and intention was of great significance for Russia's British advocates. For those who openly professed a religious allegiance, it was hard to resist. It is unsurprising, therefore, that G.K. Chesterton failed to see the irony in describing Russia as 'a pillar of universal civilisation; [...] she is not only a Christian but liberal State.'[90]

Such notions certainly held great appeal for Stephen Graham, who was a different kind of reporter to Pares, Washburn or Dillon. For a start he was freelance. Secondly, he was not officially accredited by the Tsarist regime, nor did he appear to have significant personal contacts within Russia's political or military hierarchy. Indeed, in the wake of 31 articles about Russia's war he produced for *The Times* in 1914–1915, the British Ambassador in Petrograd, Sir George Buchanan, informed the Foreign Office that Graham's work had given 'deep offence to many of our best friends in this country'.[91] Yet, of all commentators, Graham was undoubtedly Tsarist Russia's keenest and most prolific defender.[92]

In 1915, Israel Zangwill asked in *The Nation*: 'Is no organ safe from Mr Stephen Graham [...] in his self-appointed *rôle* of defender of Holy Russia?'[93] Amidst Graham's output it was not difficult to fathom both his attitude to Imperial Russia and its Jews. In 1916, he wrote:

> I believe in Holy Russia, and as far as Russia is concerned do not care for anything else. I hate to see her being commercialised and exploited, and to see her vulgar rich, increasing at the expense of the life-blood of the nation. Without any question the new class of middle-class coming into being through Russia's industrial prosperity is the worst of its kind in Europe. They are worse than anything in Germany, and it is they who are beginning to have the power in Russia. It is the green and inexperienced who think that power wrested from the Tsar and his Court is grasped by the idealist of Russia. It is grasped by the capitalists, often by the foreign capitalists, by business interest in any case.[94]

Taken in isolation, this quotation might seem benign enough. Like the Chesterbelloc and other commentators who romanticised Russia, Graham regarded its recent modernisation somewhat disdainfully. In particular, he disliked those who were greedy at Russia's expense. The Russia he loved, no doubt he would have argued, was slowly disappearing. For sure, this is the least damning interpretation of these words. However, when compared to similar tropes deployed across the entire corpus of Graham's work, it is evident that the terms 'capitalists', 'foreign capitalists' and 'vulgar rich' were actually synonyms for 'Jews'.

In a number of writings produced in 1915, for example, Graham was far less coded when discussing Russia's Jewish question and the war. In an article published in the *English Review*, he wrote of the 'great danger' the Jews presented to the Russian Empire, their role in revolutionary movements and their questionable war-time patriotism. As for the wider world, he warned, Jews were 'availing themselves of all the opportunities of civilisation, and going forward to be masters'.[95] Later that year in a book entitled *Russia and the World*, he outlined the 'brevities of the Jewish situation':

i. Russian has promised little to the Jews and will give little.
ii. England has sympathy with the Jews.
iii. America will help the Jews [in Russia] if she can.

    iv. The Jews are working hard for themselves.

    v. I suggest that if the Turkish Empire falls, a Jewish government should be established in Palestine.

These were not wholly unreasonable suggestions, apart from, of course, the fourth item on the list. But, once again, the significance of these comments only becomes truly evident when viewed in relation to all of Graham's output. In relation to the Zionist aspect, for example, it seems clear that Graham's generosity on this matter was the consequence of his belief that the Jew was 'accursed' because he had 'no land of his own'. His own experiences on the Eastern Front had reinforced such an opinion:

> when the Russians were retreating in Poland I asked a common soldier the reason. His answer was – 'The Jews betray us. That's what comes of having an accursed people *without any land of the own* [italics in original]; they dog our steps and sell us at every turn. If we are winning they come round and praise us, and try to help us; if we begin to lose they run to the enemy and say, "Don't you ill-treat us; we are your friends; we can help you; we have valuable information." ' The Jews ought to have a place of their own and a Government of their own. They ought not to be always fighting for their separate interests in the life of foreign nations. They are a great people, and are now, as never before, on the upgrade in civilisation. They ought to be officially united. The world of Gentiles also is interested to see them as a nation, and would welcome any steps the Jews might take towards the realisation themselves as such.[96]

Of course, the dilemma as to whether or not Jews should have their own nation was hardly confined to the thoughts of individuals like Graham. Plenty of Jews, throughout Europe and the United States, were posing these very same questions at this particular moment in history. Yet, whilst this is an important consideration, it is far from the most significant aspect of this extract. What, we might more appropriately ask, was the motivation behind Graham's desire for Jews to have their own nation? In his case, it was linked to alleged Jewish (mis) conduct during the war in Eastern Europe, to disloyalty and the pursuit of self-interest at any price. Such perspectives tied Graham to the same elements of Russian Judeophobic discourse embraced by both Pares and Washburn.

    Graham often caused controversy and, indeed, perhaps he even courted it. Unlike the other three observers, his articles and correspondence in newspapers were always signed. In many ways, there seems to have been some truth to Zangwill's assertion that Graham believed himself to be the self-appointed defender of Holy Russia. Indeed, he went to considerable lengths to counter any charges made against the Tsarist regime's war-time record. In January 1915, an article in *The Nation*, for example, highlighted a report of a pogrom in Łódź, Russian Poland.[97] Graham was swift to respond to this claim. In the first place, he asserted, there had been no reports of pogroms in the British or Russian press, and thus, the allegation was a 'piece of propaganda remote from the truth'. This was reinforced by the simple fact that no pogroms had taken place at all. There were no tales 'of a massacre of the Jews', either in Łódź or, for that matter, anywhere else in Eastern Europe:

> No harm has been done to the Jews during this war; they have every reason to believe that the Allies, who are fighting for the principle of nationality, will be the protectors of their rights also. Something will no doubt be done to help the Jews as a nation. But the dissemination of calumny by a few political zealots is likely to give Liberal Russia a bad idea of Jewish political candour, and, consequently, to set back the national cause of Jewry and strengthen the hands of antisemites.[98]

It comes as no surprise that in the following week's issue, Graham was taken to task by Israel Zangwill. Indeed, the playwright publicly quarrelled with this particular defender of Russia as much as he did with the Chesterbelloc.

In this instance, Zangwill was particularly aggrieved at Graham's claim that 'no harm' had been done to the Jews during the war, a 'cool assertion' which almost, he said, froze his ink.[99] His response outlined many detailed complaints against Graham, most particularly in light of his defence of the Anglo-Russian alliance. Zangwill accepted that Britain was 'hopelessly united' to Russia, commercially and politically, but the principal problem with Graham's argument was that he tried to make his readers 'love the wrong Russia'. To a British conscience uneasy about Russia', said Zangwill, 'Mr. Graham comes as a providential pacifier, a soothing syrup.'[100] Graham dismissed these accusations in yet another book. Once again, he emphasised the spiritual dimension of his Russian cause and cited Zangwill as responsible for pursuing a 'violently misrepresentative campaign in Russia against the conception of Russia as a country that can be spiritually helpful to us'.[101] No doubt, as we shall see, many Anglo-Jewish observers would have regarded the latter part of this observation somewhat ruefully.

The Great War: the Anglo-Jewish answer

In August 1914, within weeks of the war's outbreak, Lucien Wolf ceased publication of *Darkest Russia*. It was a gesture that met with approval throughout the Anglo-Jewish community, as the urgent pressure to fall patriotically into line dominated the immediate response to the Great War.[102] Additionally, notwithstanding the many decades of hostility towards Tsarist Russia, in August and September 1914 a degree of optimism was actually discernible in some quarters with regard to the prospects for its Jewish question. The *Jewish Chronicle* expressed the hope that as Russia had been 'drawn into the orbit of enlightened peoples', it would surely return from the war 'with the scales of intolerance lifted from its eyes'.[103] This early outlook burgeoned under the influence of occasional intelligence emanating from official circles in Petrograd, which promised independence for Poland, as well as the sweeping away of the Pale of Settlement and other restrictions.[104] Inevitably, by late October and early November 1914 this hopeful position was pretty much crushed by the realities of the war.

Whilst the mainstream press was fairly restrained in reporting the difficulties endured by East European Jews at the hands of Austrian, German and Russian troops, oftentimes making no mention at all, this was not the case for its Anglo-Jewish equivalent. However, since neither the *World* nor the *Chronicle* had its own correspondents attached to the Russian imperial army, or freelancing on their behalf at the heart of battle, they each depended upon information from external agencies and correspondents.[105] One of the most important early contributions came from the renowned Danish scholar, Georges Brandes, who, in late October 1914, published several pieces in the Copenhagen newspaper *Politiken*. Whilst the *JC* and *JW* had already expressed their great fear for the Jews caught amidst hostilities, it was Brandes' articles that gave cause to wonder whether events had strayed beyond the 'normal' parameters of warfare. Hitherto, reports of individual crimes perpetrated by Austrian and German troops had been published.[106] But Brandes' analysis revealed that civilian and combatant Poles and Russians in the *Kongresówka* and the Pale were apparently engaged in a mass assault on their Jewish neighbours. He described, for instance, the corpses of dozens of Jewish adults and children hanging from telegraph poles, as well as the total destruction of individual towns.[107]

Such reportage intensified in late 1914 and early 1915. By this point, the grim knowledge that life for Eastern European Jews was universally desperate had crystallised in the Anglo-Jewish imagination: 'beggary,

starvation, ruin, desolation [existed] over the whole of the vast population of our people in the stricken territory'.[108] Millions of people were,
in essence, trapped and subject to the vagaries of military intervention.
But what could British Jews do? This was a question, asked many times
over in the course of the war, to which there was never a single satisfactory answer. The reasons for this lay not only in the vast miles of
territory that separated British and Russian/Polish Jews but also in the
patriotic exigencies the community encountered. Inherently important
in this response were the divisions within Anglo-Jewish society, not least
the gulf between the established, assimilated Jews of the West End and
the immigrant, unacculturated Jews of the East End.

In relation to Brandes' articles, for example, the reaction was far from
united. The Conjoint Foreign Committee, which best represented the
interests of the establishment at this point, was reluctant to publicise
this perspective of the Polish Jewish encounter with the war. In a letter Claude G. Montefiore, president of the AJA, Lucien Wolf concluded:
'I have read Brandes' article, but am afraid in view of the resolution
we arrived at at the Conjoint the other night, we cannot do anything
with it officially.'[109] The resolution, though not recorded, was seemingly
a decision to avoid embroiling the CFC in any public controversy connected to Russia's Jewish question. Certainly, this was the view expressed
on public platforms. At a meeting of the Board of Deputies in early
1915, David L. Alexander advised the community that it would be
'unpatriotic to introduce into the discussion [...] any question in relation to the internal policy of Russia or any other of our allies'.[110] This
was, of course, a dilemma that had dogged the Anglo-Jewish establishment since the Kishinev pogrom. But by this stage, the *Jewish Chronicle*
was somewhat less compliant in its attitude towards the Conjoint and
Board of Deputies. Leopold J. Greenberg, its editor since 1907, was more
spirited in his style than his predecessors and, in consequence, the *JC*
published a good deal of damning evidence on the Tsarist Army's activities. It was little wonder, therefore, that the establishment often found
itself isolated from mainstream Anglo-Jewish political currents during
the war.

This was best exemplified in its relationship with the community
of the East End of London. Indeed, in response to the question of
how British Jews could materially and politically assist their Polish and
Russian co-religionists, it was the working-class Jew of the East End who
first stepped up to the plate. Reacting to reports of two million destitute
Jews in divided Poland, the London Relief Fund was set up in December
1914. Headed by Herman Landau, founder and head of the Poor Jews'

Temporary Shelter that had taken in hundreds of impoverished immigrant Jews since its inception in 1885, the Fund set about raising money and publicising the cause. On 31 December 1914, a mass meeting was convened in the Pavilion Theatre in Mile End. Hundreds attended and a number of prominent speakers occupied the platform, including Landau, the Chief Rabbi, Joseph Hertz, and the Zionists Joseph Cowen and Selig Brodetsky.[111] Part of the proceedings were undertaken in Yiddish, and the audience were asked to donate a percentage of their wages for the next 2 months.[112] As the *JC* put it: 'the Jews of East London have imposed upon themselves the self-denying ordinance of giving week-by-week, of their meagre earnings, to the relief fund.'[113] The powerful impact of this meeting reverberated beyond the capital and Jewish organisations set up their own funds throughout the British Empire, in Manchester, Leeds, Birmingham, Glasgow, as well as cities in Canada, South Africa and Australia. There were also links to Russian individuals and organisations, including the Jewish Colonisation Association.[114] All monies received were paid via Baron Aleksandr Gintsburg, leader of the Petrograd Jewish community, who headed the Russian relief organisation, the Central Jewish Committee for the Relief of Victims of the War (*Evreiskii komitet pomoshchi zhertvam voiny*, known as EKOPO).[115]

Clearly, there were some members of the establishment present at Mile End, given that Landau was in the AJA and Cowen on the Board. And the Chief Rabbi was hardly outwith its sphere of influence. At the same time, their presence at this meeting and role in the organisation of a relief fund was an indication of the divisions that existed amongst even the highest ranks of Anglo-Jewry. Despite Lord Rothschild's £1000 donation to its coffers and Leopold de Rothschild's message of support, the Fund's links to the CFC, the Board and the AJA, were somewhat incidental.[116] Indeed, the failure of the community's elite to publicly support the Fund, let alone contribute significant monies, was regularly criticised in the press and at public meetings.[117] In a letter to the *JC*, one correspondent observed that the Conjoint and its members 'thought more of what the "Goyim" say than of what Judaism demands'.[118]

This was not quite justifiable, since Lucien Wolf and others were actively engaged in highlighting the plight of East European Jews to influential figures, both within and without the Jewish world. But it occurred behind the scenes of the CFC, in communications with the AIU and the American Jewish Committee, as well as in Wolf's correspondence and visits to the Foreign Office.[119] From the outside, it looked as though the key institutions of Anglo-Jewish society had, at best, adopted an indifferent stance. At worst, it appeared as though there were other priorities, none of which seemed readily apparent to those not party its mysterious activities. This disquiet was the reason the Conjoint published a letter in late January 1915 that attempted to explicate the reasons for its actions. It advised that 'nothing was being neglected [...] that all available resources for reaching the desired ends are being diligently utilised.'[120] Naturally, the non-specificity of this missive was hardly likely to assuage the frustration of the press and those active in the Fund. The Jews of Poland and Russia required more than vague words.

Yet, it was not until late 1915 that the establishment finally decided to instigate its own relief committee and publicise its involvement. But why? What finally impelled the creation of the British Fund for the Relief of Jewish Victims of the War in Russia, which was connected to the Conjoint? By mid-1915, it was evident that the situation in the East had got much worse. Week by week, fresh atrocity stories appeared in the columns of the Anglo-Jewish press, with reports of pogroms particularly dominating the headlines.[121] The regular indictment of espionage was discussed in a similarly intensive fashion.[122] A good deal of this information was gleaned from Russian visitors to the United Kingdom, who stood on various platforms in support of the East End Relief Fund. One such figure was the Zionist Nahum Sokolow, another Alexis Aladin, leader of the Trudovik Party, both of whom spoke at gatherings in Manchester and elsewhere.[123] But it was the outrage of Anglo-Jews that finally compelled a wider discussion of the elite's supposed indifference. In June 1915, a regular columnist in the *Chronicle*, Simon Gilbert, an East Ender who wrote under the pen-name 'Mentor', filed an article that left no room to doubt the crisis in the East. Moreover, he clearly intended to break the establishment's silence on the matter, recognising, for instance, that he might be 'denounced as unpatriotic':

[...] the inclination has naturally been to give to the Russian Government as an ally of this country the benefit of the doubt. [...] But there are limits. And the limit is reached when silence involves traitorousness to Truth. [The military Order of the Day of March 1915] decreed nothing less than the expulsion of all Jews from the military zones in Galicia, Bukovina and Poland. The excuse for this terrible determination was an easy one to find ready to hand. It was the alleged disloyalty of the Jewish population. [It] was directed not at any locality, or at any general section of the population. It was a decree against Jews as Jews.

These Russian actions, which had resulted in the expelling of 200,000 Jews, were so terrible, that it would 'require the pen of a Dante to adequately narrate'. What was more, Russia had wholly betrayed the principles which had underpinned its alliance with Britain.[124]

Once again, it was evident that this perspective was forged under the influence of Russian sources, quite possibly the same dossier that Lucien Wolf had at his disposal at this time. In mid-1915, he received a typewritten document of about 300 pages that included a whole host of military orders, newspaper articles culled from Jewish newspapers in Russia and personal testimony.[125] It was a dramatic account and was probably partly responsible for the urgent letter the AJA/Board of Deputies sent to the Foreign Office in June 1915, which stressed that the situation in Eastern Europe was 'so terrible and serious that we venture to think that it warrants exceptional action'.[126] But it was not until September 1915 that the 'official' institutions of Anglo-Jewry finally decided to take their own exceptional action and set up a relief committee. Even then, it was enacted under careful precautions that stressed the philanthropic over the political. There was to be no question of usurping the cause in order to highlight the manner in which Tsarist Russia was currently handling its Jewish question. This remained a diplomatic matter, to be dealt with *in camera* in official circles alone. During a London meeting with P.L. Bark, the Tsarist Minister of Finance, for instance, Claude Montefiore and Leopold de Rothschild were keen to stress that Anglo-Jewry had from the outset of the war 'abstained [...] from all agitation [...] on the question of Jewish emancipation in Russia'. And, though they presented a list of future desiderata, there was no question of criticising the regime's war-time conduct.[127]

By October 1915, the new campaign was up and running. Amongst its committee members could be found the most illustrious Anglo-Jewish names – Rothschilds, Sassoons, Montefiores, as well as various members of parliament, the Chief Rabbi, *Haham* Gaster, Israel Zangwill and, of course, Lucien Wolf. Like its predecessor, it was connected to its Russian equivalent, EKOPO, even sharing the same name. A member of that organisation, Dr Reuben Blank, served on the British committee.[128] An urgent appeal was issued and this time N.M. Rothschild granted £5000.[129] In early November 1915, a much publicised meeting was convened in London, at which it was claimed that £60,000 had been raised.[130] At last, the wider community could be proud of these achievements, and the *Chronicle* noted that it was 'nothing to wonder at the conscience of British Jewry that has been stirred'.[131] Unfortunately, this celebration was but a temporary respite in the fractured relationship between the elite and the wider community.

At the same time the new committee was being organised in London, similar activity was occurring in Edinburgh. The Russian Jews' Relief Fund was the brainchild of one Leon Levison, a converted Levantine Jew, who had been connected for over a decade to evangelical circles in Scotland.[132] In mid-November 1915, a meeting was held at New Court (headquarters of N.M. Rothschild's) at which the conjoining of the London and Edinburgh funds was decided upon. Levison, his deputy, the Reverend H. Wilkinson, Leopold de Rothschild and Claude Montefiore were present, though the Chief Rabbi refused to attend.[133] Shortly afterwards, Rothschild and Montefiore's names were found on Levison's publicity material, amidst a litany of bishops, canons and reverends from various Scottish churches.[134] Undoubtedly, it was a coup for the Edinburgh fund, but, as can be imagined, the response of Anglo-Jewish society was one of sheer horror.

The Anglo-Jewish press was, to put it mildly, startled at the naivety of the community's most distinguished representatives. Levison was a well-known 'conversionist', maintained the *JC*, and the nature of his work was surely obvious in the allusion to 'casting bread upon the waters' found in his fund's publicity material.[135] Much was therefore made of the Chief Rabbi's absence at the New Court meeting. Surely, it was argued, he was aware of Levison's outlook, though there is no extant documentary evidence to support this thesis.[136] Yet again, the Anglo-Jewish elite appeared out-of-step with general Jewish feeling in Britain and the subsequent controversy created much ill-feeling and resentment.[137] More crucially, the main crisis at hand, Jewish relief in Poland and Russia, was once more overshadowed by internal division and dissension.

There was just a single possible solution to this incident and within a matter of weeks, the Montefiore and Rothschild names vanished forever from the Edinburgh fund's newspaper advertisements. Not long afterwards, N.M. Rothschild's contributed the quite enormous sum of £20,000 to the London-based fund.[138] Understandably, one can detect a calming of the storm in the pages of the Anglo-Jewish press and, by the turn of the New Year, most internal animosity seems to have been convincingly put to one side – for the moment at least.[139] Henceforth, the priority was saving the lives and livelihoods of East European Jews. Towards the end of 1916, the fund was operating quite efficiently and, as one historian has pointed out, raised approximately £100,000 in a little over 12 months.[140] How this panned out on a practical level is, of course, difficult to discern without examining Russian archival material. No doubt many Russian and Polish Jews benefited to some degree from the humanitarian assistance provided by their British co-religionists. By this stage, however, the British spotlight of enquiry on Russian internal affairs was about to shift, as events in Petrograd were shortly to take a dramatic turn.

The February Revolution: Russia's Jewish question solved?

On 15 March 1917 (2 March OS), Tsar Nicholas II signed the abdication papers that finally brought to a swift end over 300 years of Romanov rule. In place of him and his regime, two separate organs of authority appeared. In the first place, there was the Provisional Government, which came into existence on the very same day of the abdication, led by the Kadet, Prince Georgii L'vov. Mostly representative of middle class and liberal aspirations, its membership was drawn from the Imperial Duma and the *zemstva* movement.[141] The Petrograd Soviet of Workers', Soldiers' and Sailors' Deputies formed the second centre of power in the former imperial capital. A glance at its name gives a clear insight into its membership and constituency. From a Western perspective, the Provisional Government was regarded as the sole source of legitimate rule, which would prove problematic in later months. But in early April 1917, Russia's French and British allies breathed a sigh of relief as one of the Provisional Government's first declarations was issued by Kadet leader Pavel Miliukov. As the new Minister of Foreign Affairs, Miliukov announced his nation's intention to continue its commitment to the war.[142] Despite the apparent joy the disposal of the Tsarist regime induced in the West, the war obviously remained the priority. Were Russia to withdraw, it would spell untold catastrophe, particular given the faintest glimmer of Allied advantage following the German retreat behind the Hindenburg Line in early 1917.

Nevertheless, the immediate response to the revolution was celebrated far and wide. Charles Saroléa, a professor at the University of Edinburgh who often gave public lectures on Russia, described the ousting of Nicholas II as the most 'glorious event in modern history'.[143] Almost immediately, the Labour Party sent a message to Russia heralding the 'great reverberation which this tremendous event must evoke in many lands'.[144] Numerous editorials in daily newspapers universally embraced these events. Even the pro-Tsarist *New Witness* welcomed the revolution.[145] And, of course, so too did the Anglo-Jewish press. A leading article in the *Jewish Chronicle* aptly summed up the widespread response of British Jewry: 'The vilest tyranny that the modern world has seen, and which withstood for so many years every effort of enlightenment and progress has at last been humbled to the dust.' The latter part of this quotation was, of course, the prime reason for Anglo-Jewry's rejoicing in March 1917. The Tsarist regime's demise also promised the vanquishing of all the restrictions, impositions and discrimination encountered, especially in the legal sphere, by the Jewish communities of Russia and Poland. 'At last', the *JC* reflected, 'the long night for the Russian Jew is ended.'[146]

To what extent did the rights of the Russian Jew appear in the mainstream response to the February Revolution? For the most part, it must be said, it rarely featured on the radar of significant consequences. Charles Saroléa, for instance, who had written an account of the Jewish question in his war-time book *Europe's Debt to Russia*, believed that the revolution would bring freedom to all the races of the Russian Empire, including Jews.[147] Stephen Graham, writing in *The Times*, similarly observed that 'Jews will be given more liberty.'[148] Another report in *The Times* approvingly noted the endeavours of the Jewish delegation presented to Prince L'vov and the Petrograd Soviet in early April 1917.[149] For the most part, however, the Jewish question was not the priority in the mainstream narrative. The single most influential factor in the response was tied to the war and the belief that the abdication and revolution were inherently patriotic acts. As was the case in Russia, the notion that Russia's poor military performance was tied to German intrigue in Petrograd had percolated into everyday British discourse.[150] The removal of the Romanovs would, in theory, eliminate a treasonous influence and its effort to undermine the progress of the war. Such military considerations similarly found their place in the Anglo-Jewish analysis of the revolution.[151]

There was evidence, therefore, that the February Revolution had a unifying effect in the British context. This was apparently the case even in Anglo-Jewish circles. And, certainly, in the early weeks after Nicholas II's abdication, there was little cause for the communal consensus to be broken. This was not to last. Yet again, the activities of the Conjoint precipitated a cleavage in Anglo-Jewish society. The disagreement on this occasion centred on leading institutions, including the CFC, and their official response – or lack thereof – to the Revolution. Just 2 weeks after the abdication, the *Chronicle* was already expressing its concern that the Board of Deputies and the AJA had not yet made any public comment on the situation in Russia. Despite the optimistic mood, the Russian Jew, it advised, still needed the support of Anglo-Jewry.[152] Moses Gaster made similar comments in a speech and warned against complacency and 'the supposition that the Revolution has absolved us from further effort'.[153] These early rumblings of discontent were compounded by events at a meeting of the AJA, at which Claude Montefiore suggested there should be no discussion about Russia.[154] This had, in fact, been the response decided upon behind closed doors by Wolf and the CFC. In a letter to Leopold de Rothschild, written a day after the abdication and following discussions with unnamed Russian contacts, Wolf noted that the new government consisted 'entirely of staunch friends of the Jews':

> If we do anything to accentuate this fact, we shall render it very dif-
> ficult for them to move on our behalf, and at the same time will
> enable the antisemitic Reactionaries to clamour that the revolution
> is the result of a Jewish conspiracy. You know that this has been their
> favourable method of discrediting all Liberal movements in Russia.[155]

Given the manner in which the CFC had handled all war-time Russian crises, this response was not unexpected. By the same token, since it was not communicated to the Anglo-Jewish press, it yet again appeared as though those institutions that were supposed to defend and aid foreign co-religionists were actually indifferent to their plight, or even their victories.

A few weeks later, in April 1917, relations were shaken once more at a meeting of the Board of Deputies. David Alexander was absent through ill-health and his place was taken by H.S.Q. Henriques, who read out the pre-prepared president's message. Referring to the 'stupendous happenings in Russia', 'the greatest event in out times', Alexander's address nevertheless underlined the belief that 'no separate expression of Anglo-Jewish opinion was required', a decision taken by the CFC. Instead, Anglo-Jewish institutions should simply ally themselves with the views expressed by the British government and House of Commons. He revealed that a telegram had been wired to Prince L'vov once the May Laws and other restrictions had been abolished in early April 1917, but there was no need to do or say anything else. Nor was there any necessity, he said, to convene a public meeting or debate.[156] The uproar that followed was incredible. Members hurled all kinds of insults at the Board's leadership, with one being called 'a liar'. Another described the Board and CFC's celebration of the revolution as 'paltry and humdrum'.[157] Despite this controversy there was, however, no movement on the CFC's stance. Wolf and his colleagues continued to play matters by ear.

This was not a wholly unrealistic response as events in Russia remained unpredictable and in a state of constant flux. Now that the Tsar had gone, a mass of new figures came to populate Russia's confused and chaotic political arena. Whilst many members of the Provisional Government, such as Miliukov and A.I. Shingarev, were familiar to Western observers, those individuals who dominated the Petrograd Soviet were an unknown and, to say the least, worrying quantity.[158] There was, therefore, cause for concern, particular in relation to the socialist spectre that appeared to be looming ever larger as 1917 progressed, particularly as the Bolsheviks promised to end Russia's participation in the war. These anxieties were expressed throughout the British narrative, both Jewish and non-Jewish. An interview in the *JC* with David Jochelman, the former head of the emigration department of the ITO, revealed the 'surging of the socialist spirit in Russia', which was a 'danger to Judaism'.[159] Elsewhere, a link was observed between Russian Jews, instability and the parties of the left. In *The Times*, a correspondent observed:

> I am grieved to have to state that the Jews are not behaving well. They have become free citizens of Russia, but do not display a sense of their responsibility befitting their new position. Similar complaints have reached me in Petrograd. Hot-headed and hysterical Jewish youths are, unfortunately, playing into the hands of the worst demagogues and of the external enemies of Russia.[160]

The Anglo-Jewish press took exception, naturally, to the first part of this quotation.[161] However, it expressed its own caution about the Jewish attitude towards the 'Maximalists' (an early term for Bolshevism). It advised Russian Jews to support the Provisional Government unconditionally.[162] Of course, this was not to be and there was an undeniably significant Jewish membership amongst the ranks of the Bolsheviks, Mensheviks and Socialist Revolutionaries.[163] There were few British observers who viewed this presence as mere coincidence. By the autumn of 1917, commentators of all political colourings began to see the Jewish hand at work amidst the troubled state of Russian politics. Once the Bolsheviks finally came to power in November 1917, there was no longer any question as to the revolution's origins. As a leader in the *New Witness* starkly proclaimed: 'We know that the Russian Revolution has been the work of Jews.'[164] With the advent of Vladimir Il'yich Lenin's *coup d'état*, a new phase of the East European Jewish question had commenced.

6
Britain and Poland: Propaganda, Pogroms and Independence, 1914–1925

Thinking of Poland and her tortured Jews,
'Twixt Goth and Cossack hounded, crucified
On either frontier, e'en the Pale denied,
Wand'ring with bloodied staff and broken shoes,
Scarred like their greatest son with stripe and bruise,
Though thrice a hundred thousand fight beside
Their Russian brethren and are glorified
By death for those who flout then and abuse.

Israel Zangwill, *The Nation*, 1915

This ancient country has [been] in the past a defender of all that is best in the civilisation of Western Christendom.

Henryk Sienkiewicz, 1915

The Polish Jews should have rights; nay, they should have privileges, but they should not have Poland.

G.K. Chesterton, *New Witness*, 1918

Divided Poland and the Great War

At the outbreak of war in 1914, all three partitioning powers placed Poland on their list of war-aims, each pledging different things. Tsarist Russia was first off the mark, when Grand Duke Nicholas, commander of the Imperial Russian army, issued a proclamation on 15 August 1914 that guaranteed future Polish autonomy.[1] A few days later, he promised imminent liberation to the 'Russians' of Galicia, assuring all inhabitants that 'room [would] be found [in] the bosom of our Mother Russia, without offending peaceable people of whatever nationality.'[2] Subsequently, Austria-Hungary got in on the act and declared its intention to

154

reunite the Congress Kingdom with Galicia, whilst Imperial Germany urged the liberation of Russian Poland as a component of its plans for a *Mitteleuropa*.[3] From a British perspective, the possibility of rebirth for an autonomous Polish state was understandably connected throughout the war to the need to proscribe German and Habsburg political ambitions in Europe. R.W. Seton-Watson, highly active in Polish émigré circles, noted that a resurgent Poland would be 'a death-blow to Germanic influences in Russia'.[4] Likewise, J.H. Retinger, head of the Polish Bureau in London and future biographer of Joseph Conrad, wrote in 1914 that Poland would be 'the greatest guarantee of permanent peace in Europe'.[5] Two years later, the historian and then Vice-Chancellor of Sheffield University, H.A.L. Fisher, spoke publicly of the future Poland as a 'buffer state'.[6] Cecil Chesterton, also writing in 1916, similarly reckoned that Poland would be essential in holding back the tide of German and Austrian domination.[7]

From the outset, the war had an immediate impact on the manner that Poland was depicted in the British narrative. In many ways, the initial salvoes on the Eastern Front reaffirmed Poland's status as a martyr, a notion that resonated with the contemporaneous sufferings of another Catholic state, Belgium. Religious imagery abounded in portrayals of both nations, as each performed heroic acts of Christian sacrifice. Henryk Sienkiewicz, for instance, reminded British readers that in the past Poland had been a 'defender of all that is best in Western Christendom'.[8] *The Scotsman*, in slight contrast, decreed Poland to be the 'saviour of Christendom' in the East.[9] Another contributor to British discourse on the war-time Polish question, Professor Gabriel Séailles of the Sorbonne in Paris, dramatically observed: 'so terrible has been [Poland's] Passion from the day she was nailed to the Cross that her poets [...] have suggested that she was bearing this affliction by Divine choice for the redemption of mankind.'[10] These sentiments, which hinged wholly on religious interpretations, suggested that Poland's anguish, just like Christ's, would eventually be of benefit to all humanity.[11]

In this aspect, the British narrative made much of the atrocities that were allegedly perpetrated in Poland, most especially by the German Imperial army. Again, this resonated with descriptions of Belgium, a nation widely assumed to have been raped, pillaged and desecrated by the barbarous 'Hun'.[12] Just as in Belgium, German troops were accused of destroying churches and perpetrating various acts of iconoclasm in Poland.[13] Such analyses naturally fed into the wider concerns and aspirations as to the war's meaning, as commentators sought, in all manner of propaganda, to define it primarily as a religious conflict, a holy war.[14]

Where did Poland's Jewish question fit into this specific rendering of the Great War in the East? As has already been observed in Chapter 5, the war had a terrible impact on Poland's Jews. In all corners of its partitioned territory, British observers encountered heart-rending tales of Jewish dispossession, destitution and displacement.[15] The *Jewish Chronicle*, for instance, noted in October 1914 that 'the Germans are acting with great cruelty towards [Polish] Jews who are dressed in long eastern coats. They beat them mercilessly whilst forcing them to dig trenches.' The wanton destruction of synagogues was also observed, though this remained a theme untouched in the mainstream narrative.[16] Inevitably, however, British Jews found it difficult to maintain a visible campaign on behalf of their Polish co-religionists, not least because it was exceedingly difficult to detach Poland usefully from the broader Eastern European context. Although aware that much of the conflict was perpetrated on Polish soil, whether in Galicia or the Congress Kingdom, defining Poland's geographical and ethnic parameters for the sake of a relief programme was problematic.

Additionally, as Anglo-Jewish institutions recognised, there were other threats to Jewish security and well-being in Poland. On the one hand, Polish Jews had to deal with manifestations of 'official' antisemitism, such as that embraced by pockets of the Russian Imperial army. There was also an internal antisemitic peril, presented by the activities of Polish National Democracy. Dmowski's party continued to promote the anti-Jewish boycott throughout the war, but also drew a propaganda advantage from the wider war-time atmosphere. This was revealed in a memorandum sent by the CFC to the Foreign Office in June 1915:

> The sufferings [of Polish Jews] are due in part to the rankling antisemitism of large sections of the Polish people [...] the Polish Nationalists, recognising an opportunity of 'eliminating' – the expression is theirs, the Jewish element which forms so large a proportion of the population of the Kingdom, and thus assuring a greater national homogeneity for the new Poland, have everywhere and systematically denounced the Jews as spies.[17]

Before the war, as a consequence of the publicity surrounding the boycott, Anglo-Jewish individuals and institutions had worried about the precise nature of Polish nationalism. Such concerns were not dispelled by the war, since in the Polish case it appeared as though the most extreme nationalist elements were not prepared to work for a greater cause by uniting with Jews. Indeed, Jews were regarded and depicted in Polish nationalist discourse as much an enemy as the German occupiers.

Understandably, in the matter of a British political campaign for the future Poland, Anglo-Jewish figures were anxious to ensure that there would be no input from Roman Dmowski and his party. After all, were the new Poland to be drawn on *Endek* lines alone, its Jewish population was sure to face unimaginable difficulties. In all likelihood they would be economically and politically banished, perhaps even forced to leave Poland altogether. Who knew what legal proscriptions would be instituted? These questions moved beyond the theoretical when the reality of National Democratic ideology was brought home to British observers during Roman Dmowski's visit to war-time London.

Roman Dmowski in Britain

Dmowski arrived in Britain in late 1915. By this stage, he had altered his national ambitions and was no longer prepared to settle for Polish autonomy within the Tsarist Empire. He wanted independence, underwritten by French, British and, hopefully, US guarantees. His British sojourn, therefore, was intended to publicise and gain official recognition for this cause. Prior to Dmowski's appearance in London, various Polish émigrés had already been active in promoting their own cases.[18] It included the Polish Information Committee (PIC), which drew British membership, such as R.W. Seton Watson and the liberal parliamentarians Lord Eversley and A.F. Whyte. One of the most prominent Poles associated with the PIC was August Zaleski, of the Polish Progressive Party (PPS), who represented the interests of Polish socialism and was especially well-known in British intellectual and Jewish circles, though he failed to impress at the Foreign Office.[19] Zaleski was Dmowski's main political rival while in London.

Dmowski's London visit, which lasted for approximately 18 months, has been extensively examined by historians. In particular, his encounter with the eminent historian, Lewis B. Namier, who then worked in the British propaganda department at Wellington House, has received some attention, as has Dmowski's presence at the Paris Peace Conference. In these years, contemporary British observers regarded him as bombastic, arrogant and awkward in matters of personal intercourse.[20] But how did Dmowski's political ideology, with its important antisemitic component, fare in the British context? To be sure, his difficult encounter with Namier was undoubtedly a product of the latter's suspicion about Dmowski's approach to Poland's Jewish question. And, since prominent Anglo-Jews had already encountered the reality of the *Endecja*'s hostility towards Jews, manifest in the boycott before and during the Great War, Lucien Wolf and others attempted to interfere in Dmowski's propaganda activities.[21]

Yet, despite these best efforts, Dmowski and his acolytes stood on influential public platforms throughout Britain, which included University and King's Colleges in London, and Oxford and Cambridge Universities.[22] He also appeared at a public and apparently heated debate in Edinburgh, where he verbally jousted with the director of the Russian Jews' Relief Fund, Leon Levison.[23] Intriguingly, on another occasion the organiser of this meeting, Professor Charles Saroléa of the University of Edinburgh, introduced the Polish nationalist leader to G.K. Chesterton.[24] At a lecture in London, Dmowski was heralded by Viscount James Bryce, historian and former British ambassador to the United States.[25] Dmowski also maintained links with various pro-Polish individuals in London, who, in turn, connected him and his party to several publications, including the newspapers *Tygodnik polski* ('Polish Weekly') and *Prawda* ('Truth'), and the journal *New Poland*. Eventually, in September 1917, Dmowski, or at least the organisation he then represented, the Polish National Committee (PNC), gained some kind of tacit recognition in government circles, though this was not officially and publicly determined until October 1917.[26] The response to this action on HMG's part, which was entirely decided behind closed doors, was widespread disapproval and disbelief. The *Manchester Guardian*, for instance, described the Foreign Office's decision as an 'unhappy [extension] of sympathies' to the Dmowski group.[27] Later on, in 1918, it dismissed Dmowski as 'a reactionary, a clerical and a violent antisemite'.[28] *New Europe*, the weekly publication edited by R.W. Seton-Watson, was similarly unimpressed and, not unexpectedly, Lucien Wolf wrote a series of concerned letters to the Foreign Office.[29] There were even attempts in both Houses of Parliament to query the decision, though this failed.[30]

Given this reaction, it might be assumed that Dmowski's specific and exclusive national idea failed to find a receptive audience in Britain. But to what extent was this the case? Did he downplay his ideological worldview, as he had appeared to do in Bernard Pares' *Russian Review*? Or, was he free to give full vent to his uncompromising stance towards the Jewish question on the public platforms that he appeared? From the limited data available it seems unlikely that he spoke with any restraint. At the lecture he delivered at Cambridge, for instance, where he was presented with an honorary degree alongside other prominent intellectual and political figures from the Tsarist Empire, he took the opportunity to explore and explain to his academic audience the on-going anti-Jewish boycott[31]:

In Russian Poland the Middle Class represents all stages of wealth, from the great industrials and merchants down to the small traders and craftsmen, includes a very numerous class of people of liberal professions. Here the Polish commercial and industrial class feels cramped, particularly because of the herding together in cities with the Jews who, driven out of Russia by anti-Jewish laws, gather in Poland. This explains such facts as the commercial boycott of the Jews in Poland, which is partly a manifestation of the economic tendency of the whole community to strengthen the Polish element in the town populations. The Jews in Poland, it must be mentioned here, in their mass do not belong to the Polish nationality: their language is Yiddish, a German dialect, and they are organised as a separate Jewish nationality against the Poles. In these conditions the struggle against the Jews is a national struggle. It must be firmly stated here that this commercial boycott is carried out without any manifestations of violence on the part of the Poles, and that everything is written about the use of brutal force by the Poles is pure invention.[32]

Unfortunately, these words represent the most substantial direct source of Dmowski's public propagandising on Poland's Jewish question whilst in the United Kingdom (as opposed to the private memoranda he sent to the Foreign Office).[33] Nevertheless, they succinctly expressed his worldview and were greatly revealing as to how he imagined Jews would or, more to the point, would not feature in an independent Poland.

In typical fashion, Dmowski combined both fact and fiction in order to polemicise his case. His assertion, for example, that the boycott had produced no violence overlooked the reality of its threat to Jewish life in Poland. And it is not inconceivable that his remark on the 'pure invention' of associated boycott stories was a sideswipe at the Jewish press, in both Poland and Britain. By the same token, it was indeed true that Congress Poland had experienced an influx of Russian and Lithuanian Jews in the late nineteenth and early twentieth centuries. As noted in Chapter 4, this was a consequence of greater economic opportunities in the *Kongresówka*, as well as the absence of restrictive laws that limited Jewish life in the Pale of Settlement.

Nevertheless, Dmowski clearly exaggerated the ramifications of this migration from the western provinces, particularly in the notion that Jews had been herded (like cattle?) and gathered together (were ghettoised?) in Polish cities. Yet, once again, there was a glimmer of accuracy here, since Jewish life in Congress Poland was indeed mostly urban, but the terminology employed by Dmowski was deliberately designed to be provocative. Additionally, he underplayed specific aspects of the Polish case in order to emphasise the Jewish 'threat'. His comments on the Polish middle class, for instance, suggested that it consisted only of ethnic Poles, when, in fact, Jews made up a considerable proportion of the 'small traders and craftsmen' and the 'people of the liberal professions' to whom he referred. Undoubtedly, as he suggested, there was an intrinsic economic relationship connecting Jews and gentiles in Poland, but Dmowski overstated its negative aspects. As we have already seen, for example, the boycott largely remained a failure at local level, precisely as a consequence of the crucial economic bonds that existed between Polish Jews and gentiles.

Despite Dmowski's rhetorical combination of hyperbole and understatement, this short paragraph carried more significance than its effort to portray Polish Jews as selfish economic opportunists. The key here lay in Dmowski's construction of the Polish nation and, most especially, the critical matter of who could and could not be a member. There was no reference to Jews as a religious minority in this paragraph, nor, for that matter, as an ethnic group. Nevertheless, this was the all-important difference upon which Dmowski's separation of Jews and Poles was based, though his lecture emphasised language as a test of nationhood. The Jews of Poland did 'not belong to the Polish nationality', since they spoke Yiddish and were 'organised as a separate nationality against the Poles'. Thus, at that precise moment, Poles were not merely engaged in a 'national struggle' with their German occupiers, but against Jews, too. Indeed, since Yiddish was apparently a 'German dialect', there was a suggestion here of a 'national' link between Germans and Jews, which, in turn, inferred that the latter were inherently disloyal towards Poland.[34] In this aspect, Dmowski underlined his belief that Jews could not, for economic and national reasons, belong to a reconstituted Polish state. There was no hint at a possible reconciliation of this division in Polish life. It was an intractable problem to which Dmowski, at this moment, presented no solution.

A year later, in July 1917, Dmowski published one of his most substantial policy statements whilst in Britain, in the form of the privately printed *Problems of Central and Eastern Europe*, which was distributed to important figures, including the Foreign Secretary, A.J. Balfour.[35] As might be anticipated, given the title, this treatise did not deal solely with Poland, but considered the innumerable problems that Europe would have to broach once peace came. In the matter of Poland, though, Dmowski reiterated his view that Jews did not form a part of the Polish nation. On this occasion, his hopeful prediction was, given the Jewish 'tendency to emigration', that this would develop on a 'large scale' in the future. How precisely this was to be effected was not discussed, nor whether it would be left to Jews to make the decision themselves; or, would there be 'encouragement' of some kind?[36]

How were such sentiments received in Britain? Did Dmowski encounter a receptive, hostile or indifferent audience? Given the human catastrophes on the Western Front that had become a mainstay of every-day British life by this point, did anybody really care about the future of a new Poland and whether it would treat its Jews fairly? Obviously, as already outlined, Dmowski caused controversy in Britain, but he was not without supporters, even when it came to the thorny matter of Poland's Jewish question. Stephen Graham, for instance, identified by Lucien Wolf as a 'lieutenant' of the Dmowski group, predicted that in future Poland would be 'a great Catholic country'.[37] Graham believed a reborn Polish state, with Panslavic links to Russia, would herald ram-ifications for Polish Jews, since although they 'would hope to profit by Polish emancipation', their presence would be incompatible with the religious and ethnic integrity of the new state. Polish Jews 'must', Graham argued, 'keep second or third place', which would subsequently encourage their mass emigration to the United States:

> The Jews, with that sweet reasonableness, kindness and common sense which distinguish their life when they are not too embit-tered by persecution, will perhaps see that no good end is served by fanning malice against Russia and they will turn their eyes rather towards the West than towards the East. So Poland will escape (1) Jewish predomination: (2) political deprivations on account of Jewish conditions.[38]

Undoubtedly, there was more than a hint of *Endek* ideology in the expression of such notions, and Graham tacitly approved of a future Polish state conceived along National Democratic lines.[39]

In a similar vein, Charles Saroléa, who invited Dmowski to speak in Edinburgh, expressed concern about the status of language in a future Polish state. Noting that some Polish Jews believed Yiddish should be placed on an equal footing with Polish, Saroléa argued that this was an impossible aspiration.[40] 'What would we say in this country', he asked, 'if the Jews of East London insisted that a German dialect and not the English language shall be the vehicle of education in the schools of the land?' Akin to Dmowski, Saroléa protested too much; after all, not a single Jewish organisation in Poland claimed that Yiddish should be used throughout all the schools in the land. Moreover, the Edinburgh professor imputed innate bonds of pro-German loyalty to Polish Jews, which he emphasised in both his description of Yiddish as a 'German dialect' – Dmowski's precise phrase in his Cambridge lecture – and the following statement: 'it seems somewhat ungrateful that in this supreme crisis of Polish history the Jews should be arrayed on the side of the enemies of Poland.'[41]

Elsewhere, some more obvious exponents of components of *Endek* ideology were to be found. The *New Witness* was no less uncompromising, even in war-time conditions, in its blustering indignation, and it discovered an intellectual comrade in arms in Dmowski and his party. In light of its emphasis on London-based political activity, it was naturally interested in all Polish émigré groups in the capital and the policies they espoused. It took, for example, an almost instant dislike to the PIC, no doubt as a consequence of its socialist connections, but also the fact that several of its members, including Zaleski, were Jews. Indeed, the *Witness* typically found evidence of 'the Jew's hand' at work in the PIC, especially in its publication *Polish News*, which it argued was 'clearly calculated to further the enemy's designs'.[42] It also suggested that the relief fund for Poland collected by the PIC was distributed exclusively to Jews.[43] That Polish Jews were all, to a man and woman, pro-German was an absolute given in the *New Witness*; there was no possibility of it being any other way. In September 1917, just prior to official recognition of Dmowski's PNC, the *Witness* declared that the 'Jewish party in Poland' (there was no attempt to describe precisely who or what this party was) was pro-German and desired 'a settlement in favour of the Central Empires'.[44] Inevitably, Yiddish also turned out to be German 'in disguise'.[45] Indeed, all the Jews of Central Europe were deemed by the *Witness* to have 'a slight preference for Germany as a big commercial firm; about as dangerous a combination as there can be'.[46]

Such insinuations directed wholesale towards Polish Jews were not the only link to *Endek* propaganda in the *New Witness*. The national question was explored extensively, most especially the matter of whether Jews could belong to a future Polish state. The answer, unequivocally, was in the negative. G.K. Chesterton noted in one of his many deliberately provocative articles that 'the Polish Jews should have rights; nay, they should have privileges, but they should not have Poland.'[47] Simply because a Jew was 'born of Polish territory', it did not make him anything but a Jew.[48] As a result, Jews did not and could not make up any part of the Polish nation; they were 'not even united in the Polish nation by any sense of mutual affection or common national tradition'.[49] In essence, the *New Witness* was the British embodiment of *Endek* ideology, and it argued that, once independence was achieved, drastic measures would be required: 'let [the Jews] repair to Palestine, leaving Poland in possession of the Poles'.[50] Like Dmowski and is compatriots, the *Witness* entirely and conspiratorially believed that Polish Jews were determined to undermine a future Polish state in every conceivable way:

> It is necessary once again to caution our readers against accepting as correct any news emanating from newsagencies under Judæa-German [*sic*] control. The Jews are making desperate efforts to disintegrate the Polish nation and to create the belief in the minds of the Western Powers that the Poles are incapable of self-government. [...] Cosmopolitan finance is doing its utmost to force the politicians to withhold freedom from our Allies. [...] The fate of Poland will be the trial test between the Jews and European civilisation.[51]

Of course, from the moment of its initial publication in 1912, the outlook of the *New Witness* was informed by racial antisemitism.[52] It required no encouragement from Roman Dmowski and his ilk in order to utter the kind of insidious and unfounded accusations evident in the above quotation. Nonetheless, it comes as no surprise to learn that the relationship between the *Witness* and Dmowski existed beyond the intellectual. There is proof, for instance, that members of Dmowski's circle wrote for the journal, or at least provided it with information.[53]

Despite these connections, however, it is impossible to be certain whether those in Britain who advocated views redolent of *Endek* ideology were directly influenced by Dmowski's London propaganda. To be sure, he made personal links with Graham and Saroléa, though in the case of the former, he had already expressed uncompromising attitudes on the Eastern European Jewish question several years earlier. As already indicated, the same was true of the *New Witness*. In some sense, it could be argued that for Graham and the Chesterbelloc, Dmowski's presence in Britain legitimised their uncompromising perspectives on Poland, Polish Jews and the entire Jewish question. In relation to Saroléa, there is no indication that he was much interested in the fate of Polish Jews (or even Poland itself) prior to the First World War. It could be conjectured, therefore, that he was indeed persuaded by Dmowski's politicking, though it remains definitively unproven.

In light of this evidence, it is clear that, despite the endeavours of Dmowski's detractors, he was not intellectually ostracised in Britain. On the contrary, his vision of the future Poland, utterly devoid of Jews, was shared by observers in the United Kingdom. To be sure, it could be argued that the Chesterbelloc and its associates, as well as Graham and Saroléa, did not occupy the mainstream of British intellectual and political life. It might therefore follow that, in Britain, the appreciation and embrace of *Endek* ideology was confined to less important patterns of discourse. To categorise Saroléa in this way, however, who was not only a university professor, but also the editor of a popular weekly journal, *Everyman*, and an inveterate public speaker, is not entirely justifiable. A century on, he may, in the main, be relegated to the footnotes of history, but in his day he was not an obscure individual.[54] The same can be said of Graham. Between 1912 until the early 1920s, much to the chagrin of Israel Zangwill, he was a ubiquitous figure in the newspaper and publishing world.

There were others, too, who publicly approved the Dmowski cause, though some made no overt endorsement or reference to his views on the Jewish question. These included the venerable socialist H.M. Hyndman and the journalist G.P. Gooch.[55] And, of course, there were the many figures who directly supported Dmowski from within the PNC and its associated organisations. Laurence Alma Tadema propagandised on his behalf, as did J.H. Harley, who edited the journal the *New Poland* precisely on pro-*Endek* lines; both supported Dmowski's position on the Jewish question.[56]

Furthermore, the argument that Dmowski failed to secure an intellectual and political place in Britain would obviously hold more water had the PNC been unsuccessful in gaining Foreign Office recognition. So, why did HMG effectively make Dmowski's committee Poland's government-in-waiting? And how did it negotiate its overtly antisemitic ideology? Of course, given that an independent Poland had not existed for over a century, Allied governments faced a number of problems in relation to the Polish question. Firstly, there was the simple matter of geography with which to contend. Where would Poland be placed on the map and which parts of pre-1914 Europe would it encompass? But perhaps more to the point, who would be its guarantor(s) and who would lead it? In considering these questions, as well as their possible answers, the Foreign Office was faced with an array of Polish political groupings, even in London. Since Polish politics had hitherto rarely featured on Britain's radar, not surprisingly it was no easy task to identify those best suited to represent Poland officially. In essence, the Foreign Office had to select the group and individuals who most closely fitted into Allied plans for the reconstruction of not only Poland, but all continental Europe.

How, therefore, were Dmowski and the PNC fingered as the most representative and useful Polish group? In part, this was a consequence of the outlook of Dmowski's opponents in Britain, most especially the PIC. August Zaleski, as will be recalled, represented the Polish Progressive Party. Headed by the renowned Polish soldier, Józef Piłsudski, the PPS was unwilling to negotiate with Russia, had strict aspirations as to the reconfiguration of Poland and, since it was prepared to include Imperial Germany in its negotiations, it was believed to be pro-German. This was the disloyal taint borne by the PIC and it was taken so seriously by HMG that its journal, the *Polish Review*, was banned in 1918.[57] In contrast, Dmowski had no intention of negotiating with Germany, was not guilty of pro-Germanism and, though hugely ambitious about Poland's geographical boundaries, reiterated his belief that its purpose was to act as a buffer state. This latter point, in particular, crucially chimed with Allied ambitions.

Somewhat inevitably at this stage, given these major strategic and territorial concerns, Poland's Jewish question came further down the agenda. In spite of Dmowski's undisguised anti-Jewish antipathies and the antisemitic ideology to which his party was wedded, he and it were regarded by some in the Foreign Office as representative of the majority of Poles.[58] In the main, the choice came down to the simple expediency of lesser evils. It was a compromise and not a full recognition or legitimisation of a Polish government-in-waiting. These were, after all, early days in planning the post-war settlement, and the Allies believed they would get what they wanted in the end. Moreover, prior even to Bolshevism's ominous arrival by late 1917, the very idea of granting approval to a socialist group was unpalatable and repugnant. Nevertheless, Lucien Wolf believed there were other mechanisms at work. In a memorandum recording an interview he held with Zaleski, Wolf suggested there was a 'very influential Catholic clique' at work in the Foreign Office, which included the leading civil servants Sir William Tyrrell, head of the Political Intelligence Department, and Sir Eric Drummond, the future first Secretary-General of the League of Nations.[59] It had been easy, according to Wolf, for Dmowski and his 'henchmen' to persuade these key officials in favour of his cause. Indeed, Zaleski reported that when a friend of his had interviewed another senior civil servant, Sir George Clerk, on the Jewish question, the reply was: 'If you were a Pole, you would also be an antisemite.'[60]

Despite this evidence (which, in any case, may be apocryphal), it remains difficult to verify that the Foreign Office empathised with

Dmowski's perspectives on the Jewish question. But what is clearly apparent is that those in Britain who opposed the *Endek* leader, who understood entirely the ideology he embraced and how it might be manifest at a day-to-day policy level in Poland, wholly failed in their efforts to undermine him and his party. Serious attempts to sideline Polish National Democracy, to highlight its dangers came all too late. In spite of Dmowski's bombast, arrogance and objectionable ideology, he successfully outwitted all his opponents. And he was, for a time, a legitimate element of British political and intellectual life – whether liberal opinion liked it, or not.

Heralds of change: pogroms

Within less than a year of HMG's approval of the PNC, a new Polish state gradually emerged from the debris of Empires. It began with the instigation of the Polish uprising against German occupation in December 1918 and, in the following year, the international opening of the ratification process at the Paris Peace Conference. Poland's rebirth was, to say the least, painful. On the path to the new republic, whose borders were not finalised until 1923, lay wars with Bolshevik Russia, Lithuania and Ukraine, and a good deal of rancorous negotiation in Paris, especially with regard to Poland's Minority Treaty.[61] Perhaps most worryingly of all, there were a series of brutal and destructive anti-Jewish pogroms in the immediate months following the Great War, though Poland was not alone in this. Swathes of Eastern Europe were subsumed to the force of swirling ethnic hatreds in the immediate aftermath of the Great War and anti-Jewish violence occurred on an alarming and intense basis. In terms of the collective human cost, what took place in this period vastly overshadowed anything that had occurred in the Tsarist Empire before 1914, and there are no agreed figures as to the number of Jews who were wantonly murdered, but it amounted to tens of thousands.[62] Events that acquired the greatest notoriety in the Polish case were those in Kielce (11 November 1918 – on Armistice Day) and Lemberg (22–24 November 1918), which witnessed respectively 4 and 72 murders.[63] Six months later, on 5 April 1919, upon the suspicion of being Bolshevik spies, 25 Jews in Pińsk were executed by firing squad by soldiers from the ragtag Polish army.[64]

From the outset, the pogroms in Poland and elsewhere roused the interest of the West. Jewish agencies in continental Europe, particularly the branch of the Central Zionist Organisation (CZO) in Copenhagen, were instrumental in the swift dissemination of information and appeals

for help.[65] In contrast to the incidents of anti-Jewish violence in Eastern
Europe during the Great War, those that happened in its wake generated
a huge amount of newspaper copy. They also prompted acts of Western
enquiry. The earliest from a British perspective was driven by the CZO
and led by Israel Cohen, a British author, historian, Zionist and recent
German prisoner of war.[66] He arrived in Poland in December 1918, prin-
cipally as a consequence of the imperatives stimulated by the Lemberg
pogrom.[67] Ten months later, in light of the Pińsk pogrom, a British
parliamentary investigation made its way to Poland, headed by the
recently appointed president of the Board of Deputies, Sir Stuart M.
Samuel (brother of Sir Herbert).[68] There were also numerous questions
tabled in both Houses of Parliament.[69] From an American perspective, Henry Morgenthau, ex-ambassador to the Ottoman Empire was
the most prominent investigator, his interest spurred by the American
Jewish Committee.[70] All these enquiries spawned further newspaper
reportage and other first-hand accounts.[71] As might be expected, the
events themselves prompted the convening of indignant meetings and
protests, especially in the United States.[72] Like any other pogrom, those
that were perpetrated in Poland generated their own controversies, not
least as it was even more difficult to fully understand what was occurring in Eastern Europe at this moment, where the national lines were
drawn, who represented what and whether they should elicit external
support or derision.

At the same time, given the Great War's ending and the sudden crash
of Empires, a flurry of new freedoms encouraged a greater urgency in
Britain to investigate the conditions, rivalries and aspirations amongst
the peoples of Eastern Europe. As one MP termed it, the continent was
undergoing an 'upheaval of nations' and, as a consequence, many of
those studying the situation at first-hand were not drawn by what was
or was not happening to Jews, but rather the broader context and how
it might impact upon future European security.[73] Thus, not all commentators who were present in Eastern Europe from late 1918 onwards had
the same agenda as Cohen, Samuel and others. For some observers, the
pogroms were of lesser import than the contemporaneous reinvigoration of the Polish nation, even if the two were undoubtedly related.
This was the case for the *Daily Mail* correspondent, J.M.N. Jeffries. It did
not follow that he did not file copy about the pogroms, but they were
not his priority. Similarly, Mrs Cecil Chesterton (aka J.K. Prothero), special correspondent of the *Daily Express* in Warsaw, made no reference
at all in her rose-tinted copy that described the civil conflict afflicting
Poland.[74]

To be sure, it was undoubtedly difficult to unravel precisely what had taken place in Poland in the latter months of 1918 and throughout 1919. The scale and repetitiveness of the attacks, their variety, ranging from murder to the ransacking of shops, the desecration of synagogues, plunder, rape and the vandalism of Jewish cemeteries, was difficult to comprehend. Geographical matters also played a part in provoking confusion, since Israel Cohen, for example, recorded anti-Jewish pogroms in over 100 Polish towns between November 1918 and January 1919 alone.[75] The questions that were asked of these events were no different to those that had been prompted by the 1881–1882, 1903–1906 and war-time pogroms; how many victims were there and who were the perpetrators? In this instance, however, there was no traditional explanation upon which to fall back; the Tsarist regime, its officials and soldiery were long gone. In the maelstrom of uncertainty in Poland, there appeared to be an authority (at least in some places) that controlled Polish military forces. So, perhaps, a top-down explanation might suffice even in this case? However, the violence sometimes appeared to break out in areas where there was no military control. What reasons could be given in these circumstances? What motivations lay behind these attacks?

Clearly, these were difficult questions to answer and deciphering the truth was hugely problematic, not least as the long-established view of Poland continued to exert influence on the British perspective. In late November 1918, for example, the *New Witness* dismissed the existence of pogroms out of hand and did not hesitate for a moment in asserting that 'throughout her history, Poland has never stained her hands with Jewish blood'.[76] For the same historic reasons, Charles Saroléa, who visited the new state in 1921, confidently remarked that, since the end of the Great War, there had been 'no anti-Jewish pogroms' in Poland.[77] A Pole resident in London sent a letter to *The Times* outlining the same sentiments.[78] And, unsurprisingly, the Polish language émigré press in London, utterly *Endek* in its orientation, similarly denied there were any pogroms, alleging the rumours to have been invented by Jews.[79] 'Pogroms', remarked another pro-*Endek* journal, the *New Poland*, were 'affairs of the Black Ages and utterly alien to the spirit of the new and freedom-loving nation', so, on that basis, they could not have happened.[80] At the other end of the spectrum, a correspondent to the *Daily Express* noted that following the murderous events in Lemberg, the 'whole Polish population [was] delighted', thereby implying that ethnic Poles were intrinsically and universally hostile towards their Jewish neighbours.[81] Nevertheless, the British perspective of the pogroms and Poland's agonising rebirth was not simply divided between those who believed there had or had not been pogroms. The response was much more complex and drew on a confluence of information and propaganda, as well as the influence of individuals such as Cohen, groups like the London-based Polish émigré community and its supporters, alongside international political and diplomatic manoeuvrings.

Cohen's visit to a Central Europe still thick with civil strife and political intrigue might have easily formed the basis of a Joseph Roth story. It took in a large area of territory, as well as an incredible assortment of intellectual and political contacts. These included the Zionist Nahum Sokolow, whom he met in Paris, PPS leader August Zaleski (in Berne), Zionist Dr Max Rosenfeld (in Vienna), Dr Leon Reich, a member of the Polish senate (in Kraków), the Polish Foreign, War and Prime Ministers, Leon Wasilewski, Jan Wroczyński, Ignacy Paderewski and its President, Józef Piłsudski (all, of course, in Warsaw). The scale of his evidence was equally as broad. He took careful steps to gather as much documentary proof as possible, to elicit opinions on the events from a range of local figures, especially Jewish leaders. As a consequence, he met destitute Jews, representatives of Jewish philanthropic organisations and individuals who were, to put it mildly, less than sympathetic to the objectives of his visit. An encounter with a Professor Władysław Nathanson, a baptised Jew, left Cohen exasperated:

> he [Nathanson] said Jews were as much to blame as Poles, because they had dealt dishonestly, and at the first opportunity, resolved to wreak revenge. He pleaded the ignorance Polish peasants, easily egged on to attacks. He argued that Jews had all [civil and political rights]: I instanced several wrongs. He maintained attacks on Jews could be explained by historical conditions, also said Jews were cowards, which I indignantly denied by referring to Jewish cases of heroism in the Great War. [...] Left him rather heated: at last realized how anti-Jewish the converted Jew is.[82]

These comments were made by Cohen in the diary he kept of his Polish journey, which appeared in print some 30 years later. His accounts of the time, published in a series of *Times'* articles and as a pamphlet by the CZO (which was presented to a public meeting at the Queen's Hall, London in April 1919), were less detailed and emotionally charged.[83]

Cohen was particularly focussed in his contemporary analysis on the causes of the pogroms and a number of factors dominated his interpretation. He deemed the withdrawal of Austrian troops from Galicia and the German military occupiers from Congress Poland as crucial to the stirring of Polish emotions. Poles were so overcome by 'securing their long awaited independence' that it 'found expression in an extensive outbreak of anti-Jewish excesses'. Jews were viewed as 'an obstacle to the realisation of their national aspirations', a belief fostered by Roman Dmowski and his party, which had 'disseminated the seeds of antisemitism'. Cohen did not fall back upon earlier pogrom motivations, nevertheless he indicted the Warsaw government for its failure to condemn the violence or compensate its victims. He also noted that some *pogromshchiki* were Polish soldiers, as was the case in Lemberg.[84] On the whole, Cohen's was a judicious, considered report and was not without insight. *The Spectator*, however, could not refrain from asserting that he 'may not have been as dispassionate an inquirer as he represents'.[85] Yet, had the weekly's contributor compared Cohen's account to those of earlier pogroms, which prior to 1905 were considerably less bloody than those of the immediate postwar period, he would have discovered shriller and more passionate precedents. Considering the intensity of events in Poland, the aftermath of which Cohen observed personally, his detachment was actually remarkable.[86] No doubt, of course, this was deliberate; he probably anticipated the very accusations that were levelled at him by *The Spectator*.

Cohen's version of events was not unique in the British narrative. H.N. Brailsford, a Labour MP, was in Poland at approximately the same time and reported his observations to *The Times*.[87] He was similarly adamant that Polish nationalism was to blame, though he adhered to the established pogrom paradigm by claiming it was an 'official policy'. But by this he did not mean that the brutality was orchestrated by ministers in Warsaw; he believed, for instance, that Piłsudski was 'a humane and liberal man'. Instead, the weight of guilt lay with the Polish army, most especially the officer class. Two weeks prior to the Pińsk pogrom, a nameless Polish general said to him: 'What are you to do with a Jewish spy in every house?' Clearly, in Brailsford's view, the general's answer was to kill them and ransack their property, as 'the Poles [had] acted on their suspicions and prejudices.'[88] Akin to Cohen, Brailsford believed that the *Endecja* had had a role in encouraging such sentiments. He noted, for example, that at the elections in 1919, the National Democrats 'scattered the crudest antisemitic leaflets. One of their coloured fly-sheets showed a serpent with a hideous Jewish head sucking the blood of the Polish peasantry.'[89]

Predictably, the *Manchester Guardian*, having opposed the PNC's recognition by the Foreign Office in late 1917, was as shrewd as Brailsford in comprehending the part played by the *Endecja* in promoting popular antisemitism in Poland. Commenting on a contribution by Cohen in the same issue, an editorial reflected on the reasons for the pogroms:

> It is partly an expression of a diseased nationalism which will brook no racial or national difference or variety. It is partly a device of the old Polish oligarchy to counter the new democratic tendencies and divert the demand for social reform. Both reasons help to explain why the pogroms are worst in Galicia. Polish nationalism is at its most Jingo in Galicia, because there the Poles are seeking to trample upon the national rights of two other peoples, the Ruthenians [Rusyns] as well as the Jews, and hope to prevent them claiming their rights by massacre and terrorism. Galicia, again, is a land of great estates, and it is calculated that pogroms may be an effective counter-irritant to Bolshevism.[90]

The *Manchester Guardian* was, as noted elsewhere, greatly sympathetic to the Zionist cause by this time and had even hired Chaim Weizmann as a columnist during the Great War. Thus, it was not surprising that it was less than impressed at the ethnic violence accompanying Poland's recreation.[91] Yet, even in these discerning lines there was a hint at alternative perspectives on the origins of the pogroms.

By this stage, late 1918 and early 1919, Bolshevism was more than a menacing spectre on the distant horizon. Although the Bolsheviks were still embroiled in the Civil War in Russia, as well as a war with Poland, their efforts to promote worldwide proletarian revolution were causing alarm in many quarters. Social and civil unrest throughout the continent and in the United Kingdom was a huge concern for the established political order. In Poland, for instance, there is no doubt that individuals suspected of Bolshevik leanings were dealt with ruthlessly, as was seen during the Pińsk pogrom. And added to these prevailing anxieties was the fear that Jews were intrinsically connected to and perhaps even the operators of Lenin's party. As will be discussed in Chapter 7, this period was greatly taken up with all manner of conspiracy theories about Jews, particularly the accusation that they were Bolshevism's controlling influence. By 1919, for instance, the infamous *Protocols of the Elders of Zion* had acquired international attention and, for a period, the notion of a Judeo-Bolshevik conspiracy gained widespread, not to say, respectable credence.

In the Polish case, British observers had more cause to worry about the advance of Bolshevism than any other on the continent. After all, at the very same time the pogroms were occurring, the Paris Peace Conference was locked in discussion about, alongside innumerable issues, Poland's future borders. And, in fact, the principal reason the 'Big Four' were dedicated to Polish independence was their belief in Poland's ability to act as a buffer state between Germany and Russia. It was hardly surprising, therefore, that anxiety was consequentially bred as to the permeability of Poland's social and political fabric. British interpretations simultaneously emphasised the Polish leadership's disdain for Bolshevism and Paderewski's reductive assertion that the 'Bolshevik idea is to kill all users of the toothbrush' probably fell on fertile ground in the British imagination.[92] These concerns were all manifest in the British analysis of the pogroms, in terms of attributing Bolshevism as both a real and imagined cause.[93] Brailsford, for instance, believed that the Pińsk general he encountered regarded all Jews as Bolsheviks, but the Labour MP refuted all possibility of this being the case. 'The average orthodox long-robed Jew of the Pale [*sic!*]', he said, 'regarded any revolutionary doctrine with horror.'[94] There was a good deal of truth to this assertion, to be sure, since the majority of Polish Jews were conservative in their social and religious outlook and hardly likely to be attracted to Bolshevism, though few other British observers embraced such a fair-minded and reasoned perspective.

Captain Peter E. Wright, who accompanied Sir Stuart Samuel's mission to Poland, was inclined to a different stance. He admitted that, at this moment, anti-Bolshevism was a fundamental component of Polish antisemitism, agreeing with Brailsford that the Polish army looked upon Lenin's movement as an 'entirely Jewish invention and affair', that antisemitism was a 'shield' against Bolshevism's influence. He was not convinced that all Jews were Bolsheviks, but nevertheless believed a mass of Jews were attracted to Bolshevism, not for ideological, but practical and material reasons:

> Bolshevism spells business for poor Jews, innumerable posts in a huge administration; endless regulations, therefore endless jobbery; big risks, for the Bolsheviks punish heavily, every offence treated as a form of treason; but big profits. The rich bourgeois Jew also manages to get on with it in his own way. [...] Many Jews who are by no means poor, try at the present time to escape into Russia, so fine are the business prospects. Such a desirable state of things must naturally have charms for the Jews in Poland, and in spite of repeated and

constant accusations, the Jewish political leaders have never publicly repudiated Bolshevism, from which I conclude that they must have many sympathisers with Bolshevism among their followers.[95]

It difficult to know where to begin with these words, since the notion that a mass of Polish Jews were actually attempting to gain entry into war-torn Bolshevik Russia in order to make money, is, to say the very least, bewildering. Given the pogroms in the Ukraine, the famine in the Russian interior, the Red Terror, as well as the widespread social disintegration and dislocation prompted by Civil War and Revolution, the historical record indicates a demographic movement in opposite directions.[96] Wright's response, therefore, though not unsympathetic towards the Jewish plight, was clouded by two significant stereotypes – the rich Jew and the poor Jew. Indeed, other aspects of his report stressed the overwhelming economic role played by the Jews of Poland and how, in turn, it inspired Polish animosity.[97]

The accusation that practically all Jews were Bolsheviks found the greatest adherence and exposition amongst overtly pro-Polish circles in Britain. In May 1919, J.H. Harley began a publication, the *New Poland*, that was unrestrained in revealing its political allegiances. Harley eulogised, for instance, on the reborn state: 'A new Poland, which all those who love the Polish people believe to be worthy of the most glorious traditions of the past, is quickly rising like that Phœnix which has ever been her emblem in the days of dismemberment and oppression.' Nevertheless, he also detected a series of threats faced by Poland, including the 'gaunt, ugly spectre of famine and want', frontier issues and the 'threatening chaos of hard and materialistic Bolshevism'.[98] It was, however, an external 'danger', which was trying to 'penetrate into Poland by means of German, Russian and Jewish agents'.[99] In other words, Bolshevism was not a 'natural' component of the Polish political landscape and its appearance was rejected wholesale by 'true' Poles. Indeed, for the most part Harley dismissed the 'rumours of pretended Jewish massacres' and where clashes had occurred, they were viewed a consequence of 'hostile demonstrations on the part of the Jews, usually carried out under the banner of the Bolsheviks'.[100]

The supposed connection between Jews and Bolshevism was not the only conspiratorial link in the British perspective on the pogroms in Poland. *The Spectator*, for instance, more than hinted at an ancient anti-Jewish stereotype by asserting that 'Poles have suffered at the hands of clever Jewish financiers,' hence their enmity.[101] For the *New Witness*, another mysterious force was at work – German–Jewish news agencies, which had apparently exaggerated the violence.[102] An identical trope was found in *The Times*.[103] And in the same newspaper, one of its East European correspondents, possibly Robert Wilton, garnered a whole set of conspiratorial perspectives:

> Hostility to Jews in Poland is comparable to the feeling aroused in London for a certain time by the behaviour of the low London East-End Jewish population during the Zeppelin raids. It has been aggravated to its present extent during the war for a number of reasons: – First, by the part which the Jews played in the Bolshevist revolution and terrorism in Russia; secondly, by the role of the Jews during the German occupation. In the requisitioning from the Polish population by the Germans and Austrians, Jews were always the agents; Jews thus became the instruments of the hated German extortions. A third reason is the profiteering begun during the war and continued now by the middlemen. Often use was made by the Jews of their position as Government agents to requisition more than the Germans required, and then retail the balance at extortionate prices. Finally, a small percentage of Jews either in the original Polish legions or in the later volunteer regiments has been made and additional reproach to the Jewish race.

This observer did not believe that there had been many pogroms in Poland, certainly not in terms of those that had precipitated Jewish deaths. Nevertheless, alongside the 'reasons' outlined above, this correspondent, like so many others, indicted the National Democratic Party for the 'spirit of [anti-Jewish] odium' that it had 'fostered in the lower class of the Polish population'.[104] Thus, although there were suggestions of innate Polish feelings directed against Jews in these sentiments, they were also encouraged by a guiding, destructive and determined force.

Regardless of the number of pogroms and victims, the events themselves generally provoked disdain in many British quarters. After all, they were hardly a source of comfort in such trying times and did not spell out much optimism for the future internal relations of a new state of which so much was internationally expected. *The Spectator*, for example, suggested that its aspirations had been somewhat dashed by the pogroms, since for many decades Poland 'stood for us as the archetype of the oppressed and despoiled nation, and her emancipation was one of the most glorious achievements of the Great War, and one of our greatest rewards for the sacrifices we ourselves made in it'. *The Spectator* hoped, therefore, that the pogroms were simply an aberration, that 'this time of passion, of violent revulsion from suppression to oppression, may quickly pass and leave [Poland] with a clearer vision.'[105] Perhaps, it wondered, the pattern of violence that had marred Poland's rebirth was merely a painful symptom of the fracturing of Empires, rather than a product of the Polish political landscape? The answer to this question was soon to be realised, as concerns about the Jewish question and Polish politics continued to be addressed throughout the subsequent decades of Poland's independence.

Poland reborn: good or bad for the Jews?

Historians have encountered many theoretical and interpretative difficulties in analysing the Jewish experience in the Second Polish Republic (1918–1939). For some, it has been impossible to consider the 20 years prior to the outbreak of the Second World War without reference to the Holocaust. As a consequence, the (dis)advantages wrought by hindsight have led one historian to characterise Jewish society of the Polish interbellum as living on the 'edge of destruction', which chimed with a literary response to the period by Isaac Bashevis Singer.[106] His panoramic account of interwar Warsaw Jewry, *The Family Moskat*, concluded with the apparently prophetic, grim sentence: 'Death is the Messiah. That's the real truth.'[107] Yet, other interpretations have attempted to drive a middle path through the controversies and martyrology of the 1920s and 1930s. Twenty-five years ago, for instance, historian Ezra Mendelsohn asked whether interwar Poland was 'good or bad for the Jews?'[108] This was by no means a trite question, since the 1920s, in particular, witnessed a great flowering of Jewish secular culture in Poland, as well as the consolidation and exercise of a conspicuous role in the Polish political system. Nevertheless, from the early 1930s, by which time a series of anti-Jewish laws were about to be implemented, Jews were left with few choices as to their place in Poland.[109] Mendelsohn ultimately concluded, therefore, that interwar Poland was good and bad for its Jews, or, as he paraphrased, it was both the best and the worst of times.

What relevance do these historiographical differences have for British observers of Poland's Jewish question in the early 1920s? To be sure, the parallels between historiography and contemporary examinations are not exact. Yet, aspects of the British interpretation were similarly informed by the Jewish–Polish experience of a different time, which was not a martyred past, but rather an apparently positive pattern of Jewish–gentile relations over several hundred years. As a consequence, much was expected of the new Poland and British observers in the 1920s found it difficult to move away from the idealised, long-established appreciation of Poland's 'model' of religious tolerance. Yet, as we have already seen, this perspective was immediately challenged as the early steps towards independence were marred by pogroms, a situation that gave little cause for British optimism, notwithstanding the ratification of the Polish Minority Treaty, in which Lucien Wolf had played a not inconsiderable role.[110] After these events had been played out, when time had becalmed the waves of inter-ethnic violence, did British observers take a fresh look at Poland and its Jewish question? Was the Jewish experience in the early years of the Second Polish Republic viewed in an optimistic or pessimistic light?

To be sure, it took many years for the clouds of confusion to clear and for the new republic to finally emerge. But, even before many European conflicts had ceased, British observers were keen to see how Poland had altered in the years since the First World War and, unlike the divided state that had borne many indignities in the nineteenth century, it was now a visible presence on the map of Europe. Yet, despite the reconfiguration of Poland's geopolitical boundaries, British observers undoubtedly remained dogged by earlier assumptions. In particular, basic demography was still an issue, notwithstanding the absence of the Pale of Settlement. Most, for instance, were inclined to exaggerate the number of Polish Jews, both before and after the final settling of the Poland's borders with Ukraine, Czechoslovakia, Lithuania and Weimar Germany.[111] In 1919, *The Times* estimated the total at 5 millions, as did Charles Saroléa 2 years later.[112] In the view of H.N. Brailsford the figure stood at more realistic 3 millions, whilst A. Bruce Boswell, a lecturer in Polish studies at the University of Liverpool, argued that Poland contained half the world's Jewry, which would have amounted to somewhere in the region of 6 millions.[113]

Clearly, these statistics bore significance beyond demography and were often utilised to highlight the apparent Jewish preponderance in Poland, as well as the consequences this might render in the future. For Saroléa, there was simply 'too much Jewish salt in the Polish dish. There is no room in the new Poland for such a vast population and that population can only be assimilated by a slow and painful process.'[114] In a similar vein, *The Times* noted that the 'percentage of [Jewish] aliens [was] far higher than any people can digest.'[115] In reality, according to the 1921 Polish census, Jews represented approximately 10 per cent of the total population, which amounted to around 2.8 million people.[116] They lived, however, predominantly in Poland's urban centres, which naturally drew the particular attention of British observers, who were more inclined to visit Warsaw, Łódź and Kraków than they were Polish countryside.[117] As a result, the manner in which evidence was gathered led to a inevitable skewing of the facts, often to a specific end.

This was not a hopeful beginning. Naturally, the starting point for these perspectives did not exactly brim with optimism nor insight. For commentators who thought Poland basically had too many Jews, there was bound to be trouble in the future. This perspective was not aided by the fact that from the outset British analyses of the new Poland emphasised both the ethnic and the religious in matters of national identity. Fundamentally, to be Polish meant also to be Christian. The author and feminist Margaret Pember-Devereux, who wrote under the pseudonym Roy Devereux, visited Poland in 1921 and observed that the adjective 'Christian must be interpreted in the sense of *not* Jewish' (italics in original).[118] H.N. Brailsford indicated that 'the traditional association of Polish nationality with the Catholic religion [made] the barrier against the Jews so difficult to lower.'[119] By the same token, at this stage most British commentators understood Jews to be racially different and, for some, collectively they were even a nation. In the Polish context, the resonance of these distinctions bore considerable consequences. Even before the Minority Treaty was signed, for example, *The Times*, warned that there were imminent problems on the horizon, highlighting, in particular, Zionist claims to the maintenance of Jews as a 'separate nationality' in Poland.[120]

The supposed separateness of the Jews in Poland was a huge issue in the British narrative and it was not merely manifest in the social and religious arena. Building on pre-existing allusions that formed a component of war-time discourse, Sarolea went as far as describing Polish Jewry as a 'formidable internal enemy'. Indeed, it was a foe more dangerous to the integrity of the state than even the external enemies of Germany or Russia.[121] And although Brailsford was generally sympathetically disposed towards Polish Jews, he still believed that the 'root of the evil [was] the excessive isolation of this essentially foreign racial element.'[122] The separation, the isolation of Polish Jews was marked in a number of ways. Inevitably, much was made of the degree to which Jews dominated Poland commercially, a situation that was to the detriment of the Polish peasantry.[123] For Boswell, this emphasised the necessity of the *Endek*-inspired boycott, which he deemed an attempt to 'free the peasant from Jewish exploitation', or an act of 'self-defence'.[124] Yet, in spite of the best efforts of Polish nationalists, little had seemingly altered in the pattern of Jewish–gentile relations since the nineteenth century, and Poland remained in hock to the Jewish money-lender.

But the alleged Jewish economic domination of Poland was not the only mark of separation between Jews from gentiles. Much was made, for instance, of the visible differences between the two. Like Hall Caine in the 1890s, commentators of the early 1920s were greatly drawn to the visual otherness of Polish Jewry. Sometimes, the response towards this kind of separateness was simply fascination, as it had been with Hall Caine, but other observers could barely conceal their repugnance at that which they considered a self-imposed distinctiveness. Devereux referred, for example, to the 'greasy curls' worn by Orthodox Jewish men. In Brailsford's view, the 'outer garb' of Polish Jews, simultaneously concealed and highlighted 'a personality which is as little Polish as the dress in European, the average Orthodox Jew [...] has grown up in a world which nowhere touches that of his Polish neighbour.'[125]

Two factors worsened this situation. Firstly, Polish Jews appeared incapable of undertaking even the most basic precautions in matters of hygiene. The filth, stench and overwhelming poverty Beatrice Baskerville had encountered in the Warsaw of the early twentieth century was not altered by the early 1920s. This was true even of the materially wealthy Jewish classes as their 'brilliant and gaudy trappings scarcely cover[ed] the meanness and dirt of the surroundings' in which they lived.[126] As for the poor:

> a visit to the Ghettoes of Warsaw and Lublin reveal conditions of filth and squalor which are undoubtedly dangerous to the health of the Christian population. No legal barrier, of course, exists to keep the Jews in the congeries of mean and evil-smelling streets which begin round the corner of a main thoroughfare and extend for miles. They herd together instinctively and, incited by their Nationalist leaders, resent any attempt on the part of the Polish sanitary authorities to enforce the most elementary precautions against the spread of disease.[127]

Mrs Roy Devereux, who travelled widely in the early 1920s, chose, like her predecessor, to stress, in uncompromising terminology, the harsh poverty that was undoubtedly a common feature of Polish-Jewish life.[128] Yet, as in the previous century, Polish Jews were still herding together and their environs remained harbingers of disease. This time, however, the anxious search was not for cholera, as it had been with Hall Caine, but typhus. Although Devereux did not believe that Jews were 'the carriers of these infections', they nevertheless moved about Poland 'in an indescribable condition of rags and dirt, and disappear[ed] into the dark and noisome corners of the town Ghettoes which thus become potential breeding grounds for every malady'.[129] In other words, the unsanitary conditions in which Jews dwelt encouraged the disease's proliferation. Again, whilst there is no doubt that poor sanitation and overcrowding plays a part in the development of typhus, in the post-war world it was a threat to all Polish society, not just Jews. Here, of course, is the point; Devereux did not link Polish gentiles to dirt, disease or squalor – only Jews.[130] Saroléa embraced this perspective, too, in his assertion that Polish Jews were 'prey to loathsome forms of skin disease'.[131] Again, there was no corrective or comparative reference to Polish gentiles in his analysis.

The second factor that exacerbated the otherness of Polish Jewry was language, which, in a multi-ethnic state like interwar Poland, was a crucial component of the national question. It prompted a fair amount of wrangling at Paris and, indeed, although Jews were permitted state-funded primary schools whose language of instruction was Yiddish, there was no provision to guarantee its equal status with Polish. This was, inevitably, a source of friction throughout the lifetime of the Second Republic. Whether moved by the limitations of the Minority Treaty, or not, British observers were less than sympathetic towards Jewish linguistic claims, not least because the established assumptions about Yiddish obscured the true picture. Charles Saroléa, for instance, more than hinted at the conspiratorial. Repeating the claims he had made during the Great War, that Yiddish was a 'German dialect', he further commented: 'lest a Christian might know what it is they are writing, they camouflage their German writing in the disguise of Hebrew characters.' To be frank, as an accomplished linguist himself (he claimed knowledge of 18 languages and was a fluent speaker of at least 3), Saroléa should have known better. To equate the use of Hebrew orthography with an act of deliberate concealment was, at best, bizarre and at worst, an insidious falsehood. But it was all in keeping with Saroléa's damning perspective on the Jewish place in Poland, as he argued that its government was 'anxious that all the barriers between Jew and Pole should be removed. But the Jew does not want to become a Pole, he prefers to remain a Jew.'[132] He expressed similar views in an article in *The Scotsman*, which was then comprehensively rebuffed by a letter from Dr Salis Daiches, Scotland's leading rabbi.[133]

Already, by the time Saroléa had penned these words, there was every indication that the Polish government's attitude towards its Jewish population was to the contrary. The discordant Polish noises at the Paris Peace Conference, combined with domestic events, indicated that Poland was not quite prepared to prevent the erection of barriers between Jews and gentiles. The Compulsory Sunday Rest Law, for example, introduced in 1924, meant that Jews were legally obliged to close their shops and businesses on the Christian Sabbath. And, a year earlier, there was an effort to institute a *numerus clausus* in Polish universities.[134] All this was accompanied by a barrage of anti-Jewish propaganda from the National Democrats, who, as part of a coalition government in the early 1920s, maintained a visible and vociferous presence in Polish politics throughout the interwar period.[135] Their most oft-repeated claims were that Jews were separatists, economic opportunists, wholly incapable of national loyalty and were not, in fact, Polish. They found a receptive audience in the Second Republic. Fundamentally, for the *Endecja*, and their constituency, Jews were an unsettling presence in Poland, they were 'disruptive', 'discordant' and 'dangerous'. These were the kind of adjectives utilised by the *Endeks*, but in these instances they were actually allusions found in the British narrative.[136] And, like the National Democrats, British observers were not referring to specific Jewish organisations and political parties, some of whom were undoubtedly a source of opposition and discordance in Poland; they meant all Jews, regardless of their religious or political affiliations.

In response to these recurrent threats to Poland's Jews, the attention of Western Jewish agencies and the League of Nations, or at least its Minorities' Section, was constantly roused throughout the interwar period. In 1925, Lucien Wolf, representing the Minorities' Section, visited Warsaw, where he struck a bargain for Jewish rights in exchange for foreign loans.[137] In his report put before the AJA, Wolf expressed a belief that the Jewish question in Poland was 'not a political problem, but a psychological problem'. Whilst old, inherited enmities continued to wreak havoc on Jewish lives, he said, given that Poland's constitution was 'one of the most liberal' there was reason, in public at any rate, for cautious optimism.[138] Of course, since Wolf was one of the architects of Poland's Minority Treaty, he evidently had a greater urgency to express publicly his faith in this internationally guaranteed protective structure.

In general, however, even in the early 1920s there was scant optimism to be found amongst British circles for the hope of easy Jewish–gentile relations in the new Poland.[139] The pogroms, the disputations about minority rights and the apparent social and cultural chasm which separated Jew from gentile, gave cause for few to imagine that Poland would be anything other than bedevilled by irresolvable ethnic division and antagonism. Yet, this did not necessarily give British observers any cause to feel pessimistic about Poland's future. In the early 1920s, it evidently experienced teething troubles, but surely this was inevitable after many years of foreign rule and oppression. In 1919, for instance, *The Spectator* summed up the universal British response that was to stand for the remainder of the interwar period: 'apart from the Jewish question, the outlook for the free and united Poland seems most promising.'[140] British observers imagined, therefore, that the Jewish question was merely a troubling side-show, when in fact, as a facet of a myriad of inter-ethnic rivalries, it lay at the core of the Second Republic's chronic instability. Without workable solutions, accepted by all parties, the future was sure to be not only bad for Jews, but bad for Poland, too.

7
Who were the Jews? *Ostjuden* in the British Mindset, 1867–1925

Stock exchange lyric: 'They all Jew it.'

Funny Folks, July 1877

I know that the farmers did not mind being jewed over their hay so long as they knew that others were being jewed over it too.

Sir Francis Acland, House of Commons, 1919

The Russian immigrant must be taken by the hand. His civilisation is not his affair, but the community's, which desires as much for its own sake as for his to improve his condition.

Jewish Chronicle, May 1885

The qualities of 'the Jew': West to East (and back?)

It goes without saying that throughout late nineteenth- and early twentieth-century continental Europe, the image of 'the Jew' was the focus of a host of social, political and economic anxieties. Jewish difference and otherness, imagined or real, precipitated concern, self-reflection and self-deflection and, most crucially, was central in many parts of the continent to the ever-shifting national idea. In relation to Imperial Germany, for instance, historians have established the significance of cultural antisemitism during the *Gründerjahren*, when it functioned as a code via which one might express a sense of national belonging.[1] In Austria-Hungary, where political antisemitism occupied a respectable niche, the manifold ethnic divisions within this complex Empire found expression in a variety of rivalries and animosities. Poles and Czechs, for instance, were not exempt from stereotyping and derision, yet in all parts of the Habsburg lands, many fell upon 'the

Jew' in order to explicate an assortment of problems.[2] Similar uncertainties troubled the perennially unsteady French Third Republic, most emphatically symbolised by the Dreyfus affair, at the heart of which lay spy-mania and concerns about the status of French masculinity.[3]

In each of these states, racialist theories found widespread adherence and the manner in which the image of 'the Jew' was configured described a series of 'fixed', essentially hereditary characteristics, which ranged from avariciousness, sexual predation and cowardliness to disloyalty, moral unreliability and the inability to embrace patriotic causes. Jews, it was argued, were not part of the nation and could not assimilate, despite their best efforts. The changing of names, abandonment of religious markers, such as *yarmulkes*, or even conversion to Christianity were not, by any means, a guarantee that 'the Jew' could be absorbed into society. On the contrary, for some these were merely sinister indications of a mysterious hand at work.

In Western Europe, the imprint of Jewish otherness, or perhaps even of Jewishness itself, found its most obvious representation in the *Ostjude*, the East European Jew. Compared to Britain and the United States, fewer East European Jews sought new lives in Germany and France, yet the arrival of *Ostjuden* to these lands, even if their sojourn was only temporary, breathed an assortment of new fears into their respective Jewish questions.[4] Observers imagined an immigrant that was impoverished, diseased, rag-swathed and insect-infested, with a singular calling to make money, who represented an entirely destabilising, dangerous, not to say, terrifying influence for mainstream German and French society.[5] Surely, it was wondered, these people could never be assimilated, let alone be German or French? Indeed, a cartoon in Édouard Drumont's antisemitic weekly, *La libre parole*, pictured a hard-working French *citoyen* in confrontation with a Jewish immigrant, who carries a 'certificate of naturalisation'. Pointing to the Jew's nose, Jacques remarks: 'But it is that hook which can never be naturalised.'[6] In other words, 'the Jew', the paradigmatic other, could never be anything but a Jew, a religious and racial outcast. These precise allusions were also readily found in the Habsburg Empire, which had its own population of *Ostjuden* in Galicia, many of whom migrated to Vienna during the period in question.[7]

Where did Britain fit into the pattern of things? To be sure, political antisemitism failed to make an appearance in the nineteenth century, only finally stuttering onto the scene in the 1920s, and even then, until the advent of Oswald Mosley, it was confined to a peripheral element.[8] Yet, racialist discourse was certainly deeply embedded in

British imaginings of 'the Jew'. As historians have indicated, in previous centuries the British had enthused about the racial admixture of their origins, but by the 1870s many commentators, as well as popular opinion, began to be concerned about the apparent 'physical degeneration' of the peoples of the British isles.[9] Responding to developments on the continent and, in particular, the forging of the nation-state, where, or so it appeared, the hallmark of nationhood was racial homogeneity, the question of who was or was not British advanced up the cultural and social agenda. In the mid-nineteenth century, similar kinds of internalised anxieties had looked towards the Irish as the agent of all that was 'foreign', un-British and unassimilable.[10] However, with the increasing visibility, literally and figuratively, of the 'alien Jew' by the 1880s, the focus of racialised discourse switched emphasis (though the Irish stereotype did not, by any means, disappear). Nevertheless, it would be folly to argue that the arrival of *Ostjuden* solely informed British prejudices on the Jewish question. Indeed, a survey of the manner in which Jewry was generally depicted in the narrative reveals that an array of negative attributes were strongly associated with 'the Jew'.

As Deborah Cohen has indicated, in common with continental developments, for British observers the most troubling aspect of Jewry, domestic or otherwise, was its adaptability. The scars of the ghetto, in the British context, were invisible and, outwith religious leaders, even the most observant Jews no longer sported signifiers of faith (apart from immigrant Jews, of course). Moreover, as was discovered during the First World War, Jews often Anglicised their surnames, so that a Meyer might become a Merrick.[11] Consequently, given this apparently chameleon-like ability to adjust one's characteristics according to the background in which one dwelt, observers sought other ways to identify 'the Jew'. Naturally, racialised discourse was essential to the process of spotting and separating Jews from the rest of the populace. So, how was this done? What ineffaceable racial traits did 'the Jew' possess in the British narrative?

In the first place, physical characteristics were crucial to the British stereotype of 'the Jew'.[12] This aspect found its most obvious rendering in cartoons that appeared in weekly journals, which visualised, though in caricatured and, therefore, deliberately exaggerated form, the corporal attributes that enabled observers to identify even the most assimilated Jew. Inevitably, the 'Jewish nose' played a fundamental role here. A series of cartoons, for instance, appeared in the populist *Funny Folks* ('the comic companion to the newspaper') throughout 1891 and 1892. They narrated the trials and tribulations of the family Onckelstein, which responded in a typically 'Jewish' fashion to various matters. These incidents were as diverse as the stymieing of money-making caused by bad weather, a stranded Mr Onckelstein in the waters of a frozen skating pond offering his rescuers five shillings ('less five per cent discount for cash'), and his encouragement of a general strike amongst the pawnbroking community. 'Everyone goes on strike – the omnibus man, the laundress', he observes, so 'pledge me your words to strike also – for longer hours, ninety per cent [interest] and no flat irons.'[13] In all these images, the Jewish nose was a prominent feature and oftentimes a central component of the joke. But in other cartoons, all apparently by the same artist, the presence of the Jewish nose was merely a given that required no further elaboration – not least, as it was hardly a newly discovered attribute.[14] A sketch from August 1891, for example, showed a group of small boys tormenting Onckelstein outside his pawnbroker's shop. There are just two parts of 'Mr O' visible in this image; his lower arm, which wields a bundle of sticks in order to thrash his tormentors, and his nose, poking out from around the door.[15] Yet, it is evident in another image, from May 1891, that whilst the pronounced nose of all Onckelstein family members was intrinsic to notions of Jewishness, it required no direct reference in the accompanying text.[16]

The racialised image of 'the Jew' in these cartoons extended beyond the condition of the proboscis. For instance, in image 4, the supposed heredity of Jewishness is evident in the fact that the children, twin boys, are exact replicas of their parents. All family members share not only the same nose but also dark, frizzy hair and well-defined, matching eyebrows. Additionally, despite their assimilated attire – significantly, there are no religious markers in any of these cartoons – the shared Jewishness of the wife and her husband appears in the form of ostentatious diamond rings, earrings and cuff-links. Another cartoon (image 5) shows the family gathered about their Christmas tree, which symbolically reaffirmed their attempts at acculturation. However, they unwittingly let slip their identity – and, therefore, their utter failure to understand various, apparently native cultural symbols – by decorating the tree with jewellery and watches, a decision, Onckelstein remarks, designed to 'improve the children's minds as early as' possible.[17] Moreover, in all these cartoons perhaps the most singularly 'Jewish' attribute was Onckelstein's profession as a pawnbroker and money-lender. Indeed, his surname was a pun on the word 'uncle', deliberately Germanised (*onkel*), a slang term for pawnbroker, which hinted, therefore, at a hereditary professional calling.

In the years these cartoons appeared the Russian Jewish question occupied a regularly prominent place in the British narrative. This was, of course, a consequence of the expulsions in the Tsarist Empire, but also

Image 4 'Jew-rusa-lamb!', *Funny Folks*, October 1891

the widespread fear that a flood of immigrants might suddenly swamp the United Kingdom, bringing untold domestic hardship and instability in its wake. So, were the Onckelsteins *Ostjuden*? The answer is not directly apparent. An indication is potentially indicated by Onckelstein's manner of speaking, illustrated as a pronounced, supposedly Yiddish accent.[18] This featured in every cartoon, including one in which the family complete their census returns (there was a national census in 1891), for which the caption ran:

> I tell's you vat, Mrs O., ve don't want eferypody to know we are foreigners, so I puts you, 'Rachael Rebecca Leah Onckelstein' down *Scotch*; der eldest tvin, 'Israel Solomon Isaac Onckelstein', I puts him down *Velsh*; die youngest, 'Myer Lazarus Moses Onckelstein', I puts down *English*; undt myself, 'Sholomon Elisha Shayoop Levi Onckelstein', I puts down *Irish*. So there can't be no chealousy anyvere.[19]

However, like the Jewish nose, the questionable diction of Jews was long-established in the British narrative; even Charles Dickens's original

A HAPPY NEW ERA.

Onckelstein: " There, ma tear ! No nonsense apout Ghristmas-trees for my family—no stupid toys, undt such trash. I hangs up jewellery undt watches—good goods. My motto is—Improve the shildren's minds so early as you can."

Image 5 'A happy new era', *Funny Folks*, January 1891

rendering of Fagin (1837–1839) possessed a curious, nasally, if unaccented, mode of speaking, though this characteristic, along with his apparently Jewish manner of gesture and the like, was excised by the author in later editions of *Oliver Twist*.[20] In this context, therefore, the Yiddish-inflected/afflicted English of the family Onckelstein was not necessarily a sure sign that they were *Ostjuden*. No, they were simply Jews that were easily categorised as mammon-driven foreigners, with a strange physiognomy, who possessed despicable and immutable personal traits. Even when they tried to 'fit in', it met with miserable failure as they just did not understand what it meant to be English/British, as further evidenced by their foolishness over the census.

In light of the visual evidence outlined above, it is by no means directly apparent as to whether, in the British narrative, the East European Jew possessed any specific and unique idiosyncrasies. Even though, there were, at the time these cartoons appeared, significant events taking shape in the Tsarist Empire that carried resonance for the British context, they were not overtly or immediately referenced. To what extent, therefore, did the British narrative embrace an image of the Russian, Polish or Romanian Jew that was, as it were, distinctly Eastern? If such a rendering was present, what influences did it draw upon? In this context, it is important to consider the degree to which the British analysis of the East European Jew burgeoned in response to an externally articulated discourse in Eastern Europe and the resonance this carried for the domestic situation. In other words, how did the manner in which *Ostjuden* were depicted function as a kind of cultural exchange between East and West?

Economic crimes: money-lending and tavern-keeping

The nineteenth century witnessed a considerable social and economic transformation in circumstances for the Jews of Eastern Europe. In Tsarist Russia, in particular, during the latter half of the century there was an extensive change in fortunes, mostly wrought by the consequences of the Emancipation of the Serfs in 1861, which altered forever the economic bonds between Jews and their neighbours. Most especially, employment opportunities for Jews diminished in fields of work that had once, in the serf-dominated economy, been their preserve and a mass of unskilled and semi-skilled labourers subsequently overstocked the market. The peddler or petty trader, for instance, who had been a familiar individual in the first half of the century, more or less disappeared. Instead, Jews now vied with gentiles for the same employment opportunities. Yet, some roles retained a Jewish flavour, particularly tavern- and shop-keeping, and, to be sure, middleman activities remained an important link between the peasant, his produce, the town/city and the merchant.[21] There were, as was noted in Chapter 2, some 'success stories' in the latter decades of the century, as the Poliakovs and Gintsburgs carved out a profitable niche in the new Russian capitalism. Yet, the majority of Russian Jews were not beneficiaries of the post-emancipation economy. For them life was tough and, as was the case for all members of the lower social orders throughout Europe, they battled daily in the face of poverty and its accompanying hardships.

Notwithstanding the reality and harshness of everyday life for the Jews of the Russian Empire, in the official mindset and conservative elements of the Tsarist press, 'the Jew' was regarded as the calculating oppressor of the peasantry. For this reason, in the period following Tsar Alexander II's Great Reforms, Russian Judeophobia emphasised the economic aspect of the Jewish presence in the Empire. The various pieces of legislation enacted by the Tsarist regime, such as the 1882 May Laws, were intended as a corrective to the alleged exploitative qualities of 'the Jew' and focussed particularly on his alleged triangular relationship with the peasant and noble. Similar efforts were made in the Romanian context, since it, too, was economically reliant on a large peasant class. Even though, as in Tsarist Russia, the Romanian economy actually depended not only upon those who could grow produce but also upon those who could sell it, the government attempted to circumscribe Jewish activities in a variety of professions throughout the period under investigation.

To what extent were these notions, both real and imagined, manifest in the British narrative of East European Jewish life? How much emphasis was placed on the economic dimension that was so significant in the Eastern context? To be sure, some commentators wholly appreciated the 'state of destitution' under which the Eastern European Jew laboured and his overwhelming material poverty sometimes provoked a sympathetic response.[22] E.J. Dillon, for instance, graphically depicted a visit he made to the Pale of Settlement in the late 1880s, though, in light of other contemporary concerns, it might just have easily been the East End of London:

> I have visited some [Jews] in the Pale and shall never forget the sights I beheld; narrow coffins called rooms, reeking with filth, in which living and dying have a bitter foretaste of the equality of death; [...] they begin their daily work in the den that is a bedroom, sitting-room, dining room, workshop and temporary coffin. This, in euphemistic phraseology, is the record of the lives of many of the best Jews of the Pale.[23]

The same view was taken by Harold Frederic, London correspondent of the *New York Times*, who noted that 'the most grinding poverty has always reigned' in the Pale, as did Arnold White.[24] He summarised the day-to-day struggle in simple, humanitarian terms: 'So far as my observations go, the Russian Jew and his children have not enough to eat.'[25] In fact, White often highlighted the impoverishment of immigrant Jews in his anti-alienist polemic, best represented by his use of the synonymous term 'foreign paupers', though it was not kindly intended.[26] All these views bore more than passing resemblance, of course, to the observations of Hall Caine and Evans-Gordon in their visits to Poland.

Inevitably, however, poverty's ubiquity in the Pale reaffirmed its existence as a ghetto, an exclusively Jewish area. Indeed, this notion was often overstated to include all the Jews of Eastern Europe, as Israel Cohen indicated in a book published in 1914. He described Jews beyond Germany and Austria as living in an 'Eastern Ghetto', where their 'homogeneity and poverty' made them easily distinguishable from West European Jewry. However, given Cohen's Zionist proclivities, it comes as no surprise to learn that, for him, the Jewish way of life in Russia, divided Poland and Romania, had 'all the intensity and distinctiveness of the life of an independent nation'.[27] By subverting the negative associations of 'the ghetto', Cohen, like many of his Zionist contemporaries, argued that the historical conditions of Eastern Europe laid the foundations for a truly national, Jewish life, as the bonds of slavery had unwittingly forged cohesiveness and homogeneity amongst Eastern European Jewry.

Cohen attempted to make a positive out of a negative. In a similar vein, the exact expression, 'Eastern ghetto', was utilised by the reporter G.F. Abbott in a perspicacious article for the *Fortnightly Review*. Having corresponded with the CZA leader Max Nordau, Abbott was convinced that the solution to the Eastern European Jewish question lay in the establishment of a Jewish state.[28] But the majority of British commentators were not so impressed by Jewry's 'distinctiveness' in Eastern Europe and, for them, the precise qualities outlined by Cohen, homogeneity and the collective yoke of poverty, actually made for a society that was exclusive, tribal and separate. This uniqueness was emphasised, not created, by religious practice, linguistic differences or particular professional avenues. Eastern Europe's Jews were, according to *The Spectator*, 'a separate nation, and accentuate their separateness by difference of food and of the weekly day of rest, sometimes of dress, but chiefly by refusing to intermarry outside their own race.'[29] These sentiments obviously reiterated the role played by racialised dogma in the British worldview; dietary laws and the like were simply symbols, and racial exclusivity was the real characteristic that lay at the heart of Jewish difference. Another commentator, however, believed it was the 'economic factor [which] must inevitably have its place in estimating the aloofness of the Jew'.[30] Akin to Eastern Europe, this was certainly an overriding component of the British narrative.

In the professional roles assigned to Jews in Eastern Europe, money-lending was inevitably placed at the very apex of British assessments. Given the long-standing, even ancient, presence of this trope in the

British imagination – one need only mention Shakespeare's Shylock and, an updated nineteenth-century representation, Anthony Trollope's Augustus Melmotte – it was hardly surprising that many observers reached for it when attempting an explication of the Jewish economic function in the East. It appeared, in fact, an instinctive assumption to make, particularly, as we shall see, for those making their judgements from afar. Nevertheless, as Harold Frederic indicated, it was an allusion that possessed widespread currency in Imperial Russia, too:

> one continually hears of the Jewish usurer. To believe the average Russian's talk, all the money-lending in that whole great empire of debtors is done by the Jews. [...] this is a wild nonsense. The rich Jewish usurers in Russia can be counted on one's fingers. But the significant thing is that these big-money lenders [...] have always been hand in glove with the Russian authorities.[31]

Frederick's assessment was incisive and revealed the economic anxieties that occupied the thoughts of conservative elements of the Tsarist Empire's political classes. Yet, like their Russian counterparts, British commentators did not imagine Jewish money-lenders in Eastern Europe to be an all-powerful Rothschild-like character, controlling a financially intricate behemoth. It was for this reason that the leading figures of Russian Jewry, such as the Poliakovs or Gintsburgs, seldom appeared in the British narrative. Rather, there was more concern with money-lending at a localised, village level, particularly the alleged tens of thousands of Jews for whom money-lending was a vocation, who held the peasantry in a constant condition of economic blackmail.

For example, in 1881, in the wake of the pogroms, it was reported that 'half the peasantry' in Russia was in debt to Jews.[32] Two years later, *The Times* claimed that 'most of the rural communes' were obligated to Jewish money-lenders, as were individual peasants as an 'invariable rule'.[33] *The Spectator* went even further: 'the very labour of the peasantry is mortgaged to Jewish money-lenders.'[34] These were exaggerations touching on fantasy, and the extent of this imagined realm stretched to include Russian landowners, who were alleged to have succumbed to the power of 'money-lenders of the SHYLOCK type' (capitals in original).[35] A generation later, Beatrice Baskerville noted that 'every Jew in Poland is more or less a money-lender', and she doubted that 'any country [was] such a happy hunting-ground for the Hebrew usurer.'[36] Similarly, in the wake of the Kishinev pogrom, Arnold White argued that each of its victims was a money-lender.[37] Analogous sentiments appeared in analyses of Romania.[38] An article in the *Manchester Guardian*, for example, asserted that the 'banking and money-lending business of the country is entirely in [Jewish] hands.'[39]

The resonance of such allusions in the British context was immediate and required no further elaboration. Such was the degree to which the image of the Jew as a money-lender was deeply entrenched as a metaphorical trope that cast all Jews as intrinsically dishonest, greedy and self-interested, even Anglo-Jewish observers used it as a yardstick for the positive measurement of Jewish society in Russia. In November 1881, E.L. Benas, an AJA member in Liverpool, investigated a recent arrival of Russian Jewish immigrants, who were *en route* to new lives in North America. Benas was astonished to learn that there was not a 'single money-lender' among the 500 emigrants he interviewed. Instead, he discovered a range of talented artisans, including blacksmiths, bricklayers, masons, joiners, saddlers, locksmiths, plumbers, painters, shoemakers, tailors, as well as agricultural labourers. Twenty per cent he adjudged to be petty traders, whilst shopkeepers made up a further 10 per cent.[40] Like other observers, Benas did not find it necessary to square assumptions about Jewish money-lending with the acknowledged existence of widespread Jewish poverty. He did not ask why, if the Eastern European Jew was so involved with money and made earning it his chief business, was he also so desperately poor? The one attribute did not cancel out the other. It was therefore straightforward to dismiss the reality, especially if geographical distance allowed the imagination to run away with itself. This was probably the reason, for instance, that a piece in *The Scotsman* during the 1881–1882 pogroms was able to assert freely that many Russian Jews were rich.[41]

The image of the Jewish money-lender functioned, from the British perspective, in both the domestic and Eastern European context. In no way was it an innovation that originated under the influence of East European discourse. After all, one can find it referenced in every European context and period.[42] It naturally crossed cultural and international boundaries and, it must be said, the profession lent itself to notions of cosmopolitanism, to which Jews were often linked in this period. From a British viewpoint, Jewish money-lending was assumed to operate at a low level in the East, both socially and morally. Its manifestations in the West were more powerful, though all activities were conducted in a secretive manner, and the ties binding the

Western and Eastern ends of this disreputable profession were all but invisible. The polemical, provocative weekly, *Truth*, highlighted this interconnectedness:

> The Jews in Russia and Poland are what the Gombeen men are in Ireland. They advance money to the peasants at usurious interest, and it is as usurers [rather] than religionists that they are persecuted [...] The Polish village Jew has the peasant entirely under his thumb, and he uses his power much as a 'West-End usurer' tries to do with us.[43]

'Gombeen' was an adjective with Gaelic origins that, in Ireland, meant usury.[44] Its usage in this citation prompted a host of negative associations about the financial entrapment of peasant Ireland, which in turn resonated with peasant Russia. Here, of course, was the link to elements of Eastern European discourse. It raised questions about the structure of a peasant-based society, about weaknesses and strengths, and how one group might exploit the other. What was more, the notion could be transferred to the British context, given the suggestion about Jewish money-lenders in the West-End of London.[45] It implied that all Jewish commercial practice was inherently underhand and despicable, that even in London it was a commonplace hazard. Indeed, *Punch* made ironic reference to an apparent historical change in circumstances. Jews had once been slaves in ancient Egypt, but now they were the gleeful masters (see image 6).

If usury was the most commonplace money-making activity associated with the Jews of Eastern Europe, it was far from the only one. Other avenues of extortion were noted and the apparent Jewish 'devotion to money-making' was expressed in a variety of ventures.[46] *The Times* observed, for instance, that Jews were 'principal dealers in spirits, keepers of vodka (drinking) shops and homes of ill-fame, receivers of stolen goods, illegal pawnbrokers and usurers'.[47] Thus, Jews were brothel-keepers, fences and thieves, and seemingly made up a large proportion Eastern Europe's criminal fraternity. As the earlier reference to the 'West End' Jew insinuated, shady Jewish business practices were ubiquitous, multi-faceted and opportunistic. 'No sooner does [the Jew] save a few roubles than he takes either to broking or the liquor trade,' argued a contributor to the *Contemporary Review*.[48] This view suggested that the two trades, money-lending and tavern-keeping, guaranteed a swift and substantial return on one's investment, a singular Jewish priority. Both, without doubt, were immoral practices, designed to exploit the foolish,

Image 6　'Israel and Egypt; or turning the tables', *Punch*, September 1888

gullible, 'simple' peasant.[49] According to E.J. Dillon, 'no nation in the world [was] more temperate than the Jewish', but:

> considering the crowded position of the Pale and the keenness of competition there, [the Jew] gladly puts his hand to any work that offers, instinctively giving preference to that for which the demand is most brisk, and seeing that in Russia there is an eternal, insatiable demand for *vodka*, the obsequious Jew steps forward, takes down his quart bottle and respectfully serves his impatient customers.[50]

Neither Jew nor peasant emerges favourably here, as the 'obsequious' economic opportunist serves the 'impatient' customer, who insatiably demands vodka. But herein lay the essence of the British perspective on the Jewish economic dominion in Eastern Europe; the Jew was an exploiter, sometimes of other's vices, the living he tried to forge was entirely dishonest, and sometimes it was undertaken for the benefit of Jewry as a whole.

The image of the tavern-keeper was deeply imbued with negative characteristics throughout Russia, divided Poland and Romania, and the Jewish publican was often held responsible for rural unproductiveness and the maintenance of peasant backwardness.[51] It was not, at first glance, an image that carried immediate meaning for the British domestic context, since by the late nineteenth century it lacked a peasantry, even if it was hardly deficient in an entrenched, problematic drinking culture in the Victorian and Edwardian city. By the same token, the British narrative was only too keen to impute immorality to Jewish business practices and imagined 'the Jew' was able to turn his hand to any profession, so long as money was to be made. He was able to adapt according to local conditions and wants. Thus, the despicable Jewish tavern-keeper may not have been a homespun figure, but his traits were appreciated as universal.

The Jewish role in lending money and other scandalous activities in Eastern Europe raised other questions in the British imagination, largely related to the alleged 'power of the Jews'. This was particularly the case when, in response to incidents of persecution, Jewish financial institutions threatened to punish various regimes by withdrawing vital loans. In 1891, for example, the Paris branch of the Rothschilds acted against Tsarist Russia.[52] In the early twentieth century, similar efforts by the London Rothschilds were observed in connection with Romania.[53] Sometimes, as was noted in Chapter 3 in relation to Major Evans-Gordon, these endeavours were utilised in a conspiratorial, suggestive manner. And, R.W. Seton-Watson, in his appreciation of Romania, remarked that its regime had needed to curb Jewish immigration in order to 'answer the sinister agitation of Jewish societies and financial interests against Romania's very existence as an independent state'.[54]

It followed, therefore, that throughout the period under investigation, apprehension was manifest as to the 'power of the Jews' in Eastern Europe, intimated in a cartoon in *Punch* that used Shylock as a clearly understood point of reference (see images in chapter 2). As *The Spectator* argued:

> It is not simply that in imperfectly organised communities [such as Russia and Romania] the Jews are the bankers, the money-lenders, innkeepers, and middlemen; but they are all this not as separate individuals, but as a highly organised guild of foreigners, spreading its tentacles over the whole country till all its material resources are at last in its grasp.[55]

There was more than a hint of conspiracy in these sentiments. Similar views were expressed by *The Times'* Habsburg correspondent, Henry Wickham Steed, who spoke in the midst of the Great War, like the Chesterbelloc, of a 'German-Jewish financial organisation that controls the economic affairs of Central Europe and extends to Austria through the Balkans and to the East'.[56] Economically, therefore, Jews were regarded as an all-pervasive force in the East (and elsewhere), to the extent that for one observer, even the entire Russian Imperial capital was in thrall to the power of the Jew:

> As likely as not, you have a Jew as your next-door neighbour [in St Petersburg], a Jew as your neighbour over the way, and a Jew as your neighbour in the tenement over your head. In the theatre, in the streets, everywhere the Jew is in evidence. The banks and institutions solely depend upon him.[57]

Petersburg's Jewish population was comparatively tiny, amounting to less than 2 per cent (c.35,000) of the whole city's populace by the early 1890s, thus such an exaggeration was highly suggestive.[58] The last sentence, in particular, was indicative of a wider, more modern form of exploitation, which sucked in territory and people beyond the boundaries of the Tsarist Empire.

Little wonder then, that parallel processes, under the influence of *Ostjuden*, were apparently taking shape in Britain. In 1911, for instance, the *Penny Illustrated Paper* ran a piece that revealed Manchester – or

'Cottonopolis' as it was known – was totally in 'the hands of the Jews', whose Eastern European origins were identified by their use of Yiddish in advertising hoardings. The extent of this takeover encompassed a large portion of the north of the city, where, it was claimed, Jews owned all the shops and were buying up residential property at an astounding rate. 'Think of it', said this observer, 'Manchester the home of plain, shrewd Lancashire workers, who have by tireless hands and active brain made it the second commercial city of the Empire, in the throttling grip of a people who are the contempt of all nations as units, but much feared as a colony absolutely united by bonds of blood and religion.'[59]

In both Britain and Eastern Europe, this form of 'complete economic superiority' was guaranteed by a number of factors.[60] First of all, sheer, unbridled avarice was crucial. The *St James's Gazette*, for instance, claimed that the Tsarist government introduced the May Laws precisely as a response to 'Jewish greed'.[61] Yet, a more pressing concern in Eastern Europe was Jewish deceit, particularly expressed in habits such as bribery. In 1891, for example, the *Pall Mall Gazette* noted that the Moscow police force was turning a pretty penny from Jews who attempted to avoid the proscriptions of the expulsion edicts.[62] Such was the prevalence of bribery at this time, *The Spectator* claimed that 'a Jew in Russia is an outlaw who buys permission to live.'[63] This editorial expressed some sympathy for the Jewish plight and highlighted the necessity of living beyond the limits of the law in order to survive, a view not entirely without foundation. However, in contrast to the 'sturdy sons of Lancashire', who possessed the ability to repel the Jewish onslaught in Manchester, Jews encountered a 'flabby, easy-going people' in Eastern Europe, who were 'always accommodating in the matter of bribes'.[64] Herein lay a major reason that Jews were easily able to overcome their gentile contemporaries in the East. The 'flabby, easy-going' official, a description suggestive of inherent weaknesses in the Russian national character, was infinitely corruptible and corrupted. Yet, it was the peasant in whom these weaknesses could most readily be detected. He could not compete with the clever Jew. As a consequence, the lives of peasants and Jews created a neat dichotomy in the British narrative. The one was rooted to the soil, the other driven by a materialist obsession for money.

A 'National' crime: Jews, peasants and rootlessness

'The peasant will have nothing to do with commerce,' wrote one observer. 'He will till the ground, or carry on a handicraft, such as that of carpenter, mason or blacksmith, but he leaves haggling and barter to the despised Israelite.'[65] To many commentators, the peasant way of life formed the antithesis of Jewish existence in Eastern Europe, though British characterisations of the peasantry sometimes varied. During the famine of the early 1890s, which occurred in several provinces of the Russian Empire, the desperation of some starving peasants was so great that they were forced to break into the grain stores of local merchants and wealthier farmers.[66] These actions were presented as a marked schism from the peasants' previously respectable and law-abiding habits; only when faced with hunger and possible death did they seek recourse to law-breaking. Indeed, the apparent general passivity of the peasantry was remarked upon in relation to events in the previous decade, as *The Scotsman* believed that although the '[*muzhik*] has his faults, cruelty cannot said to be prominent among them'. According to this commentator, the peasant was not even guilty of 'religious intolerance'.[67] In a similar vein, some commentators utterly idolised the peasant, as already noted in Chapter 5 with the case of G.K. Chesterton, for whom peasant proprietorship was regarded as a solution to modernity's destructive advance.[68] Inevitably, Stephen Graham was equally awe-struck:

> The Russians are an agricultural nation, bred to the soil, [...] and having yet no ambition to live in towns. They are as strong as giants, simple as children, mystically superstitious by renown of their unexplained mystery [...]. They are obediently religious, seriously respectful to their elders, true to the soil they plough.[69]

Sometimes, however, the alleged naïveté and innocence of the peasant prompted consternation. According to the writer Charles Reade, the 'peasant [was] a silly, improvident brute' and a 'varnished savage'.[70] For Arnold White, he was 'ignorant and credulous'. But the overriding perspective rendered peasants simpleminded, yet honest, susceptible to the evils of drink, yet a good Christian and, although the peasant might engage in a pogrom or two, from the regime's perspective he was adjudged politically reliable. Arnold White again: the peasants 'are industrial and faithful, and devoted to their Emperor. [...] The [*muzhik*] delights in manual labour, in vodka, in the worship of icons.'[71]

All these attributes were not, of course, associated with Jews. Although Jews were acknowledged as industrious, it was always a pursuit closely allied with self-serving objectives and their loyalty was similarly directed. As far as the Tsar or other rulers were concerned, observers pointed out that Jews had no reason to feel grateful, so why would they be? To be sure, it was believed that Jews were not inclined to physical labour, nor did they embrace alcohol – save as a means to exploit others – and they most certainly did not worship icons.[72] The religious division betwixt peasant and Jew appeared occasionally, though observers often believed the former was merely superstitious, rather than Christian. A Christian missionary, Charles Byford, who visited the Russian Empire in the decade before the First World War, was inevitably drawn to the religious symbols of separation between Jew and peasant:

> I have seen in a railway station lamps burning before the Holy Icon, a priest conducting a service in the waiting-room, but in the corner, a Jew, with praying shawl over his shoulders, face to the wall, *wailing* his prayers, apparently unconscious of the wonder gaze of the 'uncircumcised'. The great gulf fixed between the two religions, the superstitious fanaticism of the ordinary [*muzhik*], the persecuting policy of the clergy and the police, all have had their effect in keeping the two races estranged.[73]

The two symbols highlighted here, the icon (Russian: *obraz*) and prayer shawl (Hebrew: *tallit*) were legitimate enough in summarising and representing each faith. But they were also symbols of division, a separateness expressed by Byford utilising the crucial word 'race'. Nevertheless, it is clear that the reason Jew and peasant remained separate in Russia was the fault of 'fanaticism' and persecution; unlike other commentators, he did not deem it the consequence of Jewish exclusivism.

Religious difference was often an implied source of friction between peasant and Jew in Eastern Europe, though it sometimes acquired greater significance during moments of crisis, such as the pogroms of 1881–1882 and beyond. Yet, in assessing the day-to-day divergences between the two, the most significant aspect was expressed in the matter of land and agriculture. Naturally, the peasant was defined by his connection to land and his eternal relationship with its functions. Soil, earth, crops, animals, the seasons and elements were all intrinsic to the peasant's existence. He understood how to grow things, worked in tandem with the agricultural (nature's) calendar and performed tasks that were ultimately useful and undertaken for the benefit of all society. The Jew, of course, understood none of these things. He was, in fact, 'indisposed to agriculture'.[74] Indeed, according to *The Spectator*, he literally produced nothing: 'no Jew produces anything, or mines, or builds, or adds to the general wealth of the world.'[75] It further observed, with barely disguised disdain: 'there is probably not a Jew ploughman in the world.'[76] Thus, whilst the majority of the population tilled the soil in Eastern Europe, the Jew did not: 'they themselves do not raise agricultural products; but they reap the benefit of others.'[77] Once again, the Jew was simply an exploiter, who stood idly by, awaiting the moment he could cheat the peasant, buy his produce cheaply and sell it on at an extortionate price.

These notions, about the inability of Jews to connect with the land, to engage in agriculture, linked to a wider European discourse. In France, for example, ideologues spoke of the deracinated or rootless Jew. Racialist thinkers and commentators, such as Drumont and Maurice Barrès, contrasted the urban, degenerate Jew and the evils he thrust upon the innocent non-Jew, to the organic, natural existence of the peasant in the countryside. The peasant nurtured animals, raised foodstuffs, was connected to the land by physical labour and, most importantly, an ancient inheritance; he had been there since time immemorial belonged to the land as much as the crops he raised. For some French ideologues, he was the embodiment of the nation itself. To paraphrase one historian of the Third Republic, according to racialised discourse the symbols of French identity were soil on the soles of shoes and coarsened hands.[78] No doubt the hands of work-shy Jews were smooth and free of calluses. In contrast, such notions were absent in Russian Judeophobia, which was not concerned with the kind of national questions inherent in such allusions, not least as the issue of who was or was not Russian was hugely problematic in the borderland areas in which most Jews lived.[79] The British preoccupation with these matters was formulated, therefore, under Western influences, though applied to parts of Europe where the peasantry formed the absolute majority.

Observers in Britain noted that the Jew had sometime had a connection to the land, but this was hundreds of years ago, from the moment he began his exile in Europe, and his subsequent failure to reconnect was scornfully regarded. As *The Times* strikingly expressed it: 'severance from the soil is evil.'[80] Inevitably, in agricultural Eastern Europe, this severance was all the more troublesome. For instance, according to W.G. Wagstaff, the British Vice-Consul at Taganrog, who investigated the origins of the 1881–1882 pogroms at HMG's behest: 'In their relations to Russia, [Jews] are compared to parasites that have settled on a plant not vigorous enough to throw them off, and which is being gradually sapped of its virility.'[81] Wagstaff imputed this unsophisticated metaphor as Russian in origin and it suggested, non-too-subtly, that the organic plant stood representative of the peasantry, whose lifeblood was slowly being drained by the Jew.[82] In general, therefore, when it came to considering agriculture, earth and land (as property and 'the nation') in Eastern Europe, there was a clear division in not only the roles ascribed to Jews and peasants, but also their resultant characteristics.[83]

Nowhere were these characteristics better demonstrated than in the contributions made to the British analysis of Poland by W.F. Bailey, an Irish barrister and itinerant journalist. Just before and during the First World War, he made an exploration of Galicia, Serbia and Romania.[84] The divided Poland described by Bailey was undoubtedly an ethnic maelstrom and, alongside the Habsburg/Tsarist border that had so trans-fixed Hall Caine, he listened to a 'babble of tongues.'[85] Observing this colourful and cosmopolitan landscape, Bailey embraced racialised discourse in his assessment of difference and diversity. Inevitably, there-fore, the ethnic Pole, especially as represented by the peasant, emerged as a favourable, even admirable, individual. Hard-working, with 'true Slavonic politeness', Polish peasants were 'a very lovable people', and their lives appeared blissful, not to say, idyllic.[86] His pastoral evocation of this land was depicted as a gentle, organic order, picked out in natural, rather soothing, colours:

> It is a Saturday afternoon, and everyone [in the village] is finishing his or her week's work. A group of women, with petticoats hitched high above their shapely brown legs, are washing clothes. [...] Crimson, pink, yellow and white – the warm colours of their garments flash joyously in the sunshine. Some men, clad in yellowish frieze breeches and short, white linen tunics girthed about the waist with a foot-wide red leather belt, are rattling homeward in their *bryczka* [cart], drawn by a troop of wiry, honey-tinted ponies whose coats shine like spun silk. Joyous smiles, a fleeting glimpse of sun-bronzed, merry faces framed in round dark grey hats gay with poppy wreaths, appear and vanish as the cart and its occupants proceed in a whirlwind of white dust towards the next village.[87]

In view of such a bucolic setting, where life retained its primordial rhythms and routines, it was difficult to image that Galicia was affected by war, though in reality it was as intensively fought-over as parts of Belgium and France.[88] It is clear from this portrait that, in Bailey's mindset, the Polish peasant and his environment were intrinsically con-nected; the one was rooted in the other. Yet, when depicting the Jewish presence in these outer-reaches of European civilisation, he was not as sympathetically inclined, and, indeed, the Jew appeared as a somewhat jarring presence in Poland's otherwise admirable existence:

> Men and boys are out on the fields, shepherds are rounding up their flocks on the gentle uplands. Only the black kaftan-clad Jew, who resides in the ugly, blue-painted house, and amasses a small fortune by smuggling diseased swine across the frontier, by dispensing bad spirits, lending money to the needy peasants, and by other similar industries, is snoozing among his progeny on the threshold of their residence.[89]

In stark contrast to the lives of the Polish peasantry, the Jewish existence was at odds with its surroundings. It was aesthetically unpleasant, associated with disease, illicit money-making endeavours and the misuse of alcohol. Observing commercial life in one unnamed Galician town, Bailey could not help noticing that:

> the Jewish element predominated. Long lines of lugubriously apparelled sons of that race sat hunkered up on the trottoirs [...] or in the gutters, looking like so many roosting crows in their greasy black kaftans and high black caps, low, square-toed shoes, and grey stockings. [...] These gentlemen of the gutter act as interpreters and guides, and they alone, amongst all the peoples and tribes which make up the population of this district, are able to speak several languages. [...] Nearby, their ugly, half-clad wives and children has set up several score of dirty booths and stalls, which were heaped up with every conceivable kind of merchandise.[90]

Again, this contrasted with the peasantry, from the counterpoint of lugubrious with joyous, black/grey with crimson/pink/yellow/honey, to the whiff of sexual immorality ascribed to the Jewish women, the 'ugly, half-clad wives'. Compare this latter point with the noble, innocent beauty of the peasant women, whose 'petticoats [were] hitched high above their shapely brown legs', an especially startling contrast.

At the root of all this contrast lay, of course, Bailey's anxieties about the Jew as a non-producer, as an individual who could not connect with the land. He observed, for instance, that in Poland, Jews were regarded as a people who could 'never invent or produce anything which would tend to the betterment of human existence and civilization'.[91] The Tsarist regime had harboured the same concerns and, in the early nineteenth century, Tsar Nicholas I was responsible for setting up several agricultural colonies in the south of the Empire, in parts of what is now modern Ukraine. The driving force behind these endeavours was again related to the fear of Jewish exploitation, coupled with a desire to make Jews 'more productive' – in other words, to turn them into peasants.[92] By mid-century, these efforts had been all but abandoned, though the colonies continued to exist. Since, in terms of the proportion of Russian Imperial Jews these agricultural colonies actually represented was tiny (approximately 3.5 per cent of the Empire's total Jewish population), very few British observers were aware of their existence.[93] But when such activities were acknowledged, it was suggested that Jewish involvement in any agricultural enterprise was doomed to failure. 'Where estates are farmed by the Jews', wrote one contributor to *The Times*, 'it is distressing to see the pitiable condition in which they are handed over on the expiration of the lease.'[94] This reiterated that which was widely believed, that Jews appeared were incapable of engaging in agricultural pursuit and forming a healthy relationship with the soil.

There was one British observer, however, who purposefully visited Russia in order to investigate the agricultural colonies in the province of Kherson. This was Arnold White, who worked on behalf of the Jewish Colonisation Association, and his task was to examine employment opportunities for Jews in the colonies Baron de Hirsch proposed to establish in South America and elsewhere.[95] As already acknowledged in Chapter 2, White is a problematical figure in the historiography of British antisemitism, not least as a consequence of his deserved reputation as a strident anti-alienist. In 1899, he published *The Modern Jew*, in which he was forthright in his racialised antisemitic worldview. For him, immigrant Jews represented a danger to the integrity of the Anglo-Saxon race, a threat to the economic stability of the world, and a host of other negative accusations that deemed them in possession of 'a complex and mysterious power'.[96] By the dawn of the twentieth century, White was categorical in his views on the Jewish question, hence his unconditional support for restrictive legislation, and his strident appearances at the Royal Commission.

Given this, it might seem that White was utterly unsuited as an emissary for Baron Hirsch's cause. At first glance, it appears as if ever there was a man with an antisemitic agenda, it was White. But in the late 1880s and early 1890s, the time that he visited the Tsarist Empire, White's antisemitic worldview was not fully formed, or, at the very least, he was prepared to compromise. As a result, his work of this period was often sympathetic towards the Jewish plight in Russia, as was clear in his contributions to *Darkest Russia* (noted in Chapter 2). At this moment,

1891, White believed that the prospects for Jewish self-improvement were good and he was far from alone in such prescriptions. In particular, like Tsarist officials of the early nineteenth century, he ascribed to the notion that agriculture would provide a means of solving Russia's Jewish question, and his visit to Kherson convinced him that Jews were more than capable of becoming productive farmers. In this southern province, he found:

> a well set-up, sunburnt, muscular agricultural population, marked by all the characteristics of a peasantry of the highest character. There are thirty thousand. So far as I could learn from the neighbouring proprietors – Russian – who employed them, they have no vices, unless early, improvident, and fruitful marriages can be deemed a vice.

Of course, implicit in the last sentence of this quotation was White's oft-expressed concern about Jewish fecundity, which he often highlighted in his pronouncements on immigration to the United Kingdom. Yet, the rest of his views were remarkably complementary towards the Jews of Kherson. Here he observed 'sober Hebrew ploughmen', Jewish blacksmiths, millers and haymakers who 'all exhibited their skill and strength'. There was no suggestion that these Jews exploited peasants, or that they sapped their vitality by plying them with vodka. On the contrary, one of the most admirable aspects of the Jews of Kherson, especially when compared to peasants, was their temperance. 'If courage', White wrote, 'moral courage, hope, temperance, are fine qualities, then the Jews are a fine people.' Moreover, by being 'moralised by sweat and sunshine', the Jew could be 'restored to the land'.[97] The import of this latter illusion, of course, bore significance beyond the ability to become farmers. It suggested that Jews could form a national connection and subsequently focus their loyalties upon it.

White arrived in the Tsarist Empire with an explicit agenda, his travel costs underwritten by a generous benefactor who was prescriptive in his ambitions. Therefore, the positive light he threw on this aspect of Imperial Russia's Jewish question is entirely understandable. Additionally, White's aims were not a million miles away from those that he had harboured in the 1880s, when, during his initial encounter with British public life, he appeared as an active promoter of another emigration scheme that involved the transference of hundreds of unemployed East End labourers to an agricultural colony in South Africa.[98] For him, emigration represented a solution to an array of social problems.

Nevertheless, it is particularly striking that Arnold White's positive perspective on Jewish farmers in Kherson was a contrast to the greater part of the British narrative on Jewish-peasant relations in Easter Europe. A cartoonist in *Funny Folks*, for instance, could not even fantasise as to how Jews might become farmers and instead rendered a panorama of a Baron Hirsch colony that was riddled with all manner of established stereotypes of 'the Jew'[99] (see image 7). By the same token, White's views are interesting since they linked not only to Russian Imperial anxieties, but many that were expressed closer to home. After all, throughout the period under investigation, Anglo-Jews were greatly concerned, like White, about the image, talents and physical prowess of East European Jews.

Anglo-Jewish perspectives: soldiering and farming

As we have seen, British Jewry felt an urgent empathy with its co-religionists in Eastern Europe, especially during various crises, and its support was manifest in a number of ways. In particular, it was engaged in several, highly creditable philanthropic actions in London and elsewhere, as well as assisting emigration schemes from Eastern Europe to various parts of the world. In this aspect, it matched the endeavours of its continental counterparts, both West and East, though it often felt isolated in aiding emigrants and, in the 1880s, occasionally accused French and German Jewry of shirking their responsibilities.[100] All these efforts, which focussed on the needs of materially poor brethren, were accompanied by mixed feelings about the East European Jew. Most particularly, throughout the period under investigation, a great deal of concern was manifest as to how the image of *Ostjuden*, both as residents of Eastern *shtetlekh* and immigrants heading westwards, might negatively impact upon that of the acculturated, 'respectable' British Jew. As the *Jewish Chronicle*, the epitome of Anglo-Jewish decency and national attainment, observed during the 1881–1882 pogroms: 'It is the Western Jews who are as much on their trial as the Jews of the East of Europe, and we have to see that History will give us a favourable verdict on our conduct in the most trying crisis.'[101]

Sympathy and a sense of duty were undoubtedly uppermost in Anglo-Jewish attitudes and intentions towards Eastern European Jews, but these feelings uneasily co-existed with an ingrained sense that they were not of 'us'. At one level, such a stance was merely expressed as inquisitiveness for that which contrasted with the established Jewish way-of-life in Britain. In 1902, for instance, just as the Royal Commission was

Image 7 Baron Hirsch's colony in Pennsylvania, *Funny Folks*, May 1891

meeting, the *Jewish World* ran a series of picturesque covers that featured sketches of 'ghetto types', which included a *melamed* (teacher), a *yeshiva* student and a *chazzan* (cantor).[102] There was no intent to impute any negative characteristics to these staple individuals of East European Jewish life and, undoubtedly, the *Jewish World*'s intentions were didactic, perhaps even celebratory. Nevertheless, they proffered images that rendered their subjects as curiosities, emphasised by the use of the problematic term 'ghetto'. Yet, these individuals were not inhabitants of the ghetto of the Pale, but of Commercial Road in London's East End; their brand of otherness was, in fact, conspicuously close to home.

The East European Jewish presence in Britain, although fascinating for some Anglo-Jewish observers, was perceived in other ways that encouraged a burgeoning unease not just related to the image of *Ostjuden*, but British Jews, too. These worries were particularly acute in the 1880s and 1890s, when Jewish immigration from Eastern Europe to the United Kingdom reached heightened levels. The alien question prompted both a defensive and offensive stance, which sought to ensure that wider opinion understood that British Jews were doing their all to strip the Eastern European Jew of his disagreeable habits.[103] Inevitably, such preoccupations provoked questions about Jewish identity and its components. What was Jewish and what was not? And, perhaps more to the point, what was British and what was not?

An editorial in the *Chronicle*, for instance, observed in 1886 that 'when we speak of the [British] nation we are too apt to think that it is composed of the comparatively well-to-do', a vision that suited many acculturated, bourgeois British Jews, who attire and demeanour was akin to the rest of middle-England. Yet, the arrival of East European Jews reminded this editorialist that the poor, of every religious group, also belonged to the nation.[104] In the matter of self-perception, of course, these remarks were greatly revelatory; British Jews were middle-class, respectable subjects, whilst immigrant, 'foreign' Jews were poor and perhaps less reliable in their national potential. In terms of Anglo-Jewish ambition, the greatest achievement was to be wholly unrecognisable as a Jew, for 'Englishness' (conflated with 'Britishness' at this time) to be borne with pride.

As a consequence, the obvious Jewishness of the East European immigrant was almost a source of shame from the Anglo-Jewish perspective. Another *JC* editorial observed in 1884 that upon visiting Spitalfields in the East End of London one would encounter 'a number of men in long coats and women in wigs, speaking a jargon which belongs to no one language under the sun'. Constituting 'a body of foreign Jews', they 'physically' lived in England, but 'mentally and morally' remained in the Russian Empire. 'Is it not a serious thing', it asked, 'that the reputation of the Jewish people rests with [the immigrant] glazier, the tailor, the peddler and the cobbler?'[105] The manner and conditions in which these Jews dwelt was also deeply worrying:

> We want the foreign poor to live like Englishmen; but we shall not make much progress towards realising our wish while we allow them to inhabit houses which, in respect of cleanliness, almost compel them to live like Russians. A Jew from Lithuania or the Black Sea littoral cannot be converted into an Englishman by the simple process of being domiciled in Whitechapel. If this is all that takes place it amounts to nothing more than his transference from Great Russia to Little Russia. If the community want to Anglicize him it must do something itself. It would like him to be inspired with an English love of soap-and-water; to see him take kindly to Western notions of sanitation. [...] The Russian immigrant must be taken by the hand. His civilisation is not his affair, but the community's, which desires as much for its own sake as for his to improve his condition.[106]

Again, these were highly revealing sentiments. Britishness could not be attained by the simple expedient of residence in London, since it was a status necessitating a certain set of obligations that would liberate the immigrant from all the habits ('the scars of oppression') he had previously acquired.[107] Any effort towards assimilation could and must be immediate, illustrated in this instance by good sanitary habits, or the purging of the ghetto's dirt, figuratively and literally, from both body and soul. Clearly, this hinted at a deeper set of anxieties that suggested a link between poor sanitation and bad national health. Were the Eastern Jew permitted to continue his unwelcome practices, it would be detrimental to not only himself, but the rest of British society. It was Anglo-Jewry's profound duty to correct this and other unwelcome conditions:

> The immigrants strike the mind of many observers with disgust. [...] Part of the repugnance they inspire may be due to their very virtues, their frugality and industry. Some of it is caused by their misfortunes, which have rendered them squalid and dirty, ill-favoured and cunning. Their exclusiveness, their ignorance of our English ways and talk, are removable by teaching and example. These defects cured, the immigrants themselves supply a remedy for many of the other

characteristics which render them unpopular. They are eminently receptive, and to approach them on the receptive side and in such a spirit as they will welcome is the task of us who have been longer established. We must hasten to help them to a true naturalisation, not only to an admission to political privileges but to incorporation into English ideas and the sentiments of a land of freedom.[108]

British Jews could, therefore, instigate practical remedies to correct these superfluous, distasteful characteristics of immigrant Jews and, in essence, make them more British. They could 'cure their defects' by erecting sanitary dwellings, funding language classes and instituting schools to remove the influence of the *cheder*, which was regarded as preserving 'all the worst traditions of Russo-Jewish life'.[109] And this had to be undertaken by all Anglo-Jewish society, in a visible, open way, in order that it would not be forced to bear, by association, the negative taint of the *Ostjude*.

These concerns were, of course, a product of the aliens question that rendered the East European Jew a noticeable presence on British streets, in shops, schools and on the Clapham omnibus. Yet the domestic worries transposed upon the image of the East European Jew were far from the only ones that bothered Anglo-Jewry in this period. At home 'in the Pale', which could be anywhere in Eastern Europe, two aspects of the Jewish image preoccupied the Anglo-Jewish imagination – agriculture and the military. As we have already seen, the question of whether Jews could be farmers was important in the mainstream narrative, as was a fixation on the Jewish suitability to soldiery. This latter point operated on a number of levels, not least the widespread issue as to whether Jews were physically and patriotically up to the arduous task of defending the nation.

In Eastern Europe, both Tsarist Russia and Romania conscripted Jews into their armies, though inhibited any professional progression. Of course, in the second case prolonged service in the army did not even guarantee citizenship. Inevitably, a multitude of fears about the Jewish inability to soldier occupied Eastern European discourse. In 1903, 'Verax' (Radu Rosetti), wrote about Jewish failures in the Romanian army: 'completely without military spirit, [Jews] are generally soft, lacking in vigour, [are] bad marchers and thieves. [...] Persons like the Jew try to gain exemption from all disagreeable chores, or heavy and dangerous service.'[110] The same notions, that Jews were shirkers and even draft-dodgers, were commonplace across the border in the Russian Empire.[111] In turn, they were embraced in British discourse:

> Summoned as recruits to the colours [in Russia], a large proportion of [Jews] shirk their duty and abscond. Enlisted in the regiments they mutilate themselves or feign illness. On the battlefield they surrender themselves. [...] Then there is the other undoubted fact that Jews emigrate in much greater numbers than any other element of the population [...] what is termed emigration is really a shirking of duty.[112]

E.J. Dillon bought the official, military perspective, just as Bernard Pares and others did during the Great War. In a similar vein, W.T. Stead, who interviewed the former Minister of the Interior, I.P. Ignatiev, in the late 1870s, followed the same line. For Stead, Jews were 'disobedient subjects. As many as 80 per cent of the recruits who did not respond to the summons to join the army in 1878 were Jews.'[113] This particular allusion, therefore, maintained durability over several generations, notwithstanding corroborative evidence to the contrary.[114]

The assumption that Jews could not make good soldiers struck at the very heart of Anglo-Jewry's anxiety about its own self-image and that of East European Jews. If individual Jews could not serve efficiently and loyally, what did that say about Jewish society as a whole? What did it reveal about the Jewish role and place in the nation in which they lived? What did it say about their physicality, their strength in body and mind? These were questions implicitly asked and answered throughout the period under investigation. In 1893, for example, Lucien Wolf wrote a piece for *The Graphic* that went to great lengths to prove historically the Jewish tendency to soldiering, tracing a line of martial capacity from Alexander the Great to Napoleon Bonaparte and beyond.[115] In relation to Eastern Europe, both the *Chronicle* and the *World* strove to counter popular perceptions. In the 1880s and 1890s, the *JC* published up-beat reports about Jewish recruitment statistics in the Russian Empire, which proved that 'the statement that Jews evade military service is quite unfounded.'[116] In 1904, the *World* carried a report about one Leiser Bolishmenikov, a non-commissioned officer in the Russian Imperial army, who celebrated 50 years' service under the Tsar and possessed 'all the medals that are awarded to soldiers, including the gold medal of St. Andrew'.[117]

The need to emphasise the Jewish fighting sprit attained prominence during the Great War, when British wariness about its ally was at its height. Once again, Jewish achievements on the field of battle were recorded.[118] In 1915, a report appeared in the *World*, sourced from the

Jewish Colonisation Association in Petrograd, which celebrated the fact that almost half-a-million Jews were fighting under the Tsar's colours. This gave the newspaper some cause for optimism, as it noted: 'We will not believe that such gigantic sacrifices will be for nought and in vain so far as the position of our people in the land of the Tsar is concerned.'[119] Whether the *World* truly imagined this aspiration was realisable is debatable. Only 6 months earlier, it had decried the insults hurled at Jewish soldiers in the Imperial Russian army by the Minister of Foreign Affairs, Sergei Sazonov, who, in an interview with Stephen Graham, suggested that Jews might be less inclined to military service than their gentile contemporaries. The *World*'s indignant response requires no elaboration: 'The words of M. Sazonov form, by their implication, a dastardly libel on our people in Russia.'[120]

Anglo-Jewish society harboured contemporaneous concerns as to whether Jews could be farmers. Just as with Arnold White and Baron Hirsch, this worry was oftentimes interlinked to emigration and it was thereby proffered as a solution to Eastern Europe's Jewish question. Similarly, the origins of these reservations matched White's, since they were underpinned by concerns about the nation, about productivity and 'usefulness'. For this reason, although in the 1880s and 1890s the *Jewish Chronicle* was mostly opposed to emigration schemes to Palestine and, indeed, to political Zionism itself, it nevertheless wrote admiringly about the achievements of the First *Aliyah* (the so-called Farmers' *Aliyah*) of the 1880s onwards.[121] It also published recurrent tales of Jewish agricultural triumphs in Canada and the United States.[122] Likewise, the *World* was inclined to laud these achievements and, in 1904, it bore a front cover that depicted an American rural success story, in the form of the National Farm School in Pennsylvania. Governed by Rabbi Josef Krauskopf, this organisation took Eastern European Jews 'from ghetto to farm', channelled their energies into learning practical applications in agriculture, which in turn produced physically fit and usefully skilled young men.[123]

Inevitably, given the emergence of the Zionist movement in this period, as well as the growth in influence of the Jewish Territorial Organisation, Anglo-Jewish observers were much interested in the accomplishments of Palestinian and other colonies. Regardless as to whether Jewish observers agreed with the political aims of creating a Jewish national home, the mere fact that Jews had demonstrated that they were able to engage with agriculture on untilled land was a worthwhile and heartening sign. Emigration schemes of all kinds, therefore, prompted both interest and hope.[124]

Nevertheless, surely those who remained in the *shtetl* could also be encouraged along more useful avenues of employment and new skills acquired, a theme extant not only in Anglo-Jewish aspirations but amongst Eastern Jewry too. As in Western Europe, Russian Imperial Jewish organisations were involved in various self-help programmes.[125] From a British perspective, of course, the need to inculcate practical skills in the East carried domestic consequences. After all, if Jews were productive in the East, there would be no need for them to travel West! If only Jews were given an opportunity, they could easily prove their abilities and talents. During the pogroms of 1881, for instance, the *JC* rebutted the notion that all Jews were money-lenders in Russia and asserted that, instead, their 'value' was evident in many economic spheres, including agriculture. It admitted that there were Jews who sold intoxicating liquor, but in the main, they were a 'useful part of the Russian population'.[126] A decade later, there were similar claims, when Count Sergei Witte, Russia's finance minister, was in search of foreign capital to underwrite his modernisation schemes. Why, the *Jewish Chronicle* wondered, did Witte need to look abroad, when the kind of commercial acumen he sought could surely be found nearby: the 'enterprise of the [Russian] Jew lay at home and awaiting a chance.'[127] Alas, despite this expression of faith in East European brethren and the best efforts of Jewish organisations both East and West, there can be no doubt that in the Anglo-Jewish imagination the image of the Eastern Jew forever remained redolent of the ghetto and its disagreeable characteristics.

The final chapter? Jews and revolution

It has long been established in the historiography of British anti-semitism that the Bolshevik takeover of October 1917 had a profound impact on attitudes and imaginings of 'the Jew'.[128] Upon its debut in English, for instance, *The Protocols of the Elders of Zion* was initially accepted, by the press, leading politicians and many British observers who visited the Soviet Union in its earliest years, as proof of Jewish-Bolshevik plotting.[129] The journalist Victor Marsden was instrumental in the proliferation of this theory, and, throughout late 1918 and 1919, he published a series of highly influential articles in the *Morning Post*, which stressed the Jewish role in a range of events in Russia, from the October revolution to the murder of the imperial family.[130] In May 1920, *The Times* ran with a story that asserted the *Protocol*'s authenticity and pondered upon the possibility of Britain falling victim to a 'Pax Judæica'.[131] One of its correspondents, Robert Wilton, published a book that adumbrated his belief in Bolshevism's Jewish origins, as did, inevitably, G.K. Chesterton and Hilaire Belloc.[132] Similarly, following a visit to the USSR in 1923, Charles Saroléa expressed the same opinion.[133] Inevitably, Lucien Wolf and other Anglo-Jewish commentators, such a Israel Zangwill, went to considerable lengths to challenge these views.[134]

That many in Britain were greatly troubled by the Bolshevik revolution and its threats was reinforced by the domestic travails and civil unrest that dogged the 1920s, perhaps best represented by the General Strike of 1926. As a wholesale menace to the established social and political order, Bolshevism was particularly feared since it was imbued with mysterious qualities, which might prompt it to seep quietly and unbidden into the nation's factories, collieries and workshops. Winston Churchill, for instance, described it as 'a plague of bacillus', whilst for Bernard Pares it was a 'disease'.[135] As has already been noted, its influence was detected outwith Russia, in Poland particularly, but also, amongst other states, in Germany and Hungary. Oftentimes, the Jewish link, whether real or imagined, was easily identified. For example, following the short-lived 1919 Bolshevik revolution in Hungary led by Béla Kun, who was actually of mixed Jewish/protestant/ethnic Hungarian parentage, the *Daily Mail* insisted on continually and erroneously referring to him as 'Bela Cohen'.[136] In *The Spectator*, he was described as a 'Jewish Bolshevik', as though the two terms were synonymous.[137] Nevertheless, despite the panic Bolshevism bred in Britain, the association between Jews and revolution was not, by any means, a new phenomenon.

As was observed in Chapter 2, by the early 1880s, East European Jewry was tentatively linked with various revolutionary ideologies and organisations, most particularly nihilism.[138] All the same, the most significant revolutionary moment of those years, the assassination of Tsar Alexander II, did not provoke a discussion in the British press as to whether the plotters were Jews or not.[139] Unsurprisingly, given the degree to which one regularly informed the other, this mirrored responses in the Russian Imperial press.[140] In fact, in general British observers actually made little of the Jewish connection to revolutionary groups in the early 1880s, perhaps because domestic incidents of terrorist violence were usually the work of Irish republicans.[141] The dread of political bomb plots and the like was thus driven by familiar, internal prejudices. Until the 1890s, therefore, revolutionary politics, whatever its objectives, appeared a continental concern, and there was no real sense that it had successfully permeated British political life. This perspective altered, of course, since socialists and anarchists became increasingly associated with political violence at the very same moment that East European Jewish emigration was on the rise. By the turn of the twentieth century, there was a noticeable Jewish involvement in various socialist parties and trades' unions in Britain, especially in London's East End.[142]

The increasing visibility of socialism in Britain meant that newspapers became more attuned to its presence. But they did not always concern themselves with its Jewish connections, notwithstanding the *Jewish Chronicle*'s claim in 1891 that the 'more genuine and truer features of socialism' were 'Jewish in their complexion'.[143] However, alarm bells did occasionally ring. In 1899, for example, the populist weekly, *Reynolds's Newspaper*, hosted a fractious discussion on the Jewish question in its letter columns. Edited by W.M. Thompson, the publication stood to the left of British politics, often championing the working-class cause, particularly as victims of exploitation. Its endeavours to stir up the class consciousness of the East End meant that 'the Jew', in numerous representations, was a frequent target of its venom. The discussion in September and October 1899, set against the background of the South African war, revealed that Jews were guilty of the 'disease of avarice', having no nationality, 'shirking manual labour' and 'parasitism'. They were also, it was argued, instinctively drawn to socialism, though one correspondent was puzzled by this, since he believed that Jewish exclusivism and 'tribalism' meant that 'no Jew can be a true, a sincere Socialist'.[144] For other correspondents, the matter was much more straightforward and it was regarded as no coincidence that the most important figures of socialism, such as Karl Marx, Ferdinand Lasalle and the like, were all Jews.[145] In this way, socialism basically became yet another component of the multi-faceted image of the mystifying, secretive and dastardly Jew.

Such simplistic explanations were the mainstay of interpretations throughout Europe and beyond that linked Jews to revolution, to socialism, anarchism and communism. Thus, these notions were far from unique in the British analysis of the Jewish question, yet they did not attain a prominent position in the narrative until the 1905 Revolution in Tsarist Russia. Following events in Odessa in late 1905, much copy was devoted in *The Times* to the supposed Jewish role in fomenting trouble – for which punishment was meted out in the form of pogroms.[146] Reflecting on these events 5 years later, Bernard Pares observed:

> In summer [1905], the reactionaries had begun to unite to defend their vested interests under the name of 'Genuine Russians'. They were urged forward by the *Moscow Gazette* and formed provincial

branches, weak in number but strong in the support of the police, who had close contact with the casual criminal class. In very many cities and towns the educated radicals were attacked by the mobs under the eyes of the police. In Kieff and Odessa, where revolutionary Jews had been prominent, it was still worse. Here, on the destruction of the Emperor's insignia, the responsibility for which has never been fixed, crowds dispersed the demonstrators, fell upon the Jews, and plundered their shops wholesale for three days; brutal murders were committed.[147]

In a similar vein, Charles Saroléa, who was present in Russia in late 1905, made several references to the alleged Jewish role in the revolution. Those he regarded as the principal revolutionary protagonists were a deemed 'a mere band of intellectuals, journalists, professors, advocates and students', almost every one of whom was a Jew.[148]

Conspiracy theories about Jews, however, were not confined to the realms of socialist revolution. As was the case with the Chesterbelloc, the link between Jews and the press was occasionally invoked and commentators even highlighted this in an Eastern European context. Harold Williams, for example, a future foreign editor of *The Times*, noted in 1914 the 'conspicuous part' Jews played in journalism in the Tsarist Empire. 'The bulk of the reporting is in their hands,' he wrote, 'and many editors, leader writers and feuilletonists are of Jewish extraction.'[149] But, again, this was not a new phenomenon. Two decades earlier, E.J. Dillon had written:

> twenty-eight years ago not a Jew in all Russia owned a newspaper. [...] but things have undergone a considerable change since then, the Jew's tactics have also changed, and I am now afraid even to hint at the number of newspaper proprietors who are followers of the Laws of Moses.[150]

The concern here, of course, was related to the potential for Jews to influence public opinion, to encourage and stir up dissension, perhaps even political trouble. After all, if the Jews controlled the press, they would surely only use it to their own ends, whatever they may be, but which were bound to be to the detriment of the rest of society.

The limits of fantasy did not end there. As has already been discussed, this period was riddled with all kinds of anxieties about 'the power of the Jews', apparently manifest in a multitude of arenas.

Stephen Graham, almost inevitably, extensively dwelt on such matters. In 1913, he recorded a conversation he had with a monk in the Caucasus:

> 'You said you were English', said he. 'You are not a Jew, I suppose?'
>
> 'Oh no', I replied with a smile. [...]
>
> 'They ought not to be allowed any education at all, and ought to be employed simply as labourers', said he. 'They have no religion, they have only politics.'
>
> 'Yes', I said with a smile. 'The only thing they seriously believe in is trade, business. Here in Russia their business is hampered, and so they work practically for freedom, – freedom for more trade – not freedom for more life or for a truer religion, but freedom for more mammon-worship. With you, however, the Jews obtain comparatively little success. With us they are unchecked. They hold the highest places in the state.'
>
> 'The English are in a dangerous way', replied the monk. 'I have heard that the Church is likely to fall. The Freemasons are at work there as in France. There is a conspiracy among the [Free] Masons and the Jews to overthrow the state-recognition of the Church. [...] What do the Jews want in the end of the ends?'
>
> 'Power, I suppose'.
>
> 'Power for what?'
>
> I confessed I couldn't say. The Jew himself doesn't consider the matter deeply. He knows he wants power and wealth; that's about the end of it.
>
> 'Power', he said, 'power and nothing more, just as Satan wished power in heaven, power and nothing more; he wished to put himself even above the Almighty. The Jew is the spirit of Satan on earth – the Jews are the hosts of Satan, and Satan will lead them on the Last Day.'
>
> 'The Devil was a Jew, you think?'
>
> 'I don't know what he was. He is a Jew today. He is a Jew in Russia. We don't want Jews and their money-lending and financing and dividend-making. We want quiet agriculture, the Holy Church, simple peasants, the Russian Tsar, the Russian language. Russian customs.'[151]

There is no way of knowing whether this exchange genuinely took place, or whether it simply resided in Graham's imagination. Indeed, it would not be wholly unfair to suggest that the opinions and speculations posited in these sentiments were simply Graham's own views, for which his 'witness' merely functioned as a mouthpiece. Nonetheless, whatever the truth of the conversation, these sentences are highly revealing. Although Graham failed to link Jews to socialism, he still suggested that they were involved in a conspiracy that took in politics, trade, business, the church, Freemasonry and even the Devil himself! In other words, Jews represented a pretty comprehensive threat to the every aspect of the established social and political order.

Each of these elements could be found in the vast Jewish conspiracy detailed in the *Protocols of the Elders of Zion*. It described the meeting of a strange group of rabbis in Prague's ancient Jewish cemetery and discussed, amongst other things, how to take over the world's banks, its industry, destroy the aristocracy and increase financial speculation. For observers who assumed a Jewish plot existed at some level in modern life, even if confined to the financial world, it was not necessary to take a giant psychological leap in order to believe that Jews were behind the Bolshevik revolution. After all, if Jews merely wanted power, then surely this was precisely what drove on the Bolsheviks, no matter the human cost. In this respect, the response to the Bolshevik revolution was all of a piece with other aspects of British attitudes towards East European Jewry. The conspicuous presence of Jews in the Bolshevik movement, most especially Leon Trotsky, facilitated the confirmation of a suspicion that had been felt, to various degrees, for several decades. 'The Jew' wanted ultimate power and was prepared to go to any lengths to achieve it. Even rootlessness could be tied to Bolshevism. After all, was it not an ideology that traversed international boundaries and national allegiances? What could be more rootless, more unpatriotic than the Bolshevik, the true internationalist? Naturally, therefore, what occurred in Eastern Europe in the decade after the Great War, especially in the former Russian Empire, played a major contribution in instilling and concentrating this conspiratorial perspective in the British mindset. At face value, perhaps the revolutionary Jew was a different kind of *Ostjude* to the money-lender, the tavern-keeper or the peddler. Then again, at heart he was still 'the Jew', whatever manner of (dis)guise he selected in the execution of his vile plans.

Abbreviations

Archives

AAIU	Archives of the Alliance Israélite Universelle, Paris, France
AJASU	Archives of the Anglo-Jewish Association, Special Collections, Southampton University Library, UK
AJC	Archives of the American Jewish Committee, New York City, USA
BOD	Archives of the Board of Deputies of British Jews, London Metropolitan Archives, London, UK
GAST	Papers of Dr Moses Gaster, Special Collections, University College London, UK
MGA	Manchester Guardian Archives, Special Collections, John Rylands University Library of Manchester, UK
PAR	Papers of Professor Sir Bernard Pares, School of Slavonic and East European Studies, University College London, UK
LWUCL	Papers of Lucien Wolf – *Darkest Russia* file, School of Slavonic and East European Studies, University College London, UK
PRO-FO	Foreign Office Files, the National Archives, Public Record Office, Kew, London, UK
RA	Rothschild Archives, New Court, London, UK
WMC	Lucien Wolf, David Mowshowitch Collection, YIVO Institute for Jewish Research, New York City, USA

Newspapers and publications

AJY	*American Jewish Yearbook*
DNB	*Oxford Dictionary of National Biography*
JW	*Jewish World*
JC	*Jewish Chronicle*
MG	*Manchester Guardian*
NYT	*New York Times*
PIP	*Penny Illustrated Paper*
PMG	*Pall Mall Gazette*
RCAI	*Royal Commission on Alien Immigration*
TLS	*Times Literary Supplement*

Notes

Introduction

1. This was asserted throughout the period under study, for example: *The Scotsman*, 14 May 1881: 8; N.S. Joseph, to *The Times*, 24 November 1890: 13; *The Times*, 11 May 1904: 7; White, Arnold, *The Views of Vanoc*, London: Kegan, Treach, Trübner, 1910: 83.
2. *The Times*, 29 April 1882: 11.
3. Naturally, Western Europe was not exempt from such investigations, though it is not the subject of this study. The Dreyfus Affair in France, for example, prompted a good deal of scrutiny and sniggering in Britain. Various ideologues in France, Berlin and Vienna were similarly an object of concern. One, the German ideologue Adolf Stöcker, actually visited in 1883 and gave several lectures (in German) in London. His presence raised a few eyebrows and opposition from British Jews, see: *JC*, 16 November 1883: 6; 16 November 1883: 9–10; 23 November 1883: 9–10; *The Times*, 13 November 1883: 9; Henry de Worms to *The Times*, 26 November 1883: 6.
4. *The Spectator*, 21 January 1882: 83. See also: *The Spectator*, 11 December 1897: 851, in which it was observed: 'There is no country in Europe, except England, certainly no large country, where the [Jewish] race, as a race, does not feel that it is in immediate and most serious danger. Even in France, where the Jews are under no disabilities [...] tens of thousands declare that France is betrayed by a Jew syndicate, and Extremists inquire, even in the Chamber, whether the French government is or is not guided in the last resort by Jew moneylenders who are anti-French. In Austria the moment the mob rises for any cause whatever it attacks Jews; they are not safe even in Vienna; in Prague they are despoiled, and even murdered, like Germans, while, unlike Germans, they are not protected by the soldiery. In Germany a powerful party makes of their expulsion its shibboleth, and but that the bureaucracy insists on external order, no Jew house, even in Berlin, would be safe for a week from pillage. In Romania [...] Jews are prohibited from entering common schools, and they are permitted to practise some trades only on condition of a servility which popular writers then hold up to the general disgust. In Russia they are treated as a slave race, penned up in assigned districts where they almost starve.' For a discussion of *The Spectator*'s attitude towards Dreyfus and other continental anti-Jewish events, see: Johnson, Sam, 'Hep! Hep!, Dreyfus and Other Jewish Questions. A View from London, 1881–1914', in S. Marten-Finnis and M. Winkler (eds), *City and Press. Interaction, Discourse, Thesis*, Bremen: Edition Lumière, 2009: 151–160.
5. Russell, C. and Lewis, H.S., *The Jew in London. A Study of Racial Character and Present-Day Conditions*, London: T. Fisher Unwin, 1900: 5.

219

6. Endelman, Todd M., *The Jews of Britain, 1656–2000*, Berkeley: University of California Press, 2002: 127.

7. *The Graphic*, 14 February 1891: 171: in light of the Guildhall meeting this article asked what the British would think of 'a memorial addressed to the Queen [Victoria] about Ireland by a meeting of philanthropic Russians?'; see also, *Reynolds's Newspaper*, 15 February 1891: 4. This was precisely the counter-argument the Russian Minister of the Interior, Count N.P. Ignatiev, utilised in 1882 in response to the British sympathy meeting held in the wake of the pogroms, see: Klier, John D., 'The Mansion House Protest of 1882: Philosemitism or the "English Disease" ', paper presented at Birkbeck College, University of London, 11 July 2007. In author's personal collection.

8. Gutwein, Daniel, 'The Politics of Jewish Solidarity: Anglo-Jewish Diplomacy and the Moscow Expulsion of April 1891', *Jewish History*, 5(2), September 1991: 23–45; Rubenstein, W.D. and Rubenstein, Hilary, *Philosemitism: Admiration and Support in the English-Speaking World for Jews, 1840–1939*, London: Macmillan, 1999; Gidley, Brian, 'The Ghosts of Kishinev in the East End: Responses to the Pogrom in the Jewish London of 1903', in Bar-Yosef, Eitan and Valman, Nadia (eds), *'The Jew' in Late-Victorian and Edwardian Culture. Between the East End and East Africa*, London: Palgrave, 2009: 98–112.

9. Garrard, John A., *The English and Immigration, 1880–1910*, London: Oxford University Press, 1971; Gainer, Bernard, *The Alien Invasion. The Origins of the Aliens Act of 1905*, London: Heinemann, 1972.

10. Holmes, Colin, *Antisemitism in British Society, 1876–1939*, London: Edward Arnold, 1979; Allett, John, 'New Liberalism, Old Prejudices: J.A. Hobson and the "Jewish Question" ', *Jewish Social Studies*, 1987(49): 99–114.

11. For example, one of Belloc's biographers in the 1980s was keen to point out that both his and Chesterton's work could be 'distinguished from the vulgar excesses of continental journalism', Wilson, A.N., *Hilaire Belloc*, London: Hamilton, 1984: 267. A more recent biographer of Belloc has asserted that 'it would be wrong to associate the complex nature of Belloc's position [on the Jews] with the crude hatred of the Nazis, that he would condemn outright': Pearce, Joseph, *Old Thunder. A Life of Hilaire Belloc*, London: Harper Collins, 2002: 197. Pearce spends little time examining the antisemitic component of Belloc's worldview and succeeds in glossing over that which he evidently finds unpalatable. To claim that Belloc's worldview was not informed by antisemitism is, to say the least, breathtakingly naïve, as is the inference that there was nothing complex about the Nazi antisemitic worldview. Another historian has asserted that Belloc and Chesterton attempted to 'import the French clerical variety' of antisemitism into Britain, but met with 'little or no success': Lewis, Bernard, *Semites and Anti-Semites*, London: Phoenix Giant, 1997: 97. Again, I would adjudge this a misreading of the evidence.

12. Cheyette, Brian, *Constructions of 'the Jew' in English Literature and Society. Racial Representations, 1875–1945*, Cambridge: Cambridge University Press, 1995; Bar-Yosef, Eitan and Valman, Nadia (eds), *'The Jew' in Late-Victorian and Edwardian Culture. Between the East End and East Africa*, London: Palgrave, 2009.

13. There have been occasional exceptions, which include: Maglen, Krista, 'Importing Trachoma. The Introduction into Britain of American Ideas of an "Immigrant Disease", 1892–1906', *Immigrants and Minorities*, 23(1), March 2005: 80–99; Gilman, Sander, *The Jew's Body*, London: Routledge, 1991, which encompasses British discourse in its comparisons.

14. Alderman, Geoffrey, 'The Anti-Jewish Riots of August 1911 in South Wales', *Welsh History Review*, 6, December 1972/1973: 190–200; Holmes, Colin, 'The Tredegar Riots of 1911', *Welsh History Review*, 11, December 1982/1983: 214–225; Glaser, Anthony, 'The Tredegar Riots of August 1911', in Henriques, Ursula R.Q. (ed.), *The Jews of South Wales*, Cardiff: University of Wales Press, 1993: 151–176; Rubinstein, William D., 'The Anti-Jewish Riots of 1911 in South Wales: A Re-examination', *Welsh History Review*, 18 December 1997: 667–699; Alderman, Geoffrey, 'The Anti-Jewish Riots of August 1911 in South Wales: A Response', *Welsh History Review*, 20, June 2001: 565–571; Gilam, Abraham, 'The Leeds Anti-Jewish Riots 1917', *Jewish Quarterly*, 29 (1981): 34–37.

15. Vincent, David, *The Rise of Mass Literacy. Reading and Writing in Modern Europe*, Cambridge: Polity, 2000: 9–10.

16. There was even a subscriber to the *JC* in St Petersburg, who, during the Kishinev crisis, complained that one copy had been mutilated by the Russian Imperial censor and others not delivered at all: *JC*, 19 June 1903: 11.

17. For a discussion of developments in newspapers, the telegraph and railways, see the definitive text on the rise of mass communication and its impact in Europe, Briggs, Asa, and Burke, Peter, *A Social History of the Media. From Gutenberg to the Internet*, Cambridge: Polity, 2005.

18. Rubenstein and Rubenstein, *Philosemitism*.

19. For example, see the various Jewish responses in the Tsarist Empire to the pogroms of 1881–1882: Klier, John D., *Russians, Jews and the Pogroms of 1881–1882*, Cambridge: Cambridge University Press, 2011. In the early twentieth century, the novelist and international celebrity Lev Tolstoi was often involved in public protests against the Russian regime, as was Maxim Gorkii. These actions were always reported in the British press, see *JW*, 5 June 1903: 205; 14 August 1903: 414–415. See also a 1915 declaration against the persecution of the Jews of the Russian Empire, signed by an array of prominent Russians, including members of the Imperial Senate, intellectuals and cultural figures: *The Observer*, 25 April 1915: 17.

20. *The Times*, 22 November 1880: 9.

21. *The Times*, 5 October 1882: 3.

22. For discussion of Marr, see Zimmerman, Moshe, *Wilhelm Marr. The Patriarch of Antisemitism*, Oxford: Oxford University Press, 1986.

23. *The Times*, 27 August 1883: 3.

24. I have only found a single usage of the term 'antisemitism' applicable to the Russian case in *The Times* between 1880 and 1890: 27 November 1890: 5. From 1891 to 1900, I can find none; of the 53 references to the term in these years, the majority (at least 80 per cent) refer to Imperial Germany. The same is the case for the 126 uses of 'antisemitic' in the final decade of the nineteenth century, though there is one connected to Romania: 7 February 1893: 5.

1 Romania: 'Cruelty to an Unprecedented Pitch', 1860s and 1870s

1. *JC*, 6 July 1866: 8.
2. *JC*, 27 July 1866: 4.
3. *JC*, 14 June 1867: 4.
4. *JC*, 9 July 1867: 4–5; *The Times*, 10 August 1867: 9, reported that two Jews were drowned.
5. For the official British take on this, see George B. Ward to Consul-General John Green, 16 July 1867, in 'Correspondence Respecting Persecution of Jews in Moldavia, 1867', *Parliamentary Command Paper*, No., 3917, London: Harris and Sons, 1867: 7–8 [henceforward, 'Correspondence 1867']; these events became hugely symbolic, see *Daily News*, 18 January 1877: 5; *PMG*, 18 January 1877: 4. Ten years later, it was referred to as the 'noyades [executions by drowning] de Galatz'; *MG*, 26 August 1879: 5; *Birmingham Daily Post*, 23 February 1879: 8.
6. *PMG*, 1 May 1868: 1–2.
7. *Hull Packet and East Riding Times*, 17 September 1869: 3; *Leeds Mercury*, 18 September 1869: 1.
8. *JC*, 9 August 1867: 4–5.
9. 'Correspondence 1867', Nos. 3890, 3897, 3917; 'Correspondence Respecting Conditions and Treatment of Jews in Serbia and Romania, 1875–76', *Parliamentary Command Paper*, No. 1742, London: Harris and Sons, 1877 [henceforward, 'Correspondence 1875–1876'].
10. *The Times*, 31 May 1872: 8.
11. *Hansard*, Volume 188, 1868: 1136, 1242; *Hansard*, Volume 209, 1872: 109, 946. For details of Goldsmid, see his *DNB* entry, by Geoffrey Alderman.
12. Montefiore's visit was widely reported: *The Times*, 31 August 1867: 10; *Daily News*, 5 September 1867: 3; Moses Montefiore to *The Times*, 21 September 1867: 9 – included a copy of his petition to Romania's ruler, Prince Carol (Charles). For a discussion of Montefiore, see Green, Abigail, 'Rethinking Sir Moses Montefiore: Religion, Nationhood and International Philanthropy in the Nineteenth Century', *American Historical Review*, 110(3), 2005: 631–658; ibid. *Moses Montefiore. Jewish Liberator, Imperial Hero*, Cambridge: Harvard University Press, 2010.
13. Fink, Carole, *Defending the Rights of Others. The Great Powers, the Jews and International Minority Protection, 1878–1938*, Cambridge: Cambridge University Press, 2004: 15–21.
14. For other efforts to historicise the Romanian experience, see *The Times*, 20 November 1886: 15; Miller, William, *The Balkans. Romania, Bulgaria, Serbia and Montenegro*, London: T. Fisher Unwin, 1894.
15. Seton-Watson, R.W., *The Rise of Nationality in the Balkans*, London: Constable & Co., 1917: 2, 3. For a collection of Seton-Watson's writings on Romania, see Bodea, Cornelia and Hugh Seton-Watson, *R.W. Seton-Watson şi Românii, 1906–1920*, Bucharest: Editura Ştiinţifică şi Enciclopedică, 1988, in two volumes.
16. Seton-Watson, *The Rise of Nationality in the Balkans*: 26.
17. *The Scotsman*, 22 July 1867: 2.

18. Hitchins, Keith, *The Romanians, 1774–1866*, Oxford: Clarendon, 1996: 71.
19. Benjamin, Lya, 'The Jews in Romania, a Historical Outline', in Giurescu, Dinu C. and Fischer-Galaţi, Stephen A. (eds), *Romania. A Historical Perspective*, New York: Columbia University Press, 1998: 539.
20. Iançu, Carol, *Jews in Romania 1866–1919. From Exclusion to Emancipation*, New York: Columbia University Press, 1996: 8, 10; Oldson, William O., *A Providential Antisemitism. Nationalism and Polity in Nineteenth-Century Romania*, Philadelphia: American Philosophical Society, 1991: 58.
21. The historiography of the Romanian Jewish experience, especially in the nineteenth century, is somewhat under-researched in English, though this is probably as much the case for wider Romanian history. Histories of Romanian Jewry are heavily weighted towards the Holocaust period, for obvious reasons. There are, however, some Romanian scholars who have begun to fill these manifold historiographical lacunae. See, for example, the work of Oişteanu, Andrei, *Imaginea evreului în cultura română. Studiu de imagologie în context est-central european*, Bucharest: Humanitas, 2001; ibid., *Inventing the Jew. Antisemitic Stereotypes in Romanian and other East-Central European Cultures*, London: University of Nebraska Press, 2009.
22. Berkowitz, Joel, 'Avrom Goldfaden and the Modern Yiddish Theatre', *Pakn Treger*, Winter 2004: 11–19.
23. Hitchins, *The Romanians*: 112–113.
24. Benjamin, 'The Jews in Romania, a Historical Outline': 539; Hitchins, Keith., *Rumania, 1866–1947*, Oxford: Clarendon, 1994: 166; Hitchins states that between 1899 and 1907 around 52,000 Jews left Romania.
25. Hitchins, *Rumania, 1866–1947*: 16.
26. Kellogg, Frederick, *The Road to Romanian Independence*, West Lafayette: Purdue University Press, 1995: 39–67.
27. Iançu, *Jews in Romania 1866–1919*: 11, 39; Fink, *Defending the Rights of Others*: 13.
28. Livezeanu, Irina, *Cultural Politics in Greater Romania. Regionalism, Nation-Building and Ethnic Struggle, 1918–1930*, Ithaca: Cornell University Press: 11.
29. Oldson, *A Providential Antisemitism*: 103, 58.
30. Eidelberg, Philip, *The Great Romanian Peasant Revolt of 1907: Origins of a Modern Jacquerie*, Leiden: Brill, 1974.
31. Fink, *Defending the Rights of Others*: 14.
32. *The Times*, 10 September 1867: 9.
33. Szajkowski, Zosa, 'Jewish Diplomacy: Notes on the Occasion of the Centenary of the *Alliance Israélite Universelle*', *Jewish Social Studies*, 22, 1960: 131–158; Graetz, Michael, *The Jews in Nineteenth-Century France. From the French Revolution to the Alliance Israélite Universelle*, Stanford: Stanford University Press, 1996: 249–288. The *Consistoire* was the central administrative body that dealt with Jewish affairs in France.
34. It was also concerned with Jewish self-help, particularly through the promotion of professional education. The AIU sponsored all kinds of schools in various states, including the Ottoman Empire and parts of the French Empire. See Rodrique, Aron, *French Jews, Turkish Jews: The Alliance Israélite Universelle and the Politics of Jewish Schooling in Turkey, 1860–1925*, Bloomington: Indiana University Press, 1990.

35. *Glasgow Herald*, 1 June 1867: 5; *Glasgow Herald*, 1 June 1870: 5.
36. Iançu, Carol, 'Adolphe Crémieux, l'Alliance Israélite Universelle et les juifs de Roumanie au début du règne de Carol Hohenzollern Sigmaringen', *Revue des Etudes Juives*, 133, 1974: 481–502.
37. Consul St Clair to Mr Green, 21 May 1867, 'Correspondence 1867', Nos. 3890: 4.
38. 'Correspondence 1867', No. 3890: 4.
39. See Gartner, Lloyd P., 'Romania, America and World Jewry: Consul Peixotto in Bucharest, 1870–1876', *American Jewish Historical Quarterly*, September 1968: 25–117.
40. *Birmingham Daily Post*, 23 March 1872: 5; *PMG*, 27 April 187: 8; *MG*, 27 April 1872: 4; *The Times*, 18 June 1872: 6; *Glasgow Herald*, 19 June 1872: 5; *The Times*, 20 September 1872: 7.
41. Fink, *Defending the Rights of others*: 19–22. For discussion of Bleichröder's relationship with Bismarck and his part in forging the new Germany, see Stern, Fritz, *Gold and Iron: Bismarck, Bleichröder and the Building of the German Empire*, London: Allen and Unwin, 1977.
42. Goldsmid corresponded privately with Crémieux in the 1860s, see various letters in AAIU, II.D.29.
43. *Daily News*, 23 February 1872: 5; *Birmingham Daily Post*, 24 February 1872: 6; *Manchester Weekly Times*, 24 February 1872: 5.
44. George, B. Ward to Consul-General John Green, 30 January 1872, 'Correspondence 1875–1876': 226.
45. Consul-General John Green to Earl Granville (Secretary of State for Foreign Affairs), 11 February 1872, 'Correspondence 1875–1876': 227–228.
46. Consul-General John Green to Earl Granville, 8 February 1872, 'Correspondence 1875–1876': 226–227.
47. *JC*, 23 February 1872: 4.
48. *JC*, 8 March 1872: 13; *The Times*, 6 March 1872: 12. A poem was dedicated to Cahul's victims, *JC*, 12 April 1872: 26; Davis, Israel, *The Jews in Romania. A Short Statement on their Recent History and Present Situation*, London: AJA/AIU, Trübner and Co., 1872: 14–24; in the second edition (1872), a petition from the Jews of Cahul was included: 32–39.
49. George B. Ward to Consul-General John Green, 30 January 1872, 'Correspondence 1875–1876': 226.
50. *PMG*, 18 April 1872: 7.
51. *Birmingham Daily Post*, 24 February 1872: 6. It was referred to as an 'act of sacrilege' in a consular letter, Consul-General John Green to Earl Granville, 11 February 1872, 'Correspondence 1875–1876': 227–228.
52. For details of the myth's manifestations in the late medieval period, see Rubin, Miri, *Gentile Tales. The Narrative Assault on Late Medieval Jews*, New Haven: Yale University Press, 1999.
53. *MG*, 14 September 1871: 5.
54. *Birmingham Daily Post*, 18 March 1872: 5.
55. The *shtadlan* was an intercessor (but not a rabbi) appointed by a local Jewish community, who represented its interests before various authorities (sometimes local, sometimes not).
56. *Birmingham Daily Post*, 23 March 1872: 5. The Jewish community of Birmingham was comparatively small in this period. In 1851, the census

indicated a population of 750–1000 Jews, and it is doubtful that it had increased greatly by 1872, see Alderman, Geoffrey, *Modern British Jewry*, Oxford: Clarendon Press, 1998: 27

57. *JC*, 5 April 1872: 4.
58. *Birmingham Daily Post*, 28 March 1872: 6.
59. Francis Goldsmid to Earl Granville, 9 February 1872; Francis Goldsmid to Earl Granville, 18 February 1872; Francis Goldsmid to Viscount Enfield (under-secretary of state in Foreign Office), 11 April 1872, 'Correspondence 1875–1876': 225, 230, 237.
60. *Hansard*, Volume 210, 1872: 1585–1604.
61. *JC*, 3 May 1872: 68.
62. In July 1871, the AJA sent a letter to Tsar Alexander II in protest at the Odessa pogrom of that year, see AAIU, II.D.21.
63. See various letters published in the *JC* in 1871 and 1872.
64. Moses Montefiore to Earl Granville, 29 February 1872; 19 March 1872, 'Correspondence 1875–1876': 231, 234–235.
65. *JC*, 15 March 1872: 1: this appeal was listed on the front page and urged all Jews to contribute, regardless as to whether or not they agreed with the principles governing the AJA's mission.
66. *JC*, 15 March 1872: 6.
67. *JC*, 31 May 1872: 124–126.
68. *The Times*, 31 May 1872: 6; *Daily News*, 31 May 1872: 3; *Leeds Mercury*, 1 June 1872: 11.
69. Davis, *The Jews in Romania*.
70. *JC*, 17 May 1872: 96.
71. For aspects of the emancipation process, see Gilam, Abraham, *The Emancipation of the Jews in England, 1830–1860*, New York: Garland Publishing, 1982; Salbstein, M.C.N., *The Emancipation of the Jews in Britain: the Question of the Admission of the Jews to Parliament, 1828–1860*, London: Associated University Press, 1982.
72. *JC*, 24 May 1872: 112.
73. *JC*, 26 April 1872: 54. Similar sentiments were expressed during the Commons' debate instigated by Goldsmid, see *Hansard*, Volume 210, 1872: 1585–1604.
74. *The Times*, 8 March 1872: 7.
75. *JC*, 14 June 1872: 150, 157.
76. See Scult, Mel, 'English Missions to the Jews; Conversion in the Age of Emancipation', *Jewish Social Studies*, 35(1), January 1973: 3–17.
77. *The Scotsman*, 23 June 1877: 7–8.
78. *The Scotsman*, 15 March 1877: 5; see also Vice-Consul Dupuis at Galatz to Sir H. Elliot [FO], 28 August 1872, 'Correspondence 1875–1876': 269.
79. *The Scotsman*, 23 June 1877: 7–8.
80. *The Scotsman*, 15 June 1877: 5.
81. *Saturday Review*, 23 March 1872: 356–357; also cited in Guedella, H., *The Romanian Government and the Jews*, London: Pottle & Sons, 1872: 20.
82. *JC*, 29 March 1872: 7–8.
83. George B. Ward to Consul-General John Green, 9 October 1868, 'Correspondence 1875–1876': 134–135.

84. Vice-Consul St John to Earl Granville [FO], 29 April 1873, 'Correspondence 1875–1876': 284–285.
85. Vice-Consul St John to Vivian Hussey [Bucharest], 20 June 1874, 'Correspondence 1875–1876': 324.
86. Francis Goldsmid to Mr E. Hammond [FO], 27 May 1873, 'Correspondence 1875–1876': 287–288.
87. *PMG*, 18 January 1877: 4; *Daily News*, 18 January 1877: 5.
88. This was common penname used by letter writers in nineteenth- and early twentieth-century newspapers, as such it is impossible to speculate usefully upon the author's identity.
89. *PMG*, 22 January 1877: 4; see also *PMG*, 26 January 1877: 2–3.
90. *PMG*, 24 January 1877: 3; *PMG*, 27 January 1877: 5.
91. *PMG*, 26 January 1877: 3.
92. *Leeds Mercury*, 4 November 1872: 4; *PMG*, 9 November 1872: 7.
93. Fink, *Defending the Rights of Others*: 16, 18.
94. For discussions of the general aspects of the Congress, see Jelavich, Barbara, *Russia and the Formation of the Romanian National State 1821–1878*, Cambridge: Cambridge University Press, 1984: 277–291; Hitchins, Rumania: 50–54.
95. Fink, *Defending the Rights of Others*: 24.
96. *Leeds Mercury*, 28 December 1876: 5; *Daily News*, 28 December 1876: 2; *Bristol Mercury*, 20 December 1876: 4.
97. *JC*, 15 March 1878: 3; Goldsmid died as a consequence of an accident at Waterloo Station (he appeared to fall under the wheels of an oncoming train) in early May 1878, so was unable to pursue his ambitions regarding the Congress, see *The Times*, 4 May 1878: 7.
98. *JC*, 7 June 1878: 7.
99. Letter from Montefiore, J.M. and Henry de Worms to Benjamin Disraeli and Lord Salisbury, *The Times*, 19 June 1878: 11; *JC*, 21 June 1878: 2.
100. *The Times*, 6 July 1878: 11. For a similar perspective, a year on from the Treaty, see *MG*, 15 August 1879: 5.
101. For discussion of the Congress, see Fink, *Defending the Rights of Others*: 22–38; Medlicott, W.N., *The Congress of Berlin and After. A Diplomatic History of the Near Eastern Settlement, 1878–1880*, London: Routledge, 1963; Iancu, Carol, *Bleichröder et Crémieux: le combat pour l'émancipation des Juifs de Roumanie devant le congrès de Berlin: Correspondance inédite, 1878–1880*, Paris: Centre de recherches et d'études Juives et Hébraïques, 1987.
102. *JC*, 5 July 1878: 5.
103. Fink, *Defending the Rights of Others*: 29.
104. *JC*, 5 July 1878: 6–7.
105. Iancu, *Jews in Romania*: 140; this was noted by the British press, see *PMG*, 22 August 1879: 4.
106. *The Scotsman*, 26 July 1879: 8; *Leeds Mercury*, 26 July 1879; *Daily News*, 26 July 1879: 4.
107. Bluntschli, J.C., *Romania and the Legal Status of the Jews in Romania. An Exposition of Public Law*, London: Anglo-Jewish Association, 1879; Bluntschli was a professor of law at the University of Heidelberg, his pamphlet originally appeared in German, as *Der Staat Rumänien und das Rechtsverhältniss der Juden in Rumänien. Ein Rechtsgutachten*, Berlin: 1879; *JC*, 17 October 1879: 7.

108. *JC*, 1 August 1879: 11.
109. *The Observer*, 24 August 1879: 5.
110. *MG*, 26 August 1879: 5; *PMG*, 2 September 1879: 8; *PMG*, 20 September 1879: 4.
111. Ion Ghica to *The Times*, 20 January 1879: 4; this letter caused a bit of a stir, see *Birmingham Daily Post*, 23 February 1879, 8.
112. *Daily News*, 6 October 1879: 5.
113. For British diplomatic approaches on the final moves to Romanian independence, see 'Correspondence Relative to Recognition of Independence of Romania, 1880', *Parliamentary Command Paper*, No. 2554, London: Harris and Sons, 1880.
114. Fink, *Defending the Rights of Others*: 32.
115. Iançu, *Jews in Romania*: 112. Lists of those granted naturalisation were provided by the *JC* in its 'Romanian Bulletin', 13 February 1903: iv.
116. *The Times*, 16 August 1884: 2.
117. See William White's papers, PRO-FO 364; Sutherland-Edwards, H., *Sir William White. His Life and Correspondence*, London: John Murray, 1902.
118. For instance, *The Times*, 4 August 1884: 7; Henry de Worms to *The Times*, 16 August 1884: 2.
119. *JC*, 30 May 1884: 7. See also *JC*, 13 June 1884: 8–10.
120. *The Scotsman*, 8 August 1885: 9. A pamphlet by an AJA member also appeared this year, Schloss, David F., *The Persecution of the Jews in Romania. A Detailed Account, Compiled from Recent Official and Other Authentic Information*, London: D. Nutt, 1885.
121. Gaster was expelled from Romania in 1885, though invited back a few years later – he did not return. For a brief biography, see his *DNB* entry, by Geoffrey Alderman. See also the many letters appealing for his assistance, usually financial, from Romanian Jews in the United Kingdom and Romania, GAST.
122. Abraham Benisch to *PMG*, 26 January 1877: 3.

2 Imperial Russia: Troubles in the South, 1880s–1890s

1. This chapter is much indebted to the work of John Klier, for which I make no apology. I was privileged to act as a 'friendly reader' for his monumental study of the 1881–1882 pogroms, *Russians, Jews and the Pogroms of 1881–1882*, Cambridge: Cambridge University Press, 2011. The manuscript and the many discussions that John and I had have greatly informed my reading of these events, especially in terms of the significance for the British context.
2. Klier, *Russians, Jews and the Pogroms of 1881–1882*.
3. Rowland, R.H., 'Geographical patterns of the Jewish population in the Pale of Settlement in late nineteenth-century Russia', *Jewish Social Studies*, 48(3–4), 1986: 207–234.
4. For an analysis of the motivations that lay behind Jewish emigration during the period this study covers, see Sorin, Gerald, *A Time for Building. The Third Migration, 1880–1920*, London: Johns Hopkins University Press, 1992; Klier, John D., 'Emigration Mania in Late Imperial Russia: Legend and Reality', in

A. Newman and S. Massil (eds), *Patterns of Migration, 1850–1914*, London: Jewish Historical Society of England/UCL, 1996: 21–30.

5. For analyses of the Bund, see Mendelsohn, Ezra, *Class Struggle in the Pale: The Formative Years of the Jewish Workers' Movement in Tsarist Russia*, New York: Cambridge University Press, 1970; Gitelman, Zvi (ed.), *The Emergence of Modern Jewish Politics. Bundism and Zionism in Eastern Europe*, Pittsburgh: University of Pittsburgh Press, 2002; Zimmerman, Joshua D., *Poles, Jews and the Politics of Nationality: The Bund and the Polish Socialist Party in Late Tsarist Russia, 1892–1914*, Madison: University of Wisconsin Press, 2004.

6. For the classic account of the political experience of Russian Imperial Jewry, see Frankel, Jonathan, *Prophecy and Politics. Socialism, Nationalism and the Russian Jews, 1861–1917*, Cambridge: Cambridge University Press, 1981.

7. For a discussion of the Jewish role in revolutionary movements in the Tsarist Empire, see Haberer, Eric E., *Jews and Revolution in Nineteenth-Century Russia*, Cambridge: Cambridge University Press, 1995.

8. See Nathans, Benjamin, *Beyond the Pale. The Jewish Encounter with Late Imperial Russia*, London: University of California Press, 2002.

9. The Anglo-Jewish press occasionally acknowledged these achievements, see a discussion of Poliakov in *JC*, 7 May 1880: 6. For discussion of the Gintsburgs, see Nathans, *Beyond the Pale*; Klier, John D., 'Krug Gintsburgov i politika shtadlanuta v imperatorskoi Rossii', *Vestnik Evreiskogo Universiteta v Moskve*, 3(10), 1995: 38–55.

10. Henry Iliowizi (1850–1911) was originally from Minsk, but spent much of his adult life in Western Europe and the United States, where he was a rabbi to various congregations in Pennsylvania. Prior to this he was a teacher in an AJA school. He was also a novelist, and his works included: *In the Pale. Stories and Legends of the Jews*, Philadelphia: Jewish Publication Society of America, 1897; *The Weird Orient. Nine Mystic Tales*, Philadelphia: H.T. Coates & Co., 1900. These publications were pretty stereotypical and unsophisticated in their depictions of Jewish–gentile relations in the Russian Empire and elsewhere, such as Morocco.

11. *JC*, 9 July 1880: 12; 16 July 1880: 12; 23 July 1880: 12.

12. *The Times*, 1 May 1880: 11.

13. *The Times*, 16 March 1880: 4.

14. *JC*, 16 January 1880: 9.

15. See, for instance, Rogger, Hans, *Jewish Policies and Right-Wing Politics in Imperial Russia*, London: Macmillan, 1986; Aronson, I. Michael, *Troubles Waters. The Origins of the 1881 Anti-Jewish Pogroms in Russia*, Pittsburgh: University of Pittsburgh Press 1990; Klier, John D. and Lambroza, Shlomo, *Pogroms. Anti-Jewish Violence in Modern Russian History*, Cambridge: Cambridge University Press, 1992; Löwe, Heinz-Dietrich, 'Pogroms in Russia: Explanations, Comparisons, Suggestions', *Jewish Social Studies*, 11(1), (2004): 16–23; and, most especially, Klier, *Russians, Jews and the Pogroms of 1881–1882*.

16. Klier, *Russians, Jews and the Pogroms of 1881–1882*.

17. Similarly, the pogroms form a considerable component of the historiography of the Russian Imperial Jewish experience, see Frankel, Jonathan, 'The Crisis of 1881–1882 as a Turning Point in Modern Jewish History', in Berger, David (ed.), *The Legacy of Jewish Migration: 1881 and Its Impact*, New York: Columbia University Press, 1983: 9–22.

18. In terms of differences, the death toll might be considered. In all the events of 1881–1882, the total number of dead was around 25: Klier, *Southern Storms*; two decades later during 2 days at Kishinev, 49 Jews were killed: Judge, Edward H., *Easter in Kishinev: Anatomy of a Pogrom*, New York: New York University Press, 1992. In the First World War, as a consequence of the so-called military pogroms (the only pogroms to have any official connection in the Tsarist regime, via its armed forces), many hundreds, possibly thousands, were murdered: Prusin, Alexander Victor, *Nationalizing a Borderland: War, Ethnicity, and Anti-Jewish Violence in East Galicia, 1914–1920*, Tuscaloosa: University of Alabama Press, 2005.
19. Klier, John D., 'The Times of London, the Russian Press, and the Pogroms of 1881–2', *Carl Beck Papers*, (308), 1984: 1–26; Klier, *Russians, Jews and the Pogroms of 1881–1882*.
20. The 1989 edition of the *Oxford English Dictionary*, for instance, noted that first reference to Russian 'pogromen', a phrase taken from a German source, was made on 17 March 1882 in *The Times*. The dictionary has since revised its view and now cites the earliest usage as 1891. See draft revision (December 2007) of the OED entry for 'pogrom', which indicates an entry in Kennan, George, *Siberia and the Exile System*, New York: Century Co., 1891, Volume 2: 236. For my analysis of how pogrom was absorbed into the English language on both sides of the Atlantic, see Johnson, Sam, 'Uses and Abuses. "Pogrom" in the Anglo-American Imagination, 1881–1925', 2011 in Harriet Murav and Eugene Avrutin (eds), *Violence and Jewish Daily Life in the East European Borderlands. Essays in Honor of John D. Klier*, Brighton: Academic Studies Press.
21. *PMG*, 23 January 1882: 4.
22. Dates relating directly to events in the Russian Empire are given in both Old Style and New Style (OS and NS); at this time, Russia still used the Julian calendar, which was, in the nineteenth century, 12 days behind the Gregorian calendar used in the West.
23. Though, once again, like many other things Tsarist censorship should not be exaggerated in this period, see Klier, John D., 'Censorship of the Press in Russia and the Jewish Question, 1855–1894', *Jewish Social Studies*, 48, 1986: 257–268. One matter that Klier's monograph *Russians, Jews and the Pogroms of 1881–1882* challenges, and from which its title is drawn, is the belief that the Russian Jewish press was unable to refer directly to the 1881–1882 pogroms; 'southern storms' was allegedly their codeword for these events, see Bartal, Israel, *The Jews of Eastern Europe, 1772–1881*, Philadelphia: University of Pennsylvania, 2005: 144. However, as is noted by Klier, this was not the case and the Russian Jewish press gave extensive coverage to the pogroms.
24. *Morning Post*, 3 May 1881: 5.
25. *Daily News*, 11 May 1881: 5.
26. *Evening Standard*, 10 May 1881: 2; *The Times*, 12 May 1881: 5.
27. For a discussion of the anti-Jewish violence in Germany in the early 1880s, see Hoffmann, Christian, 'Political Culture and Violence against Minorities. The Antisemitic Riots in Pomerania and West Prussia': 67–92, in Christian Hoffmann, Werner Bergman and Helmut Walser Smith (eds), *Exclusionary Violence. Antisemitic Riots in Modern German History*, Ann Arbour: University of Michigan Press, 2002.

28. *Daily News*, 23 May 1881: 5; *The Graphic*, 28 May 1881: 514.

29. *JW*, 6 May 1881: 4–5. The connections between German and Russian Judeophobia were widely assumed by commentators in the 1880s and beyond. They are explored in: Klier, John D., 'Russian Judeophobes and German Antisemites: Strangers and Brothers', *Jahrbucher für Geschichte Osteuropas*, 37(4), 1989: 524–540.

30. *Evening Standard*, 16 May 1881: 4; *Daily News*, 16 May 1881: 8; *St James's Gazette*, 17 May 1881: 6; *Morning Post*, 18 May 1881: 5; *Daily Telegraph*, 18 May 1881: 4; *Daily News*, 21 May 1881: 5.

31. *Daily News*, 17 May 1881: 5; *JW*, 24 June 1881: 5.

32. *The Graphic*, 14 May 1881: 474; *Daily News*, 16 May 1881: 8; *St. James's Gazette*, 17 May 1881: 6; *Morning Post*, 24 May 1881: 4; *Morning Post*, 26 May 1881: 4.

33. Klier, *Southern Storms*; Aronson, *Troubled Waters*: 107.

34. *The Times*, 2 May 1881: 8; *The Times*, 3 May 1881: 5.

35. *Daily News*, 16 May 1881: 8; *Daily Telegraph*, 21 May 1881: 5.

36. *Daily Telegraph*, 24 May 1881: 6.

37. Wortman, Richard, *The Crisis of Russian Populism*, Cambridge: Cambridge University Press, 1967.

38. *Morning Post*, 26 May 1881: 4; *Daily Telegraph*, 24 May 1881: 6.

39. *Daily Telegraph*, 18 May 1881: 3.

40. *The Scotsman*, 14 May 1881: 8.

41. *Daily Telegraph*, 14 May 1881: 5.

42. *The Times*, 24 May 1881: 11.

43. *The Graphic*, 28 May 1881: 514.

44. *Weekly Register*, 28 May 1881: 21.

45. *JW*, 3 June 1881: 5.

46. *JW*, 6 May 1881: 4–5.

47. *JC*, 13 May 1881: 4.

48. *Daily News*, 20 May 1881: 3.

49. *St James's Gazette*, 23 May 1881: 6.

50. *Illustrated London News*, 4 June 1881: 549; see also *Illustrated London News*, 18 June 1881: 610, 616. These images, three in all, were the first Western visual depictions of the pogroms, and are discussed in: Klier, John, 'Iskusstvo i pogromyi: khudozhestvennoe otobrazhenie antievreiskogo nasiliia v imperskoi Rossii (1871–1903)': 442, in Oleg Budnitskii et al. (eds), *Russko-Evreiskaia kul'tura*, Moscow: Rosspen, 2006.

51. *Morning Post*, 4 May 1881: 5.

52. *Morning Post*, 3 May 1881: 5; *Evening Standard*, 10 May 1881: 2; *Evening Standard*, 16 May 1881: 4; *Daily News*, 19 May 1881: 5; *The Graphic*, 4 June 1881: 564.

53. *Daily News*, 25 May 1881: 5.

54. *Evening Standard*, 2 June 1881: 5; *Morning Post*, 3 June 1881: 5; *Daily News*, 8 June 1881: 5.

55. *Daily Telegraph*, 24 May 1881: 6.

56. *Morning Post*, 18 May 1881: 5.

57. *The Scotsman*, 3 October 1881: 5.

58. *The Times*, 24 May 1881: 11.

59. *Morning Post*, 23 May 1881: 5; *Evening Standard*, 24 May 1881: 2; *Daily Telegraph*, 25 May 1881: 5. Alexander III met with Baron Gintsburg and

other leading Petersburg Jews in May 1881, see Klier, *Russians, Jews and the Pogroms of 1881–1882.*

60. *The Graphic*, 14 May 1881: 474.
61. *JC*, 20 May 1881: 11.
62. *JW*, 6 May 1881: 4–5.
63. *JW*, 3 June 1881: 5.
64. *Hansard*, Volume 256, 1881: 563–565. This question was tabled by Baron Henry de Worms, who initially asked about one Leon Lewisohn, a British Jew expelled from Moscow by the authorities. In typical parliamentary fashion, de Worms used one question in order to add a follow up. See a similar question, 1073–1075. For discussion of the public meeting and the Granville deputation, see several articles in the *JC*, 27 May 1881: 3, 8–9, 11–13. The mainstream press commended these protests, but did not believe that any good could come of it; it is 'not our business to make formal protests against the laws of other nations', *Daily News*, 25 May 1881: 5.
65. The AJA declared a meeting 'undesirable', see AJA Minute Book, 24 May 1881: 317, AJASU, MS137/AJ95/ADD/1. The reasons for the failure to convene a meeting in 1881 are discussed in an unpublished paper by John Klier, 'The Mansion House Protest of 1882: Philosemitism or the "English Disease"', in author's possession. See also Feldman, David, *Englishmen and Jews. Social Relations and Political Culture, 1840–1914*, New Haven/London: Yale University Press, 1994.
66. As will be discussed, the *Jewish World*'s correspondent's work was syndicated to other British newspapers and was attributed to Bankanovich. A Jewish newspaper in the Russian Empire, *Russkii Evrei*, noted the visit of an émigré journalist called Bankanovich, see Klier, *Russians, Jews and the Pogroms of 1881–1882.*
67. For a selection of individual pieces, see *JW*, 15 June 1881: 4–5; 5 August 1881: 5–6; 26 August 1881: 5–6; 9 September 1881: 5–6; 16 October 1881: 5–6; 23 October 1881: 5–6. The article about Berezovka appeared in the issue of 26 September 1881: 5–6.
68. See Klier, *Russians, Jews and the Pogroms of 1881–1882.* The role of the *Jewish World*'s Special Correspondent is discussed in the chapter dealing with the legends of the pogroms. Klier argues that Bankanovich's work was crucial in generating the belief, in the West at any rate, that Tsarism used pogroms as an official policy.
69. For a discussion of *Kievlianin*, see Klier, John D., *Imperial Russia's Jewish Question*, Cambridge: Cambridge University Press, 1995: 187ff.
70. *JW*, 8 July 1881: 5–6.
71. *JW*, 15 July 1881: 5–6.
72. *JW*, 5 August 1881: 5–6.
73. *JW*, 26 August 1881: 5–6.
74. *JW*, 22 July 1881: 4–5.
75. Louis Cohen to *The Times*, 30 July 1881: 9.
76. *JW*, 2 September 1881: 4–5.
77. For discussion of Ignatiev, see Klier, *Russians, Jews and the Pogroms of 1881–1882*; Aronson, *Troubled Waters.*
78. The circular was dated 6 September 1881 (OS 25 August 1881), and was enclosed in letter from Wyndham to Granville, 5 October 1881, in 'Correspondence Regarding the Treatment of Jews in Russia, 1882', *Parliamentary*

Command Papers, Nos. C3132, C3250, London: Harris and Sons, 1882: 16. [Hereafter, 'Correspondence 1882'].

79. For details of the pogrom, see Ochs, Michael, 'Tsarist Officialdom and anti-Jewish Pogroms in Poland', in Klier and Lambroza, *Pogroms: Anti-Jewish Violence in Modern Russian History*: 164–190.

80. *St James's Gazette*, 26 December 1881: 8: this was republished from a report in the *Evening Standard*.

81. *Daily Telegraph*, 29 December 1881: 4.

82. *JW*, 6 January 1882: 4–5.

83. *JW*, 13 January 1882: 4–5.

84. For a biography of Jacobs, see his *DNB* entry by Anne Kershen.

85. *The Times*, 11 January 1882: 4; see also editorial in this issue, 9; the second article, appeared on 13 January 1882: 4. These articles were soon published as pamphlet: *Russian Atrocities, 1881. Supplementary Statement Issued by the Russo-Jewish Committee*, London: Wertheimer, 1882.

86. *The Scotsman*, 6 January 1882: 6, 10 January 1882: 5; 12 January 1882: 3; *Daily News*, 19 January 1882: 8; *Evening Standard*, 19 January 1882: 8.

87. *The Scotsman*, 12 January 1882: 4.

88. It did not follow, of course, that the press was not open to alternate perspectives and perhaps the most significant in 1882 came from an émigré Russian noblewoman who lived in London, Olga Novikova. She signed herself as 'O.K' in letters to *The Times*. See, for instance, her refutation of Jacob's articles, *The Times*, 18 January 1882: 10. For details of Novikova, see Stanislawski, Michael, *Zionism and the Fin de Siècle. Cosmopolitanism and Nationalism from Nordau to Jabotinsky*, London: University of California Press, 2001: 49–56; Stead, W.T. *The MP for Russia. Reminiscences and Correspondence of Madame Olga Novikoff*. London: Andrew Melrose, 1909, in two volumes.

89. *Birmingham Daily Mail*, 25 January 1882: 2.

90. *Morning Post*, 2 February 1882: 4.

91. *The Spectator*, 14 January 1882: 43.

92. *PMG*, 23 January 1882: 7.

93. *PMG*, 28 January 1882: 1–2; 30 January 1882: 1–2. Of course, Jacobs was not an eyewitness to the pogroms or their aftermath, but he presented his case as such.

94. *JW*, 13 January 1882: 5.

95. *Daily Telegraph*, 2 January 1882: 4.

96. *Daily News*, 31 December 1881: 6; *JC*, 6 January 1882: 4.

97. For an analysis of Tsarist rule in Poland and the western provinces, see Weeks, Theodore, *Nation and State in Late Imperial Russia: Nationalism and Russification on Russia's Western Frontier 1863–1914*, DeKalb: Northern Illinois University Press, 1996.

98. *JC*, 11 November 1881: 7. For details of the formation of the RJC, see AJA Minute Book, 15 November 1881: 4, AJASU, MS137/AJ95/ADD/2; CFC Minute Book, 6 November 1881, BOD, ACC3121/C11A/001.

99. *JC*, 6 January 1882: 4.

100. *Evening Standard*, 23 January 1882: 2; *St. James's Gazette*, 25 January 1882: 4; *Daily News*, 25 January 1882: 2; *The Times*, 25 January 1882: 9.

101. *JW*, 27 January 1882: 5.

102. Earl of Shaftesbury to *The Times*, 16 January 1882: 8.

103. *Daily Telegraph*, 18 January 1882: 4.
104. *St. James's Gazette*, 2 February 1882: 3; *Daily Telegraph*, 2 February 1882: 4; *Morning Post*, 2 February 1882: 4; *Daily News*, 2 February 1882: 2; *Evening Standard*, 2 February 1882: 4; *JW*, 3 February 1882: 4–5.
105. AJA Minute Book, 24 January 1882: 13, AJASU, MS137/AJ95/ADD/2.
106. *The Scotsman*, 3 January 1882: 6; *MG*, 3 February 1882: 6; *Birmingham Daily Mail*, 7 February 1882: 2.
107. *JC*, 27 January 1882: 8.
108. *MG*, 13 February 1882: 8.
109. *Hansard*, Volume 267, 1882: 30–70.
110. 'Correspondence 1882'.
111. *Hansard*, Volume 266, 1882: 25–230, 244.
112. *Hansard*, Volume 267, 1882: 30–70.
113. *JW*, 10 March 1882: 5.
114. *Hansard*, Volume 267, 1882: 30–70.
115. *Liverpool Mercury*, 1 July 1890: 3; *Birmingham Daily Post*, 16 July 1890: 8. See also 'The Tsar and the Jews', *Blackwood's Edinburgh Magazine*, October 1890: 441–452.
116. *The Times*, 30 July 1890: 10; *Daily News*, 1 August 1890: 6; *Birmingham Daily Post*, 31 July 1890: 3; *Manchester Weekly Times*, 1 August 1890: 4.
117. *Leeds Mercury*, 31 July 1890: 4; see also, *Daily News*, 1 August 1890: 4, which spoke of Tsar Alexander III's mind having been 'poisoned'.
118. *Hansard*, Volume 347, 1890: 1366; 1896–1897; *Daily News*, 2 August 1890: 4.
119. *Daily News*, 21 August 1890: 5. This was, of course, technically true; the Tsarist regime proposed to revitalise legislation already on the statute book, not to create a whole new body of law on Jewish residence restrictions.
120. In the wake of his father's death, Herman Adler was not formally appointed as the next Chief Rabbi until May 1891. It was announced in the press, *PMG*, 12 May 1891: 6. He addressed the Bayswater Synagogue on Jewish persecution in Russia, see *The Times*, 7 October 1890: 7. For an exposition of Oswald John Simon's views, see his letter to *The Times*, 6 October 1890: 13.
121. *Daily News*, 13 November 1890: 3, 4.
122. *The Times*, 11 December 1890: 10; *JC*, 12 December 1890: 8; *Leeds Mercury*, 11 December 1890: 7; *PMG*, 11 December 1890: 7; *Birmingham Daily Post*, 11 December 1890: 4. For a Russian Jewish perspective of the meeting, written a decade or so later, see Dubnow, S.M, *History of the Jews of Russia and Poland. From the Earliest Times until the Present Day*, Bergenfield, NJ: Avotaynu, 2000: 399–402.
123. *Daily News*, 11 February 1891: 5; *Preston Chronicle*, 21 February 1891: 2.
124. Löwe, Heinz-Dietrich, *The Tsars and the Jews: Reform, Reaction, and Anti-semitism in Imperial Russia, 1772–1917*, London: Harwood Academic Publishers, 1993: 70–71.
125. Meetings were organised throughout Britain, including Glasgow, Cardiff and Liverpool, see *Glasgow Herald*, 13 June 1891: 10; *Western Mail*, 22 June 1891: 4; *Liverpool Mercury*, 29 January 1892: 6.
126. *The Spectator*, 25 April 1891: 578; *Daily News*, 28 April 1891: 5; *Birmingham Daily Post*, 1 May 1891: 4; *The Spectator*, 2 May 1891: 619–620; *The Times*, 8 May 1891: 9; *Hampshire Telegraph*, 9 May 1891: 2; *PMG*, 23 May 1891: 6; *Glasgow Herald*, 28 May 1891: 6.

127. Olga Novikova to *The Times*, 22 November 1890: 9; 2 December 1890: 4; 10 December 1890: 3.

128. *Birmingham Daily Post*, 1 May 1891: 4; *Aberdeen Journal*, 4 May 1891: 4; *PMG*, 26 May 1891: 5; *Daily News*, 1 June 1891: 4.

129. *Hansard*, Volume 353, 1891: 1617–1618; *Glasgow Herald*, 6 June 1891: 8.

130. *PMG*, 1 June 1891: 6; *PMG*, 2 June 1891: 2, 6.

131. Wertheimer, Jack, *Unwelcome Strangers. East European Jews in Imperial Germany*, New York/Oxford: Oxford University Press, 1987: 50–51.

132. *Birmingham Daily Post*, 6 June 1891: 8; *Liverpool Mercury*, 6 June 1891: 4.

133. *Aberdeen Journal*, 4 May 1891: 4. See also Earl of Dunraven, 'The Invasion of Destitute Aliens', *Nineteenth Century*, June 1892: 985–1000.

134. Jeyes, S.H., 'Foreign Pauper Immigration', *Fortnightly Review*, July 1891: 13–24; Anglo-Russian, 'The Tsar and the Jews', *Contemporary Review*, 59, October 1891: 309–326.

135. *PMG*, 5 May 1891: 6; *Aberdeen Journal*, 11 May 1891: 4. This did happen, but it was nothing to do with the cause of Russian Jews, but rather French military interests, see Ferguson, Niall, *The House of Rothschild. The World's Banker, 1849–1998*, London: Penguin, 1998: 380. For Anglo-Jewish interventions, see Gutwein, Daniel, 'The Politics of Jewish Solidarity: Anglo-Jewish Diplomacy and the Moscow Expulsion of April 1891', *Jewish History*, 5(2), September 1991: 23–45.

136. Norman, Theodore, *An Outstretched Arm: A History of the Jewish Colonization Association*, London: Routledge & Kegan Paul, 1985. For a contemporary report on the JCA's foundation, see *Birmingham Daily Post*, 12 November 1891: 6.

137. *Liverpool Mercury*, 22 April 1891: 5; *Birmingham Daily Post*, 1 May 1891: 4; *Daily News*, 27 May 1891: 5; *The Spectator*, 30 May 1891: 746–747.

138. *Northern Echo*, 1 May 1891: 3.

139. White, Arnold, 'Jewish Colonization and the Russian Persecution', *New Review*, August 1891: 97–105.

140. An article by White was described as 'valuable and instrumental' in *JC*, 6 May 1892: 5; the article was, White, Arnold, 'The Truth about the Russian Jew', *Contemporary Review*, May 1892: 695–708. White's Russian visit was also closely monitored, see *JC*, 26 June 1891: 15; *JC*, 3 July 1891: 14; *JC*, 10 July 1891: 8.

141. Johnson, Sam, 'Confronting the East. *Darkest Russia*, British Opinion and Tsarist Russia's "Jewish Question", 1890–1914', *East European Jewish Affairs*, December 2006: 199–211.

142. *Darkest Russia*, 14 August 1891: 6.

143. *Darkest Russia*, 20 May 1892: 1, 5.

144. *Darkest Russia*, 20 May 1892: 1, 5.

145. Geffcken, Friedrich, 'Russia under Alexander III', *New Review*, August 1891: 234–243.

3 Romania and Kishinev: Crises Intertwined, 1900–1906

1. For details of immigration, the aliens debate and Royal Commission, see Garrard, John A., *The English and Immigration, 1880–1910*, London: Oxford

University Press, 1971; Gainer, Bernard, *The Alien Invasion. The Origins of the Aliens Act of 1905*, London: Heinemann, 1972; Black, Eugene C., *The Social Politics of Anglo-Jewry, 1880–1920*, London: Blackwell, 1988; Kershen, Anne J., (ed.), *London the Promised Land? The Migrant Experience in a Capital City*, London: Ashgate, 1997; Gartner, Lloyd P., *The Jewish Immigrant in England*, London: Vallentine Mitchell, 2001.

2. For these interviews, see *RCAI*, Volume II.

3. *RCAI*, Volume I: 3–4.

4. Holmes, Colin, *Antisemitism in British Society, 1876–1939*, London: Edward Arnold, 1979, part 1.

5. For example, *JC*, 4 May 1900: 15–16; 25 May 1900: 10–14.

6. For details of the impact of Jewish nationalism in the United Kingdom, see Vital, David, *Zionism. The Formative Years*, Oxford: Clarendon, 1982: 146–162ff; Black, Eugene C., 'A Typological Study of English Zionists', *Jewish Social Studies*, 9(3), 2003: 20–55.

7. Vital, David, 'Zangwill and Modern Jewish Nationalism', *Modern Judaism*, 4(3), October 1984: 243–253.

8. See, for example, Israel Zangwill to *The Times*, 4 February 1902: 10; 22 July 1902: 14; 23 March 1903: 10; 4 April 1903: 9; Lucien Wolf to *The Times*, 20 March 1903: 12; 11 April 1903: 8.

9. *RCAI*, Volume II: 529. However, according to Evans-Gordon in *The Alien Immigrant*, London: Heinemann, 1903: 189, Jewish immigration from Romania stood at 3126 in 1900, 1162 in 1901.

10. Lord Edmund Fitzmaurice asked HMG whether Romanian Jewish policy was 'contrary to the Treaty of Berlin'. HMG's response concluded that as Romanian Jews were un-naturalised citizens, no complaints had been received on this matter; clearly, the Romanian purpose of the Treaty had been forgotten. See *Hansard*, Volume 87, 1900: 26. A similar perspective was recorded 2 years later; this time the question was from Captain Herbert Jessel, *Hansard*, Volume 110, 1902: 682–683.

11. *RCAI*, Volume II: 460–462; for Evans-Gordon's entire report, see 451–466.

12. CFC letter to Lord Roseberry, 8 December 1893; CFC letter to Lord Kimberly, 24 May 1895, BOD, ACC3121/C11/12/96/1.

13. See various correspondence between Morris Duparc of the AJA and Jacques Bigart of the AIU, AIUA/A/VI.H.38–40. During this period, the AJA received copies of the regular reports sent to Paris by the AIU's representative in Bucharest, Isaac Astruc, see, for example, AIUA/R/V.C. 28–30.

14. See, for instance, *JC*, 17 January 1902: 21; *JC*, 7 March 1902: 8.

15. *JC*, 4 April 2002: 17.

16. L.J. Greenberg, et al., to *The Times*, 11 April 1902: 8.

17. AJA to Austrian AIU, AJA Minute Book, 8 February 1902: 175, AJASU, MS137/AJ95/ADD/3.

18. L.J. Greenberg, et al., to *The Times*, 11 April 1902: 8.

19. Note of Landau's verbal report, AJA Minute Book, 11 May 1902: 161, AJASU, MS137/AJ95/ADD/3. A copy of the *procès verbal* of the conference, dated 16 April 1902, is located at BOD, ACC3121/C11/12/96/4. It sheds little light on the proceedings and its principal proposal was to organise a press campaign, led by the Berlin representatives, Paul Nathans and Hermann Cohn.

20. *JC*, 18 April 1902: 11.
21. *JC*, 11 April 1902: 16–17.
22. *JC*, 11 July 1902: 25.
23. *JC*, 18 July 02: 16; *JW*, 18 July 1902: 321.
24. *JW*, 6 June 1902: i–ii.
25. *JW*, 11 July 1902: 304–307.
26. Some related material is located in RA, files XI/III/108 (000/73) 18901902; XI/III/109 (000/73) 1901–1902.
27. This was not the first time the Rothschild family was involved in Romanian Jewish politics, see Ferguson, Niall, *The House of Rothschild. The World's Banker, 1849–1998*, London: Penguin, 1998: 176–177.
28. For Sir John Kennedy's take on this proposed legislation, see his memorandum to the FO, 12 March 1902, PRO-FO, file 104–159. He generally thought Romania's policy 'obnoxious', see letter to Lord Lansdowne, 21 September 1902, PRO-FO, file 104–159.
29. Lord Rothschild to Lord Lansdowne, 10 March 1902; Lord Rothschild to Sir Thomas Sanderson, 24 March 1902; 10 April 1902; 2 May 1902, PRO-FO, file 104–159.
30. BOD/AJA to Lord Lansdowne, 22 May 1902, PRO-FO, file 104–159.
31. BOD/AJA to Lord Lansdowne, 30 June 1902, PRO-FO, file 104–159: ten-page memorandum attached, dated 23 June 1902.
32. Memorandum from Kennedy to Captain Herbert Jessel MP, undated, PRO-FO, file 104–159.
33. *The Times*, 10 June 1902: 7; *JC*, 6 June 1902: 8.
34. Lazare, Bernard, *Die Juden in Rumänien*. Berlin: H.S. Hermann, 1902; *La question israélite en Roumanie*. Bucarest: Imprimerie E.S. Cerbu, 1902; 'The Jews in Romania', *Contemporary Review*, February 1903: 237–248.
35. *JC*, 15 August 1902: 8.
36. For the full version of Hay's note, see Wolf, Lucien (ed.), *Notes on the Diplomatic History of the Jewish Question, with Texts of Treaty Stipulations and other Official Documents*, London: Jewish Historical Society of England, 1919: 23–44.
37. *The Scotsman*, 19 September 1902: 5.
38. *The Times*, 18 September 1902: 3.
39. US concern in the Romanian Jewish question is reflected in the annual publication of the American Jewish Committee: *AJY*, 3, 1901: 25–108; the introduction to 5, 1903: 17–39, records the optimism felt by American Jewry at the Hay's Note and its swift dissipation following Kishinev. For a discussion of Schiff, the most important American Jewish leader of this era, see Cohen, Naomi W., *Jacob H. Schiff. A Study in American Jewish Leadership*, Hanover/London: UPNE, 1999.
40. *JC*, 2 October 1902: 14.
41. *JW*, 26 September 1902: 9; third bulletin also in this issue; next issue appeared 5 December 1902, then 13 February 1903.
42. This issue provoked comment in the mainstream press, mainly a result of its prominent signatures: *The Scotsman*, 23 September 1902: 5; so, too, did the December issue: *The Scotsman*, 5 December 1902: 8.
43. *JW*, 5 December 1902: ii.
44. On the first occasion, 1900, he was not elected.

45. For example, in 1899, Evans-Gordon presided over a concert for a Jewish home for the elderly, *JC*, 22 December 1899: 28; a year later, he distributed the prizes for Jewish schools in Stepney, *JC*, 28 December 1900: 34.
46. Lord Rothschild to the *JC*, 28 September 1900: 5.
47. *JC*, 6 March 1903: 18.
48. *JC*, 15 May 1903: 14.
49. Very little has been written about the British Brothers' League, but see entry by Colin Holmes on the topic, in Levy, Richard S. (ed.), *Antisemitism. A Historical Encyclopaedia of Prejudice and Persecution*, Oxford: ABC-Clio, 2005: 86.
50. For Evans-Gordon's appearance at BBL meetings, see *JC*, 17 January 1902: 21.
51. *JC*, 31 October 1902: 20.
52. *JC*, 28 November 1902: 19.
53. A year after Evans-Gordon's visit to the Tsarist Empire, where he met the much derided Minister of the Interior, Viacheslav von Plehve – renowned for his antisemitic views – the Zionist leader Theodor Herzl arrived in St Petersburg. This is perhaps the most infamous contemporary case of a Jewish leader 'supping with the Devil'. For details of Herzl and Plehve's meeting, see Vital, *Zionism. The Formative Years*: 249–251. In 1904, a leading member of Anglo-Jewish society, Lucien Wolf, also met with Plehve, see Roth, Cecil (ed.), *Essays in Jewish History by Lucien Wolf with a Memoir*, London: Jewish Historical Society, 1934: 64–69.
54. *Hansard*, Volume 113, 1902: 219–220; *Hansard*, Volume 123, 1903: 931; *JC*, 5 December 1902: iii.
55. *The Times*, 19 September 1902: 3: 22 September 1902: 3; 23 October 1902: 3, 7; 26 September 1902: 3; 27 September 1902: 5; 9 October 1902: 11; 5 December 1902: 4; 29 December 1902: 4.
56. Compare, for instance, the two bulletins that appeared on 5 December 1902 and 13 February 1903.
57. Gaster, Moses, 'The Jews in Romania', *North American Review*, November 1902: 665–666.
58. *The Times*, 9 October 1902: 11.
59. Sir John Kennedy to Lord Lansdowne, 24 September 1902; 2 October 1902, PRO-FO, file 104–159.
60. Isaac Astruc to AIU, date illegible, AIUA/R/V.C.28.
61. 'Verax', *La Roumanie et les Juifs*, Bucharest: I.V. Socecu, 1903: 109–110, 169, 250–251, 199. It was published in English in 1904, and distributed to British MPs, which, as can be imagined, failed to impress the *JC*, 25 March 1904: 10–11, 22. Interestingly, Verax attacked Evans-Gordon, who indignantly rebuffed him in a letter to the *JC*, 25 March 1904: 20. A similar publication appeared in 1906; Lahovary, Jean, *The Jewish Question in Romania*, London: Aggett and Co., 1906.
62. Sir John Kennedy to Lord Lansdowne, 2 October 1902, PRO-FO, file 104–159.
63. B'nei Zion, founded in 1887, was the British incarnation of *Hovevei Zion*, one of the earliest Jewish nationalist organisations, founded in the Tsarist Empire in 1881.

64. *JC*, 14 November 1902: 19.

65. *JC*, 14 November 1902: 19: In the mainstream press, Samuel's act was greeted with similar approval: 'If the Romanians do not like their representatives to be ignored by the Chief Magistrate of the City, they should mend their ways, and see that the Jews who have the misfortune to live within their frontiers are treated as citizens, and not as outlaws': *Daily Chronicle*, 22 November 1902: 4. See also *The Times*, 21 November 1902: 3.

66. *JW*, 30 January 1903: 353.

67. *JC*, 30 January 1903: 20.

68. *JC*, 22 May 1903: i. Out of a total population of 147,000 in Kishinev, there were 50,000 Jews, 50,000 Moldavians and 8000 Russians; Lambroza, Shlomo, 'The Pogroms of 1903–1906': 204, in Klier, John D., and Lambroza, Shlomo, *Pogroms. Anti-Jewish Violence in Modern Russian History*, Cambridge: Cambridge University Press, 1992.

69. For details of Kishinev, see Judge, Edward H., *Easter in Kishinev. Anatomy of a Pogrom*, New York: New York University Press, 1992; for the number of victims – dead and injured: 72–75.

70. Penkower, Monty Noam, 'The Kishinev Pogrom of 1903: A Turning Point in Jewish History', *Modern Judaism*, 24(3), 2004: 187.

71. *JC*, 29 May 1903: 10–11; photographs taken by the journalist Michael Davitt were reproduced on 26 June 1903: 8–9. Davitt, a former Irish MP, was one of the first Western observers to arrive in Kishinev, a couple of months after the pogrom. He published a book, *Within the Pale: The True Story of the Antisemitic Persecution in Russia*, London: Hurst & Blackett, 1903, which further added to the myth that the pogrom was centrally orchestrated.

72. This image was clearly so shocking in 1903 that it was not published in the *JC*, though the *JW* reproduced it as a front cover, but only as a simple line-drawing, which rendered a very different and less impressive effect than the original photograph: *JW*, 29 May 1903: front page.

73. For a discussion of the American response to Kishinev, see Schoenberg, P.E., 'The American Reaction to the Kishinev Pogrom of 1903', *American Jewish Historical Quarterly*, 63(3), March 1974: 262–283. For a contemporary response, see Adler, Cyrus, *The Voice of America on Kishinev*, Philadelphia: Jewish Publication Society of America, 1904.

74. *The Times*, 24 April 1903: 5; *The Scotsman*, 24 April 1903: 7; *JC*, 1 May 1903: 7; *JW*, 1 May 1903: 112; *MG*, 24 April 1903: 9; *Daily Express*, 24 April 1903: 1. A similar paragraph appeared in the *NYT*, 24 April 1903: 6.

75. Unfortunately, since the *Jewish Chronicle* and the *Jewish World's* archives were destroyed during the London Blitz on 29 December 1940, it is often only possible to speculate on the source or individuals responsible for the many connections between London and St Petersburg.

76. Although, as was discussed in Chapter 2, the 1882 Warsaw pogrom was instrumental in the development of a single pogrom narrative, it was not regarded as an isolated event.

77. *JC*, 1 May 1903: 7.

78. *MG*, 12 May 1903: 7; *Daily Express*, 28 May 1903: 1: this report asserted that a placard had been discovered, signed by local Orthodox priests, which exhorted local Christians to attack Jews.

79. *The Times*, 2 May 1903: 7; *JW*, 8 May 1903: 137; *The Times*, 18 May 1903: 9; Judge, *Easter in Kishinev*: 39–44. Dubossary was about 25 kilometres from Kishinev.
80. *JC*, 8 May 1903: 7.
81. Klier, John D., 'Solzhenitsyn and the Kishinev Pogrom. A Slander against Russia?', *East European Jewish Affairs*, 33(1), 2003: 49–59; Judge, *Easter in Kishinev*: 135–140; Lambroza, 'The Pogroms of 1903–1906': 196–197.
82. *JC*, 8 May 1903: 7.
83. *JC*, 15 May 1903: 9.
84. *JC*, 22 May 1903: 7.
85. *JC*, 22 May 1903: 7.
86. *Daily Express*, 25 May 1903: 1; this story also appeared in *Daily News*, 25 May 1903: 12.
87. *Daily Mail*, 2 May 1903: 2.
88. *JW*, 15 May 1903: 156; *JW*, 22 May 1903: 165. See also *Free Russia*, 1 June 1903: 62; *MG*, 21 May 1903: 7; *The Anglo-Russian*, June 1903: 717–718.
89. *JC*, 8 May 1903: 7.
90. *JC*, 8 May 1903: 7. See also *Daily Telegraph*, 12 May 1903: 10.
91. *The Spectator*, 23 May 1903: 806.
92. *Free Russia*, 1 June 1903: 63.
93. White, Arnold, 'Kishinev and After', *National Review*, August 1903: 953.
94. Judge, *Easter in Kishinev*: 73.
95. 'Despatch from His Majesty's Consul-General at Odessa, forwarding a Report on the Riots at Kishinev. Russia, No. 1', *Parliamentary Command Paper*, No. 1721, London: HMSO, 1903.
96. *The Times*, 18 May 1903: 9.
97. All of these newspapers were warned by the Russian censor in light of their coverage, a matter discussed in the British press: *JW*, 15 May 1903: 156; 22 May 1903: 165; *The Times*, 12 May 1903: 5.
98. *Daily Telegraph*, 12 May 1903: 10.
99. Many of the images cited above appear in H.M. Bialik's famous poem about Kishinev, 'The City of Slaughter', which can be found in *Prooftexts*, 25, 2005: 8–29 (this issue is dedicated to various examinations of the poem and its author). See, for instance, 'A tale of cloven-belly, feather filled' (line 59); 'Of nostrils nailed' (line 60) and so on. In contrast, these images are absent in another literary rendering of the pogrom, published in the British periodical press: Korolenko, [V.G.], 'House No. 13. An Episode in the Massacre of Kishinev', *Contemporary Review*, February 1904: 266–280. There are plenty of references to feathers, blood, broken glass, some mutilations, but there is no cadaver stuffed with feathers.
100. *JW*, 8 May 1903: 131; see also *Daily News*, 4 May 1903: 5.
101. *The Times*, 24 April 1903: 5.
102. *JC*, 1 May 1903: 7.
103. *JW*, 8 May 1903: 137; *Daily Mail*, 2 May 1903: 2.
104. Lambroza, 'The Pogroms of 1903–1906': 204.
105. *JW*, 8 May 1903: 137.
106. Krushevan is well known to historians of antisemitism, though there is no satisfactory assessment of his journalistic endeavours in the Tsarist Empire. Alongside *Bessarabets*, he also edited *Znamia* ('The Banner'), which was

equally antisemitic and was the first newspaper to publish a version of the *Protocols of the Elders of Zion*. See de Michelis, Cesare G., 'Les Protocoles des sages de Sion: philologie et histoire', *Cahiers du monde russe*, 38(3), 1997: 263–306; ibid., *The Non-Existent Manuscript: A Study of the Protocols of the Sages of Zion*, Lincoln: University of Nebraska Press, 2004.

107. *JW*, 22 May 1903: 164.
108. *JC*, 15 May 1903: 9.
109. *JC*, 22 May 1903: 7.
110. *Free Russia*, 1 June 1903: 63; *The Times*, 18 May 1903: 9. A year after the pogrom, a Russian commentator described Krushevan's activities in a journal article: Tugan-Baranowskii, M., 'Antisemitism in Contemporary Russia', *Monthly Review*, January 1904: 74.
111. *JW*, 8 May 1903: 131.
112. *The Times*, 18 May 1903: 9.
113. *The Spectator*, 23 May 1903: 806.
114. Lambroza, 'The Pogroms of 1903–1906': 196, 200–202.
115. *The Times*, 18 May 1903: 10; *JW*, 22 May 1903: 164; *JC*, 22 May 1903: 8.
116. Judge, *Easter in Kishinev*: 89ff.
117. *JC*, 5 June 1903: 17.
118. *JC*, 15 May 1903: 21; *JW*, 22 May 1903: 175; *The Spectator*, 30 May 1903: 846; *MG*, 21 May 1903: 7.
119. *JW*, 22 May 1903: 164.
120. *MG*, 25 September 1903: 5; see also *JC*, 2 October 1903: 10, 15.
121. *The Times*, 7 December 1903: 10; it was reproduced in full in the *JC*, 11 December 1903: 14.
122. Lambroza, 'The Pogroms of 1903–1906': 208–212.
123. Lambroza, 'The Pogroms of 1903–1906': 218, 223.
124. Judge, *Easter in Kishinev*: 5–61; according to the head physician at the Kishinev city hospital, the bodies of four victims were brought to the hospital on the first day. Judge disputes this evidence.
125. It is an intriguing suggestion in this extract that 'feather beds' appear as a mark of 'social distinction', emphasising another way in which Jews were separate from gentiles. To destroy mattresses was to cut 'at the pride and purse of the Jew'. However, it was simply not the case that only Jews had feather mattresses; many inhabitants in Kishinev had feather beds! The suggestion that they were only owned by wealthy Jews reveals a great deal about the author's mindset; as does the notion that it might be considered a 'fine sport', even by the perpetrators. To my knowledge, after 25 years of reading nineteenth-century Russian literature (both Jewish and non-Jewish) in which one is most likely to find information about mattresses (!), they were stuffed with feathers, horse-hair or straw. In all probability, wealthier town-dwellers owned feather mattresses and pillows, since they would have been purchased from a shop; whilst in the countryside, peasants would have made their own – or did not have one at all.
126. *The Times*, 2 June 1903: 6; *JW*, 5 June 1905: 209.
127. *JW*, 26 June 1903: 279.
128. *The Anglo-Russian*, July–August 1903: 729.
129. *The Times*, 18 May 1903: 10.

130. *JW*, 29 May 1903: 188. At a meeting of the CFC, Lucien Wolf was instructed to meet with the Chief Commissioner of the Metropolitan Police prior to the Hyde Park meeting, so that he 'might warn the organizers to moderate their language': entry dated 15 June 1903, CFC Minute book, 1878–1916, BOD, ACC3121/C11/2/5.
131. *JW*, 29 May 1903: 195.
132. Entry dated 15 June 1903, CFC Minute book, 1878–1916, BOD, ACC3121/C11/2/5.
133. The RJC still existed in 1903, and publicly promoted philanthropic calls for the victims of Kishinev; but, like its activities in 1881–1882, and those of the Board, AJA and so on, in 1903, were conducted beyond the public gaze. See *JW*, 26 June 1903: 280.
134. Ironically, the *Catholic Herald*, 12 June 1903: 9, congratulated the London Jewish community on the organisation of the Hyde Park Demonstration, in the belief that it reflected a unified action: 'It requires courage and initiative to take this step, and evidently the Jews of London have both. If Catholics decided upon such an action in similar circumstances, there would be enough head-shaking and adverse criticism from the "antediluvians" to nip the effort in the bud. There is sufficient lack of zeal in Catholic circles to damp down a prairie fire. Someday, no doubt, we shall take our courage in both hands and resolve to do something to make our influence felt. Meantime, we keep adding to the pavement of Hades by blocks of good intentions.'
135. *JC*, 5 June 1903: 17.
136. Black, 'A Typological Study of English Zionists': 26–28.
137. *The Times*, 22 June 1903: 14; for a discussion of the East End response, see Fishman, William J., *East End Jewish Radicals, 1875–1914*, London: Duckworth, 1975: 250–252.
138. Black, *the Social Politics of Anglo-Jewry*: 213.
139. *Hansard*, Volume 122, 1903: 1093; Volume 123, 1903: 1310–1311.
140. 'Despatch from His Majesty's Consul-General at Odessa': 3–4.
141. Lambroza, 'The Pogroms of 1903–1906': 210–211. The trial took place behind closed doors, and just a handful of perpetrators were prosecuted and sentenced.
142. The Dogger Bank Incident occurred when the Russian navy bombarded several British fishing boats in the North Sea. The Russians had apparently mistaken the trawlers for Japanese torpedo boats.
143. For discussion of the 1905 revolution, see Ascher, Abraham, *The Russian Revolution of 1905*, Stanford: California University Press, 1988 and 1992.
144. All these statistics are taken from Lambroza, 'The Pogroms of 1903–1906': 228–231.
145. Weinberg, Robert, 'Workers, Pogroms and the 1905 Revolution in Odessa', *Russian Review*, 46(1), January 1987, 53: footnote 2: there are no precise statistics, as Weinberg elaborates – but the significance was, of course, that unlike Kishinev and all the pogroms of 1881–1882, they numbered in the hundreds. In 1905, *The Times*, 7 November 1905: 5, estimated that 1000 were killed in Odessa.

146. It was held in the Queen's Hall, London, and led by the Bishop of Ripon. Lord Rothschild was also present, see *JW*, 12 January 1906: 403; *JC*, 12 January 1906: 20–21; *The Spectator*, 13 January 1906: 42. For the privately expressed views of the London Rothschilds, see the correspondence to their Paris cousins in RA, file X1/130A/0, where there are references to the 'blindness of the Tsar', 'sinister forces' and the Black Hundreds.

147. In a search of *The Times* digital database, 'pogrom' appears in 50 articles between July 1905 and December 1906; between January 1903 and December 1904, it occurs in just three articles. The same search of the *JC* resulted in 186 hits in 1905–1906; 17 in 1903–1904. For the *MG*, between 1905 and 1906, 114 hits, 1903–1904, 3 hits; *The Scotsman*, 75 (1905–1906), 2 (1903–1904).

148. An indication of the degree to which the word was absorbed into English was the manner in which it could be used humorously [*sic*!]. For instance, the *Musical Times* referred to the destruction of a collection of aged pianos as 'a pianoforte pogrom', 1 June 1914: 374; in 1913, H.H. Munro, who wrote under the pseudonym 'Saki' and had been a Russian correspondent of the *Morning Post*, wrote a short story, 'The Unrest Cure', in which a pogrom is suggested. Though not actually used, it would be clear to readers that this was his point of reference; it can be found in *The Chronicle of Clovis*; I discuss this in my 'Uses and Abuses. "Pogrom" in the Anglo-American Imagination, 1881–1925', forthcoming in Harriet Murav and Eugene Avrutin (eds), *Violence and Jewish Daily Life in the East European Borderlands. Essays in Honor of John D. Klier*, Brighton: Academic Studies Press, 2011.

149. *JC*, 3 November 1905: 6.

150. *JC*, 10 November 1905: 9–14.

151. *The Times*, 3 November 1905: 7; 8 November 1905: 9; 9 November 1905: 5; 10 November 1905: 5; 15 November 1905: 5.

152. *The Times*, 22 November 1905: 4.

153. Moses Gaster to *The Times*, 25 November 1905: 18.

154. A reply by the correspondent was published on 11 December 1905: 5.

155. *The Times*, 30 November 1905: 4.

156. Lucien Wolf to *The Times*, 7 December 1905: 12; see also his letter on 21 December 1905: 7.

157. Lambroza, 'The Pogroms of 1903–1906', 225; see also Rogger, Hans, 'Was there a Russian Fascism? The Union of the Russian People', *Journal of Modern History*, 36, December 1964: 398–415.

158. Weinberg, 'Workers, Pogroms and the 1905 Revolution in Odessa'.

159. *JC*, 10 November 1905: 23.

160. *The Times*, 30 December 1905: 9. Hooliganism (*khuliganstvo*) was a major component of Russian popular and, to a degree, official anxieties at this moment. It was particularly associated with the lawlessness connected to the modern city, see Neuberger, Joan, *Hooliganism: Crime, Culture and Power in St Petersburg, 1900–1914*, Berkeley: University of California Press, 1993.

161. Lambroza, 'The Pogroms of 1903–1906': 225.

162. [Pares, Bernard and Baring, Maurice], 'The Russian Government and the Massacres', *Quarterly Review*, 205, July/August 1906: 594. Although this article did not bear the name of either men, Pares revealed their co-authorship

in his memoirs: Pares, Bernard, *My Russian Memoirs*, London: Jonathan Cape, 1931: 138.
163. Pares, Bernard, *Russia and Reform*, London: Constable, 1907: 527–528.
164. Lucien Wolf in Semenov, E.P., *The Russian Government and the Massacres. A Page of the Russian Counter-Revolution*, London: John Murray, 1907: xi.
165. *Darkest Russia*, 24 January 1912: 1.
166. This was also observed in *The Anglo-Russian*, June 1903: 715.

4 Partitioned Poland: Physical and Ideological Encounters, 1880s–1914

1. Klier, John D., *Russia Gathers her Jews. The Origins of the 'Jewish Question' in Russia, 1772–1825*, De Kalb: Northern Illinois University Press, 1986.
2. Rowland, R.H., 'Geographical Patterns of the Jewish Population in the Pale of Settlement in Late Nineteenth-Century Russia', *Jewish Social Studies*, 48(3–4), 1986: 207–234; 'Naslenie', *Evreiskiaia entsiklopediia*, St. Petersburg, 1906–1913, Vol. XI: 537.
3. For an analysis of the *shtetl* throughout the Tsarist period and beyond, see Estraikh, Gennady and Krutikov, Mikhail, *The Shtetl: Image and Reality*, Oxford: Legenda, 2001.
4. *The Times*, 9 October 1890: 13; Joseph, N.S. to *The Times*, 5 November 1890: 13; Dillon, E.J. *Russian Characteristics*, London: Chapman and Hall, 1892: 645. *The Times*, 30 July 1890: 9; *JW*, 12 February 1904: 403; *The Lancet*, 6 February 1904: 397; Pares, Bernard, *Russia and Reform*, London: Constable,. 1907: 64; see also *The Anglo-Russian*, February 1899: 214.
5. *The Times*, 1 April 1892: 15. Actually, the Pale was almost twice the size of Texas.
6. In this regard, we should perhaps not be too critical of nineteenth-century observers, since maps in recent textbooks and distinguished monographs continue to depict Congress Poland within the Pale; they shall remain nameless!
7. The 15 provinces were: Bessarabia, Vil'na, Vitebsk, Volhynia, Grodno, Ekaterinoslav, Kovno, Minsk, Mogilev, Podolia, Poltava, Taurida, Kherson, Chernigov and Kiev. In modern terms, these covered parts of Lithuania, Ukraine, Belorussia, Moldova and Poland.
8. Eisenbach, Arthur, *The Emancipation of the Jews in Poland, 1780–1870*, Oxford: Basil Blackwell, 1991.
9. The population of the *Kongresówka* in the late nineteenth century was around 1.3 million, 'Naslenie', *Evreiskiaia entsiklopediia*, Vol. XI: 537.
10. Teter, Magda, *Jews and Heretics in Catholic Poland: A Beleaguered Church in the Post-Reformation Era*, Cambridge: Cambridge University Press, 2006. In contrast, blood libel accusations were extremely rare in Orthodox Christian Russia.
11. Porter, Brian, *When Nationalism Began to Hate. Imagining Modern Politics in Nineteenth-Century Poland*, New York/Oxford: Oxford University Press, 2000.
12. *JC*, 1 August 1890: 20; Cohen, Israel, *Jewish Life in Modern Times*, London: Methuen and Co., 1914: 7; Eversley, Lord, *The Partitions of Poland*, London: T. Fisher Unwin, 1915: 40.

13. *Everyman*, 31 January 1913: 490.
14. *Russian Review*, II(2): 83–84.
15. In 1909, Sienkiewicz acquired the support of Israel Zangwill and Wells, H.G. in a campaign against Prussian rule in Poland, see *Prusse et Pologne*, Paris: Agence polonaise de presse, 1909.
16. Gardner, M.M., *Adam Mickiewicz, the National Poet of Poland*, London: J.M. Dent & Sons, 1911; *Poland. A Study in National Idealism*, London: Burns & Oates, 1916; *Anonymous Poet of Poland. Zygmunt Krasinski*, Cambridge: University Press, 1919; *Kosciuszko: A Biography*, London: George Allen & Unwin Ltd., 1920; *The Patriot Novelist of Poland. Henryk Sienkiewicz*, London: Dent, 1926. Even a glance at the titles sheds light on Gardner's Polonophilia.
17. Kompert, Leopold, *Scenes from the Ghetto. Studies of Jewish Life*, London: Remington & Co., 1882; Franzos, Karl Emil, *The Jews of Barnow*, London: Blackwood and Sons, 1882. See Hess, Jonathan M., 'Leopold Kompert and the Work of Nostalgia: The Cultural Capital of German Jewish Ghetto Fiction', *Jewish Quarterly Review*, 97(4), 2007: 576–625; Robertson, Richie, *The 'Jewish Question' in German Literature, 1749–1939. Emancipation and its Discontents*, Oxford: Oxford University Press, 1999.
18. Franzos, *The Jews of Barnow*: 85–86.
19. Wertheimer, Jack, *Unwelcome Strangers. East European Jews in Imperial Germany*, New York/Oxford: Oxford University Press, 1987: 150.
20. *The Times*, 23 August 1882: 3.
21. Franzos, Karl Emil, *For the Right*, London: J. Clarke & Co., 1889; see W.G. Gladstone's review in *Nineteenth Century*, April 1889: 615–617.
22. *The Graphic*, 23 September 1882: 299; *PMG*, 2 October 1882: 4. Over 30 years later, a review noted that Franzos 'painted Barnow as he saw it, but he did not see it as it was': *JW*, 15 October 1913: 17–18.
23. Barnow was Franzos' fictional name for Czortków, the town in which he was born and lived until he was a teenager. It was around 50 kilometres from the border of the Russian Empire/Pale of Settlement. It was located in Podolia, a part of Poland divided between Russia and Austria by the first partition. Today, it is called Chotkiv and is in Ukraine.
24. 'Jewish Tales and Jewish Reform', *Blackwood's Edinburgh Magazine*, November 1882: 639.
25. *Daily News*, 29 August 1882: 3.
26. For a good overview of the history of Galicia during the Habsburg period, see Wróbel, Piotr, 'The Jews of Galicia under Austrian-Polish Rule, 1869–1918', *Austrian History Yearbook*, 25, 1994: 97–138.
27. *Illustrated London News*, 10 October 1891: 468.
28. According to some contemporary observers, Caine's visit was orchestrated by the Russo-Jewish Committee, though others decried this. See *Review of Reviews*, November 1891: 442–443, in which Hall Caine was described as a 'Special Commissioner to the Russian Jews'. A columnist in the *Birmingham Daily Post*, 2 December 1891: 3, was dubious about this accolade, describing it as 'erroneous' and noting that: 'if the Russian official regards him in this character [his] stay in the country is not likely to be a lengthy one.' No corroborative evidence that Hall Caine was invited by the RJC has been located in either the AJA archives, or Hall Caine's personal

archive, deposited in the Manx National Heritage Library, Isle of Man, MS 09542.

29. *The Scapegoat* was first serialised in the *Illustrated London News*, then published in two volumes by Heinemann in 1891. For a positive review of *The Scapegoat*, see *JC*, 30 October 1891: 15: 'no such loving picture of Jewish life in the East has ever been drawn before.'

30. *JC*, 25 December 1891: 7; *JC*, 13 May 1892: 9. The Maccabaeans was/is a charitable organisation, with a Zionist membership.

31. Markel, Howard, *Quarantine! East European Jewish Immigrants and the New York City Epidemics of 1892*, Baltimore: John Hopkins University Press, 1999; Kraut, Alan M., *Silent Travelers. Germs, Genes and the 'Immigrant Menace'*, Baltimore: John Hopkins University Press, 1994, especially chapter six; Maglen, Krista, 'Importing Trachoma. The Introduction into Britain of American Ideas of an "Immigrant Disease", 1892–1906', *Immigrants and Minorities*, 23(1), March 2005: 80–99.

32. Evans, Richard J., *Death in Hamburg. Society and Politics in the Cholera Years, 1830–1910*, Oxford: Oxford University Press, 1987.

33. During the Black Death, Jews were accused of transmitting the disease by poisoning wells, see Richards, Jeffrey, *Sex, Dissidence and Damnation. Minority Groups in the Middle Ages*, Oxford: Routledge, 1994: 98–105.

34. *The Times*, 17 September 1892: 8.

35. *The Times*, 17 September 1892: 8; *The Times*, 19 September 1892: 4.

36. *The Times*, 17 September 1892: 8.

37. Hall, Caine, 'Russian Jewry. Scenes of Home Life in Poland and the Pale', *Pall Mall Magazine*, September 1893: 641–655; for part two, see October 1893 issue: 863–872.

38. Franzos, *The Jews of Barnow*: xix–xxi.

39. *Liverpool Mercury*, 28 September 1892: 7.

40. Most of Caine's subsequent work was devoted to various fictional examinations of life in the Isle of Man, about as far removed from Galicia as one could get.

41. Caine, 'Russian Jewry', *Pall Mall Magazine*, September 1893: 649.

42. In the early 1880s, the journalist W.T. Stead, who often wrote in Russian themes visited the Empire and encountered the Minister of the Interior, Ignatiev, N.P. see Stead, W.T., *Truth About Russia*, London: Cassell & Co., 1888: 305–306; in 1891, Arnold White also met with Russian ministers during his visit, see White, Arnold, 'Jewish Colonisation and the Russian Persecution', *New Review*, August 1891: 99; and, as was discussed in the chapter 3, in 1902 both Evans-Gordon and Lucien Wolf met with Von Plehve prior to their own Russian travels.

43. Baskerville, Beatrice C. *The Polish Jew. His Social and Economic Value*, London: Chapman & Hall, 1906: 6. Baskerville was Rome correspondent for the *New York World* (1914–1931) and the *Daily Telegraph* (1933–1940). She also made contributions to the literary world, including *Passover. A Novel*, London: Thornton Butterworth, 1920, a non-too-subtle rehashing of the Beilis Affair (see Chapter 5) relocated to Poland from Ukraine.

44. *TLS*, 26 October 1906: 359. An American review was less flattering about Baskerville's book, condemning her for 'naïveté', 'lack of discrimination',

and use of 'second-hand antisemitic sources', *Political Science Quarterly*, September 1908: 551–553; see also *NYT*, 19 January 1907: 5.

45. Evans-Gordon served in the Madras Staff Corps in British India, which included a stint on the North–West Frontier – now in Pakistan, on the border with Afghanistan.

46. Evans-Gordon, W., *The Alien Immigrant*, London: Heinemann, 1903: 55.

47. Many commentators were confused about the Jewish population of the Russian Empire and precisely how many respectively lived in Poland and the Pale. See, for example, two authors who believed that all Jews of the Russian Empire lived in Congress Poland: 'The State of Russia', *Edinburgh Review*, January 1907: 236; *The Times*, 29 October 1914: 7.

48. And, it must be said, in addressing and interrogating witnesses during the process of the Royal Commission, Evans-Gordon's questions tended to be of a leading, rather than inflammatory nature.

49. *RCAI*, Vol. II: 451–466.

50. The *JC*, 9 January 1903: 18, described Galician *luftmenschen* in connection with a report by the Austrian Zionist, Dr Fuchs, J.S.: 'No wonder that from out this welter of poverty and hate there emerges the Jewish *Luftmensch*, the poor shiftless creature, destitute of spirit, bereft of self-respect, sunk in ignorance and barren religious formalism, living from hand to mouth and never knowing from day to day whence the morrow's bread is to come.'

51. *RCAI*, Vol. II: 460.

52. Evans-Gordon, *The Alien Immigrant*: 135.

53. Arnold White's evidence, for instance, was challenged by Lord Rothschild, *RCAI*, Vol. II: 23, 25, 28, 41–42, 44, 48–51.

54. Baskerville, *The Polish Jew*: 3, 6, 65, 139.

55. Baskerville, *The Polish Jew*: 64.

56. Baskerville, *The Polish Jew*: 64–65.

57. An evident falsehood or misreading of the revolution in Congress Poland, described by one historian as the 'most lawless' part of the Empire by late 1905, see Ascher, Abraham, *The Russian Revolution of 1905*, Stanford: California University Press, 1988, Vol. 1: 134.

58. Baskerville, *The Polish Jew*: 126.

59. *RCAI*, Vol. II: 86ff, the testimony of George Brown, a photographer's assistant in the East End, emphasised the degree to which Jews monopolised trade and pushed others out of business, as well as the degree to which Jews were 'content to pig together' in overcrowded conditions (88); R.H. Onion, who worked as a 'clicker' (leather-cutter) in the shoe trade made similar assertions (89ff) and according to him, Jews made deliberate attempts 'to swindle', etc.

60. Roberts, Ian W., *History of the School of Slavonic and East European Studies, 1915–1990*, London: University of London, 1991. Nowadays, of course, SSEES is part of University College London.

61. Much of this is discussed in Pares, *Russia and Reform*; see also Pares, Bernard, 'A Peasants' Meeting in Russia', *Contemporary Review*, December 1905: 783–798, as well as a later, reflective publication, Pares, Barnard, *My Russian Memoirs*, London: Jonathan Cape, 1931.

62. See Hughes, Michael, 'Bernard Pares, Russian Studies and the Promotion of Anglo-Russian Friendship, 1907–1914', *Slavonic and East European Review*,

78(3), July 2000: 510–536. For Pares' own perspective on the visit to Russia, see his letter to *The Times*, 13 January 1912: 5.

63. Ascher, Abraham, *The Revolution of 1905. Authority Restored*, Stanford: Stanford University Press, 1992, Vol. II: 51, 88. The National Democrats also had representation in the Austrian *Reichsrat*, and in 1907 they won 25 seats in Galicia.

64. Taken from Pares' introduction to Dmowski, Roman, 'The Political Evolution of Poland', *Russian Review*, II(4): 54; see also similar sentiments in G.W., 'The Rise of the Pan-Polish Party', *English Review*, May 1909: 381–384.

65. Pares, Bernard, *Day by Day with the Russian Army, 1914–1915*, London: Constable, 1915: 1.

66. Pares, *My Russian Memoirs*: 138; Dmowski was also described as 'the Polish Cavour' in G.W., 'The Rise of the Pan-Polish Party': 383. In *My Contacts with Polish Politics, 1907–1917*, Kraków, 1933 [publisher unknown], Pares described many personal encounters with Dmowski, including a stay in his Warsaw apartment on the eve of the German invasion in August 1915: 11–12.

67. Leroy-Beaulieu, Henri, 'Introduction', in Dmowski, Roman, *La question polonaise*, Paris: Librairie Armand Colin, 1909: v.

68. For a discussion of the National Democratic ideological vision of Poland prior to the 1905 revolution, see Porter, Brian, A., 'Who Is a Pole and Where Is Poland? Territory and Nation in the Rhetoric of Polish National Democracy before 1905', *Slavic Review*, 51(4), Winter 1992: 639–653.

69. *Przegląd Wszechpolski* and *Myśli nowoczesnego Polaka* are discussed extensively in Porter, *When Nationalism Began to Hate*; Dmowski's *La question polonaise* was originally published in Polish as *Niemcy, Rosja i kwestia Polska*, ('Germany, Russia and the Polish Question') but was never translated into English. This did not disqualify it from acquiring interest in British circles, since a good knowledge of French was not unusual for commentators or journalists.

70. Porter, *When Nationalism Began to Hate*: 200, 228, 182.

71. For a study of the SDF, see Crick, Martin, *The History of the Social Democratic Federation*, Keele: Keele University Press, 1994; there is no study of the BBL, though it is referenced in Holmes, Colin, *Antisemitism in British Society, 1876–1939*, London: Edward Arnold, 1979.

72. G.W., 'The Rise of the Pan-Polish Party', *English Review*, May 1909: 381–384. The Brandes' quotation is from his book, *Poland. A Study of the Land, People and Literature*, London: Heinemann, 1903: 106.

73. Porter, 'Who Is a Pole and Where Is Poland?': 645ff.

74. There is a small collection of archival papers related to the *Russian Review*, but unfortunately they add very little to our understanding of how the journal operated, its criteria for the selection of contributions and the like. Little correspondence is extant and there is certainly nothing from Dmowski or Balicki. See PAR/2/1-24.

75. Dmowski, Roman, 'The Political Evolution of Poland', Parts I–III, *Russian Review*, II(4): 54–68; III(1): 84–99; III(2): 73–86.

76. Balicki, Zygmunt, 'The Revival of Political Thought in Poland', *Russian Review*, III(2): 87–115.

77. Dmowski, *La question polonaise*: 180–183.

78. Balicki, 'The Revival of Political Thought in Poland': 110, 112.
79. Marriott, J.A.R., 'The Problem of Poland', *Edinburgh Review*, February 1915: 358–359. This is the only British review of Dmowski's *La question polonaise* I have been able to find; it was not reviewed, for instance, in the *TLS*. It is evident that Pares was familiar with this source, since he footnoted it in Balicki's article, 'The Revival of Political Thought in Poland': 108.
80. 'Uwagi' [Observations], *A Review of the British War Literature on the Polish Problem*, London: Polish Information Committee, 1916: 4–5.
81. See, for instance, one of the few references to Dmowski before the Great War in the *JC*, 29 December 1907: 11.
82. Evans-Gordon, *The Alien Immigrant*: 134–135.
83. Baskerville, *The Polish Jew*: 138–139.
84. Corrsin, Stephen D., *Warsaw Before the First World War: Poles and Jews in the Third City of the Russian Empire, 1880–1914*, Boulder, Col.: East European Monographs, 1989: 89–104; Weeks, Theodore R., *From Assimilation to Antisemitism. The "Jewish Question" in Poland, 1850–1914*, DeKalb: Northern Illinois University Press, 2006: 163–169.
85. There is evidence that the boycott was even manifest in the United States, in cities like Chicago and New York, where there were large Polish communities, see AJC, AJC Minutes, II(23 April 1911–9 May 1915): 205–206.
86. Blobaum, Robert, 'The Politics of Antisemitism in Fin-de-Siècle Warsaw', *Journal of Modern History*, 73(2), June 2001: 275–306.
87. Balicki, 'The Revival of Political Thought in Poland': 110–111.
88. Williams, Harold, *Russia of the Russians*, London: Isaac Pitman, 1914: 380.
89. See, for example, the following reports in the *JC*, 4 October 1912: 11; 27 December 1912: 12 (report of physical violence); 3 January 1913: 17 (report that a pogrom planned for Christmas, but was thwarted); 6 June 1913: 6 (report that eight Jews burned to death in arson attack); 1 August 1913: 25 (report of failed pogrom).
90. *JC*, 18 September 1914: iii.
91. See Johnson, Sam, 'Confronting the East. *Darkest Russia*, British Opinion and Tsarist Russia's "Jewish Question", 1890–1914', *East European Jewish Affairs*, December 2006: 199–211.
92. *Darkest Russia*, 3 January 1912: 2.
93. Actually, the Russian government took considerable steps to restrain the boycott, especially as it was concerned that the localised violence might turn into pogroms, see Blobaum, 'The Politics of Antisemitism in Fin-de-Siècle Warsaw': 305. The *JC* recorded some of these interventions, see 3 January 1912: 17.
94. *Darkest Russia*, 5 March 1913: 39.
95. *Darkest Russia*, 26 February 1913: 83.
96. For Wolf's views on the origins of pogroms, see his introduction to Semenov, E.P., *The Russian Government and the Massacres. A Page of the Russian Counter-revolution*, London: John Murray, 1907.
97. *Darkest Russia*, 16 July 1913: 115.
98. The first mention of Dmowski appeared in *Darkest Russia*, 27 August 1913, 140. In all other articles relating to Poland and its aspirations for autonomy, the nationalists appeared in rather simplistic terms.

99. The danger posed to Polish Jews by National Democracy featured in Board of Deputies' confidential memoranda from early on in the war, see, for instance, Conjoint Committee Report, 3 June 1915, BOD, ACC/3121/C11/3/1/3.
100. See *The Times*, 4 June 1914: 8; *The Times*, 5 June 1914: 9; David L. Alexander and Claude G. Montefiore to *The Times*, 9 June 1914: 7.
101. Israel Zangwill to *The Times*, 19 August 1914: 7.
102. Zangwill's insight did not go down well in some British quarters, and the response it provoked from one correspondent presaged many of the difficulties the War was to herald for not only Polish and Russian Jews but also their British counterparts. The Oxford historian Bodley, J.E.C. viewed Zangwill's attitude as treasonous, see Bodley, J.E.C. to *The Times*, 21 August 1914: 4; see also Zangwill's reply, 28 August 1914: 5.

5 Imperial Russia: The International Arena and the Great War, 1907–1917

1. *The Nation*, 22 August 1914: 755–756.
2. Wells, H.G., *The War That Will End War*, London: Palmer, 1914.
3. *The Nation*, 22 August 1914: 755.
4. *New Witness*, 20 August 1914: 474–475; *Everyman*, 21 August 1914: 548.
5. For discussion of Anglo-Russian diplomacy and rivalry in this period, see Neilson, Keith, *Strategy and Supply. The Anglo-Russian Alliance, 1914–17*, London: Allen and Unwin, 1984; Ibid., *Britain and the Last Tsar. British Policy and Russia, 1894–1917*, Oxford: Clarendon Press, 1995; Siegel, Jennifer, *Endgame: Britain, Russia and the Final Struggle for Central Asia*, London: I.B. Tauris, 2002.
6. *The Graphic*, 12 January 1907: 46. Wolf was not alone, by any means, in his suspicion of Russia, see *The Nation*, 27 April 1907: 338.
7. This visit was opposed by many in the United Kingdom. A mass meeting held in Trafalgar Square was organised by the Independent Labour Party, the Social Democratic Federation, the Christian and Socialist League and a number of women's organisations, see, for example, *Glasgow Herald*, 26 July 1909: 7.
8. Lucien Wolf to *Morning Leader*, 30 July 1909: 4; Bernard Pares to *Morning Leader*, 3 August 1909: 4; Wolf to *Morning Leader*, 4 August 1909: 4; Pares to *Morning Leader*, 6 August 1909: 4; Pares to *The Times*, 26 July 1909: 6; 28 July 1909: 12; Wolf to *The Times*, 15 January 1908: 5; 29 February 1908: 5; 21 March 1908: 10. There was also a private exchange of letters, which related to Wolf's criticism of the content of Pares' *Russian Review* – Wolf believed it too supportive of the regime – though only Pares' side of the correspondence is preserved; Bernard Pares to Lucien Wolf, 10 May 1912, WMC, RG348, f. 112a.
9. Lucien Wolf to *Morning Leader*, 30 July 1909: 4. Many of these themes, of course, appeared in *Darkest Russia*.
10. For discussion of Wolf's attitude at this time, see Levene, Mark, *War, Jews and the New Europe. The Diplomacy of Lucien Wolf, 1914–1919*, Oxford: Oxford University Press, 1992: 54; Beloff, Max, *Lucien Wolf and the*

Anglo-Russian Entente, 1907–1914, London: Jewish Historical Society of England, 1951: 27; see also for the disagreement with Pares, Hughes, Michael, 'Bernard Pares, Russian Studies and the Promotion of Anglo-Russian Friendship, 1907–1914', *Slavonic and East European Review*, 78(3), July 2000: 510–536.

11. *JC*, 6 September 1907: 13.
12. *JC*, 16 August 1907: 8–9.
13. Chaim Weizmann, Zionist leader and future first president of Israel, forged an important friendship with C.P. Scott, before the Great War, which helped opened doors to the British political elite. Some limited correspondence between the two men exists in MGA.
14. Brailsford, H.N., *The Fruits of Our Russian Alliance*, London: Anglo-Russian Committee, 1912: 27, 28, 29–31, 32. The capitalisation of 'ghetto' should be noted here, in addition to its synonymy with 'Pale'.
15. For details, see Melançon, Michael, 'The Ninth Circle: the Lena Goldfield Workers and the Massacre of 4 April 1912', *Slavic Review*, 53(3), Autumn 1994: 766–795.
16. This was claimed by V.V. Shul'gin, editor of the reactionary Russian newspaper *Kievlanin*, see *The Times*, 11 October 1913: 7.
17. *AJY* (1914–1915, Vol. 16): 19, for instance, asserted that the 'case divided Russia into two camps', which was not without some accuracy. Though, like in France during Dreyfus, the political response to Beilis could not always be delineated in a straightforward manner.
18. The most significant historiography on the Beilis Case is as follows; Samuel, Maurice, *Blood Accusation: The Strange History of the Beilis Case*, Philadelphia: Jewish Publication Society of America, 1966; Rogger, Hans, 'The Beilis Case: Antisemitism and Politics in the Reign of Nicholas II', *Slavic Review*, 25(4), December 1966: 615–629; Murav, Harriet, 'The Beilis Ritual Murder Trial and the Culture of Apocalypse', *Cardozo Studies in Law and Literature*, 12(2), Autumn–Winter, 2000: 243–263; Katsis, Leonid, *Krovavyi navet i russkaia mysl': Istoriko-teologicheskoe issledovanie dela Beilisa*, Moscow/Jerusalem: Mosty kul'tura/Gesharim, 2006.
19. *The Times*, 6 May 1912: 7.
20. These petitions were reprinted in the *JC*, 10 May 1912: 14–16. The Russian letter was signed by, amongst others, Maxim Gorky, Alexei Tolstoy, leader of the Kadet party P.N. Miliukov, and several members of the Imperial Senate.
21. Stuart M. Samuels to *The Times*, 7 May 1912: 5.
22. *The Times*, 29 October 1913: 5; *The Times*, 3 November 1913: 7; *JW*, 5 November 1913: 17–18; for a discussion of the meeting, see Rait, R.S. (ed.), *Memorials of Albert Venn Dicey*, London: Macmillan, 1925: 220–221. Dicey often supported the anti-Tsarist campaign and wrote the introduction to Wolf, Lucien, *The Legal Sufferings of the Jews in Russia. A Survey of their Present Situation, and a Summary of Laws*, London: Fisher Unwin, 1912.
23. *Glasgow Herald*, 28 October 1913: 13.
24. *NYT*, 13 October 1913: 4.
25. *AJY* (1914–1915, Vol. 16): 79–82.
26. *NYT*, 17 October 1913: 6.
27. *AJY* (1914–1915, Vol. 16): 85–89; it appeared in the *JW*, 24 September 1913: 15–16; *JC*, 26 September 1913: 2, 21.

28. *NYT*, 11 October 1913: 6. For Hilsner, see Červinka, Frantisek, 'The Hilsner Affair': 135–161, in Dundes, Alan, *The Blood Libel Legend. A Casebook in Antisemitic Folklore*, Madison: University of Wisconsin Press, 1991; Kieval, Hillel, 'Death and the Nation. Ritual Murder as Political Discourse in the Czech Lands', *Jewish History*, 10(1), March 1996: 75–91.

29. Some newspapers were restrained in the amount of material published on the affair, such as the *Catholic Herald*, which seldom referred to events in Kiev: 4 October 1914: 4; 1 November 1913: 4; 15 November 1913: 2.

30. Byford, Charles T., *The Soul of Russia*, London: Kingsgate Press, 1914: 77; *Glasgow Herald*, 11 October 1913: 6; *Russian Review*, I(3): 194–196; *Russian Review*, II(4): 221–226.

31. *JC*, 6 October 1911: 11.

32. *JC*, 17 October 1913: 11–15; 24 October 1913: 19–21; 31 October 1913: 26–45; 7 November 1913: 21–30.

33. *JC*, 10 October 1913: 9.

34. See, for example, *Darkest Russia*, 14 February 1912: 1; 27 August 1913: 140.

35. Lucien Wolf to Joseph Jacobs, 3 December 1913, LWUCL.

36. Dillon, E.J., *Russian Characteristics*, London: Chapman and Hall, 1892. It was published under pseudonym Lanin, E.B. with many of the chapters reproductions of articles from the *Fortnightly Review* and other journals.

37. *The Observer*, 10 March 1912: 11.

38. *Darkest Russia*, 13 March 1912: 3.

39. Baron Alphonse Heyking to *The Times*, 8 May 1912: 5.

40. Moses Gaster to *The Times*, 9 May 1912: 5; Lucien Wolf to *The Times*, 10 May 1912: 5. Heyking's views were also ridiculed in the Russian press, in *Novyi Voskhod*, 17 May 1912 (4 May 1912 OS): 43–44; and *Rech'*, 9 May 1912 (27 April 1912 OS): 2; 11 May 1912 (29 April 1912 OS): 2; 14 May 1912 (1 May 1912 OS): 2. My thanks to Aleksandr Ivanov for these references. This was not the only time that Heyking was involved in controversy about the Russian-Jewish question in 1912, see Heyking, Alphonse, 'Anglo-Russian Progress', *Fortnightly Review*, January 1912: 106–114, which followed a familiar Russian conservative line; a riposte appeared 2 months later: Gelberg, S, 'The Russian-Consul General and the Russian Jews', *Fortnightly Review*, March 1912: 543–552.

41. *New Witness*, 16 October 1913: 739. 'The Chesterbelloc' ('a very amusing pantomime elephant') was the collective term applied to the ideas of Belloc and Chesterton by George Bernard Shaw, see Corrin, J.P., *G.K. Chesterton and Hilaire Belloc. The Battle Against Modernity*, London: Ohio University Press, 1981; Cheyette, Brian, *Constructions of 'the Jew' in English Literature and Society. Racial Representations, 1875–1945*, Cambridge: Cambridge University Press, 1995: 150–205.

42. The *New Witness* was founded in 1911 as the *Eye-Witness*. A major preoccupation at this time for Belloc and Chesterton was the so-called Marconi Case, involving the naval contract for telegraph stations throughout the British Empire. The Chesterbelloc believed several members of the government – all Jews – had corrupted the contract. See Lunn, Kenneth, 'The Marconi Scandal and Related Aspects of British Antisemitism, 1911–1914', unpublished PhD thesis, University of Sheffield, 1978.

43. *New Witness*, 16 October 1913: 739.

44. See, for example, *New Witness*, 16 October 1913: 749–751; 23 November 1913: 778–780; 15 January 1914: 366–368.

45. This was in connection with characterisation of a Russian nobleman, Baron Levendal, whose attitudes towards Jews were uncompromising; at one stage, he says, 'those Jew vermin – all my life I have suffered from them'. There was, however, more than a hint of stereotype in most of Zangwill's characters. See Zangwill, Israel and Nahson, Edna (eds), *From the Ghetto to the Melting Pot: Israel Zangwill's Jewish Plays*, Detroit: Wayne State University Press, 2005.

46. *New Witness*, 5 March 1914, 566–567.

47. Israel Zangwill to *New Witness*, 12 March 1914: 593.

48. *New Witness*, 12 March 1914: 593–594.

49. It complained, for instance, about Leon Trotsky's change of name from 'Braunstein' (*sic* – he was called Bronstein), and, closer to home, Lewis B. Namier, whom it alleged to have originally been named 'Ludwig Bernstein' (*sic* – he was born Ludwik Niemirowski); *New Witness*, 26 April 1918: 586–587. Namier, who worked at Wellington House, a British propaganda unit, for most of the Great War bore the brunt of some unpleasant attacks by the *Witness*. Born in Galicia, Namier came to the United Kingdom before the war and was regularly indicted by the Chesterbelloc for his supposed lack of national instinct and tendency to 'cosmopolitanism'.

50. *Everyman*, 21 August 1914: 548; see also Chesterton, G.K., *The Barbarians of Berlin*, London 1914: 27–28.

51. *New Witness*, 30 March 1916: 667.

52. The authorities could not find a single Russian Orthodox priest who was willing to formulate a theological argument in favour of the Blood Libel. This was undoubtedly a reflection of the rarity of the accusation in Eastern Christendom – not to say the attitudes taken towards the case in Russia.

53. Klier, John D., 'Cry Bloody Murder', *East European Jewish Affairs*, 36(2), December 2006: 216; *JC*, 7 November 1913: 9; *New York Times*, 4 November 1913: 6. The term 'vaudeville' was taken from the Ukrainian newspaper, *Kievskaia mysl'*.

54. Klier, 'Cry Bloody Murder': 217–218: images of the original court records can be found at 224–225.

55. By this stage, the Case had entered the popular psyche, in the form of Yiddish theatre. The production, for instance, of 'Mendel Beilis' in a theatre in London's East End, was noted in the *MG*, 16 November 1913: 14. This play was also produced in New York City, see Berkowitz, Joel, 'The "Mendel Beilis Epidemic" on the Yiddish Stage', *Jewish Social Studies*, 8(1), Autumn, 2001: 199–225.

56. *New Witness*, 13 November 1913: 93; this was refuted in the following week's edition by Maurice Baring, see his letter, 27 November 1913: 115.

57. *JC*, 14 November 1913: 9; *The Times*, 11 November 1913: 7, referred to 'medievalism in a modern city'. Similar views were expressed in *The Scotsman*, 11 November 1913: 6.

58. *JC*, 14 November 1913: 9.

59. *The Times*, 12 November 1913: 9; *JW*, 12 November 1913: 5.

60. See, for instance, Almog, Shmuel, 'Antisemitism as a dynamic phenomenon: the "Jewish Question" in England at the end of the First World War', *Patterns of Prejudice*, 21(4), 1987: 3–18; Aronsfield, C.C., 'Jewish Enemy Aliens in England during the First World War', *Jewish Social Studies*, 181, 1956: 275–283; Cesarani, David, 'An Embattled Minority: the Jews in Britain During the First World War', *Immigrants and Minorities*, 8, 1989: 61–81; Holmes, Colin, *Antisemitism in British Society*, London: Edward Arnold, 1979, Part Two; see also Johnson, Sam, 'Making or Breaking the Silence: British Jews and East European Jewish Relief, 1914–1917', *Modern Judaism*, February 2010: 95–119, which elaborates on some of the themes considered below.

61. *JC*, 7 August 1914: 5.

62. These letters were in response to allegations of disloyalty that appeared in various British newspapers, including *The Times*, see Holmes, *Antisemitism in British Society*, Chapter 8.

63. Wasserstein, Bernard, *Herbert Samuel. A Political Life*, Oxford: Oxford University Press, 1992; Cesarani, David, *The 'Jewish Chronicle' and Anglo-Jewry, 1841–1991*, Cambridge: Cambridge University Press, 1994: 114–121; Levene, *War, Jews and the New Europe*: Chapter 3; for a discussion of the conscription of un-naturalised Jews, see Shukman, Harold, *War or Revolution. Russian Jews and Conscription in Britain, 1917*, London: Vallentine Mitchell, 2006.

64. Watts, Martin, *The Jewish Legion and the First World War*, London: Palgrave Macmillan, 2004; Keren, Shlomit and Keren, Michael, 'The Jewish Legions in the First World War as a Locus of Identity Formation', *Journal of Modern Jewish Studies*, 6(1), March 2007: 69–83.

65. Lohr, Eric, *Nationalizing the Russian Empire. The Campaign Against Enemy Aliens in World War I*, Harvard University Press: London, 2003: 31–54; Ibid., 'Patriotic Violence and the State: The Moscow Riots of May 1915', *Kritika*, 4(3), Summer 2003: 607–626.

66. Klier, John D., *Imperial Russia's Jewish Question*, Cambridge: Cambridge University Press, 1995, 332–349; Petrovsky-Shtern, Yohanan, *Jews in the Russian Army, 1827–1917. Drafted into Modernity*, Cambridge: Cambridge University Press, 2008; for discussion of the role conscription played in mythologising the Russian Imperial Jewish experience, see Litvak, Olga, *Conscription and the Search for Modern Russian Jewry*, Bloomington: Indiana University Press, 2006.

67. See Petrovsky-Shtern, Yohanan, 'The "Jewish Policy" of the Late Imperial War Ministry: The Impact of the Russian Right', *Kritika*, 3(2), Spring 2002: 217–254; Sanborn, Joshua A., *Drafting the Russian Nation. Military Conscription, Total War, and Mass Politics*, DeKalb: Northern Illinois University Press, 2002: 119–122.

68. See Prusin, Alexander Victor, *Nationalizing a Borderland: War, Ethnicity, and Anti-Jewish Violence in East Galicia, 1914–1920*, Tuscaloosa: University of Alabama Press, 2005. For a first-hand account, by one of the most important Russian Jewish commentators in this period, see An-sky, S., [Shloyme-Zanvl Rappoport] (ed. & trans. by Joachim Neugroschel) *The Enemy at his Pleasure. A Journey through the Jewish Pale of Settlement during World War I*, New York: Metropolitan Books, 2003.

69. See Rechter, David, *The Jews of Vienna and the First World War*, London: Littman Library, 2001. For an analysis of Habsburg's Jewry experience during the Great War, see Rozenblit, Martha, *Reconstructing a National Identity: The Jews of Habsburg Austria during World War I*, New York: Oxford University Press, 2001.

70. For discussion of the Russian Jewish refugee's experience, see Gatrell, Peter, *A Whole Empire Walking. Refugees in Russia during World War I*, Bloomington: Indiana University Press, 2005: 145–150.

71. See Klier, John D., 'Kazaki i pogromy. Chem otlichalis' "voennye" pogromy?', in Budnitskii, O.V., et al., *Mirovoi krizis 1914–1920 godov i sud'ba vostochnoevropeiskogo evreistva*, Moscow: Rosspen, 2005: 47–70.

72. For some coverage in the mainstream press, see *The Times*, 26 November 1914: 5; *The Observer*, 1 November 1914: 5. However, see a series of articles published in *The Times* and the *New Statesmen* in 1916, which although dealing extensively on the German occupation of Congress Poland made not a single mention of Jews, despite reference to Łódź and Warsaw: *Poland under the Germans*, London: Joseph Causton & Sons, 1916. In a similar vein, see the diplomatic correspondence related to the occupation and food shortages in Poland, published in 1916, which again made no reference to the hardships faced by Jews: 'Correspondence Respecting the Relief of Allied Territories in the Occupation of the Enemy', *Parliamentary Command Paper*, No. 8348, London: Harrison and Sons/HMSO, 1916.

73. See Pares, Bernard, 'Au jour le jour avec l'armée russe', *Revue de Paris*, 15 March 1916: 397–424; Ibid., 'Russian Hopes and Aims', *Edinburgh Review*, July 1916: 99–113.

74. Pares, Bernard, *Day by Day with the Russian Army, 1914–1915*, London: Constable, 1915: x: 'It was delightful to be with these splendid men. I never saw anything base all the while I was with the army. There was no drunkenness; everyone was at his best, and it was the simplest and noblest atmosphere in which I have ever lived.' Reflecting on this account, a reviewer noted: 'nothing in the war has been finer the behaviour of the Russian soldiers', *TLS*, 25 November 1915: 423.

75. Russian soldiers renamed the streets in occupied Galicia, replacing the old signs with imaginative names such as 'Tolstoi Street' and the like, see Prusin, *Nationalizing a Borderland*; 2005; An-sky, *The Enemy at his Pleasure*.

76. Pares, *Day by Day with the Russian Army*: x.

77. Washburn, Stanley, *Field Notes from the Russian Front*, London: Andrew Melrose, 1915: 64.

78. Pares, *Day by Day with the Russian Army*: 33, 90.

79. Pares, Bernard, 'Reaction and Revolution', in A.W. Ward, G.W. Prothero, S. Leather, *Cambridge Modern History*, Volume XII, Cambridge: Cambridge University Press, 1910: 339.

80. Washburn, *Field Notes from the Russian Front*: 84; 230; see also Washburn, Stanley, *The Russian Campaign*, London: Andrew Melrose, 1915: 75.

81. Pares, *Day by Day with the Russian Army*: 158.

82. Manuscript of *Day by Day with the Russian Army*, entry dated 16 September 1914, PAR/5/3/2.

83. Bernard Pares to Benjamin Wilenski, 20 October 1916, WMC, RG348, f.73; Lucien Wolf to David Alexander, 6 December 1916, WMC, RG348, f.73.

84. Lucien Wolf to David Alexander, 6 December 1916, WMC, RG348, f.73.
85. Wolf also challenged, in September and October 1915, another author, John Buchan, for the public expression of similar views in Volume VI of the *Nelson's History of the War*, London: Nelson & Sons, 1915: 23. See correspondence from Wolf to Buchan and vice versa in BOD, ACC3121/C11/2/7.
86. And these views were pretty entrenched. Over a decade later, Pares wrote his memoirs in which he reflected upon the conduct of Jews on the Eastern Front: 'There were innumerable cases of espionage by Jews, and also wholesale desertions, which were made very easy by the huge retreat of summer and autumn [of 1915]. I found almost regularly that about 80 per cent had gone over to the enemy or let themselves be taken prisoner during the retreat. One cannot blame them after the way in which Jews were treated in Russia, and I think the German cause, as aiming at a great, unified world empire was one which would appeal to many of the Jews. I was more than once rebuked from England for sending in the data, but I found defenders among our own Jews, who most certainly showed no lack of patriotism.' Pares, Bernard, *My Russian Memoirs*, London: Jonathan Cape, 1931: 350, 376.
87. Dillon, E.J., *The Eclipse of Russia*, London: J.M. Dent, 1918: 6–7. Witte died in 1915, but clearly doors were open for Dillon in the highest echelons of Russian society and politics.
88. *The Observer*, 12 September 1915: 8.
89. *The Observer*, 1 November 1914: 5.
90. *New Witness*, 16 November 1916: 68; see also Dearmer, Percy, 'The Soul of Russia', *Nineteenth Century and After*, January 1915: 72–83; Saroléa, Charles, 'The Soul of Russia', *Review of Reviews*, March 1916: 193–197.
91. For a selection of Graham's articles in *The Times*, see 12 February 1914: 7; 23 June 1914: 7; 12 September 1914: 7; 15 September 1914: 6; 13 October 1913: 7; 31 October 1914: 7; 15 December 1914: 5. Sir George Buchanan to the Foreign Office, 8 November 1915, PRO-FO, file 371/2455: 'It is certainly regrettable that the task of interpreting the Russian people to the British Public should have been assumed by a writer whose interpretation appears to give deep offence to many of our best friends in this country. I would suggest that it might be advisable, privately and confidentially, to call the attention of the Editor to the Times to the effect produced in Russia by Mr Graham's articles.' The *JW* was none too impressed by Graham's articles either, see 4 November 1914: 4–5.
92. It comes as no surprise that he suspected a Jew's hand lay behind the Yushchinskii murder, possibly for ritual purposes, see Graham, Stephen, 'Russia and the Jews', *English Review*, February 1915: 27–44. The *JW* sneered as this perspective: *JW*, 10 February 1915: 7.
93. Israel Zangwill to *The Nation*, 20 February 1915: 650.
94. Graham, Stephen, *Russia in 1916*, London: Cassell, 1916: 148; see also ibid, 'Russia's Religion of Suffering', *London Quarterly Review*, January 1916: 22–30.
95. Graham, 'Russia and the Jews': 27–44.
96. Graham, Stephen, *Russia and the World*, London: Cassell, 1915: 146. These sentiments also appeared in an article by Graham in the *Sunday Times*, 20 December 1914: 7.

97. *The Nation*, 30 January 1915: 548.
98. Stephen Graham to *The Nation*, 13 February 1915: 619–620. He argued along similar lines in a letter to the *JW*, 10 February 1915: 23.
99. Israel Zangwill to *The Nation*, 20 February 1915: 651.
100. Israel Zangwill to *The Nation*, 13 March 1915: 748–749.
101. Graham, *Russia in 1916*: 144.
102. *JC*, 7 August 1914: 6.
103. *JC*, 4 September 1914: 5; see also *JW*, 9 September 1914: 1.
104. *The Times*, 18 August 1914: 6; *JC*, 4 September 1914: 13; *JW*, 9 September 1914: 3.
105. By this stage, in fact, the two newspapers were owned by the same company and consequently their sources were identical; they included the AIU, the AJC in the United States, Leo Motzkin, head of the Zionist Bureau in Copenhagen, as well as various Russian sources like the Bund.
106. *JC*, 20 October 1914: 11.
107. *JW*, 25 November 1914: 5; see also *JC*, 20 November 1914: 6. The pieces were also sent to Lucien Wolf and the Conjoint Committee, see Louis Troukel[?] to *JC*, AJA, Herbert Bentwich, Board of Deputies, 4 November 1914, BOD, ACC3121/C11/2/5. It also appeared in the *NYT*, 19 March 1915: 9.
108. *JW*, 6 January 1915: 5.
109. Lucien Wolf to Claude G. Montefiore, 16 November 1914, BOD, ACC3121/C11/2/5.
110. *JC*, 26 February 1915: 6.
111. Brodetsky was also a lecturer in mathematics at Bristol University at this time, then at Leeds University from 1920; in 1940, he became president of the Board of Deputies. For a good biography, see his *DNB* entry, by Leon Mestel.
112. *JW*, 6 January 1915: 12.
113. *JC*, 8 January 1915: 8.
114. *JC*, 8 January 1915: 14.
115. *JW*, 17 March 1915: 18. For a discussion of EKOPO's activities, see Zipperstein, Steven J., 'The Politics of Relief: The Transformation of Russian Jewish Communal Life during the First World War', in Jonathan Frankel (ed.), *The Jews and the European Crisis, 1914–1921. Studies in Contemporary Jewry*, Volume IV, Oxford: University Press 1988: 22–40; see also Pevzner, Evgeniia, 'Jewish Committee for the Relief of War Victims (1914–1921)', *Pinkas*, 1, 2006: 114–142.
116. A list of donors appeared regularly in the press, the first substantial one in *JC*, 13 March 1915: 3–5.
117. Whilst the Rothschilds committed £1000 to the fund, compare this to the £10,000 that was granted to the relief of Jewish refugees from Belgium, see *JW*, 18 November 1914: 4.
118. Isaiah Wassilevsky to *JC*, 1 January 1915: 18.
119. Much of this is discussed in Levene, *War, Jews and the New Europe*, especially Chapters 1 and 2.
120. *JW*, 27 January 1915: 22.
121. See, for example, *JW*, 24 March 1915: 10. The *World* utilised Russian Jewish sources in these reports, taking evidence from *Novyi Voskhod* and *Rassvet*.

122. *JW*, 1 September 1915: 8.
123. *JC*, 27 August 1915: 22; *JW*, 12 May 1915: 22. The Trudoviks were socialist, with a presence in the Duma.
124. *JC*, 23 July 1915: 7–8. It was also published in the *New York Times Magazine*, 15 August 1915: 15. Unsurprisingly, the *Chronicle*'s editor, Leopold Greenberg, had problems with the Russian censor over this issue (there were subscribers to the *JC* in Petrograd): see Lucien Wolf to Leopold de Rothschild, 13 August 1915, BOD, ACC3121/C11/3/1/1.
125. Undated dossier, BOD, ACC3121/C11/12/119(1–4).
126. Claude G. Montefiore and Alexander, D.L. to Foreign Office, 3 June 1915, BOD, ACC3121/C11/3/1/3.
127. Lucien Wolf to Foreign Office, 14 October 1915, BOD, ACC3121/C11/2/6; Lucien Wolf to Cyrus Adler, 3 October 1915, AJC, Louis Marshall Papers, Box 3.
128. Blank spent a good deal of time in Britain during the Great War and was a main point of contact for Lucien Wolf, supplying an information about conditions in Russia, acting as a link between the CFC and the AIU, as well as visiting the Foreign Office from time to time.
129. *JC*, 8 October 1915: 2.
130. *JC*, 5 November 1915: 11.
131. *JC*, 5 November 1915: 16; 18; *JW*, 3 November 1915: 18; *The Observer*, 7 November 1915: 19.
132. For information about Levison, see the biography by his son: Levison, Frederick, *Christian and Jew. The Life of Leon Levison, 1881–1936*, Edinburgh: Pentland Press, 1989; and his own war-time writings, Levison, Leon, *The Tragedy of the Jews in the European War Zone*, Edinburgh: Russian Jews Relief Fund, 1915; Ibid., *The Jewish Problem and the World War*, London: Morgan & Scott, 1916.
133. *JC*, 19 November 1915: 13; *JC*, 10 December 1915: 14.
134. *The Scotsman*, 4 December 1915: 1.
135. *JC*, 10 December 1915: 9, 14.
136. *JW*, 8 December 1915: 8–9.
137. *JC*, 31 December 1915: 7.
138. *JW*, 2 February 1916: 9.
139. The Anglo-Jewish press continued to follow the progress of Levison's fund, see *JC*, 16 February 1917: 9–10. It was less than thrilled when Levison was awarded a knighthood for his services to East European Relief, see *JC*, 22 August 1919: 16.
140. Black, Eugene C., *The Social Politics of Anglo-Jewry, 1880–1920*, London: Blackwell, 1988: 328.
141. The *Zemstva* were the local councils set up in 1864 under Tsar Alexander II's Great Reforms and managed schools, hospitals and the like. They were associated with the liberal movement in Russia.
142. *The Times*, 9 April 1917: 5.
143. Saroléa, Charles, *The Russian Revolution and the War*, London: Allen and Unwin, 1917: 5.
144. *The Times*, 19 March 1917: 9.
145. *New Witness*, 22 March 1917: 563–564.
146. *JC*, 23 March 1917: 11.

147. Saroléa, Charles, *Europe's Debt to Russia*, London: Heinemann, 1916: 161–187; Saroléa, *The Russian Revolution and the War*: 8.
148. *The Times*, 19 March 1917: 8.
149. *The Times*, 11 April 1917: 5.
150. Figes, Orlando and Boris Kolonitskii, *Interpreting the Russian Revolution: the Language and Symbols of 1917*, London: Yale University Press, 1999: 158–167.
151. *JC*, 23 March 1917: 11.
152. *JC*, 30 March 1917: 5.
153. *JC*, 30 March 1917: 6.
154. *JC*, 30 March 1917: 16.
155. Lucien Wolf to Leopold de Rothschild, 16 March 1917, BOD, C11/2/11.
156. *JC*, 27 April 1917: 11. The telegram from Leopold de Rothschild to Prince L'vov, 12 April 1917, is located in BOD, C11/3/1/3. The press were told about this 2 weeks later, and the text appears in the *JC*, 27 April 1917: 10, though it notes that it was dated 10 April 1917. A similar letter was sent to L'vov, signed by Montefiore, Alexander and Rothschild, 25 April 1917, CFC Minute Book, BOD, ACC3121/C11A/2.
157. *JC*, 27 April 1917: 12.
158. Shingarev was Minister of Agriculture in the Provisional Government and, along with Miliukov, was one of the Duma deputies of visited the United Kingdom prior to the war.
159. *JC*, 25 May 1917: 6.
160. *The Times*, 28 March 1917: 6. The author of the piece was Robert Wilton, who was less than sympathetic in his attitudes towards Jews. A protest against Wilton was published by the Russian Committee of Journalists in various Russian newspapers, 17 May 1917, CFC Minute Book, BOD, ACC3121/C11A/2.
161. See *JC*, 30 March 1917: 5. So, too, did Jewish leaders in Petrograd and telegrams were exchanged on the matter between the CFC, Aleksandr Gintsburg and Maxim Vinaver, 25 April 1917, CFC Minute Book, BOD, ACC3121/C11A/2.
162. *JC*, 27 August 1917: 5; 31 August 1917: 5.
163. Whether many 'Jewish' revolutionaries considered themselves to be Jewish is another matter entirely, and too broad and detailed a topic to be considered here.
164. *New Witness*, 14 February 1918: 355.

6   Britain and Poland: Propaganda, Pogroms and Independence, 1914–1925

1. It was published in *The Times*, 17 August 1914: 8.
2. *The Times*, 19 August 1914: 6.
3. Fink, Carole, *Defending the Rights of Others. The Great Powers, the Jews and International Minority Protection, 1878–1938*, Cambridge: Cambridge University Press 2004: 69–71.
4. Seton-Watson, R.W., *Poland's Case for Independence*, London: Allen & Unwin, 1916: 16–17.

5. Retinger, J.H., 'Poland and the Present War', *English Review*, December 1914: 83. See also *The Resurrection of Poland*. *For a Lasting Peace*, Paris: Société générale d'imprimerie et d'édition Levée, 1915; Belloc, Hilaire, *The Two Maps of Europe*, London: Pearson, 1915: 29, which includes a map of the future Europe with Poland drawn as 'quasi-independent, but a holding of Russia'; Wickham Steed, Henry, 'A Programme for Peace', *Edinburgh Review*, April 1916: 381, which suggested the 'constitution of a unified self-governing Poland under the Russian sceptre'.
6. *Polish News*, 24 February 1916: 2.
7. *New Witness*, 14 September 1916: 617. According to Chesterton's wife, his belief in Poland 'contended that [it] would provide the key to war-time conditions in Europe', Chesterton, [Ada E.], *The Chestertons*, London: Chapman and Hall, 1941: 241.
8. See Henryk Sienkiewicz's preface to *Poland Ravaged and Bereaved! A Lecture Delivered at Copenhagen on 19th November 1915 by Countess Julie Ledochowska*, London: Saint Catherine Press, 1915: 23.
9. *The Scotsman*, 3 January 1916: 2.
10. Séailles, Gabriel, 'Poland', in *The Resurrection of Poland. Poland for the Poles*, London: George Allen and Unwin, 1916: 10–11.
11. Alma Tadema, Laurence, *Poland, Russia and the War*, London: St Catherine's Press, 1915: 7–8. Laurence Alma Tadema was the daughter of the renowned Victorian painter and pre-Raphaelite, Lawrence Alma Tadema.
12. For discussion of alleged German atrocities and their impact on allied discourse, see Horne, John and Kramer, Alan, *The German Atrocities of 1914: A History of Denial*, New Haven/London: Yale University Press, 2001; Harris, Ruth, 'The "Child of the Barbarian": Rape, Race and Nationalism in France during the First World War', *Past and Present*, 141, November 1993: 170–206.
13. *The Times*, 21 November 1914: 7.
14. Burleigh, Michael, *Sacred Causes: The Clash of Religion and Politics, from the Great War to the War on Terror*, London: Harper Collins, 2007.
15. *The Times*, 26 November 1914: 5; *The Times*, 21 November 1914: 7; *Observer*, 1 November 1914: 5; *JC*, 23 October 1914: 7.
16. *JC*, 20 October 1914: 11.
17. Memorandum of CFC, signed by David Alexander and C.G. Montefiore, to Foreign Office, 3 June 1915: 1, BOD, ACC/3121/C11/3/1/3.
18. Davies, Norman, 'The Poles in Great Britain', *Slavonic and East European Review*, 50(118), 1972: 63.
19. Calder, Kenneth J., *Britain and the Origins of the New Europe, 1914–1918*, Cambridge: Cambridge University Press, 1976: 87ff.
20. Black, Eugene C., 'Lucien Wolf and the Making of Poland: Paris, 1919', *Polin*, 2, 1987: 5–36; Latawski, Paul, 'The Dmowski-Namier Feud, 1915–1918', *Polin*, 2, 1987: 37–49; Latawski, Paul, 'Roman Dmowski, the Polish Question and Western Opinion, 1915–1918'; Black, Eugene C., 'Squaring a Minorities Triangle: Lucien Wolf, Jewish Nationalists and Polish Nationalists'; Wandycz, Peter, 'Dmowski's Policy at the Paris Peace Conference: Success or Failure?', in Latawski, Paul (ed.), *The Reconstruction of Poland, 1914–1923*, London: Macmillan, 1992: 1–40, 117–132; Davies, 'The Poles in Great Britain'; Levene, Mark, *War, Jews and the New Europe*.

The Diplomacy of Lucien Wolf, 1914–1919, Oxford: Oxford University Press, 1992; Ng, Amy, 'A Portrait of Sir Lewis Namier as a Young Socialist', *Journal of Contemporary History*, 40(4): 621–636.

21. Lucien Wolf to Claude G. Montefiore, 24 October 1917, BOD, ACC3121/C11/2/12.
22. Wolf tried to prevent Dmowski's appearance at King's, see Lucien Wolf to Israel Zangwill, 13 March 1916, WMC, RG348, f. 50k; one of Dmowski's colleagues, G. Holewinski gave a lecture entitled 'The Present and Future of Poland', at Wadham College, University of Oxford, 10 June 1918, see R.A. Leeper [FO] to Lucien Wolf, 20 June 1918, BOD, ACC3121/C11/3/1/3.
23. Saroléa, Charles, *Letters on Polish Affairs*, Edinburgh: Oliver & Boyd, 1922: 95. I have searched the columns of *The Scotsman* and the *Glasgow Herald*, but have found no report of this meeting. In contrast, there is record of a lecture delivered by Zaleski in Edinburgh, *The Scotsman*, 27 October 1917: 6.
24. For details of the encounter with Chesterton, which seems to have been an invitation to dinner, rather than a public meeting, see Chesterton, G.K., *Autobiography*, London: Hutchison, 1937: 317: 'Dr Saroléa brought [Dmowski] to my house; where the Belgian, in his impish way, had taunted the Pole with his antisemitism, saying persuasively: "After all, your religion came from the Jews." To which the Pole answered: "My religion came from Jesus Christ, who was murdered by the Jews." ' One wonders whether this was the only moment in the evening's proceedings that reference was made to Jews and the Jewish question....
25. *NYT*, 9 March 1916: 7; *MG*, 9 March 1916: 6. In 1915, Bryce assisted in compiling a report for the HMG on alleged German atrocities in Belgium and northern France. Although the text of the meeting with Dmowski is only sketchily recorded, it seems likely that their mutual views on the activities of the 'barbarous Hun' drew them together.
26. Davies, 'The Poles in Great Britain'; Calder, *Britain and the Origins of the New Europe*. It was announced in *The Times*, 23 October 1917: 6.
27. *MG*, 15 February 1918: 4.
28. *MG*, 8 August 1918: 4.
29. *New Europe*, 6 September 1917: 256; 'many dangers lurk in Mr Dmowski's policy'; Lucien Wolf to A.J. Balfour, 31 October 1917; Lucien Wolf to Lord Robert Cecil, 26 November 1917; 21 December 1917, BOD, ACC3121/C11/2/12.
30. CFC Memorandum, 22 November 1917, BOD ACC3121/C11/2/12: according to this account, A.F. Whyte and Samuel Hoare tried to table questions about Dmowski, but were asked to withdraw them 'in the public interest' by A.J. Balfour and Lord Robert Cecil.
31. This included leader of the Kadet Party, Pavel Miliukov, the political economist Piotr Struve and historian Aleksandr Lappo-Danilevskii, for details see *Cambridge University Reporter*, 16 August 1916: 1042–1044; *MG*, 12 August 1916: 8.
32. Dmowski, Roman, 'Poland, Old and New', in Duff, J.D., (ed.), *Russian Realities and Problems*, Cambridge: Cambridge University Press, 1916: 115–116.
33. See, for example, Dmowski to FO, 21 March 1916; 11 March 1916, in PRO-FO file 371/2747/53414. Discussion of these memoranda in Calder, *Britain and the Origins of the New Europe*; Levene, *War, Jews and the New Europe*.

34. In a 1919 discussion at the Paris Peace Conference between Louis Marshall, president of the AJC, and Dmowski, the latter argued that the *Endek* 'opposition to Yiddish lies in the fact that its basis is German and that the natural tendency of continuing its use [in Poland] would be to make the Jews German instead of Polish in their sympathies in the event that differences should ever arise between the Poles and the Germans'; cited in *Evidence of Pogroms in Poland and Ukraina*, New York: AJC, 1919: 181. For a discussion of Marshall at Paris, see Fink, Carole, 'Louis Marshall: An American Jewish Diplomat in Paris, 1919', *American Jewish History*, 94(1–2), March–June 2008: 21–40.

35. Davies, 'The Poles in Great Britain': 75. It was described by the historian Sir Paul Vinogradoff in letter to Lewis Namier, 10 November 1917, as a 'mixture of political sophistry and historical perversion': Sir Lewis Namier Papers, Special Collections, Manchester University.

36. Dmowski, Roman, *Problems of Central and Eastern Europe*, London: privately printed, July 1917: 78–79.

37. Lucien Wolf to Claude G. Montefiore, 24 October 1917, BOD, ACC3121/C11/2/12; JFC memorandum, 3 September 1918, BOD, ACC3121/C11/12/64.

38. *The Times*, 29 October 1914: 7.

39. These sentiments were repeated, almost verbatim, in Graham, Stephen, *Russia and the World*, London: Cassell & Co: 132–133, 146. They were also criticised in the *JW*, 4 November 1914: 5.

40. It should be noted, of course, that the use of Yiddish was politicised in the lands of the former Tsarist Empire, especially for the Bund, which regarded it as a 'sine qua non for the creation of a mass labour movement': Fishman, David E., *The Rise of Modern Yiddish Culture*, Pittsburgh: University of Pittsburgh Press, 2005: 49. Yet, given the diversity of Jewish political opinion in the new Poland, it was not true to assert that Yiddish was a plank in every programme; for the assimilationist group, the Folkists, its language of choice was Polish, whereas Zionist groups, with a view to the colonisation of Palestine, promoted Hebrew as the vernacular Jewish language.

41. *Everyman*, 7 July 1916: 226; this was a review of Zangwill's *The War for the World*; Saroléa, Charles, *Europe's Debt to Russia*, London: Heinemann, 1916: 164–165. Saroléa was invited by Levison to take a trip to Eastern Europe on behalf of the Russian Jews' Relief Fund, but did not take up the offer, see Leon Levison to Charles Saroléa, 24 July 1916, SAR, file 130.

42. *New Witness*, 21 September 1916: 618.

43. *New Witness*, 14 September 1916: 597. This allegation was challenged by PIC member Robert Seton-Watson, who nevertheless asserted that those who ran the fund were capable of 'drawing the necessary distinctions between Jews and who are Polish alike in language and traditions and Jews who are merely Germans in disguise': *New Witness*, 28 September 1916: 693–694.

44. *New Witness*, 27 September 1917: 513–514.

45. *New Witness*, 25 October 1917: 609; *New Witness*, 26 April 1917: 586–587.

46. *New Witness*, 19 July 1918: 224.

47. *New Witness*, 10 January 1918: 243.

48. *New Witness*, 27 September 1917: 513–514.
49. *New Witness*, 21 September 1916: 618; 10 January 1918: 242–243.
50. *New Witness*, 10 January 1918: 242–243.
51. *New Witness*, 20 December 1918: 147–148.
52. It originally appeared in 1911 as the *Eye Witness*, but changed its name a year later.
53. R.A. Leeper to Lucien Wolf, 20 June 1918, BOD, ACC3121/C11/3/1/3. This was, of course, after Dmowski had left Britain, but representatives of the PNC remained in Britain.
54. For an insight into the political and intellectual associations Saroléa maintained, see my article on his relationship with Czechoslovakia and its leadership, especially T.G. Masaryk: Johnson, Sam, ' "Playing the Pharisee"? Charles Saroléa, Czechoslovakia and the Road to Munich, 1915–1939', *Slavonic and East European Review*, Vol. 82, (2), April 2004: 292–314.
55. For Hyndman's speech, see *Prawda*, 1 March 1918: 3: for Gooch, see *Tygodnik polski*, 10 March 1918: 3.
56. Calder, *Britain and the Origins of the New Europe*: 83ff.
57. *MG*, 8 July 1918: 4.
58. Calder, *Britain and the Origins of the New Europe*: 88.
59. It is worth noting that Wolf highlighted religious and not ethnic/racial animosity as the reason for anti-Jewish sentiment in the Foreign Office. Perhaps it was encouraged – though this is mere speculation – by the kind of anti-Catholic suspicions that were readily found in British society at this point; he make also have (un)consciously made a link to the Chesterbelloc and its associates.
60. CFC memorandum, 22 November 1917, BOD ACC3121/C11/2/12.
61. The Polish Minority Treaty was signed in June 1919, for details see Fink, *Defending the Rights of Others*, especially chapter eight; for Lucien Wolf's part in the process, see Levene, *War, Jews and the New Europe*; for the contemporary Anglo-Jewish response to its role at the Paris Peace Conference, see *Report of the Delegation of the Jews of the British Empire on the Treaties of Versailles, Saint-Germain-en-Laye and Neuilly and the Annexed Minority Treaties*, London: The Joint Foreign Committee of the Board of Deputies of British Jews and the Anglo-Jewish Association, 1920. For the Polish-Soviet war, see Davies, Norman, *White Eagle, Red Star. The Polish-Soviet War, 1919–20*, London: MacDonald, 1972.
62. It should be remembered that many pogroms occurred in what is now modern Ukraine, Lithuania and Belarus, as well as Poland. The historiography usually makes a distinction between events in Ukraine and Poland, though at the time the border between the two states was indistinct. For emphasis on the Ukrainian pogroms, see Gergel, Nahum, 'The Pogroms in Ukraine in 1918–21', *Yivo Annual of Jewish Social Science* 6 (1951): 237–252; Abramson, Henry, *A Prayer for the Government. Ukrainians and Jews in Revolutionary Times, 1917–1920*. Cambridge, MA: Harvard University Press, 1999; Prusin, Alexander Victor, *Nationalizing a Borderland. War, Ethnicity, and Anti-Jewish Violence in East Galicia, 1914–1920*, Tuscaloosa: University of Alabama Press, 2005; Budnitskii, O.V., *Rossiiskie evrei mezhdu krasniymi i beliymi*, Moscow: Rosspen, 2006.

63. Fink, *Defending the Rights of Others*: 107, 112. The British press initially reported that 'thousands' had been killed in Lemberg, see *MG*, 29 November 1918: 4; *Daily Express*, 2 December 1918: 1. The figure was later revised to 500, then 35: *MG*, 9 March 1919: 10.

64. Fink, *Defending the Rights of Others*: 176. For the historiography dealing with the Polish pogroms, see Golczewski, Frank, *Polnisch-Jüdische Beziehungen, 1881–1922*, Wiesbaden: Franz Steiner, 1981: for the Lemberg pogrom, 185–205; Tomaszewski, Leszek, 'Pińsk, Saturday 5 April 1919', *Polin* 1, 1986: 227–251; Lewandowski, Józef, 'History and Myth: Pińsk, April 1919', *Polin* 2, 1987: 50–72; Hagen, William, 'Murder in the East: German-Jewish Liberal Reactions to the Anti-Jewish Violence in Poland and Other East European Lands, 1918–1920', *Central European History*, 34 (1), 2001: 1–30; ibid, 'The Moral Economy of Popular Violence: The Pogrom in Lwów, November 1918', in Blobaum, Robert (ed.), *Antisemitism and Its Opponents in Modern Poland*, Ithaca, NY: Cornell University Press, 2005: 124–147; Różański, Przemysław, 'Wilno, 19–21 kwietnia 1919 roku', *Jewish History Quarterly*, 1 (2006): 13–34; these latter two items discusses events in two cities that were part of Poland during the interwar period, but are now respectively in Ukraine and Lithuania.

65. The Board of Deputies archive contains numerous telegrams appealing for aid and attention, see BOD ACC3121/C11/2/13, ACC3121/C11/4/2, ACC3121/C11/12/56, ACC3121/C11/12/60-66; see also *The Times*, 3 June 1919: 11. For coverage in the *JC*, 22 November 1918: 8; 29 November 1918: 8–9; 6 December 1918: 8–11.

66. Cohen's experience as a POW led him to write about his experiences, but he also produced a remarkably insightful pamphlet about German attitudes towards Jews: Cohen, Israel, *Antisemitism in Germany*, London: Offices of the 'Jewish Chronicle' and the 'Jewish World', 1918; Cohen, Israel, *The Ruhleben Prison Camp: A Record of Nineteen Months Internment*, London: Methuen, 1917.

67. Cohen, Israel, *A Report on the Pogroms in Poland*, London: Central Office of the Zionist Organisation, April 1919; Cohen, Israel, 'My Mission to Poland (1918–1919)', *Jewish Social Studies*, 1951 (2): 149–172.

68. Samuel, Sir Stuart, 'Report on Mission to Poland, 1 July 1920', *Papers by Command*, Vol. 51, 1121, *Parliamentary Command Paper*, No. 674, London: HMSO, 1920 [hereafter, 'Samuel Report'].

69. *Hansard*, Volume 113, 1919: 433–434; Volume 115, 1919: 1081; Volume 116, 1919: 78, 165–166, 824–825, 2181–2182; Volume 117, 1919: 596–597, 951, 1798–1799; Volume 118, 1919: 178–179, 793–794, 887–889; Volume 119, 1919: 879–880, 1127, 1675–1676; Volume 120, 1919: 1648–1649; Volume 121, 1919: 121; Volume 122, 1919: 1606; Volume 125, 1920: 1321–1322; Volume 126, 1920: 1862–1863; Volume 128, 1920: 1686–1687; Volume 131, 1920: 2622, 2579.

70. For the former ambassador's own perspective, see Morgenthau, Henry, *All in a Life-Time*, New York: Doubleday, 1922: 348–384. For the wider American response, see Wentling, Sonja P., 'Prologue to Genocide of Epilogue to War? American Perspectives on the Jewish Question in Poland, 1919–1921', *Journal of the Historical Society*, 8(4), December 2008: 523–544.

71. For a sample of the intensive coverage in the US press, see *NYT*, 1 June 1919: 1–2; for efforts to assuage US concerns about events in Ukraine, see Batchinsky, Julian, Margolin, Arnold, Vishnitzer, Mark and Zangwill, Israel, *The Jewish Pogroms in Ukraine*, Washington DC: Friends of Ukraine, 1919; for an alternative perspective, see *Evidence of Pogroms in Poland and Ukraina*.

72. For details of the meetings in the United States, see *AJY*, Volume 20, 1919–1920: 188–193; in Britain, the community promoted a day of mourning, see *The Times*, 26 June 1919: 14.

73. *Hansard*, Volume 113, 1919: 434.

74. *Daily Express*, 2 April 1919: 4; 5 April 1919: 4. Her husband, Cecil Chesterton, died in early December 1918 on the Western Front, so it is somewhat remarkable that she was at work in Poland at this time.

75. Cohen, *A Report on the Pogroms in Poland*: 11–20.

76. *New Witness*, 29 November 1918: 90–91.

77. Saroléa, Charles, *Letters on Polish Affairs*, Edinburgh: Oliver & Boyd, 1922: 88–89.

78. *The Times*, 7 December 1918: 6.

79. *Tygodnik Polski*, 8 December 1918: 1. Comparable sentiments were expressed in the *Morning Post*, 20 March 1919: 6; 11 April 1919: 6.

80. *New Poland*, 10 May 1919: 18.

81. *Daily Express*, 2 December 1918: 1.

82. Cohen, 'My Mission to Poland': 159.

83. *The Times*, 23 December 1919: 7; 8 February 1919: 7; *Morning Post*, 10 April 1919: 9; *JC*, 11 April 1919: 6–7.

84. Cohen, *A Report on the Pogroms in Poland*: 7–9, 23, 34.

85. *The Spectator*, 31 May 1919: 699.

86. For an interview with Cohen, see *JC*, 30 May 1919: 14, 16–17.

87. For a biography of Brailsford, see Leventhal, F.M., *The Last Dissenter. H.N. Brailsford and his World*, Oxford: Clarendon Press, 1985.

88. H.N. Brailsford to *The Times*, 1 July 1919: 8.

89. Brailsford, H.N., 'Poland as a Barrier', *New Republic*, 3 May 1919: 10–13; see also Brailsford, H.N., *Across the Blockade. A Record of Travels in Enemy Europe*, London: Allen & Unwin, 1919: 82; H.N. Brailsford to *The Nation*, 12 April 1919: 42–43.

90. *MG*, 30 November 1918: 6. See also *MG*, 16 November 1918: 6; 12 December 1918: 6; 11 February 1919: 6.

91. In the early months of the War, C.P. Scott wrote to Weizmann that the Poland's Jewish population would be 'a tremendously important question later on if there comes to be a question of reconstituting a re-united Poland', 15 November 1914, MGA.

92. *MG*, 9 January 1919: 6.

93. *Morning Post*, 14 April 1919: 8.

94. H.N. Brailsford to *The Times*, 1 July 1919: 8.

95. 'Samuel Report': 29.

96. For an analysis of the emigration in the early years of revolution, see Gatrell, Peter, *A Whole Empire Walking: Refugees in Russia during World War I*, Bloomington: Indiana University Press, 2005, especially chapter eight; for discussion of the impact of famine and refugeedom during the Civil

War, as well as the international response to the crisis, see Patenaude, Bertrand M., *The Big Show in Bololand. The American Relief Expedition to Soviet Russia in the Famine of 1921*, Stanford: Stanford University Press, 2002; for the experience of a single city during the Civil War, see Raleigh, Donald J., *Experiencing Russia's Civil War. Politics, Society and Revolutionary Culture in Saratov, 1917–1922*, Princeton: Princeton University Press, 2002.

97. 'Samuel Report': 21. A similar perspective was expressed in a letter to *The Times* by W. Majdewicz, secretary of the PIC in London, 26 June 1919: 17. It was followed by a refutation from Stuart M. Samuel and Claude G. Montefiore of the BOD and AJA, 28 June 1919: 8.

98. *New Poland*, 10 May 1919: 1.

99. *New Poland*, 17 May 1919: 27.

100. *New Poland*, 19 July 1919: 206; 10 May 1919: 17–18. It also accused Brailsford of an 'inexplicable tenderness' towards Bolshevism, 31 May 1919: 76–77.

101. *The Spectator*, 31 May 1919: 699.

102. *New Witness*, 29 November 1918: 90–91.

103. *The Times*, 2 December 1918: 9.

104. *The Times*, 21 July 1919: 11.

105. *The Spectator*, 31 May 1919: 699.

106. Heller, Celia S., *On the Edge of Destruction. The Jews of Poland between the Two World Wars*, New York: Columbia University Press, 1977.

107. Singer, I.B., *The Family Moskat*, London: Vintage, 2000: 611 (originally published in 1950).

108. Mendelsohn, Ezra, 'Interwar Poland: Good or Bad for the Jews?', Abramsky, Ch., Jachimczyk, M. and Polonsky, A., (eds), *The Jews in Poland*, Oxford: Oxford University Press, 1986: 130–139; Hagen, William, 'Before the Final Solution: Toward a Comparative Analysis of Political Antisemitism in Interwar Germany and Poland', *Journal of Modern History*, 68(2), 1996: 351–381.

109. For discussion of this legislation and the increasing political hostility towards Jews in 1930s Poland, see Melzer, Emmanuel, *No Way Out. The Politics of Polish Jewry, 1935–1939*, Cincinnati: Hebrew Union College Press, 1997.

110. *The Spectator*, 5 July 1919: 2; for Wolf's role at the Paris Peace Conference and the manoeuvrings that finally led to the signing of Poland's Minority Treaty, see Levene, *War, Jews and the New Europe*.

111. The National Democrats had broad geographical ambitions, as did many other Poles, and the war with Bolshevik Russia was partially fought in order to reclaim the lands lost to Russia in the wake of the Partitions. Had this occurred, the new Poland would have been made up of extensive parts of the former Polish-Lithuanian Commonwealth, which in turn would have inevitably meant that a good number of Ukrainian, Belorussian and Lithuanian Jews would have fallen under Polish rule. It is not entirely surprising, therefore, that there was occasional confusion over demographic matters, though six million is an entirely ludicrous statistic in adjudging Poland's Jewish population.

112. *The Times*, 22 May 1919: 13; Saroléa, *Letters on Polish Affairs*: 91.

113. Brailsford, *Across the Blockade*: 86; Boswell, Bruce A., *Poland and the Poles*, London: Methuen, 1919: 23; see also Battine, Cecil, 'Poland and the Peace', *Nineteenth Century & After*, March 1919: 617; Devereux, Roy, *Poland Reborn*, London: Chapman & Hall, 1922: 201; the latter two commentators both estimated the number at four millions.
114. Saroléa, *Letters on Polish Affairs*: 37.
115. *The Times*, 2 December 1918: 9.
116. Mendelsohn, Ezra, *The Jews of East Central Europe between the Two World Wars*, Bloomington: Indiana University Press, 1986: 23.
117. Mendelsohn, *The Jews of East Central Europe between the Two World Wars*: 23; Jews represented respectively 30, 33 and 25 per cent of the total population in these cities.
118. Devereux, *Poland Reborn*: 197.
119. Brailsford, *Across the Blockade*: 79.
120. *The Times*, 22 May 1919: 13.
121. Saroléa, *Letters on Polish Affairs*: 36; ibid., 'The Jewish Crisis in Eastern Europe', *New York Times Current History*, January 1923: 593. An article rebuffing Saroléa's argument appeared 2 months later, written by the former Deputy Minister of Foreign Affairs of the short-lived independent Ukrainian government: Margolin, Arnold, 'The Jewish Problem in Eastern Europe', *New York Times Current History*, March 1923: 962–967.
122. Brailsford, *Across the Blockade*: 85–85.
123. Devereux, *Poland Reborn*: 209.
124. Boswell, *Poland and the Poles*: 190.
125. Brailsford, *Across the Blockade*: 79.
126. Boswell, *Poland and the Poles*: 191.
127. Devereux, *Poland Reborn*: 209–210.
128. See her letter to *The Times*, 19 September 1923: 6.
129. Devereux, *Poland Reborn*: 211.
130. For an admiring review of Devereux's book, see *TLS*, 4 May 1922: 284.
131. *The Scotsman*, 21 October 1922: 8.
132. Saroléa, *Letters on Polish Affairs*: 94.
133. *The Scotsman*, 21 October 1922: 8; Salis Daiches to *The Scotsman*, 24 October 1922: 6.
134. Mendelsohn, *The Jews of East Central Europe between the Wars*: 43.
135. For discussion of the political rhetoric in the Polish Second Republic, especially its antisemitic component, see Kamińska-Szmaj, Irena, *Judzi, zohydza, ze czci odziera: Język propagandy politycznej w prasie 1919–1923*, Wrocław: Towarzystwo Przyjaciół Polonistyki Wrocławskiej, 1994; Domagalska, Małgorzata, 'Antisemitic Discourse in Polish Nationalist Weeklies between 1918 and 1939', *East European Jewish Affairs*, 36(2): 191–197.
136. Boswell, *Poland and the Poles*: 97, 191; Devereux, *Poland Reborn*: 197.
137. JFC memorandum, 'Mission in Warsaw', 1925, BOD, ACC3121/C11/12/75; *JC*, 12 June 1925: 17; Fink, *Defending the Rights of Others*: 290.
138. *JC*, 10 July 1925: 13.
139. Saroléa described it as an 'artificial state' in *Europe and the League of Nations*, London: Bell & Sons, 1919: 167.
140. *The Spectator*, 26 October 1919: 458–459.

7 Who were the Jews? *Ostjuden* in the British Mindset, 1867–1925

1. Volkov, Shulamit, *Germans, Jews, and Antisemites. Trials in Emancipation*, Cambridge: Cambridge University Press, 2006: 82–118.
2. Pulzer, P.G.J., *The Rise of Political Antisemitism in Germany and Austria*, Cambridge, Mass: Harvard University Press, 1988; Boyer, John W., *Political Radicalism in Late Imperial Vienna*, Chicago: University of Chicago Press, 1981; Pauley, Bruce F., *From Prejudice to Destruction. A History of Austrian Antisemitism*, London: University of North Carolina Press, 1992; Frankl, Michal, *"Emancipace od židů." Český antisemitismus na konci 19. Století*, Prague: Paseka, 2007.
3. Forth, Christopher E., *The Dreyfus Affair and the Crisis of French Manhood*, Baltimore: John Hopkins University Press, 2004.
4. For studies of Germany, see Aschheim, Steven E., *Brothers and Strangers: The East European Jew in German and German Jewish Consciousness, 1800–1923*, Madison/London: University of Wisconsin Press, 1982; ibid., 'Eastern Jews, German Jews and Germany's Ostpolitik in the First World War', *Leo Baeck Institute Year Book*, 28, 1983: 351–365; Maurer, Trude, *Ostjuden in Deutschland, 1918–1933*, Hamburg: Christians, 1986; Wertheimer, Jack, *Unwelcome Strangers. East European Jews in Imperial Germany*, New York/Oxford: Oxford University Press, 1987.
5. Approximately 10,000 East European Jews came to France in the period before the Great War, see Green, Nancy L., *The Pletzl of Paris. Jewish Immigrant Workers in the 'Belle Époque'*, New York: Holmes & Meier, 1986. The German equivalent was approximately 70,000, Aschheim, *Brothers and Strangers*: 42.
6. *La libre parole illustrée*, 14 October 1893: 16. For an assessment of Drumont, see Winock, Michel, *Nationalism, Antisemitism and Fascism in France*, Stanford: Stanford University Press, 1998: 85–102.
7. Pauley, *From Prejudice to Destruction*: 65; from 1867 to 1910 around 30,000 Galician Jews moved to Vienna.
8. Lebzelter, Gisela C., *Political Antisemitism in England, 1918–1939*, London: Macmillan, 1978.
9. Cohen, Deborah, 'Who Was Who? Race and Jews in Turn-of-the-Century Britain', *Journal of British Studies*, 41, October 2002: 460–483; Knepper, Paul, 'British Jews and the Racialisation of Crime in the Age of Empire', *British Journal of Criminology*, 47(1), 2007: 61–79.
10. De Nie, Michael Willem, *The Eternal Paddy: Irish Identity and the British Press, 1798–1882*, Madison: University of Wisconsin Press, 2004.
11. See Holmes, Colin, *Antisemitism in British Society, 1876–1939*, London: Edward Arnold, 1979.
12. For an analysis of the physical traits ascribed to Jews, see Gilman, Sander, *The Jew's Body*, London: Routledge, 1991.
13. *Funny Folk*, 6 June 1891: 200; 17 January 1891: 24; 20 June 1891: 216. The pawnbroker joke was not just focussed on the irony of a Jew attempting to make money by striking, there was a pun here too, on the word pledge; customers 'pledged' their items to the pawnbroker.

14. Compare the sentiments expressed in some commentary in *Punch*, 5 June 1875: 245–246 and the riposte from an anonymous Jewish correspondent, 19 June 1875: 261.
15. See a comparable image, *Funny Folk*, 20 February 1892: 64.
16. For other 'nose' jokes, see *Funny Folk*, 16 May 1891: 176; 4 July 1891: 232; 25 July 1891: 256.
17. *Funny Folk*, 3 January 1891: 8. Of course, the Christmas tree was not a native British symbol; it was imported into Royal Family culture by the Hanoverians and popularised during Victoria's reign by Albert, Prince Consort.
18. This trait was noted in other cartoons, see 'What's in a name', *Punch*, 27 October 1883: 194; 'A Jew all over', *Illustrated Chips*, 10 September 1892: 4; 'A Jew's craving', *Illustrated Chips*, 3 February 1894: 4.
19. *Funny Folks*, 11 April 1891: 128.
20. Fagin mixes the order of words, has a distinct manner of emphasis and employs occasional dialect, which hints at a foreign background, rather than making him a creature of the *shtetl*. For a discussion of Dickens' characterisation of Fagin, see Felsenstein, Frank, *Antisemitic Stereotypes. A Paradigm of Otherness in English Popular Culture, 1660–1830*, Baltimore: John Hopkins University Press, 1999: 238ff.
21. For a discussion on the impact of the Emancipation on Jewish life in Russia, see Klier, John D., *Imperial Russia's Jewish Question*, Cambridge: Cambridge University Press, 1995: especially part three, 'The era of change and turmoil'.
22. *Aberdeen Journal*, 4 May 1891: 4.
23. Dillon, E.J., 'Jewish Colonization and the Russian Persecution', *New Review*, August 1891: 108–109. See also an account that described the rags, dirt and despair of Jewish emigrants in Charlottenburg, Berlin: *Birmingham Daily Post*, 6 June 1891: 8.
24. Frederic, Harold, *The New Exodus. A Study of Israel in Russia*, London: Heinemann, 1892: 27.
25. White, Arnold, *The Modern Jew*, London: Heinemann, 1899: 57; White, Arnold, 'Jewish Colonisation and the Russian Persecution', *New Review*, August 1891: 99.
26. Arnold White to *The Times*, 30 May 1887: 3; 30 November 1887: 5; 8 December 1893: 15.
27. Cohen, Israel, *Jewish Life in Modern Times*, London: Methuen & Co., 1914: 33–34.
28. Abbott, G.F., 'The Jewish Problem', *Fortnightly Review*, April 1910: 749.
29. *The Spectator*, 25 August 1883: 1085–1086.
30. Byford, Charles T., *The Soul of Russia*, London: Kingsgate Press, 1914: 77.
31. Frederic, *The New Exodus*: 68.
32. Laister, James, 'The Anti-Jewish Agitation', *Modern Thought*, July 1881: 194.
33. *The Times*, 17 August 1883: 7.
34. *The Spectator*, 25 July 1883: 1086.
35. *The Times*, 17 August 1883: 7.
36. Baskerville, Beatrice, *The Polish Jewish. His Social and Economic Value*, London: Chapman & Hall, 1906: 66–67. In her novel, *Passover*, London: Thornton Butterworth, 1920, which rehashes the Beilis Affair, set in Poland,

one of her characters argues, (58): 'We can't look upon the Jewish question from a western European point of view because we've got so many of them. If we don't react against their peaceful penetration we shall have no economic independence left.' See also Wallace, Donald Mackenzie, *Our Russian Ally*, London: Macmillan, 1914: 16.

37. White, Arnold, 'Kishinev and After', *National Review*, August 1903: 956.
38. *Birmingham Daily Post*, 23 February 1879: 8; *The Times*, 16 August 1884: 2.
39. *MG*, 15 August 1879: 5; 26 August 1879: 5.
40. *JC*, 11 November 1881: 8–9.
41. *The Scotsman*, 12 January 1882: 4.
42. Penslar, Derek J., *Shylock's Children. Economics and Jewish Identity in Modern Europe*, Berkeley: University of California Press, 2001: especially 50–89.
43. *Truth*, 26 January 1882: 139.
44. See Chapman, S.J., 'Agricultural Credit in Ireland', *Economic Journal*, December 1914: 637–639.
45. For a similar line of argument, which accused the Chancellor of the Exchequer of putting 'the nation in the hands of the Jews', see Radclyffe, Raymond, 'In the Hands of the Money-Lender', *English Review*, May 1916: 602.
46. *The Spectator*, 28 January 1882: 83.
47. *The Times*, 20 February 1882: 7.
48. Anglo-Russian, 'The Tsar and the Jews', *Contemporary Review*. October 1891: 326; see also *Morning Post*, 26 May 1881: 4.
49. Stead, W.T., *The Truth about Russia*, London: Cassell & Co., 1888: 305.
50. Dillon, E.J., *Russian Characteristics*, London: Chapman and Hall, 1892: 504–505.
51. Klier, *Imperial Russia's Jewish Question*: 311–320.
52. *Birmingham Daily Post*, 6 May 1891: 8; *Leeds Mercury*, 6 May 1891: 5; *Aberdeen Journal*, 11 May 1891: 4.
53. *The Scotsman*, 5 December 1902: 8.
54. Seton-Watson, R.W., *Romania and the Great War*, London: Constable & Co., 1915: 26.
55. *The Spectator*, 25 August 1883: 1085.
56. Wickham Steed, Henry, 'Austria an Europe', *Edinburgh Review*, January 1917: 2. These sentiments were repeated in his memoirs, *Through Thirty Years*, Volume II, London: Heinemann, 1924: 390–391.
57. Anglo-Russian, 'The Tsar and the Jews': 323, 326.
58. Beizer, Mikhail, *The Jews of St. Petersburg: Excursions through a Noble Past*, Philadelphia: Jewish Publication Society of America, 1989: 7. It was only in 1920 that the Jewish population of the city exceeded 2 per cent.
59. *PIP*, 7 January 1911: 16. This piece was followed, several weeks in succession, by disdainful and angry letters that refuted the accusations: 14 January 1911/58; 21 January 1911: 78; 4 February 1911: 144; 18 February 1911: 205. For a similar fear in relation to London, see *Northern Echo*, 1 May 1891: 3.
60. Pares, Bernard, 'Reaction and Revolution', in A.W. Ward, G.W. Prothero and S. Leather (eds), *Cambridge Modern History*, Volume XII, 'The Latest Age', Cambridge: Cambridge University Press, 1910: 339–341.
61. *St. James's Gazette*, 10 January 1882: 6.

62. *PMG*, 23 May 1891: 6; see also *Daily News*, 23 May 1891: 5.
63. *The Spectator*, 25 April 1891: 578.
64. *PIP*, 7 January 1911: 16; Anglo-Russian, 'The Tsar and the Jews': 325.
65. *The Spectator*, 21 March 1885: 383.
66. *PMG*, 6 November 1891: 6; interestingly, the term *kulak* was employed here, a word that literally means 'fist', but was associated with peasants who had managed to get on better than their neighbours. Of course, it is a word that acquired great significance in the Stalinist 1930s, especially during Collectivisation.
67. *The Scotsman*, 12 January 1882: 4.
68. See, for instance, *Everyman*, 18 October 1912: 4–5. A belief in peasant proprietorship was a core value of the Distributist movement, which Chesterton formed with Hilaire Belloc in the 1920s. The nascent ideas of the movement were explored by Belloc in *The Servile State*, published in 1912. For a discussion of Distributism, see Corrin, J.P., *G.K. Chesterton and Hilaire Belloc. The Battle Against Modernity*, Athens: Ohio University Press, 1981.
69. Graham, Stephen, *Undiscovered Russia*, London: John Lane, 1912: ix–xi.
70. *PMG*, 23 January 1882: 4.
71. White, *The Modern Jew*: 38. *Muzhik* is Russian for 'peasant', and stems from *muzh* – man.
72. According to *The Spectator*, 21 March 1885: 383–384: 'the despised Israelite never condescends to agriculture, or other hard physical labour, and is, indeed, physically unfitted for any work demanding strength.'
73. Byford, *The Soul of Russia*: 377.
74. Stead, *The Truth About Russia*: 305; *Review of Reviews*, March 1891: 265.
75. *The Spectator*, 28 January 1882: 83. The same perspective was expressed almost 40 years later by Captain Peter Wright in his report on the post-war Polish pogroms, see Samuel, Sir Stuart, 'Report on Mission to Poland, 1 July 1920', *Papers by Command*, Vol. 51, 1121, *Parliamentary Command Paper*, No. 674, London: HMSO, 1920: 35.
76. *The Spectator*, 15 October 1881: 1295.
77. *The Times*, 20 February 1882: 7.
78. Birnbaum, Pierre, *Antisemitism in France. A Political History from Léon Blum to the Present*, Oxford: Blackwell, 1992: 130.
79. The reasons for this are complex and lie in the manner in which Jews were identified in 'official' Judeophobic discourse in Russia, a matter I discussed at length with John Klier. There was a continual theme, for instance, of the Jews as 'rootless', 'aliens' and '*inorodtsy*' (i.e. non-Orthodox, non-Slavs, non-Russians), and they were always contrasted with the 'native' population. But since Jews lived largely on the borderlands (in modern Ukraine, Belarus, etc.), 'native-soil-ism' was not really too concerned with far-away Jews. Since, as already noted, concern about Jews 'on the land' was related not to land ownership, but to the exploitation of the peasantry (who were 'Russians' – but not fully so), 'national' issues were difficult to apply. For a discussion about Jews and peasants in Russian Judeophobic discourse, see Klier, *Imperial Russia's Jewish Question*: 300ff.
80. *The Times*, 30 July 1890: 9.

81. *The Times*, 20 February 1882: 7.
82. Klier, *Imperial Russia's Jewish Question*: 300ff.
83. *The Spectator*, 15 October 1881: 1295.
84. The journey was detailed in Bailey, W.F., *The Slavs of the Eastern War Zone*, London: Chapman & Hall, 1916.
85. Bailey, W.F., 'Where Russia Borders Austria', *Fortnightly Review*, May 1915: 820; ibid., 'Life in Eastern Galicia', *Fortnightly Review*, July 1915: 106.
86. Bailey, 'Where Russia Borders Austria': 825.
87. Bailey, W.F., 'Polish Memories', *Fortnightly Review*, December 1915: 1048.
88. R.C. Long was more effective in depicting the comings and goings of various armies in Galicia, see 'Two Battle Fronts: A Letter from Warsaw', *Fortnightly Review*, April 1915: 568–582; 'Soldiers: A Letter from Poland', *Fortnightly Review*, June 1915: 951–963.
89. Bailey, 'Polish Memories': 1049.
90. Bailey, 'Where Russia Borders Austria': 819.
91. Bailey, *The Slavs of the Eastern War Zone*: 19–20.
92. Klier, *Imperial Russia's Jewish Question*: 290–291.
93. Aronson, I. Michael, *Troubles Waters. The Origins of the 1881 Anti-Jewish Pogroms in Russia*, Pittsburgh: University of Pittsburgh Press, 1990: 36–37. The statistic is taken from the 1897 census.
94. *The Times*, 20 February 1882: 7; see also *The Spectator*, 21 January 1882: 1.
95. For a discussion of the mechanics of White's visit, see Perlmann, Moshe, 'Arnold White, Baron Hirsch's Emissary', *Proceedings of the American Academy of Jewish Research*, Vol. 46, 1979–1980: 473–489.
96. White, *The Modern Jew*: xii–xvi.
97. White, 'Jewish Colonisation and the Russian Persecution': 98–100, 104.
98. See, for instance, *The Times*, 19 February 1885: 10; 23 September 1885: 5.
99. *The Graphic* was also sceptical about the prospects of Jews becoming farmers, see 30 May 1891: 602.
100. Black, Eugene C., *The Social Politics of Anglo-Jewry, 1880–1920*, London: Blackwell, 1988: 243–270. There were various institutions in Britain which aimed to materially, and sometimes morally, assist immigrant East European Jews. These included the Poor Jews' Temporary Shelter and the Board of Guardians. In 1885, mindful of an unceasing trickle of emigrants from Eastern Europe, the *JC* advocated the creation of an 'international emigration fund', which would witness a collective effort on the part of all Western Jewry to assist transit and the like to, preferably, North America: *JC*, 13 February 1885: 11–12.
101. *JC*, 17 March 1881: 11.
102. *JW*, 29 August 1902: front cover & 422; 5 September 1902: front cover & 438–439; 12 September 1902: front cover & 454–455.
103. See a series of articles by Leopold Greenberg, which attempted to deconstruct and refute the alienist argument, but also to prove the worthiness of the East European Jewish immigrant for a new life in the United Kingdom; see, for example, *JC*, 6 January 1899; 12–13; 13 January 1899: 10; 20 January 1899: 13; 10 February 1899: 22–23; 17 February 1899: 10; 3 March 1899: 23–24; 26 May 1899: 13.
104. *JC*, 8 December 1886: 9.
105. *JC*, 12 December 1884: 11.

106. *JC*, 20 February 1885: 11.
107. *JC*, 12 December 1884: 11.
108. *JC*, 8 April 1891: 12.
109. *JC*, 19 December 1884: 9.
110. Verax, *La Roumanie et les Juifs*, Bucharest: I.V. Socecu, 1903: 199.
111. For discussion of the Russian Imperial context, see Klier, Imperial Russia's Jewish Question: 332–349.
112. Dillon, E.J., 'Foreign Affairs; Emancipation or Disenfranchisement for Russian Jews', *Contemporary Review*, June 1908: 759–760.
113. *Review of Reviews*, March 1891: 265. For the same perspective on Romania and the Habsburg Empire, see *PMG*, 22 January 1877: 4.
114. Jews served in all European armies in the nineteenth century, and most especially during the Great War. In the first few weeks of the war alone, for instance, around 10,000 German Jews volunteered for service in the German Imperial army: Chickering, Roger, *Imperial Germany and the Great War*, Cambridge: Cambridge University Press, 2004: 128.
115. *The Graphic*, 23 December 1893: 782.
116. *JC*, 13 April 1883: 4. See also *JC*, 23 February 1883, 3; 15 May 1891: 18; 17 February 1899: 10.
117. *JW*, 12 February 1904: 401.
118. *JW*, 9 September 1914: 4. The Jewish press was not alone in this, see an appreciative piece about Jewish heroisim in the Russian Imperial army in *The Nation*, 10 October 1914: 29.
119. *JW*, 9 June 1915: 12. It even published a poem, by Florence Kiper Frank, which lauded the courage of the Russo-Jewish conscript, see 6 January 1915: 9.
120. *JW*, 20 January 1915: 8; *Sunday Times*, 17 January 1915: 9–10.
121. *JC*, 2 December 1881: 9; *JC*, 31 March 1882: 9; *JC*, 28 August 1885: 12. The *JC* was opposed to political Zionism from the outset and, in the wake of the first Zionist Congress at Basle in 1897, constantly strove to demonstrate its ideological frailties. This outlook only changed once Leopold Greenberg, a founder of the English Zionist Federation, became editor in 1907. For discussion, see Cesarani, David, *The 'Jewish Chronicle' and Anglo-Jewry*. Cambridge: Cambridge University Press, 1994: 86–88.
122. See, for example, *JC*, 6 June 1884: 5; *JC*, 27 November 1885: 5; *JC*, 30 October 1884: 7; *JC*, 27 November 1885: 5.
123. *JW*, 16 September 1904: front cover; 480.
124. For examples of analyses of various schemes, see Conder, C.R., 'Jewish Colonies in Palestine', *Blackwood's Edinburgh Magazine*, June 1891: 856–870; Herzl, Theodor, 'The Zionist Congress', *Contemporary Review*, October 1897: 587–600; Prag, Joseph, 'The Jewish Colonies in Palestine', *Contemporary Review*, May 1898: 706–717.
125. A number of schemes and organisations in Eastern Europe sought to modernise Jewish life, the most significant of which were the Society for the Dissemination of Enlightenment amongst the Jews of Russia (known as OPE), and the Society for the Promotion of Artisan and Agricultural Work among the Jews (known as ORT), see Veidlinger, Jeffrey, *Jewish Public Culture in the Late Russian Empire*, Bloomington: Indiana University Press, 2009;

Shapiro Leon, *The History of ORT. A Jewish Movement for Social Change*. New York: Schoken Books, 1980; Dekel-Chen, Jonathan, 'JCA-ORT-JAS-JDC: One Big Agrarianizing Family', *Jewish History*, 21(3/4), 2007: 263–278.

126. *JC*, 11 December 1881: 11; see also *JC*, 28 August 1885: 9.

127. *JC*, 19 August 1891: 16. Similar perspectives can be found in an overview of the worldwide economic Jewish contribution, intended as a rebuttal to Werner Sombart's *Die Juden und das Wirtschaftsleben*, see Cohen, Israel, 'The Economic Activities of Modern Jewry', *Economic Journal*, March 1914: 41–56.

128. Lebzelter, *Political Antisemitism in England*: part one; Holmes, *Antisemitism in British Society*: part three; Wilson, Keith M., 'The Protocols of Zion and the *Morning Post*, 1919–20', *Patterns of Prejudice*, 19(3), 1985: 5–14; Kadish, Sharman, *Bolsheviks and British Jews. The Anglo-Jewish Community, Britain and the Russian Revolution*, London: Frank Cass, 1992; Cohn, Norman, *Warrant for Genocide. The Myth of the Jewish World Conspiracy and the Protocols of the Elders of Zion*, London: Serif Publishing, 1996. For a survey of British perspectives gathered by the Foreign Office, see 'A Collection of Reports on Bolshevism in Russia. (Russia No. 1, 1919)', *Parliamentary Command Paper*, No. 8, London: HMSO, 1919.

129. The *Protocols* were later proven a forgery in *The Times*, with other publications similarly disputing their veracity. *The Nation*, 20 August 1921: 729, mocked the 'silliness of the [White movement's] Western dupes', since the *Protocols* were partially disseminated in the West via the influence of White émigrés.

130. See, for example, *Morning Post*, 18 November 1918: 8; 19 November 1918: 5; 21 November 1918: 8; 23 November 1918: 3; 7 December 1918: 6; 20 March 1919: 6; 25 March 1919: 6; 26 March 1919: 6; 27 March 1919: 5; 4 April 1919: 6.

131. *The Times*, 8 May 1920: 15.

132. Wilton, Robert, *Russia's Agony*, London: Edward Arnold, 1918: 54ff; Chesterton, G.K., *The New Jerusalem*, London: Hodder & Staughton, 1920: 227–228; see also Belloc, Hilaire, *The Jews*, London: Constable, 1922: 171.

133. Saroléa, Charles, *Impressions of Soviet Russia*, London, Nash & Grayson, 1924. Saroléa was privately challenged by Israel Zangwill, who advised: 'By quoting the absurd statement that the "Jews have come out of the war the only victors", or by continuing to exaggerate the proportion of Jewish Bolshevists, you help to hound on the coming European massacre'; Israel Zangwill to Charles Saroléa, 21 June 1924, SAR 82(ii).

134. Wolf, Lucien, *The Jewish Bogey, and the Forged Protocols of the Learned Elders of Zion, published by N.S. Nilus. A Reply to Articles in 'The Morning Post' on the 'Causes of the World Unrest'*, London: Board of Deputies, 1920; ibid., *The Myth of the Jewish Menace in World Affairs; or the Truth about the Forged Protocols of the Elders of Zion*, New York: Macmillan, 1921. For various correspondence and material in Wolf's files dealing with the *Protocols of the Elders of Zion*, see WMC, RG348, f.52, 5/339; f.169, 18/802; f.237. 26/256.

135. Churchill, W.S., *The World Crisis: the Aftermath*, London: Thornton Butterworth, 1929: 73; Pares, Bernard, *The League of Nations and Other Questions of Peace*, London: Hodder & Staughton, 1919: 135.

136. For example, *Daily Mail*, 29 April 1919: 8; 2 May 1919: 6. Kun's original surname was Kohn, which he Magyarised in 1906, though since Kun's mother was protestant, he was not even *halakhically* Jewish.

137. *The Spectator*, 26 April 1919: 515; 10 May 1919: 582; 9 August 1919: 166.

138. *Leeds Mercury*, 31 May 1879: 12; *Glasgow Herald*, 5 March 1880: 4; *Northern Echo*, 15 November 1880: 3.

139. The assassination received intense coverage, see *PMG*, 14 March 1881: 1; *Liverpool Mercury*, 17 March 1881: 6; *The Graphic*, 26 March 1881: images of the assassination throughout; *The Times*, 25 January 1882: 9.

140. Klier, John D., and Lambroza, Shlomo, *Pogroms. Anti-Jewish Violence in Modern Russian History*, Cambridge: Cambridge University Press, 1992: 39. Only one of the assassins was Jewish, Gesia Gelfman.

141. Irish republican groups were associated with a number of bomb-plots and actual terrorism in the 1880s, including an attack on Salford Barracks in 1881, and a plan to murder Queen Victoria in 1887 (the 'Jubilee Plot').

142. Fishman, William J., *East End Jewish Radicals, 1875–1914*, London: Duckworth, 1975.

143. *JC*, 12 June 1891: 11.

144. *Reynolds's Newspaper*, 8 October 1899: 3.

145. *Reynolds's Newspaper*, 22 October 22, 1899: 4.

146. *PIP*, 18 November 1905: 309; *The Times*, 22 November 1905: 4; 30 November 1905: 4.

147. Pares, 'Reaction and Revolution': 359.

148. Saroléa, Charles, 'The geographical foundations of Russian politics', *Scottish Geographical Magazine*, April 1906: 196.

149. Williams, Harold, *Russia of the Russians*, London: Isaac Pitman, 1914: 117–118.

150. Dillon, *Russian Characteristics*: 505.

151. Graham, Stephen, *Changing Russia*, London: John Lane, 1913: 134–137.

Select Bibliography

Archives

Archives of the Board of Deputies of British Jews, London Metropolitan Archives.
Archives of the Anglo-Jewish Association, Special Collections, Southampton University.
Correspondence and papers of Dr Moses Gaster, Special Collections, University College London.
Papers of Sir Lewis Namier, Special Collections, Manchester University.
Manchester Guardian archives, Special Collections, Manchester University.
The National Archives, Kew, London.
Papers of Lord Nathaniel Rothschild, Rothschild Archives, New Court, London.
Papers of Professor Sir Bernard Pares, Special Collections, School of Slavonic and East European Studies, University College London.
Archives of the *Alliance Israélite Universelle*, Paris, France.
Papers of Lucien Wolf/David Mowshowitch, YIVO Institute for Jewish Research, New York City, USA.
Archives of the American Jewish Committee, New York City, USA.

Official publications

'Correspondence Respecting Persecution of Jews in Moldavia, 1867', *Parliamentary Command Papers*, Nos. 3890, 3897, 3917, London: Harris and Sons, 1867.
'Correspondence Respecting Condition and Treatment of Jews in Serbia and Romania, 1875–1876', *Parliamentary Command Paper*, No. 1742, London: Harris and Sons, 1877.
'Correspondence Relative to Recognition of Independence of Romania, 1880', *Parliamentary Command Paper*, No. 2554, London: Harris and Sons, 1880.
'Correspondence Regarding the Treatment of Jews in Russia, 1882', *Parliamentary Command Papers*, Nos. C3132, C3250, London: Harris and Sons, 1882.
Royal Commission on Alien Immigration, London: HMSO, 1903: Volume I, The Report; Volume II, Minutes of Evidence; Volume III, Appendix to Minutes of Evidence; Volume IV, Index and Analysis.
'Despatch from His Majesty's Consul-General at Odessa, forwarding a Report on the Riots at Kishinev. Russia, No. 1', *Parliamentary Command Paper*, No. 1721, London: HMSO, 1903.
'Correspondence Respecting the Relief of Allied Territories in the Occupation of the Enemy', *Parliamentary Command Paper*, No. 8348, London: Harrison and Sons/HMSO, 1916.

'A Collection of Reports on Bolshevism in Russia. (Russia No. 1, 1919)', *Parliamentary Command Paper*, No. 8, London: HMSO, 1919.

Samuel, Sir Stuart, 'Report on Mission to Poland, 1 July 1920', *Papers by Command*, Vol. 51, 1121, *Parliamentary Command Paper*, No. 674, London: HMSO, 1920.

Hansard's Parliamentary Debates, 3rd Series, London: Cornelius Buck.[*]

1868: Volume 188.
1872: Volumes 209, 210.
1878: Volume 239.
1881: Volumes 256, 262–264.
1882: Volumes 266–269, 272.
1890: Volumes 347, 350.
1891: Volume 353.

Hansard's Parliamentary Debates, 4th Series, London: Wyman & Sons.

1892: Volume 3.
1893: Volumes 8, 10, 17.
1898: Volumes 58, 59.
1900: Volume 87.
1902: Volumes 109, 110, 112, 113.
1903: Volumes 122, 123.
1904: Volume 133.
1905: Volume 147.
1906: Volumes 150, 155, 158, 159.
1907: Volume 177.
1908: Volumes 186, 187.

Hansard's Parliamentary Debates, 5th Series, London: HMSO.

1909: Volumes 11, 13.
1911: Volumes 23, 30.
1912: Volume 42.
1913: Volume 36.
1914: Volumes 62, 64.
1915: Volumes 77, 83.
1916: Volumes 84–86, 88.
1917: Volumes 90, 91, 94, 99.
1918: Volumes 101, 104, 106, 107.
1919: Volumes 113, 115–122.
1920: Volumes 125, 126, 128, 131.
1921: Volume 140.
1922: Volumes 150, 151, 156.
1923: Volumes 161, 166.
1924: Volume 176.
1925: Volumes 182, 189.

---

[*] Naturally, I have perused all volumes of *Hansard* from the 1860s onwards, but only those which contain material appertaining to the Jewish question, in Eastern Europe and elsewhere, are indicated.

Selected daily newspapers and weekly journals

Aberdeen Journal
The Anglo-Russian
Birmingham Daily Mail
Birmingham Daily Post
Catholic Herald
Daily Chronicle
Daily Express
Daily Mail
Daily News
Daily Telegraph
Evening Standard
Everyman
Free Russia
Funny Folks
The Graphic
Illustrated London News
Jewish Chronicle
Jewish World
Leeds Mercury
Liverpool Mercury
Manchester Guardian
Manchester Weekly Times
Morning Leader
Morning Post
The Nation
New Europe
New Poland
New Witness
New York Times
The Observer
Pall Mall Gazette
Penny Illustrated Paper
Polish News
Prawda
Punch
Review of Reviews
Saturday Review
Glasgow Herald
The Scotsman
The Spectator
St James' Gazette
The Scotsman
The Spectator
Sunday Times
The Times

Truth
Tygodnik Polski
Weekly Register
Western Mail

Material published before 1939

Abbott, G.F., 'The Jewish Problem', *Fortnightly Review*, April 1910: 742–754.

Adler, Cyrus (ed.), *American Jewish Yearbook*, Philadelphia: Jewish Publication Society of America: all volumes from 1901 to 1925.

Adler, Cyrus, *The Voice of America on Kishinev*, Philadelphia: Jewish Publication Society of America, 1904.

Alma Tadema, Laurence, *Poland, Russia and the War*, London: St Catherine's Press, 1915.

American Jewish Committee, *The Jews in the Eastern War Zone*, New York: American Jewish Committee, 1916.

Anglo-Russian, 'The Tsar and the Jews', *Contemporary Review*, October 1891: 309–326.

Bailey, W.F., 'Where Russia Borders Austria', *Fortnightly Review*, May 1915: 817–826.

——, 'Some Glimpses of Russian Poland To-Day', *Fortnightly Review*, September 1915: 465–475.

——, 'Life in Eastern Galicia', *Fortnightly Review*, July 1915: 97–109.

——, 'Some Glimpses of Russian Poland To-Day', *Fortnightly Review*, September 1915: 465–475.

——, *The Slavs of the Eastern War Zone*, London: Chapman & Hall, 1916.

Balicki, Zygmunt, 'The Revival of Political Thought in Poland', *Russian Review*, Vol. II(2): 87–115.

Baskerville, Beatrice. C., *The Polish Jew. His Social and Economic Value*, London: Chapman & Hall, 1906.

——, *Passover. A Novel*, London: Thornton Butterworth, 1920.

Batchinsky, Julian, Margolin, Arnold, Vishnitzer, Mark and Zangwill, Israel, *The Jewish Pogroms in Ukraine*, Washington DC: Friends of Ukraine, 1919.

Battine, Cecil, 'Poland and the Peace', *Nineteenth Century & After*, March 1919: 612–625.

Belloc, Hilaire, *The Two Maps of Europe*, London: Pearson, 1915.

Belloc, Hilaire, *The Jews*, London: Constable, 1922.

Bluntschli, J.C., *Romania and the Legal Status of the Jews in Romania. An Exposition of Public Law*, London: Anglo-Jewish Association, 1879.

Bluntschli, J.C., *Der Staat Rumänien und das Rechtsverhältniss der Juden in Rumänien. Ein Rechtsgutachten*, Berlin: 1879.

Boswell, A. Bruce, *Poland and the Poles*, London: Methuen, 1919.

Brailsford, H.N., *The Fruits of Our Russian Alliance*, London: Anglo-Russian Committee, 1912.

Brailsford, H.N., *Across the Blockade. A Record of Travels in Enemy Europe*, London: Allen & Unwin, 1919.

Brailsford, H.N., 'Poland as a Barrier', *New Republic*, 3 May 1919: 10–13.

Brandes, Georg, *Poland. A Study of the Land, People and Literature*, London: Heinemann, 1903.

Buchan, John, *Nelson's History of the War*, Volume VI, London: Nelson & Sons, 1915.

Byford, Charles T., *The Soul of Russia*, London: Kingsgate Press, 1914.

Caine, Hall, 'Russian Jewry. Scenes of Home Life in Poland and the Pale', *Pall Mall Magazine*, September 1893: 641–655; October 1893: 863–872.

Chapman, S.J., 'Agricultural Credit in Ireland', *Economic Journal*, December 1914: 637–639.

Chesterton, G.K., *The Barbarians of Berlin*, London: Cassell & Co., 1914.

Chesterton, G.K., *The New Jerusalem*, London: Hodder & Staughton, 1921.

Churchill, W.S., *The World Crisis: the Aftermath*, London: Thornton Butterworth, 1929.

Cohen, Israel, *Jewish Life in Modern Times*, London: Methuen & Co., 1914.

——, 'The Economic Activities of Modern Jewry', *Economic Journal*, March 1914: 41–56.

——, *The Ruhleben Prison Camp: A Record of Nineteen Months' Internment*, London: Methuen, 1917.

——, *Anti-Semitism in Germany*, London: Offices of the "Jewish Chronicle" and the "Jewish World", 1918.

——, *A Report on the Pogroms in Poland*, London: Central Office of the Zionist Organisation, April 1919.

——, 'The Jews under the Minorities Treaties', *Contemporary Review*, January 1929: 75.

Conder, C.R., 'Jewish Colonies in Palestine', *Blackwood's Edinburgh Magazine*, June 1891: 856–870.

Davis, Israel, *The Jews in Romania. A Short Statement on their Recent History and Present Situation*, London: AJA/AIU, Trübner and Co., 1872.

Davitt, Michael, *Within the Pale: The True Story of the Antisemitic Persecution in Russia*, London, Hurst & Blackett, 1903.

Dearmer, Percy, 'The Soul of Russia', *Nineteenth Century and After*, January 1915: 72–83.

Devereux, Roy, *Poland Reborn*, London: Chapman & Hall, 1922.

Dillon, E.J., [written under the pseudonym, E.B. Lanin], 'Jewish Colonization and the Russian Persecution', *New Review*, August 1891: 105–117.

——, *Russian Characteristics*, London: Chapman and Hall, 1892.

——, 'Foreign Affairs; Emancipation or Disenfranchisement for Russian Jews', *Contemporary Review*, June 1908: 759–760.

Dmowski, Roman, *La question polonaise*, Paris: Librairie Armand Colin, 1909.

——, 'The Political Evolution of Poland', Parts I-III, *Russian Review*, Vol. II(4): 54–68; Vol. III(1): 84–99; Vol. III(2): 73–86.

——, *Problems of Central and Eastern Europe*, London: Privately Printed, July 1917.

Duff, J.D., (ed.), *Russian Realities and Problems*, Cambridge: Cambridge University Press, 1916.

Earl of Dunraven, 'The Invasion of Destitute Aliens', *Nineteenth Century*, June 1892: 985–1000.

Evans-Gordon, W.E., *The Alien Immigrant*, London: Heinemann, 1903.

Eversley, Lord, *The Partitions of Poland*, London: T. Fisher Unwin, 1915.

Evidence of Pogroms in Poland and Ukrainia, New York: American Jewish Congress, 1919.

Evreiskaia entsiklopediia, St Petersburg: Obshchestva dlia Nauchniykh Evreiskikh Izdanii, 1906–1913, in 16 volumes.

Franzos, Karl Emil, *The Jews of Barnow*, London: Blackwood and Sons, 1882.

——, *For the Right*, London: J. Clarke & Co., 1889.

Frederic, Harold, *The New Exodus. A Study of Israel in Russia*, London: Heinemann, 1892.

Gardner, M.M., *Adam Mickiewicz, the National Poet of Poland*, London: J. M. Dent & Sons, 1911.

——, *Poland. A Study in National Idealism*, London: Burns & Oates, 1916.

——, *Anonymous Poet of Poland. Zygmunt Krasinski*, Cambridge: University Press, 1919.

——, *Kosciuszko: A Biography*, London: George Allen & Unwin Ltd., 1920.

——, *The Patriot Novelist of Poland. Henryk Sienkiewicz*, London: Dent, 1926.

Gaster, Moses, 'The Jews in Romania', *North American Review*, November 1902: 604–675.

Geffcken, Friedrich, 'Russia under Alexander III', *New Review*, August 1891: 234–243.

Gelberg, S, 'The Russian-Consul General and the Russian Jews', *Fortnightly Review*, March 1912: 543–552.

Graham, Stephen, *Undiscovered Russia*, London: John Lane, 1912.

——, *Changing Russia*, London: John Lane, 1913.

——, *Russia and the World*, London: Cassell, 1915.

——, 'Russia and the Jews', *English Review*, February 1915: 324–333.

——, *Russia in 1916*, London: Cassell, 1916.

——, 'Russia's Religion of Suffering', *Quarterly Review*, January 1916: 22–30.

Gregory, J.D., *On the Edge of Diplomacy. Rambles and Reflections, 1902–1928*, London: Hutchinson, 1929.

Guedella, H, *The Romanian Government and the Jews*, London: Pottle & Sons, 1872.

'G.W.', 'The Rise of the Pan-Polish Party', *English Review*, May 1909: 381–384.

Herzl, Theodor, 'The Zionist Congress', *Contemporary Review*, October 1897: 587–600.

Heyking, Alphonse, 'Anglo-Russian Progress', *Fortnightly Review*, January 1912: 106–114.

Iliowizi, Henry, *In the Pale. Stories and Legends of the Jews*, Philadelphia: Jewish Publication Society of America, 1897.

——, *The Weird Orient. Nine Mystic Tales*, Philadelphia: H.T.Coates & Co., 1900.

'Jewish Tales and Jewish Reform', *Blackwood's Edinburgh Magazine*, November 1882: 639–653.

The Jews of Romania. Report of Public Meeting Held at the Mansion House, on Thursday May 30, 1872, London: Asher I Myers, Office of the "Jewish Chronicle", 1872.

Jeyes, S.H., 'Foreign Pauper Immigration', *Fortnightly Review*, July 1891: 13–24.

Kompert, Leopold, *Scenes from the Ghetto. Studies of Jewish Life*, London: Remington & Co., 1882.

Korolenko, [V.G.], 'House No. 13. An Episode in the Massacre of Kishinev', *Contemporary Review*, February 1904: 266–280.

Kozicki, Stanislas, *The Social Evolution of Poland in the Nineteenth Century. Lectures Delivered at University College London*, London: Hodder and Stoughton, 1918.

Lahovary, Jean, *The Jewish Question in Romania*, London: Aggett and Co, 1903.

Lazare, Bernard, *Die Juden in Rumänien*, Berlin: H. S. Hermann, 1902.
——, *La question israélite en Roumanie*, Bucarest: Imprimerie E. S. Cerbu, 1902.
——, 'The Jews in Romania', *Contemporary Review*, February 1903: 237–248.
Long, R.C., 'Two Battle Fronts: A Letter from Warsaw', *Fortnightly Review*, April 1915: 568–582.
Long, R.C., 'Soldiers: A Letter from Poland', *Fortnightly Review*, June 1915: 951–963.
Levison, Leon, *The Tragedy of the Jews in the European War Zone*, Edinburgh: Russian Jews' Relief Fund, 1915.
Levison, Leon, *The Jewish Problem and the World War*, London: Morgan & Scott, 1916.
Margolin, Arnold, 'The Jewish Problem in Eastern Europe', *New York Times Current History*, March 1923: 962–967.
Marriott, J.A.R., 'The Problem of Poland', *Edinburgh Review*, February 1915: 358–384.
——, 'Prussia, Poles and Ireland', *Edinburgh Review*, January 1917: 158–177.
Miller, William, *The Balkans. Romania, Bulgaria, Serbia and Montenegro*, London: T. Fisher Unwin, 1894.
Morgenthau, Henry, *All in a Life-Time*, New York: Doubleday, 1922.
Pares, Bernard, 'A Peasants' Meeting in Russia', *Contemporary Review*, December 1905: 783–798.
——, *Russia and Reform*, London: Constable, 1907.
——, 'Reaction and Revolution', in A.W. Ward, G.W. Prothero, S. Leather, *Cambridge Modern History*, Volume XII, Cambridge: Cambridge University Press, 1910: 339–341.
——, *Day by Day with the Russian Army, 1914–1915*, London: Constable, 1915.
——, 'Russian Hopes and Aims', *Edinburgh Review*, July 1916: 99–113.
——, *The League of Nations and Other Questions of Peace*, London: Hodder & Staughton, 1919.
——, *My Russian Memoirs*, London: Jonathan Cape, 1931.
——, *My Contacts with Polish Politics, 1907–1917*, Kraków: [publisher unknown], 1933.
Pares, Bernard and Baring, Maurice, 'The Russian Government and the Massacres', *Quarterly Review*, July/August 1906: 586–615.
Julie Ledochowska, *Poland Ravaged and Bereaved! A Lecture Delivered at Copenhagen on 19th November 1915 by Countess Julie Ledochowska*, London: Saint Catherine Press, 1915.
Poland under the Germans, London: Joseph Causton & Sons, 1916.
Polish Information Committee, *Poland's Case for Independence*, London: Allen & Unwin, 1916.
Prag, Joseph, 'The Jewish Colonies in Palestine', *Contemporary Review*, May 1898: 706–717.
Radclyffe, Raymond, 'In the Hands of the Money-Lender', *English Review*, May 1916: 599–602.
Rait, R.S. (ed.), *Memorials of Albert Venn Dicey*, London: Macmillan, 1925.
Report of the Delegation of the Jews of the British Empire on the Treaties of Versailles, Saint-Germain-en-Laye and Neuilly and the Annexed Minority Treaties, London: The Joint Foreign Committee of the Board of Deputies of British Jews and the Anglo-Jewish Association, 1920.

The Resurrection of Poland. For a Lasting Peace, Paris: Société générale d'imprimerie et d'édition Levé, 1915.

Retinger, J.H., 'Poland and the Present War', *English Review*, December 1914: 78–84.

Roth, Cecil (ed.), *Essays in Jewish History by Lucien Wolf with a Memoir*, London: Jewish Historical Society, 1934.

Russell, C. and Lewis, H.S., *The Jew in London. A Study of Racial Character and Present-Day Conditions*, London: T. Fisher Unwin, 1900: 5.

Russian Atrocities, 1881. Supplementary Statement Issued by the Russo-Jewish Committee, London: Wertheimer, 1882.

Saroléa, Charles, *The French Revolution and the Russian Revolution. A Historical Parallel and a Forecast*, Edinburgh: Oliver & Boyd, 1906.

——, 'The Geographical Foundations of Russian Politics', *Scottish Geographical Magazine*, April 1906: 194–205.

——, 'The Soul of Russia', *Review of Reviews*, March 1916: 193–197.

——, *Europe's Debt to Russia*, London: Heinemann, 1916.

——, *The Russian Revolution and the* War, London: Allen and Unwin, 1917.

——, *Europe and the League of Nations*, London: G. Bell & Sons, 1919.

——, *Letters on Polish Affairs*, Edinburgh: Oliver & Boyd, 1922.

——, 'The Jewish Crisis in Eastern Europe', *New York Times Current History*, January 1923: 590–595.

——, *Impressions of Soviet Russia*, London, Nash & Grayson, 1924.

Schloss, David F., *The Persecution of the Jews in Romania. A Detailed Account, Compiled from Recent Official and other Authentic Information*, London: D. Nutt, 1885.

Semenov, E.P., *The Russian Government and the Massacres. A Page of the Russian Counter-Revolution*, London: John Murray, 1907.

Seton-Watson, R.W., 'Modern Romania', *The Rise of Nationality in the Balkans*, London: Constable & Co., 1917.

Sienkiewicz, Henryk, *Prusse et Pologne*, Paris: Agence polonaise de presse, 1909.

Stead, W.T., *The Truth About Russia*, London: Cassell & Co., 1888.

——, *The M.P. for Russia. Reminiscences and Correspondence of Madame Olga Novikoff*, London: Andrew Melrose, 1909, in two volumes.

Sutherland-Edwards, H., *Sir William White. His Life and Correspondence*, London: John Murray, 1902.

Swietochowski, G. de, 'Poland and her Rôle in Europe', *Fortnightly Review*, September 1915: 502–512.

'The Tsar and the Jews', *Blackwood's Edinburgh Magazine*, October 1890: 441–452.

Tugan-Baranowskii, M., 'Antisemitism in Contemporary Russia', *Monthly Review*, January 1904: 70–77.

Under the Duma and the Entente. The Persecution of the Jews in Russia. An Account of the Legalised Torture of Six Million Human Beings, London: T. Fisher Unwin, 1912.

'Uwagi' [Observations], *A Review of the British War Literature on the Polish Problem*, London: Polish Information Committee, 1916.

'Verax', *La Roumanie et les Juifs*, Bucarest: I.V. Socecu, 1903.

Wallace, Donald Mackenzie, *Our Russian Ally*, London: Macmillan, 1914.

Washburn, Stanley, *Field Notes from the Russian Front*, London: Andrew Melrose, 1915.

——, *The Russian Campaign*, London: Andrew Melrose, 1915.

Wells, H.G., *The War That Will End War*, London: Palmer, 1914.

White, Arnold, 'Jewish Colonisation and the Russian Persecution', *New Review*, August 1891: 97–105.

——, 'The Truth about the Russian Jew', *Contemporary Review*, May 1892: 695–702.

White, Arnold, 'Europe and the Jews', *Contemporary Review*, November 1897: 733–742.

——, ' "A Typical Alien Immigrant" ', *Contemporary Review*, February 1898: 241–250.

——, *The Modern Jew*, London: Heinemann, 1899.

——, 'Kishinev and After', *National Review*, August 1903: 950–958.

——, *The Views of Vanoc*, London: Kegan, Treach, Trübner, 1910.

Wickham Steed, Henry, *The Habsburg Monarchy*, London: Constable, 1914 (3rd ed.).

——, 'A Programme for Peace', *Edinburgh Review*, April 1916: 373–392.

——, *Through Thirty Years*, London: Heinemann, 1924 (in two volumes).

Wilkinson, Samuel H., *The Polish-Jewish Tragedy*, London: Morgan and Scott, n.d.

Williams, Harold, *Russia of the Russians*, London: Isaac Pitman, 1914.

Wilton, Robert, 'Dominant Facts in Russia', *Edinburgh Review*, January 1918: 131–145.

——, *Russia's Agony*, London: Edward Arnold, 1918.

Wolf, Lucien, *The Legal Sufferings of the Jews in Russia. A Survey of their Present Situation, and a Summary of Laws*, London: Fisher Unwin, 1912.

——, (ed.), *Notes on the Diplomatic History of the Jewish Question, with Texts of Treaty Stipulations and other Official Documents*, London: Jewish Historical Society of England, 1919.

——, *The Jewish Bogey, and the Forged Protocols of the Learned Elders of Zion, published by N.S.Nilus. A Reply to Articles in 'The Morning Post' on the 'Causes of the World Unrest'*, London: Board of Deputies, 1920.

——, *The Myth of the Jewish Menace in World Affairs; or the Truth about the Forged Protocols of the Elders of Zion*, New York: Macmillan, 1921.

——, *Russo-Jewish Refugees in Eastern Europe. Report on the Fourth Meeting of the Advisory Committee of the High Commissioner for Russian Refugees of the League of Nations, 20 April 1923*, London: Joint Foreign Committee, 1923.

——, *Russo-Jewish Refugees in Eastern Europe. Report on the Meeting of the Advisory Committee of the High Commission for Russian Refugees held in Geneva on 3 September 1924, and on certain emigration questions arising during the Fifth Session of the Assembly of the League of Nations*, London: Joint Foreign Committee, 1924.

Zangwill, Israel, *The War for the World*, London: Heinemann, 1916.

Secondary material

Abramson, Henry, *A Prayer for the Government. Ukrainians and Jews in Revolutionary Times, 1917–1920*, Cambridge, MA: Harvard University Press, 1999.

Alderman, Geoffrey, 'The anti-Jewish Riots of August 1911 in South Wales', *Welsh History Review*, 6, December 1972/1973: 190–200.

——, 'The anti-Jewish Riots of August 1911 in South Wales: a Response', *Welsh History Review*, 20, June 2001: 565–571.

——, *Modern British Jewry*, Oxford: Clarendon Press, 1998.

Allett, John, 'New Liberalism, Old Prejudices: J.A. Hobson and the "Jewish Question"', *Jewish Social Studies*, 49, 1987: 99–114.

Almog, Shmuel, 'Antisemitism as a Dynamic Phenomenon: The "Jewish Question" in England at the End of the First World War', *Patterns of Prejudice*, 21(4), 1987: 3–18.

An-sky, S., *The Enemy at his Pleasure. A Journey through the Jewish Pale of Settlement during World War I*, (edited & translated by Joachim Neugroschel) New York: Metropolitan Books, 2003.

Aronsfeld, C.C., 'Jewish Enemy Aliens in England during the First World War', *Jewish Social Studies*, 18, 1956: 275–283.

Aronson, I. Michael, *Troubles Waters. The Origins of the 1881 Anti-Jewish Pogroms in Russia*, Pittsburgh: University of Pittsburgh Press, 1990.

Ascher, Abraham, *The Russian Revolution of 1905*, Stanford: California University Press, 1988 & 1992, in two volumes.

Aschheim, Steven, *Brothers and Strangers: The East European Jew in German and German Jewish Consciousness, 1800–1923*, Madison/London: University of Wisconsin Press, 1982.

——, 'Eastern Jews, German Jews and Germany's Ostpolitik in the First World War', *Leo Baeck Institute Year Book*, 28, 1983: 351–365.

Avrutin, Eugene M., 'Racial Categories and the Politics of (Jewish) Difference in Late Imperial Russia', *Kritika*, 8(1) Winter 2007: 13–40.

Balmuth, Daniel, '*Novoe Vremia's* War Against the Jews', *East European Jewish Affairs*, 35(1), June 2005: 33–54.

Bar-Yosef, Eitan and Valman, Nadia (eds), '*The Jew' in Late-Victorian and Edwardian Culture. Between the East End and East Africa*, London: Palgrave, 2009.

Bartal, Israel, *The Jews of Eastern Europe, 1772–1881*, Philadelphia: University of Pennsylvania, 2005.

Beizer, Mikhail, *The Jews of St. Petersburg: Excursions through a Noble Past*, Philadelphia: Jewish Publication Society of America, 1989.

Beloff, Max, *Lucien Wolf and the Anglo-Russian Entente, 1907–1914*, London: Jewish Historical Society of England, 1951.

Benjamin, Lya, 'The Jews in Romania, a Historical Outline', in Giurescu, Dinu C. and Fischer-Galaţi, Stephen A., *Romania. A Historical Perspective*, New York: Columbia University Press, 1998.

Berkowitz, Joel, 'The "Mendel Beilis Epidemic" on the Yiddish Stage', *Jewish Social Studies*, Autumn 2001, 8(1) : 199–225.

——, 'Avrom Goldfaden and the Modern Yiddish Theatre', *Pakn Treger*, Winter 2004: 11–19.

Bialik, H.M., 'The City of Slaughter', *Prooftexts*, 25, 2005: 8–29.

Birnbaum, Pierre, *Antisemitism in France. A Political History from Léon Blum to the Present*, Oxford: Blackwell, 1992.

Black, Eugene C., 'Lucien Wolf and the Making of Poland: Paris, 1919', *Polin*, 2, 1987: 5–36.

——, *The Social Politics of Anglo-Jewry, 1880–1920*, London: Blackwell, 1988.

——, 'A Typological Study of English Zionists', *Jewish Social Studies*, 9(3), 2003: 20–55.

Blobaum, Robert, 'The Politics of Antisemitism in Fin-de-Siècle Warsaw', *Journal of Modern History*, 73(2), June 2001: 275–306.

Bodea, Cornelia and Hugh Seton-Watson, *R.W. Seton-Watson si Românii, 1906–1920*, Bucharest: Editura Ştiinţifică şi Enciclopedică, 1988, in two volumes.

Boyer, John W., *Political Radicalism in Late Imperial Vienna*, Chicago: University of Chicago Press, 1981.

Briggs, Asa and Burke, Peter, *A Social History of the Media. From Gutenberg to the Internet*, Cambridge: Polity, 2005.

Budnitskii, Oleg (ed.), *Russko-Evreiskaia kul'tura*, Moscow: Rosspen, 2006.

Budnitskii, O.V., *Rossiiskie evrei mezhdu krasniymi i beliymi*, Moscow: Rosspen, 2006.

Burleigh, Michael, *Sacred Causes: The Clash of Religion and Politics, from the Great War to the War on Terror*, London: Harper Collins, 2007.

Calder, Kenneth J., *Britain and the Origins of the New Europe, 1914–1918*, Cambridge: Cambridge University Press, 1976.

Červinka, František, 'The Hilsner Affair', 135–161, in Dundes, Alan, *The Blood Libel Legend. A Casebook in Antisemitic Folklore*, Madison: University of Wisconsin Press, 1991.

Cesarani, David, 'An Embattled Minority: the Jews in Britain During the First World War', *Immigrants and Minorities*, 8, 1989: 61–81.

——, *The 'Jewish Chronicle' and Anglo-Jewry, 1841–1991*, Cambridge: Cambridge University Press, 1994.

Chesterton, Ada, E., *The Chestertons*, London: Chapman and Hall, 1941.

Cheyette, Brian, 'H.G. Wells and the Jews: Antisemitism, Socialism and English Culture', *Patterns of Prejudice*, 22(3): 22–35.

Cheyette, Brian, *Constructions of 'the Jew' in English Literature and Society. Racial Representations, 1875–1945*, Cambridge: Cambridge University Press, 1995.

Chickering, Roger, *Imperial Germany and the Great War*, Cambridge: Cambridge University Press, 2004.

Cohen, Deborah, 'Who Was Who? Race and Jews in Turn-of-the-Century Britain', *Journal of British Studies*, 41(4), October 2002: 460–483.

Cohen, Israel, 'My Mission to Poland (1918–1919)', *Jewish Social Studies*, 2, 1951: 149–172.

Cohen, Naomi W., *Jacob H. Schiff. A Study in American Jewish Leadership*, Hanover/London: UPNE, 1999.

Cohn, Norman, *Warrant for Genocide. The Myth of the Jewish World Conspiracy and the Protocols of the Elders of Zion*, London 1996.

Corrin, J.P., *G.K. Chesterton and Hilaire Belloc. The Battle Against Modernity*, London: Ohio University Press, 1981.

Corrsin, Stephen D., *Warsaw Before the First World War: Poles and Jews in the Third City of the Russian Empire, 1880–1914*, Boulder, Col.: East European Monographs, 1989.

Crick, Martin, *The History of the Social Democratic Federation*, Keele: Keele University Press, 1994.

Davies, Norman, 'The Poles in Great Britain 1914–1919', *Slavonic and East European Review*, 50(118), 1972: 63–89.

——, *White Eagle, Red Star. The Polish-Soviet War, 1919–20*, London: MacDonald, 1972.

——, 'Great Britain and the Polish Jews 1918–20', *Journal of Contemporary History*, April 1973: 119–142.

Dekel-Chen, Jonathan, 'JCA-ORT-JAS-JDC: One Big Agrarianizing Family', *Jewish History*, 21(3/4), 2007: 263–278.

Domagalska, Malgorzata, 'Antisemitic Discourse in Polish Nationalist Weeklies between 1918 and 1939', *East European Jewish Affairs*, 36(2): 191–197.

Dubnow, S.M., *History of the Jews of Russia and Poland. From the Earliest Times until the Present Day*, Bergenfield, NJ: Avotaynu 2000.

Eidelberg, Philip, *The Great Romanian Peasant Revolt of 1907: Origins of a Modern Jacquerie*, Leiden: Brill, 1974.

Eisenbach, Arthur, *The Emancipation of the Jews in Poland, 1780–1870*, Oxford: Basil Blackwell, 1991.

Estraikh, Gennady and Krutikov, Mikhail (eds), *The Shtetl: Image and Reality*, Oxford: Legenda, 2001.

Endelman, Todd M., *The Jews of Britain, 1656–2000*, Berkeley: University of California Press, 2002.

Evans, Richard J., *Death in Hamburg. Society and Politics in the Cholera Years, 1830–1910*, Oxford: Oxford University Press, 1987.

Feinberg, David, 'Historical Survey of the Colonization of the Russian Jews in Argentina', *Publication of the American Jewish Historical Society*, XLIII(1), September 1953: 473–489.

——, *Englishmen and Jews. Social Relations and Political Culture, 1840–1914*, New Haven/London: Yale University Press, 1994.

Feldman, Eliyahu, 'British Diplomats and British Diplomacy and the 1905 Pogroms in Russia', *Slavonic and East European Review*, 65(4), 1987: 579–608.

Felsenstein, Frank, *Antisemitic Stereotypes. A Paradigm of Otherness in English Popular Culture, 1660–1830*, Baltimore: Johns Hopkins University Press, 1999.

Ferguson, Niall, *The House of Rothschild. The World's Banker, 1849–1998*, London: Penguin, 1998.

Figes, Orlando and Kolonitskii, Boris, *Interpreting the Russian Revolution: the Language and Symbols of 1917*, London: Yale University Press, 1999.

Fink, Carole, 'Louis Marshall: An American Jewish Diplomat in Paris, 1919', *American Jewish History*, 94(1–2), March–June 2008: 21–40.

——, *Defending the Rights of Others. The Great Powers, the Jews and International Minority Protection, 1878–1938*, Cambridge: Cambridge University Press, 2004.

Fishman, David E., *The Rise of Modern Yiddish Culture*, Pittsburgh: University of Pittsburgh Press, 2005.

Fishman, William J., *East End Jewish Radicals, 1875–1914*, London: Duckworth, 1975.

Forth, Christopher E., *The Dreyfus Affair and the Crisis of French Manhood*, Baltimore: Johns Hopkins University Press, 2004.

Fountain II, Alvin Marcus, *Roman Dmowski: Party, Tactics, Ideology 1895–1907*, New York: East European Monographs, Columbia University Press, 1980.

Frankel, Jonathan, *Prophecy and Politics. Socialism, Nationalism and the Russian Jews, 1862–1917*, Cambridge: Cambridge University Press, 1981.

Frankel, Jonathan, 'The Crisis of 1881–1882 as a Turning Point in Modern Jewish History', in Berger, David (ed.), *The Legacy of Jewish Migration: 1881 and Its Impact*, New York: Columbia University Press, 1983: 9–22.

——, *The Damascus Affair. 'Ritual Murder', Politics, and the Jews in 1840*, Cambridge: Cambridge University Press, 1997.

Frankl, Michal, *"Emancipace od židů." Český antisemitismus na konci 19. Století*, Prague: Paseka, 2007.

Gainer, Bernard, *The Alien Invasion. The Origins of the Aliens Act of 1905*, London: Heinemann, 1972.

Garrard, John A., *The English and Immigration, 1880–1910*, London: Oxford University Press, 1971.

Gartner, Lloyd. P., 'Roumania, America and World Jewry: Consul Peixotto in Bucharest, 1870–1876', *American Jewish Historical Quarterly*, September 1968: 25–117.

Gatrell, Peter, *A Whole Empire Walking. Refugees in Russia during World War I*, Bloomington: Indiana University Press, 2005.

Gergel, Nahum, 'The Pogroms in Ukraine in 1918–21', *YIVO Annual of Jewish Social Science* 6, 1951: 237–252.

Gidley, Brian, 'The Ghosts of Kishinev in the East End: Responses to the Pogrom in the Jewish London of 1903', in Bar-Yosef, Eitan, and Valman, Nadia (eds), *'The Jew' in Late-Victorian and Edwardian Culture. Between the East End and East Africa*, London: Palgrave, 2009: 98–112.

Gilam, Abraham, 'The Leeds Anti-Jewish Riots 1917', *Jewish Quarterly*, 29, 1981: 34–37.

——, *The Emancipation of the Jews in England, 1830–1860*, New York: Garland Publishing, 1982.

Gilman, Sander, *The Jew's Body*, London: Routledge, 1991.

Gitelman, Zvi (ed.), *The Emergence of Modern Jewish Politics. Bundism and Zionism in Eastern Europe*, Pittsburgh: University of Pittsburgh Press, 2002.

Glaser, Anthony, 'The Tredegar Riots of August 1911', in Henriques, Ursula R.Q. (ed.), *The Jews of South Wales*, Cardiff: University of Wales Press, 1993: 151–176.

Golczewski, Frank, *Polnisch-Jüdische Beziehungen, 1881–1922*, Wiesbaden: Franz Steiner, 1981.

Graetz, Michael, *The Jews in Nineteenth-Century France. From the French Revolution to the Alliance Israélite Universelle*, Stanford: Stanford University Press, 1996.

Green, Abigail, 'Rethinking Sir Moses Montefiore: Religion, Nationhood and International Philanthropy in the Nineteenth Century', *American Historical Review*, 110(3), 2005: 631–658.

——, *Moses Montefiore. Jewish Liberator, Imperial Hero*, Cambridge: Harvard University Press, 2010.

Green, Nancy L., *The Pletzl of Paris. Jewish Immigrant Workers in the 'Belle Époque'*, New York: Holmes & Meier, 1986.

Gutwein, Daniel, 'The Politics of Jewish Solidarity. Anglo-Jewish Diplomacy and the Moscow Expulsion of April 1891', *Jewish History*, 5(2), September 1991: 23–45.

Haberer, Eric E., *Jews and Revolution in Nineteenth-Century Russia*, Cambridge: Cambridge University Press, 1995.

Hagen, William, 'Before the Final Solution: Toward a Comparative Analysis of Political Antisemitism in Interwar Germany and Poland', *Journal of Modern History*, 68(2), 1996: 351–381.

——, 'Murder in the East: German-Jewish Liberal Reactions to the Anti-Jewish Violence in Poland and Other East European Lands, 1918–1920', *Central European History*, 34, 2001: 1–30.

——, 'The Moral Economy of Popular Violence: The Pogrom in Lwów, November 1918', in Blobaum, Robert (ed.), *Antisemitism and Its Opponents in Modern Poland*, Ithaca, NY: Cornell University Press, 2005: 124–147.

Harris, Ruth, 'The "Child of the Barbarian": Rape, Race and Nationalism in France during the First World War', *Past and Present*, 141, November 1993: 170–206.

Heller, Celia S., *On the Edge of Destruction. The Jews of Poland between the Two World Wars*, New York: Columbia University Press, 1977.

Hess, Jonathan M., 'Leopold Kompert and the Work of Nostalgia: The Cultural Capital of German Jewish Ghetto Fiction', *Jewish Quarterly Review*, 97(4), 2007: 576–625.

Hitchins, Keith, *The Romanians, 1774–1866*, Oxford: Clarendon, 1996.

——, *Rumania, 1866–1947*, Oxford: Clarendon, 1994.

Hoffmann, Christian, Bergman, Werner and Walser Smith, Helmut (eds), *Exclusionary Violence. Antisemitic Riots in Modern German History*, Ann Arbour: University of Michigan Press, 2002.

Holmes, Colin, *Antisemitism in British Society, 1876–1939*, London: Edward Arnold, 1979.

——, 'The Tredegar Riots of 1911', *Welsh History Review*, 11, December 1982/1983: 214–225.

Horne, John and Kramer, Alan, *The German Atrocities of 1914: A History of Denial*, New Haven and London: Yale University Press, 2001.

Hughes, Michael, 'Bernard Pares, Russian Studies and the Promotion of Anglo-Russian Friendship, 1907–1914', *Slavonic and East European Review*, 78(3), July 2000: 510–536.

Iancu, Carol, 'Adolphe Crémieux, l'Alliance Israelite Universelle et les juifs de Roumanie au début du règne de Carol Hohenzollern Sigmaringen', *Revue des Etudes Juives*, 133, 1974: 481–502.

——, *Bleichröder et Crémieux: Le combat pour l'émancipation des Juifs de Roumanie devant le congrès de Berlin: Correspondance inédite, 1878–1880*, Paris: Centre de Recherches et D'études Juives et Hébraïques, 1987.

——, *Jews in Romania 1866–1919: From Exclusion to Emancipation*, New York: Columbia University Press, 1996.

Jelavich, Barbara, *Russia and the Formation of the Romanian National State 1821–1878*, Cambridge: Cambridge University Press, 1984.

Johnson, Sam, ' "Playing the Pharisee"? Charles Saroléa, Czechoslovakia and the Road to Munich, 1915–1939', *Slavonic and East European Review*, 82(2), April 2004: 292–314.

——, 'Confronting the East. *Darkest Russia*, British Opinion and Tsarist Russia's "Jewish Question", 1890–1914', *East European Jewish Affairs*, December 2006: 199–211.

——, 'Hep! Hep!, Dreyfus and other Jewish Questions. A View from London, 1881–1914', in S. Marten-Finnis and M.Winkler (eds), *City and Press. Interaction, Discourse, Thesis*, Bremen: Edition Lumière, 2009: 151–160.

——, 'Making or Breaking the Silence: British Jews and East European Jewish Relief, 1914–1917', *Modern Judaism*, February 2010: 95–119.

——, 'Uses and Abuses. "Pogrom" in the Anglo-American Imagination, 1881–1925', forthcoming in Harriet Murav and Eugene Avrutin (eds), *Violence and Jewish Daily Life in the East European Borderlands. Essays in Honor of John D. Klier*, Brighton: Academic Studies Press.

Judge, Edward H., *Easter in Kishinev: Anatomy of a Pogrom*, New York: New York University Press, 1992.

Kadish, Sharman, *Bolsheviks and British Jews. The Anglo-Jewish Community, Britain and the Russian Revolution*, London: Frank Cass, 1992.

Kamińska-Szmaj, Irena, *Judzi, zohydza, ze czci odziera: Jezyk propagandy politycznej w prasie 1919–1923*, Wroclaw: Towarzystwo Przyjaciól Polonistyki Wrocławskiej, 1994.

Katsis, Leonard, *Krovavyi navet i russkaia mysl': Istoriko-teologicheskoe issledovanie dela Beilisa*, Moscow/Jerusalem: Mosty kul'tura/Gesharim, 2006.

Kellogg, Frederick, *The Road to Romanian Independence*, West Lafayette, Ind.: Purdue University Press, 1995.

Keren, Shlomit and Keren, Michael, 'The Jewish Legions in the First World War as a Locus of Identity Formation', *Journal of Modern Jewish Studies*, 6(1), March 2007: 69–83.

Kieval, Hillel, 'Death and the Nation. Ritual Murder as Political Discourse in the Czech Lands', *Jewish History*, 10(1), March 1996: 75–91.

Klier, John D., '*The Times* of London, the Russian Press, and the Pogroms of 1881–2', *Carl Beck Papers*, 308, 1984: 1–26.

——, *Russia Gathers her Jews. The Origins of the 'Jewish Question' in Russia, 1772–1825*, De Kalb: Northern Illinois University Press, 1986.

——, 'Censorship of the Press in Russia and the Jewish Question, 1855–1894', *Jewish Social Studies*, 48, 1986: 257–268.

——, 'Russian Judeophobes and German Antisemites: Strangers and Brothers', *Jahrbucher für Geschichte Osteuropas*, XXXVII(4), 1989: 524–540.

Klier, John D. and Lambroza, Shlomo, *Pogroms. Anti-Jewish Violence in Modern Russian History*, Cambridge: Cambridge University Press, 1992.

Klier, John D., 'Krug Gintsburgov i politika shtadlanuta v imperatorskoi Rossii', *Vestnik Evreiskogo Universiteta v Moskve*, 3(10), 1995: 38–55.

——, 'Emigration Mania in Late Imperial Russia: Legend and Reality', in A. Newman and S. Massil (eds), *Patterns of Migration, 1850–1914*, London: Jewish Historical Society of England/UCL, 1996: 21–30.

——, 'Solzhenitsyn and the Kishinev Pogrom. A Slander Against Russia', *East European Jewish Affairs*, 33(1), 2003: 49–59.

——, 'Kazaki i pogromy. Chem otlichalis' 'voennye' pogromy?', in O.V. Budnitskii et al. (eds), *Mirovoi krizis 1914–1920 godov i sud'ba vostochnoevropeiskogo evreistva*, Moscow: Rosspen, 2005: 47–70.

——, 'Cry Bloody Murder', *East European Jewish Affairs*, 36(2), December 2006: 213–229.

——, *Russians, Jews and the Pogroms of 1881–1882*, Cambridge: Cambridge University Press, 2011.

Knepper, Paul, 'British Jews and the Racialisation of Crime in the Age of Empire', *British Journal of Criminology*, 47(1), 2007: 61–79.

Kraut, Alan M., *Silent Travelers. Germs, Genes and the 'Immigrant Menace'*, Baltimore: Johns Hopkins University Press, 1994.

Latawski, Paul, 'The Dmowski-Namier Feud, 1915–1918', *Polin*, 2, 1987: 37–49.

——, (ed.), *The Reconstruction of Poland, 1914–23*, London: Macmillan, 1992.

Lebzelter, Gisela C., *Political Antisemitism in England, 1918–1939*, London: Macmillan, 1978.

Leventhal, F.M., *The Last Dissenter. H.N. Brailsford and his World*, Oxford: Clarendon Press, 1985.

Levene, Mark, *War, Jews and the New Europe. The Diplomacy of Lucien Wolf, 1914–1919*, Oxford: Oxford University Press, 1992.

Levison, Frederick, *Christian and Jew. The Life of Leon Levison, 1881–1936*, Edinburgh: Pentland Press, 1989.

Levy, Elkan D., 'Antisemitism in England at War, 1914–1916', *Patterns of Prejudice*, 4(5), 1970: 27–30.

Levy, Richard S. (ed.), *Antisemitism. A Historical Encyclopaedia of Prejudice and Persecution*, Oxford: ABC-Clio, 2005.

Livezeanu, Irina, *Cultural Politics in Greater Romania. Regionalism, Nation-Building and Ethnic Struggle, 1918–1930*, Ithaca: Cornell University Press.

Lewandowski, Józef, 'History and Myth: Pinsk, April 1919', *Polin*, 2, 1987: 50–72.

Lewis, Bernard, *Semites and Antisemites*, London: Phoenix Giant, 1997.

Litvak, Olga, *Conscription and the Search for Modern Russian Jewry*, Bloomington: Indiana University Press, 2006.

Lohr, Eric, 'The Russian Army and the Jews; Mass Deportations, Hostages and Violence during World War 1', *Russian Review*, 60, July 2001: 404–419.

——, 'Patriotic Violence and the State: The Moscow Riots of May 1915', *Kritika*, 4(3), Summer 2003: 607–626.

——, *Nationalizing the Russian Empire. The Campaign Against Enemy Aliens in World War I*, London: Harvard University Press, 2003.

Löwe, Heinz-Dietrich, *The Tsars and the Jews: Reform, Reaction, and Antisemitism in Imperial Russia, 1772–1917*, London: Harwood Academic Publishers, 1993.

——, 'Pogroms in Russia: Explanations, Comparisons, Suggestions', *Jewish Social Studies*, 11(1), 2004: 16–23.

Lunn, Kenneth (ed.), *Race and Labour in Twentieth-Century Britain*, London: Frank Cass, 1986.

Maglen, Krista, 'Importing Trachoma. The Introduction into Britain of American Ideas of an "Immigrant Disease", 1892–1906', *Immigrants and Minorities*, 23(1), March 2005: 80–99.

Markel, Howard, *Quarantine! East European Jewish Immigrants and the New York City Epidemics of 1892*, Baltimore: JHUP, 1999.

Matthew, H.C.G., and Harrison, Brian (eds), *Oxford Dictionary of National Biography*, Oxford: Oxford University Press, 2004.

Maurer, Trude, *Ostjuden in Deutschland, 1918–1933*, Hamburg: Christians, 1986.

Medlicott, W.N., *The Congress of Berlin and After. A Diplomatic History of the Near Eastern Settlement, 1878–1880*, London Routledge, 1963.

Melançon, Michael, 'The Ninth Circle: the Lena Goldfield Workers and the Massacre of 4 April 1912', *Slavic Review*, 53(3), Autumn 1994: 766–795.

Melzer, Emmanuel, *No Way Out. The Politics of Polish Jewry, 1935–1939*, Cincinnati: Hebrew Union College Press, 1997.

Mendelsohn, Ezra, *Class Struggle in the Pale: The Formative Years of the Jewish Workers' Movement in Tsarist Russia*, New York: Cambridge University Press, 1970.

——, *The Jews of East Central Europe between the Two World Wars*, Bloomington: Indiana University Press, 1986.

——, 'Interwar Poland: Good or bad for the Jews?', in Abramsky, C., Jachimczyk, M., and Polonsky, A. (eds), *The Jews in Poland*, Oxford: Oxford University Press, 1986: 130–139.

de Michelis, Cesare G., 'Les Protocoles des sages de Sion: philologie et histoire', *Cahiers du monde russe*, 38(3), 1997: 263–306.

——, *The Non-Existent Manuscript: A Study of the Protocols of the Sages of Zion*, Lincoln: University of Nebraska Press, 2004.

Murav, Harriet, 'The Beilis Ritual Murder Trial and the Culture of Apocalypse', *Cardozo Studies in Law and Literature*, 12(2), Autumn–Winter, 2000: 243–263.

Nathans, Benjamin, *Beyond the Pale. The Jewish Encounter with Late Imperial Russia*, London: University of California Press, 2002.

Neilson, Keith, *Strategy and Supply. The Anglo-Russian Alliance, 1914–17*, London: Allen and Unwin, 1984.

——, *Britain and the Last Tsar. British Policy and Russia, 1894–1917*, Oxford: Clarendon Press, 1995.

Neuberger, Joan, *Hooliganism: Crime, Culture and Power in St. Petersburg, 1900–1914*, Berkeley: University of California Press, 1993.

Ng, Amy, 'A Portrait of Sir Lewis Namier as a Young Socialist', *Journal of Contemporary History*, 40(4): 621–636.

de Nie, Michael Willem, *The Eternal Paddy: Irish Identity and the British Press, 1798–1882*, Madison: University of Wisconsin Press, 2004.

Norman, Theodore, *An Outstretched Arm: A History of the Jewish Colonization Association*, London: Routledge & Kegan Paul, 1985.

Oldson, William O., *A Providential Antisemitism. Nationalism and Polity in Nineteenth-Century Romania*, Philadelphia: American Philosophical Society, 1991.

Oişteanu, Andrei, *Imaginea evreului în cultura română. Studiu de imagologie în context est-central european*, Bucharest: Humanitas, 2001.

——, *Inventing the Jew. Antisemitic Stereotypes in Romanian and other East-Central European Cultures*, London: University of Nebraska Press, 2009.

Patenaude, Bertrand M., *The Big Show in Bololand. The American Relief Expedition to Soviet Russia in the Famine of 1921*, Stanford: Stanford University Press, 2002.

Pauley, Bruce F., *From Prejudice to Destruction. A History of Austrian Antisemitism*, London: University of North Carolina Press, 1992.

Pearce, Joseph, *Old Thunder. A Life of Hilaire Belloc*, London: Harper Collins, 2002.

Penkower, Monty Noam, 'The Kishinev Pogrom of 1903: A Turning Point in Jewish History', *Modern Judaism*, 24(3), 2004: 187–225.

Penslar, Derek J., *Shylock's Children. Economics and Jewish Identity in Modern Europe*, Berkeley: California University Press, 2001.

Perlmann, Moshe, 'Arnold White, Baron Hirsch's Emissary', *Proceedings of the American Academy of Jewish Research*, 46, 1979–1980: 473–489.

Petrovsky-Shtern, Yohanan, 'The "Jewish Policy" of the Late Imperial War Ministry: The Impact of the Russian Right', *Kritika*, 3(2), Spring 2002: 217–254.

Petrovsky-Shtern, Yohanan, *Jews in the Russian Army, 1827–1917. Drafted into Modernity*, Cambridge: Cambridge University Press, 2008.

Pevzner, Evgeniia, 'Jewish Committee for the Relief of War Victims (1914–1921)', *Pinkas*, 1, 2006: 114–142.

Porter, Brian, A., 'Who Is a Pole and Where Is Poland? Territory and Nation in the Rhetoric of Polish National Democracy before 1905', *Slavic Review*, 51(4), Winter 1992: 639–653.

——, *When Nationalism Began to Hate. Imagining Modern Politics in Nineteenth-Century Poland*, New York/Oxford: Oxford University Press, 2000.

Prusin, Alexander Victor, *Nationalizing a Borderland: War, Ethnicity, and Anti-Jewish Violence in East Galicia, 1914–1920*, Tuscaloosa: University of Alabama Press, 2005.

Pulzer, P.G.J., *The Rise of Political Antisemitism in Germany and Austria*, Cambridge: Harvard University Press, 1988.

Raleigh, Donald J., *Experiencing Russia's Civil War. Politics, Society and Revolutionary Culture in Saratov, 1917–1922*, Princeton: Princeton University Press, 2002.

Rechter, David, *The Jews of Vienna and the First World War*, London: Littman Library, 2001.

Richards, Jeffrey, *Sex, Dissidence and Damnation. Minority Groups in the Middle Ages*, Oxford: Routledge, 1994.

Roberts, Ian W., *History of the School of Slavonic and East European Studies, 1915–1990*, London: University of London, 1991.

Robertson, Richie, *The 'Jewish Question' in German Literature, 1749–1939. Emancipation and its Discontents*, Oxford: Oxford University Press, 1999.

Rodrique, Aron, *French Jews, Turkish Jews: The Alliance Israélite Universelle and the Politics of Jewish Schooling in Turkey, 1860–1925*, Bloomington: Indiana University Press, 1990.

Rogger, Hans, 'Was there a Russian Fascism? The Union of the Russian People', *Journal of Modern History*, 36, December 1964: 398–415.

——, 'The Beilis Case: Antisemitism and Politics in the Reign of Nicholas II', *Slavic Review*, 25(4), December 1966: 615–629.

——, *Jewish Policies and Right-Wing Politics in Imperial Russia*, London: Macmillan, 1986.

Roshwald, Aviel, *Ethnic Nationalism and the Fall of Empires. Central Europe, Russia and the Middle East, 1914–1923*, London: Routledge, 2001.

Rowland R.H., 'Geographical Patterns of the Jewish Population in the Pale of Settlement in Late Nineteenth-century Russia', *Jewish Social Studies*, 48(3–4), 1986: 207–234.

Różański, Przemysław, 'Wilno, 19–21 kwietnia 1919 roku', *Jewish History Quarterly*, 1, 2006: 13–34.

Rozenblit, Martha, *Reconstructing a National Identity: The Jews of Habsburg Austria during World War I*, New York: Oxford University Press, 2001.

Rozin, Mordechai, *The Rich and Poor. Jewish Philanthropy and Social Control in Nineteenth-Century London*, Brighton: Sussex Academic Press, 1999.

Rubinstein, William D., 'The anti-Jewish Riots of 1911 in South Wales: a Re-examination', *Welsh History Review*, 18, December 1997: 667–699.

Rubenstein, W.D., and Rubenstein, Hilary, *Philosemitism: Admiration and Support in the English-Speaking World for Jews, 1840–1939*, London: Macmillan, 1999.

Rubin, Miri, *Gentile Tales. The Narrative Assault on Late Medieval Jews*, New Haven: Yale University Press, 1999.

Salbstein, M.C.N., *The Emancipation of the Jews in Britain: the Question of the Admission of the Jews to Parliament, 1828–1860*, London: Associated University Press, 1982.

Samuel, Maurice, *Blood Accusation: The Strange History of the Beilis Case*, Philadelphia: Jewish Publication Society of America, 1966.

Sanborn, Joshua A., *Drafting the Russian Nation. Military Conscription, Total War, and Mass Politics*, DeKalb, Illinois: Northern Illinois University Press, 2002.

Shapiro Leon, *The History of ORT. A Jewish Movement for Social Change*, New York: Schoken Books, 1980.

Schoenberg, P.E., 'The American Reaction to the Kishinev Pogrom of 1903, *American Jewish Historical Quarterly*, 63(3), March 1974: 262–283.

Scult, Mel, 'English Missions to the Jews; Conversion in the Age of Emancipation', *Jewish Social Studies*, 35(1), January 1973: 3–17.

Shukman, Harold, *War or Revolution. Russian Jews and Conscription in Britain, 1917*, London: Vallentine Mitchell, 2006.

Siegel, Jennifer, *Endgame: Britain, Russia and the Final Struggle for Central Asia*, London: I.B. Tauris, 2002.

Singer, I.B., *The Family Moskat*, London: Vintage, 2000.

Sorin, Gerald, *A Time for Building. The Third Migration, 1880–1920*, London: Johns Hopkins University Press, 1992.

Stanislawski, Michael, *Zionism and the Fin de Siècle. Cosmopolitanism and Nationalism from Nordau to Jabotinsky*, London: University of California Press, 2001.

Stern, Fritz, *Gold and Iron: Bismarck, Bleichröder, and the Building of the German Empire*, London: Allen and Unwin, 1977.

Szajkowski, Zosa, 'Jewish Diplomacy: Notes on the Occasion of the Centenary of the *Alliance Israélite Universelle*,' *Jewish Social Studies*, 22, 1960: 131–158.

Teter, Magda, *Jews and Heretics in Catholic Poland: A Beleaguered Church in the Post-Reformation Era*, Cambridge: Cambridge University Press, 2006.

Tomaszewski, Leszek, 'Pińsk, Saturday 5 April 1919', *Polin*, 1, 1986: 227–251.

Udelson, Joseph H., *Dreamer of the Ghetto. The Life and Works of Israel Zangwill*, London: University of Alabama Press, 1990.

Veidlinger, Jeffrey, *Jewish Public Culture in the Late Russian Empire*, Bloomington: Indiana University Press, 2009.

Vincent, David, *The Rise of Mass Literacy. Reading and Writing in Modern Europe*, Cambridge: Polity, 2000.

Vital, David, *Zionism. The Formative Years*, Oxford: Clarendon, 1982.

——, 'Zangwill and Modern Jewish Nationalism', *Modern Judaism*, 4(3), October, 1984: 243–253.

Volkov, Shulamit, *Germans, Jews, and Antisemites. Trials in Emancipation*, Cambridge: Cambridge University Press, 2006.

Wasserstein, Bernard, *Herbert Samuel. A Political Life*, Oxford: Oxford University Press, 1992.

Watts, Martin, *The Jewish Legion and the First World War*, London: Palgrave Macmillan, 2004.

Weeks, Theodore R., 'Fanning the Flames: Jews in the Warsaw Press, 1905–1906', *East European Jewish Affairs*, 28(2), 1998–1999: 63–81.

——, *Nation and State in Late Imperial Russia: Nationalism and Russification on Russia's Western Frontier 1863–1914*, DeKalb: Northern Illinois University Press, 1996.

——, *From Assimilation to Antisemitism. The "Jewish Question" in Poland, 1850–1914*, DeKalb: Northern Illinois University Press, 2006.

Weinberg, Robert, 'Workers, Pogroms and the 1905 Revolution in Odessa', *Russian Review*, 46(1), January 1987: 53–75.

Weinerman, Eli, 'Racism, Racial Prejudice and Jews in Late Imperial Russia', *Ethnic and Racial Studies*, XVII(3), 1994: 442–495.

Wentling, Sonja P., 'Prologue to Genocide of Epilogue to War? American Perspectives on the Jewish Question in Poland, 1919–1921', *Journal of the Historical Society*, 8(4), December 2008: 523–544.

Wertheimer, Jack, *Unwelcome Strangers. East European Jews in Imperial Germany*, New York/Oxford: Oxford University Press, 1987.

Wilson, A.N., *Hilaire Belloc*, London: Hamilton, 1984.

Wilson, Keith M., '*The Protocols of Zion* and the *Morning Post*, 1919–20, *Patterns of Prejudice*, 19(3), 1985: 5–14.

Winock, Michel, *Nationalism, Antisemitism and Fascism in France*, Stanford: Stanford University Press, 1998.

Wortman, Richard, *The Crisis of Russian Populism*, Cambridge: Cambridge University Press, 1967.

Wróbel, Piotr, 'The Jews of Galicia under Austrian-Polish Rule, 1869–1918', *Austrian History Yearbook*, 25, 1994: 97–138.

Zangwill, Israel and Nahson, Edna (ed.), *From the Ghetto to the Melting Pot: Israel Zangwill's Jewish Plays*, Detroit: Wayne State University Press, 2005.

Zimmerman, Joshua D., *Poles, Jews and the Politics of Nationality: The Bund and the Polish Socialist Party in Late Tsarist Russia, 1892–1914*, Madison: University of Wisconsin Press, 2004.

Zimmerman, Moshe, *Wilhelm Marr. The Patriarch of Antisemitism*, Oxford: Oxford University Press, 1986.

Zipperstein, Steven J., 'The Politics of Relief: The Transformation of Russian Jewish Communal Life during the First World War', in Jonathan Frankel (ed.), *The Jews and the European Crisis, 1914–1921. Studies in Contemporary Jewry*, Volume IV, Oxford: University Press, 1988: 22–40.

Unpublished sources

Klier, John D., 'Are Jews a Race? The Absence of Racialism in Russian Judeophobia', seminar paper, St Antony's College, University of Oxford, 27 April 2007. In author's personal collection.

——, 'The Mansion House Protest of 1882: Philosemitism or the "English Disease"', paper presented at Birkbeck College, University of London, 11 July 2007. In author's personal collection.

Lunn, Kenneth, 'The Marconi Scandal and Related Aspects of British Antisemitism, 1911–1914', unpublished PhD thesis, University of Sheffield, 1978.

Index

CPSIA information can be obtained at www.ICGtesting.com
Printed in the USA
LVOW10*1715230514

387111LV00009B/258/P